All the Way with JFK?

All the Way with JFK?

Britain, the US, and the Vietnam War

PETER BUSCH

OXFORD

UNIVERSITY PRESS

OXFORD
UNIVERSITY PRESS

Great Clarendon Street, Oxford OX2 6DP

Oxford University Press is a department of the University of Oxford.
It furthers the University's objective of excellence in research, scholarship,
and education by publishing worldwide in

Oxford New York

Auckland Bangkok Buenos Aires Cape Town Chennai
Dar es Salaam Delhi Hong Kong Istanbul Karachi Kolkata
Kuala Lumpur Madrid Melbourne Mexico City Mumbai Nairobi
São Paulo Shanghai Taipei Tokyo Toronto

Oxford is a registered trade mark of Oxford University Press
in the UK and in certain other countries

Published in the United States
by Oxford University Press Inc., New York

British Library Cataloguing in Publication Data
Data available

Library of Congress Cataloging in Publication Data
Data available

ISBN 0-19-925639-x

1 3 5 7 9 10 8 6 4 2

Typeset by Hope Services (Abingdon) Ltd.
Printed in Great Britain
on acid-free paper by
T. J. International Ltd,
Padstow, Cornwall

Acknowledgements

I would not have been able to write this book without the support of many friends and colleagues. In particular, I would like to thank Dr Antony Best, and Dr Odd Arne Westad of the London School of Economics. The encouraging comments of Professor Richard Aldrich were also very helpful, as was the financial support of the Cusanuswerk.

I am grateful to Dr Noriko Yokoi, Dr Joseph Maiolo, Stefan Vogenauer, Bernd Ewers, Dr Barbara Lorenzkowski, Ursula Fischer, Liesel Meyer-Hermann, and Dr Sabine Freitag for their encouragement, their comments, and their friendship.

During my work in various archives, I encountered many helpful archivists and librarians. I would like to thank my former colleagues at the Public Record Office in London, and also Mike Parrish of the Lyndon B. Johnson Library, and Jessie Day of the Australian Archives. I am especially indebted to Jessie as well as to Graeme Eskrigge and Caren Phillips of the New Zealand Department of External Affairs and Trade for 'rush-accessing' a lot of the relevant material for me. For the insights into the work of the Foreign Office and the Saigon embassy I would like to thank Sir Edward Peck and Reginald Burrows. Their prompt answers to my queries, their willingness to talk to me, and their generous supply of photographic material particularly helped in the final stages of this work. I would also like to thank Lord Douglas-Hamilton and Lord Moore of Wolvercote for providing me with information and photos. Talking to Isabel Oliphant proved not only interesting and informative, but also very pleasant. I am particularly indebted to her for letting me have photos of her late father, Sir Robert Thompson.

I would also like to thank Ann and Alan Sherriff for introducing me to many a National Trust treasure, lovely countryside pubs, and for putting me and my belongings up so many times. Elizabeth Midgley made me feel very welcome at her lovely home in Washington. Moreover, the challenging early morning discussions—sweetened by fresh waffles—provided me with a lot of stamina for demanding days at the archives.

Finally and most importantly, I would like to thank my family, and in particular my parents, Alfons and Elsbeth. Without their backing, support, and love, writing and finishing this book would have been unthinkable.

P.B.

Contents

List of Plates

List of Maps

Abbreviations

AATTV	Australian Army Training Team Vietnam
AID	Agency for International Development
AMDA	Anglo-Malayan Defence Agreement
	Anglo-Malaysian Defence Agreement
ANZAM	Australia, New Zealand, Malaya
ANZUS	Australian, New Zealand, United States (security treaty)
ARVN	Army of the Republic of Vietnam
AUSNA	Australian National Archives
BArchMA	Bundesarchiv—Militärarchiv
BRIAM	British Advisory Mission Vietnam
CBS	Columbia Broadcasting System
CFA	Cease-Fire Agreement (Geneva 1954)
CIA	Central Intelligence Agency
CNA	Canadian National Archives
CO	Colonial Office
CRO	Commonwealth Relations Office
Depcirctel	Department of States circular telegram
Deptel	Department of States telegram
DRV	Democratic Republic of Vietnam (North Vietnam)
EA	Ministry of External Affairs
EEC	European Economic Community
Embtel	Embassy telegram
FO	Foreign Office
HI	Hoover Institution on War, Revolution and Peace
ICC	International Control Commission
JCS	Joint Chiefs of Staff
JFKL	John F. Kennedy Presidential Library
JIC	Joint Intelligence Committee
LBJL	Lyndon B. Johnson Presidential Library
MAAG	Military Assistance Advisory Group
MACV	Military Assistance Command Vietnam
MfAA	Ministerium für Auswärtige Angelegenheiten
MOD	Ministry of Defence
MPO	Military Planning Office
NATO	North Atlantic Treaty Organization
NIE	National Intelligence Estimate
NLF	National Liberation Front of South Vietnam
NSAM	National Security Action Memorandum
NSC	National Security Council
NSF	National Security File
NZNA	New Zealand National Archives

OSS	Office of Strategic Services
PA	Politisches Archiv des Auswärtigen Amtes
PAP	People's Action Party
PATO	Pacific Area Treaty Organization
PKI	Partai Komunis Indonesia
PLAF	People's Liberation Armed Forces
POF	Presidential Office Files
PP	Pentagon Papers
PRC	People's Republic of China
PRO	Public Record Office
RG	Record Group
RVN	Republic of Vietnam (South Vietnam)
SAPMO	Stiftung Archiv Parteien/Massenorganisationen
SEAFET	Southeast Asia Friendship and Economic Treaty
SEATO	South-East Asia Treaty Organization
SNIE	Special National Intelligence Estimate
USOM	United States Operations Mission
USVR	United States—Vietnam Relation

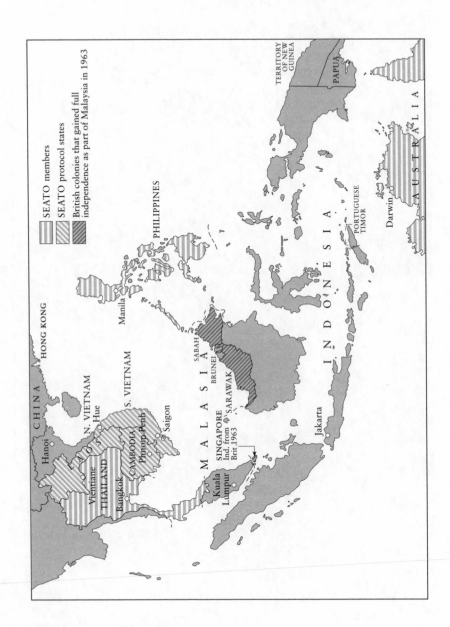

MAP I Southeast Asia in 1963

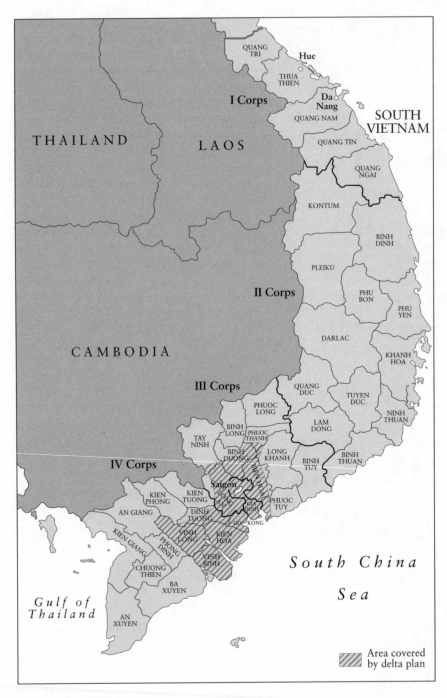

MAP II   South Vietnam

Introduction

NGUYEN AI QUOC had no idea that the British police had located him in Hong Kong. So in the summer of 1931, a couple of months after having supervised the formation of the Indochinese Party in Hong Kong, Nguyen 'the Patriot' saw no reason to take any precautions. Communist manifests were scattered all over the flat he shared with a young woman who called herself Ly Sam and claimed to be his niece. He continued to organize the activities of the communist international from here. On 6 June 1931 British police officers surrounded the building in Kowloon, a crowded residential area in the crown colony. At 2 a.m. they climbed up the stairs to the second floor and stormed into the apartment that was officially the abode of a certain T. V. Wong. Here they arrested Nguyen and his 'niece'. The couple professed to be Chinese, but the two could not fool the British authorities. They had found Nguyen Ai Quoc's address in the papers of his Comintern colleague Joseph Ducroux when he was arrested in Singapore. Moreover, they had a photograph of the leading Vietnamese nationalist they were looking for. The man the British apprehended in the flat in Kowloon indeed looked like Nguyen Ai Quoc, later known as Ho Chi Minh.[1]

One and a half years later, in late January 1933, the S.S. *An Hui* slowed down outside Lei Yue Mun strait. It was Chinese New Year's eve and most people were indoors. The steamer destined for Amoy had just left Hong Kong harbour. Now, after dark, it was ready to take another passenger on board. Guarded by plainclothes policemen, Ho Chi Minh was taken out to the ship in a motor launch the Hong Kong government had hired. The authorities were glad to get rid of him. He had spent eighteen months in British custody while his solicitors successfully fought the Hong Kong governor's order to deport him to Vietnam. The matter was finally settled in London just before the Judicial Committee of the Privy Council was ready to hear the case. It was decided to help Ho Chi Minh go where he wanted. He had to leave Hong Kong because the British would not tolerate his subversive activities from a safe haven. Yet deportation that amounted to extradition was considered repugnant to British principles. Therefore, the British assisted Ho Chi Minh in leaving secretly to avoid detection by French spies. After having spent a comfortable time in Hong Kong, he was now free to pursue his revolutionary aims.[2]

On 13 September 1945, eleven days after Ho Chi Minh had achieved one of his aims by proclaiming the Democratic Republic of Vietnam, Major-General

[1] Dennis J. Duncanson, 'Ho-chi-Minh in Hong Kong, 1931–32', *China Quarterly*, 5 (1974), 89. William J. Duiker, *Ho Chi Minh* (New York: Hyperion, 2000), 200.

[2] Duncanson, 'Ho-chi-Minh in Hong Kong', 97–100. Duiker, *Ho Chi Minh*, 201–9.

Douglas Gracey's Dakota landed in Saigon. Japanese and French delegations were at Tan Son Nhut airfield to greet him. There was also a group of Vietnamese nationalists trying to approach the British Major-General, but he chose to ignore them. Gracey's task was to take over the southern half of Vietnam from the Japanese army and to prepare the return of the French to their colony. Moreover, he had to maintain law and order in Saigon, a difficult undertaking. He had only a small British force at his disposition in Saigon and was facing three potentially dangerous groups. The Japanese army in Vietnam had not been defeated and was still a formidable fighting force. The French colons and the freed POWs had been humiliated by the Japanese and were eager to get back in power. The Vietminh claimed to have formed the legitimate government of Vietnam and were in control of key buildings, like the radio station, the town hall, and several prisons.

Just a few days after Gracey's arrival, the Vietnamese nationalists had lost what little control they had in Saigon. The British disarmed Vietminh policemen and systematically took over government buildings from them. These buildings were then given to the French. More importantly, Gracey backed the 'French *coup*' of 23 September 1945, when re-armed French POWs and civilians attacked the remaining Vietminh posts. Several days of street fighting followed. The British were unhappy about the violence that had erupted. Yet British soldiers intervened on behalf of the French and killed hundreds of Vietnamese nationalists in the months to come.[3]

These two episodes illustrate Britain's at times pivotal involvement in Indochina, although the region was not London's main concern in Southeast Asia. This involvement did not end with World War II, nor did it come to a close in 1954, when France finally granted independence to the Indochinese states. It even continued when the United States began their intervention in Vietnam on behalf of the non-communist government in Saigon in the 1960s, and it is Britain's involvement in the escalating war this study undertakes to explore.

The literature on the wars in Vietnam after 1945 and the involvement of the western and communist blocs in them is vast, and with more and more records becoming available continues to grow.[4] In view of America's traumatic experience and the Vietnam War's effect on American domestic politics and the US role

---

[3] Peter M. Dunn, *The First Vietnam War* (London: C. Hurst, 1985), 140–205.

[4] For excellent discussions of the literature and the schools of thought with regard to the Vietnam War, see Robert J. McMahon, 'U.S.–Vietnamese Relations: A Historiographical Survey', in Warren I. Cohen (ed.), *Pacific Passage: The Study of American–East Asian Relations on the Eve of the Twenty-First Century* (New York: Columbia University Press, 1996), 313–36, and Gary R. Hess, 'The Unending Debate: Historians and the Vietnam War', in Michael J. Hogan (ed.), *America in the World: The Historiography of American Foreign Relations since 1941* (Cambridge: Cambridge University Press, 1995), 358–94. The best surveys of the Vietnam War are still George C. Herring, *America's Longest War: The United States and Vietnam, 1950–1975*, 2nd edn. (New York: Knopf, 1986), and George McT. Kahin, *Intervention: How America Became Involved in Vietnam* (New York: Knopf, 1986). Also useful is Marilyn B. Young, *The Vietnam Wars, 1945–1990* (New York: HarperCollins, 1991).

in the world, it is not surprising that the majority of books on the topic are written from an American perspective and deal mainly with US Vietnam policy.[5]

This book is different in that it concentrates on Britain's policy towards the Vietnam War between 1961 and 1963. Providing the first in-depth analysis of the available British government records on Vietnam for this period, supplemented by records from the United States, Canada, Australia, and New Zealand,[6] the study pursues three aims. First and foremost, it seeks to determine the British government's reaction to the deteriorating situation in Vietnam and to President John F. Kennedy's way of responding to the conflict. Second, it aims to put British Vietnam policy into the context of Whitehall's policy towards Southeast Asia, particularly with regard to the formation of the Federation of Malaysia and the confrontation between Malaysia and Indonesia. Third, as a result of analysing British policy this study provides new insights into our understanding of the Vietnam War. It puts Kennedy's Vietnam decisions into perspective and reveals that the conflict had not only an impact on the United States but also on Britain's relations with both its American and its Commonwealth allies.

The Vietnam policy of the United Kingdom, Washington's major ally in the region, has found little scholarly attention. One reason for the lack of interest in studying British policy towards the Vietnam War, particularly in the early 1960s, appears to be the perception that the British government lost interest in Vietnamese affairs after having sponsored the Geneva peace settlement of 1954. Combs underscored this view concluding that in 1955 'London wisely washed its hands of the whole business in Vietnam and began to behave as though it had never had much to do with post-Geneva Indochina'.[7]

Scholars who deal with Britain's policy towards Indochina focus on the 1954 Geneva conference, the Laos crisis of 1960–1, and, if studies on a later period mention Britain at all, they discuss the policy of Harold Wilson's Labour government that was formed in late 1964. This leaves a gap in our knowledge of Britain's policy towards the Vietnam War which not only incorrectly underlines Combs's assertion that Britain had lost interest in Indochina after 1955; it also creates a misleading notion of continuity in Britain's Indochina policy from Anthony Eden to Harold Wilson.[8]

---

[5] Even Logevall's recent study that also makes use of French and British archival sources and focuses on the 'long 1964' asks America-oriented questions, arguing that President Lyndon B. Johnson, although aware of possible alternatives, 'chose' war in Vietnam to maintain his credibility. Fredrik Logevall, *Choosing War: The Lost Chance for Peace and the Escalation of War in Vietnam* (Berkeley: University of California Press, 1999), 387–9.

[6] Much of the Australian material and the entire New Zealand material was made publicly available for the first time for this study.

[7] Arthur Combs, 'The Path Not Taken: The British Alternative to U.S. Policy in Vietnam, 1954–1956', *Diplomatic History*, 19/1 (1995), 57.

[8] John Dickie, *'Special' No More: Anglo-American Relations: Rhetoric and Reality* (London: Weidenfeld & Nicolson, 1994), 89–137, provides a good example of merely discussing Britain's role in Geneva in 1954, and then looking at Wilson's policy, leaving out the decade in-between. The exception is Ian Selby, 'British Policy towards Indochina: South Vietnam and Cambodia, 1954–1959', Ph.D. thesis (Cambridge, 1998), yet Selby's study ends with the beginning of the insurrection in South Vietnam.

At the 1954 Geneva conference, Anthony Eden, the British Foreign Secretary, managed to broker a settlement that ended the French Indochina war and enabled Paris to disengage from its colony. Co-chairing the conference with Viacheslav Molotov, the Soviet Foreign Minister, Eden was determined to play the role of the peacemaker. Memories of the Korean War were fresh, and Eden wanted to defuse a conflict that threatened to escalate into a confrontation between the People's Republic of China (PRC) and the United States. Soviet and Chinese motives to restrain the Vietminh and persuade them to agree to the Geneva ceasefire agreements were similar. Eden also strove to demonstrate Britain's continued status as a world power and its influence in the region. London's refusal to support Washington's call for 'united action' to come to the help of the beleaguered French showed Britain's willingness to defy Washington's wishes and its apparent ability to prevent US military action in Indochina.[9]

The Laos crisis of 1960–1 also seemed to prove that British foreign policy in Southeast Asia was dominated by the desire to prevent a 'second Korea'. It was widely believed at the time, and a number of scholars underscore this belief, that Britain's reluctance to support American military intervention in Laos in 1961 played a crucial role in persuading John F. Kennedy to seek a negotiated settlement to the conflict between leftist, rightist, and neutralist forces in that remote country.[10]

[9] For an overview of British policy towards the Indochina conflict, see John W. Young, *Winston Churchill's Last Campaign: Britain and the Cold War, 1951–1955* (Oxford: Clarendon Press, 1996), 260–5. See for more detailed accounts of British policy towards the Geneva conference: James Cable, *The Geneva Conference of 1954 on Indochina* (Basingstoke: Macmillan, 1986); Kevin Ruane, 'Anthony Eden, British Diplomacy and the Origins of the Geneva Conference of 1954', *Historical Journal*, 37/1 (1994), 153–72; Geoffrey Warner, 'Britain and the Crisis over Dien Bien Phu, April 1954: The Failure of United Action', in Lawrence S. Kaplan et al. (eds.), *Dien Bien Phu and the Crisis of Franco-American Relations, 1954–1955* (Wilmington, Del.: Scholarly Resources, 1990), 55–77, and by the same author: 'From Geneva to Manila: British Policy toward Indochina and SEATO, May–September 1954', in ibid. 148–67, and also by Warner, 'The Settlement of the Indochina War', in John W. Young (ed.), *The Foreign Policy of Churchill's Peacetime Administration* (Leicester: Leicester University Press, 1988), 233–63. The American perspective of the Geneva conference is given by Robert F. Randle, *Geneva 1954: The Settlement of the Indochinese War* (Princeton: Princeton University Press, 1969); Melanie Billings-Yun, *Decision against War: Eisenhower and Dien Bien Phu, 1954* (New York: Columbia University Press, 1988); and George C. Herring, '"A Good Stout Effort": John Foster Dulles and the Indochina Crisis, 1954–55', in Richard Immerman (ed.), *John Foster Dulles and the Diplomacy of the Cold War* (Princeton: Princeton University Press, 1990), 213–33. For the French side, see Philippe Devillers and Jean Lacouture, *End of a War: Indochina 1954* (New York: Praeger, 1969), and for the Chinese, Shao Kuo-kang, 'Zhou Enlai's Diplomacy and the Neutralization of Indochina 1954–55', *China Quarterly*, 107 (1986), 483–504; Zhai Qiang, 'China and the Geneva Conference of 1954', *China Quarterly*, 129 (1992), 103–22; and Zhai Qiang, *China and the Vietnam Wars, 1950–1975* (Chapel Hill: University of North Carolina Press, 2000), 51–63.

[10] For very good discussions of the Laos crisis, see Peter Edwards with Gregory Pemberton, *Crises and Commitments: The Politics and Diplomacy of Australia's Involvement in Southeast Asian Conflicts 1948–1965* (North Sydney: Allen & Unwin, 1992), 208–28; and Leszek Buszynski, *SEATO: The Failure of an Alliance Strategy* (Singapore: Singapore University Press, 1983), 73–94. See also David L. Anderson, *Trapped by Success: The Eisenhower Administration and Vietnam, 1953–1961* (New York: Columbia University Press, 1991), 191; Arthur J. Dommen, *Conflict in Laos: The Politics of Neutralization* (London: Pall Mall Press, 1964), 190–9; Kahin, *Intervention*, 124–7; David Kaiser, *American Tragedy: Kennedy, Johnson, and the Origins of the Vietnam War* (Cambridge, Mass.: Harvard University Press, 2000), 36–57; Khong Yuen Foong, *Analogies of War: Korea, Munich, Dien*

Studies on British foreign and defence policy or Anglo-American relations in the 1960s hardly discuss the influence of the Vietnam War on the 'special relationship'. The nuclear deterrent, NATO, and Europe are the main issues. Vietnam and Southeast Asia are regarded as nothing more than side shows. What is more, if Vietnam is mentioned, it is in the context of Prime Minister Wilson's unwillingness to provide even a token deployment of British troops in 1965 despite President Johnson's pleading. Various explanations for Wilson's policy have been put forward. Baylis suggests that Britain's main aim was to persuade Washington to give up its preoccupation with Asia and concentrate on Europe.[11] Bartlett and Pickering stress that the United States made its support of troubled Sterling dependent on Britain's willingness to keep its military presence east of Suez. The analysis of possible 'deals' between London and Washington by Dumbrell supports the proposition that Vietnam, Sterling, and Britain's military commitments in Southeast Asia were somehow linked. Easter's detailed study of British defence policy east of Suez during the confrontation between Malaysia and Indonesia shows that the Americans certainly intimated after September 1965 that they expected Britain to maintain its military base in Singapore in exchange for their support for Sterling. However, there was never a written agreement.[12] Dimbleby and Reynolds argue that Britain consistently failed to come up to Washington's expectations regarding Vietnam and they name Wilson's peace initiatives as a case in point.[13] In his memoirs Wilson maintains that his aim was always to get the conflicting parties to the conference table, and that he had to find a middle way between the Labour-left's demand that the government condemn US Vietnam policy, and the Foreign Office's pressure to support it.[14]

The focus of the literature to date on the Geneva conference of 1954, the Laos crisis, and then on the Wilson years therefore conveys the impression that Britain

Bien Phu and the Vietnam Decisions of 1965 (Princeton: Princeton University Press, 1992), 80–3; William Rust and the editors of US News Books, *Kennedy and Vietnam* (New York: Scribners, 1985), 31; Orrin Schwab, *John F. Kennedy, Lyndon Johnson, and the Vietnam War, 1961–65* (Westport, Conn.: Praeger, 1998), 5; and Young, *The Vietnam Wars*, 78–9.

[11] John Baylis, *Anglo-American Defence Relations 1939–1984: The Special Relationship* (London: Macmillan, 1984), 154.

[12] Christopher J. Bartlett, *British Foreign Policy in the Twentieth Century* (Basingstoke: Macmillan Education, 1989), 110–11. Jeffrey Pickering, *Britain's Withdrawal from East of Suez: The Politics of Retrenchment* (Basingstoke: Macmillan, 1998), 148–9. John Dumbrell, 'The Johnson Administration and the British Labour Government, Vietnam, the Pound and East of Suez', *Journal of American Studies*, 30/2 (1996), 229–31. David Easter, 'British Defence Policy in South East Asia and the Confrontation, 1960–66', Ph.D. thesis (London School of Economics, 1998), 410. See also Diane B. Kunz, ' "Somewhat Mixed Up Together": Anglo-American Defence and Financial Policy during the 1960s', *Journal of Imperial and Commonwealth History*, 27/2 (1999), 213–32.

[13] David Dimbleby and David Reynolds, *An Ocean Apart: The Special Relationship between Britain and America in the Twentieth Century* (London: BBC Books, 1988), 247–50.

[14] Harold Wilson, *The Labour Government, 1964–1970: A Personal Record* (London: Weidenfeld & Nicolson, 1971), 84–5. See also the US President's account of the 1967 peace initiative involving Wilson and Kosygin: Lyndon B. Johnson, *The Vantage Point: Perspectives of the Presidency, 1963–1969* (New York: Holt, Rinehart & Winston, 1971), 253–6. For a discussion of how seriously Wilson took his peace initiatives, see John W. Young, 'The Wilson Government and the Davies Peace Mission to North Vietnam, July 1965', *Review of International Studies*, 24/4 (1998), 560–2.

was in constant pursuit of peace in Indochina. This book shows that British policy towards the Vietnam War during the Kennedy years was different. The British government ruled out a negotiated settlement, advised Kennedy to conceal his military build-up in Vietnam, and put the blame for the breakdown of the ceasefire on Hanoi, however flimsy the evidence was for this. Simultaneously, Britain increased its involvement by sending counter-insurgency experts to Saigon. These experts were convinced of the eventual success of the strategic hamlet programme and claimed in 1963 that Saigon was winning the war.

The discussion of John F. Kennedy's Vietnam policy has been dominated by the essentially unanswerable question of what he might have done in a second term in office. Hollywood film director Oliver Stone has kept the argument alive that Kennedy would have avoided the Vietnam quagmire, and so has Robert McNamara, Kennedy's and Johnson's Secretary of Defense. 'I think it highly probable,' writes McNamara in his memoirs, 'that, had President Kennedy lived, he would have pulled us out of Vietnam.'[15] Whatever side one takes, there can be no doubt that Kennedy left Lyndon B. Johnson with the legacy of a significantly increased American commitment to the survival of a non-communist Republic of Vietnam (RVN).[16]

Kennedy's two most important Vietnam decisions were to increase the number of American military advisers from less than 1,000 when he took office in 1961 to more than 16,000 in 1963, and to support a military coup against Ngo Dinh Diem, the South Vietnamese President, in November 1963. For most of his time in office, Kennedy treated Vietnam as an important but not as the most crucial foreign policy issue. That place was taken by Berlin and Cuba.[17] However, early in his presidency a report by Edward Lansdale, the Deputy Assistant for Special Operations in the Pentagon, drew Kennedy's attention to the situation in Vietnam. With Kennedy's decision to seek a negotiated agreement in Laos, defeating the insurgency in Vietnam gained greater importance. The Kennedy administration hoped that the RVN would implement the counter-insurgency plan that the American military had developed under President Dwight D. Eisenhower. Kennedy created a Task Force Vietnam in April and dispatched Vice-President Lyndon B. Johnson to Saigon in May 1961 in order to reassure Ngo Dinh Diem of his support and to promise Saigon more financial and military assistance. When

[15] Robert S. McNamara, *In Retrospect: The Tragedy and Lessons of Vietnam* (New York: Vintage Books, 1995), 96. The same argument was made by John M. Newman, *JFK and Vietnam: Deception, Intrigue and the Struggle for Power* (New York: Warner Books, 1992), 455–60, and reiterated by Kaiser, *American Tragedy*, 279–81, 329. Not surprisingly, a strong counter-argument was produced by Noam Chomsky, *Rethinking Camelot: JFK, the Vietnam War, and US Political Culture* (London: Verso, 1993).

[16] Lloyd C. Gardner, *Pay Any Price: Lyndon Johnson and the Wars for Vietnam* (Chicago: Ivan R. Dee, 1995) avoids the question of what Kennedy might have done, stressing instead that, not least because of his violent death, his legacy had a crucial effect on Johnson's Vietnam decisions.

[17] On the Berlin Crisis and the Cuban Missile Crisis in the context of Anglo-American relations, see John P. S. Gearson, *Harold Macmillan and the Berlin Wall Crisis, 1958–1962* (London: Macmillan, 1998) and L. V. Scott, *Macmillan, Kennedy and the Cuban Missile Crisis: Political, Military and Intelligence Aspects* (Basingstoke: Macmillan, 1999).

the situation deteriorated still further in the autumn of 1961, Kennedy decided to increase American military aid significantly. However, Kennedy resisted calls for the introduction of regular US combat forces from the American Joint Chiefs of Staff (JCS) and Maxwell Taylor, the President's military representative. Similarly, he rejected suggestions to search for a negotiated settlement. Kennedy's middle-of-the-road approach left both these options open. Nevertheless, the programme he endorsed was a clear breach of the 1954 Geneva ceasefire agreement. Not only did it increase the number of American military advisers beyond the Geneva limits, the introduction of modern military equipment also violated the ceasefire agreement.

American aid helped to stave off the RVN's defeat in 1962, and, indeed, the military situation in South Vietnam seemed to improve. This optimism was also due to the conviction that the new strategy of defending each village and hamlet in the RVN against insurgents, the strategic hamlet programme, was a major step forward. Yet hopes that President Diem would broaden the base of his autocratic and repressive regime were shattered in 1963. Political turmoil in the wake of Buddhist protests against Diem's regime threatened to undermine the counter-insurgency effort. Many officials in Washington had been critical of Diem's regime for years. His brutal handling of the Buddhist protests and indications that the RVN President and his brother were considering a deal with the Democratic Republic of Vietnam (DRV) finally convinced the Kennedy administration to distance itself from the Diem regime, thereby encouraging a military coup in November 1963. But far from bringing political stability to Saigon, Diem's demise destabilized the RVN still further. No competent government emerged in the months after the coup, leaving Kennedy's successor with a legacy of a largely increased American military commitment to a weak and inefficient military government in Saigon.[18]

The Kennedy years provide a natural backdrop to the study of Britain's policy towards the escalating insurgency in South Vietnam. Yet this is not the only reason for focusing on the years 1961 to 1963. 1961 marked not only the opening of a new chapter in British Vietnam policy with the establishment of the British Advisory Mission (BRIAM) in Saigon, but was also the year in which London endorsed the Malaysia concept, embarking on a new post-colonial policy towards the region. When this new era began in September 1963 with the formation of Malaysia, Britain found itself confronted with the escalation of Indonesia's confrontation policy against Malaysia. An analysis of Britain's policy towards this

[18] On Kennedy's Vietnam policy, see Lawrence J. Bassett and Stephen E. Pelz, 'The Failed Search for Victory: Vietnam and the Politics of War', in Thomas G. Paterson (ed.), *Kennedy's Quest for Victory: American Foreign Policy, 1961–1963* (New York: Oxford University Press, 1989), 223–52; Robert Buzzanco, *Masters of War: Military Dissent and Politics in the Vietnam Era* (New York: Cambridge University Press, 1996), 81–151; Chomsky, *Rethinking Camelot*; Herring, *America's Longest War*, 73–107; Kahin, *Intervention*, 129–81; Kaiser, *American Tragedy*, 36–283; Herbert R. McMaster, *Dereliction of Duty: Lyndon Johnson, Robert McNamara, the Joint Chiefs of Staff, and the Lies That Led to Vietnam* (New York: HarperPerennial, 1998), 1–41; Newman, *JFK and Vietnam*; Schwab, *John F. Kennedy*, 1–68; and Young, *The Vietnam Wars*, 75–104.

conflict up to 1966 is beyond the scope of this study, and has already been provided.[19] However, the consequences that confrontation had on Britain's policy towards Vietnam are explored. Although the investigation of these consequences takes the story briefly into 1964, the detailed discussion of British Vietnam policy ends with the dramatic events of the autumn of 1963. In Saigon, the South Vietnamese army overthrew the Ngo Dinh Diem government and killed the President and his brother at the beginning of November. In Dallas, President Kennedy was assassinated three weeks later. In London, the Macmillan era came to a close in October when the Prime Minister resigned, leaving his successor, Sir Alec Douglas-Home, to deal with the worsening situation in Vietnam and the British defence commitment to an escalating conflict between Indonesia and Malaysia.

Like Kennedy, British Prime Minister Harold Macmillan did not place the Vietnam conflict at the very top of his foreign policy agenda. Even at the height of the Buddhist crisis, when Vietnam had become a major problem for Kennedy, Macmillan and his ministers, although aware of the situation, rarely became directly involved. Yet contrary to Combs's assertion, Britain did not 'wash its hands' of the situation in Vietnam. This is illustrated by investigating four major aspects of Britain's Vietnam policy between 1961 and 1963: Britain's policies as a member of the South East Asia Treaty Organisation (SEATO) and as co-chairman of the Geneva conference, the British involvement in the counter-insurgency effort in Vietnam through the British Advisory Mission, and, finally, Whitehall's attitude towards Ngo Dinh Diem's regime. Rather than offering a purely chronological account, the various roles Britain played—diplomatically, politically, and militarily—are best examined by focusing on each of these roles separately. Widening the lens and putting Britain's Vietnam policy into the context of British policy towards Southeast Asia and the Commonwealth countries in the area is also vital to explain Whitehall's policy towards the Vietnam War between 1961 and 1963. Therefore, the chapters in this study are organized to combine an analysis of Britain's policy towards Southeast Asia, and particularly the creation of Malaysia, with a thematic examination of the four major aspects of British Vietnam policy outlined above.

The detailed discussion of these four aspects—SEATO, the ICC, BRIAM, and attitudes towards the Diem regime—shows, on the one hand, that Britain remained concerned about the situation in the RVN after the 1954 Geneva conference, and that the Macmillan government had to consider ways of responding to the deterioration of the security situation in South Vietnam. This, on the other hand, makes it clear that Britain was in a position to attempt to influence Kennedy's Vietnam policy. Ascertaining the British government's response to the mounting insurgency in the RVN and placing this response into the wider context of British policy towards Southeast Asia—the two main aims of this study—

---

[19] See Easter, 'British Defence Policy in South East Asia'. Matthew Jones, *Conflict and Confrontation in South East Asia, 1961–1965: Britain, the United States and the Creation of Malaysia* (Cambridge: Cambridge University Press, 2002). James A. C. Mackie, *Konfrontasi: The Indonesia–Malaysia Dispute, 1963–1966* (Kuala Lumpur: Oxford University Press, 1974).

will reveal that the British government did not counsel restraint and failed to show Kennedy more peaceful ways out of the potential quagmire in Vietnam. Put another way, it will become clear that Britain agreed with a military solution to the conflict and saw no reason to continue to play the role of the peacemaker in Indochina between 1961 and 1963. It will also become clear that British foreign policy was designed to maintain Britain's great power status, in spite of decolonization and dwindling military resources, and that Southeast Asia played a crucial role in Whitehall's global thinking. Here, Britain could make a valuable contribution to western cold war interests, be it against the Democratic Republic of Vietnam or the increasingly pro-Chinese Indonesians, and prove its value as an important and reliable American ally.

I

Britain's Defence Policy in Southeast Asia: The Malaysia Plan, SEATO, and Vietnam

THE UNITED KINGDOM, the United States, Australia, New Zealand, France, Thailand, Pakistan, and the Philippines signed the Southeast Asia Collective Defence Treaty in Manila in September 1954. It stipulated that the signatories would act to meet 'common danger' in the event of an armed attack. They would also consult if the independence or integrity of any party in the treaty area was threatened in any other way than by armed attack. The treaty area did not only comprise the territory of the signatories. A protocol to the Manila treaty also included Cambodia, Laos, and the 'free territory under the jurisdiction of the State of Vietnam'. These 'protocol states' were barred from joining the South East Asia Treaty Organization (SEATO) because the Geneva Accords of 1954 prohibited them from entering military alliances.[1] While Laos and South Vietnam went along with the provisions of the Manila treaty, Cambodia was determined to demonstrate its neutrality and rejected the protection offered by SEATO.[2]

SEATO was formed in reaction to the Geneva Agreements of 1954.[3] It was designed, particularly in Washington's view, to deter communist aggression in the region. John Foster Dulles, US Secretary of State at the time, called SEATO a 'no trespassing' sign warning the Soviet Union and particularly the PRC not to

---

[1] South-East Asia Collective Defence Treaty, Article 4 and Protocol. The text of the treaty is in: John A. S. Granville and Bernard Wasserstein, *The Major International Treaties since 1945: A History and Guide with Texts* (London: Methuen, 1987), 121–2.

[2] Young, *The Vietnam Wars*, 46; see also David P. Chandler, *The Tragedy of Cambodian History: Politics, War and Revolution Since 1945* (New Haven: Yale University Press, 1993), 75.

[3] Apart from the formation of the organization in 1954 and its role in the Laos crisis of 1960–1, SEATO has not attracted a great deal of scholarly attention. The focus on SEATO's non-intervention in Laos has led to the general view that the organization was a failure. Britain is usually blamed for preventing SEATO action and promoting a negotiated settlement. The titles of the two most comprehensive studies on SEATO's history underscore this by referring to SEATO as a 'paper tiger' and 'failure'. Leszek Buszynski, *SEATO: The Failure of an Alliance Strategy* (Singapore: Singapore University Press, 1983) is the best general study to date, but is based on secondary sources. Mark Pearson, *Paper Tiger: New Zealand's Part in SEATO, 1954–1977* (Wellington: New Zealand Institute of International Affairs, 1989) has provided a useful official history written from New Zealand primary sources. There are also a few studies written during SEATO's lifetime: George Modelski (ed.), *SEATO: Six Studies* (Melbourne: F. W. Cheshire for the Australian National University, 1962), and Justus M. Van der Kroef, *The Lives of SEATO* (Singapore: Institute of Southeast Asian Studies, 1976).

expand their influence in Southeast Asia still further.[4] For the British SEATO provided the only formal defence relationship with the United States in Southeast Asia. It was hoped that through SEATO Britain would be in a position to influence American cold war policy in the region.[5] Simultaneously, the inclusion of the 'protocol states' in SEATO's treaty area confronted the British government with the possibility of military involvement in Laos and Vietnam.[6] With the Laos crisis and the mounting insurrection in the Republic of Vietnam (RVN) at the beginning of the 1960s, SEATO intervention indeed became a distinct possibility.

This chapter challenges the oft-repeated view that British forces would have never taken part in active SEATO operations. The analysis of the Macmillan government's policy towards SEATO shows that there is some evidence suggesting that Britain would have taken part in SEATO intervention in Indochina if the US had insisted.

In general, Britain's policy towards Southeast Asia hinged upon the continued unrestricted use of the military base in the crown colony of Singapore. The British relied on this base for their contribution to the defence of Malaya, and without the base Britain's contribution to SEATO was a dead letter. However, in the early 1960s the British were confronted with two problems. On the one hand, the prospect of Singapore's gaining of independence raised the question whether Britain would be allowed to maintain its base in the city-state. On the other hand, the government of Prime Minister Harold Macmillan recognized that Britain had to make cuts in its defence expenditure east of Suez. The perfect solution to these two problems seemed the creation of Malaysia.

THE MALAYSIA PLAN

In 1960, the bulk of Britain's forces in Southeast Asia were stationed in Singapore. This commercially important gateway between the Indian Ocean and the South China Sea was Britain's premier base east of Suez. It contained the Far East Headquarters of the Royal Navy, the Army, and the Royal Air Force.[7] Prime Minister Macmillan had decided in 1960 to maintain the British contribution to the nuclear deterrent against China, and he did not change this policy in the following years. Again, Singapore was vital because even medium-range bombers equipped with nuclear weapons could reach the southern half of the PRC.[8] The forces in Singapore had not just the task of deterring communist expansion, they

---

[4] Anderson, *Trapped by Success*, 71.

[5] MOD paper 'United Kingdom Obligations and Policies in the Area'. Annex to MOD Memorandum. 7.7.60. Public Record Office, Kew (hereafter PRO): CAB 134/1644.

[6] House of Commons Debates, 29.11.61, Vol. 659, Col. 49. Brief for Parliamentary Question by Warner. 27.11.61. PRO: FO 371/160132, DV1015/11.

[7] John Darwin, *Britain and Decolonisation* (Basingstoke: Macmillan, 1988), 283.

[8] PM(W)(62)20: MOD brief for Anglo-American talks in Washington. 17.4.62. PRO: CAB 133/246.

also had to fulfil colonial and Commonwealth obligations. London was responsible for the defence of the crown colonies of North Borneo and Sarawak, of the State of Singapore itself, and of the Sultanate of Brunei, technically a British protectorate. Moreover, since 1949 the British had been coordinating military planning with the Australians and New Zealanders in the ANZAM area (an acronym for Australia, New Zealand, and Malaya). In this context, the three countries had formed a Commonwealth brigade in 1955 as a strategic reserve, which was stationed in Malaya.[9] In addition to SEATO and ANZAM, the Anglo-Malayan Defence Agreement (AMDA) of 1957 committed the United Kingdom to assist Malaya against external aggression.[10]

Financial constraints made it increasingly difficult for the British to maintain the level of military forces necessary to live up to these commitments and responsibilities. While it was undisputed in the British government that defence cuts had to be made, the Conservative Macmillan government wanted to preserve Britain's world role. In this respect the British ability to use its military forces east of Suez in addition to Britain's political influence in its present and former colonies in Asia was vital.[11] In order to reduce defence expenditure and maintain Britain's unhampered use of the Singapore military base, which was essential for the ability of British forces to take part in possible SEATO intervention in Vietnam, Britain embraced the plan to form the new federation of Malaysia. In fact, the formation of Malaysia became the cornerstone of Britain's policy in Southeast Asia in 1961.

Lord Selkirk, the last British Commissioner-General for Southeast Asia, found that the formation of a 'Greater Malaysia' was a marvellous idea. The Federation of Malaysia was designed to bring together Malaya, the former British colony that had become independent in 1957, and the remaining British dependencies in Southeast Asia, Singapore, Sarawak, North Borneo, and Brunei. Lord Selkirk never tired of promoting Malaysia in telegram after telegram and letter after letter. He impressed on Foreign Secretary Selwyn Lloyd that Malaysia was 'the only evolution which can give stability to the area'.[12] In a personal letter to Prime Minister Harold Macmillan on 12 September 1961 Selkirk insisted that the new federation was 'of first importance for the orderly development of [Southeast Asia]'.[13]

The idea of a federation of the British possessions in Southeast Asia was not new.[14] Malcolm Macdonald, then British Commissioner-General for Southeast

---

[9] On ANZAM and the strategic reserve in Malaya, see Edwards, *Crises and Commitments*, 60 f. and 162 ff.

[10] On AMDA, see Chin Kin Wah, *The Defence of Malaysia and Singapore: The Transformation of a Security System 1957–1971* (Cambridge: Cambridge University Press, 1983).

[11] Richard Aldous and Sabine Lee, '"Staying in the Game": Harold Macmillan and Britain's World Role', in Richard Aldous and Sabine Lee (eds.), *Harold Macmillan and Britain's World Role* (Basingstoke: Macmillan, 1996), 154.

[12] Letter: Selkirk (Singapore) to Lloyd. 17.6.60. PRO: FO 371/152141, D1022/16.

[13] Letter: Selkirk (Singapore) to Macmillan. 12.9.61. PRO: PREM 11/3737.

[14] In 1887 Lord Brassey of the North Borneo Chartered Company had proposed the merger of British Malaya with the British territories in Borneo. This idea was quickly rejected and had no lasting effect. James Ongkili, *Nation-building in Malaysia* (Singapore: Oxford University Press, 1985), 151.

Asia, had called for a Greater Malaysia in 1951, but his proposal had met with lit-tle enthusiasm.[15] Concrete plans for the creation of Malaysia emerged in 1960–1. Although the advantages the scheme held for Britain's position in the area were great, the scheme itself was initiated by the leaders of Malaya and Singapore. On 27 May 1961 the Malayan Prime Minister, Tunku Abdul Rahman, made his first public proposal for the creation of Malaysia in a speech at the Foreign Corres-pondents' Association in Singapore. Barely three months later, the Tunku, as Abdul Rahman was popularly known, reached an agreement in principle on the Malaysia concept with Singapore's Prime Minister Lee Kuan Yew.[16]

Officially, Kuala Lumpur insisted on the inclusion of the British territories in Borneo not out of a keen desire to acquire the territories per se, but only so that they would maintain the Malays' numerical superiority within the new Federa-tion which included the Chinese population in Singapore. This rationale has been accepted by most of the scholars who have worked on the topic.[17] At the time it was also put forward by Lord Selkirk, who noted that the Tunku did not have 'the slightest interest in the Borneo territories as such'.[18] The Deputy Commis-sioner for Singapore held the same view and had the impression that the Tunku was reluctant to enlarge his federation.[19]

Yet there is evidence suggesting that the Tunku had other aims on his agenda besides just the maintenance of a racial composition favourable to the Malayans. As early as June 1960, the Tunku revealed his plans for a greater federation to Lord Perth, Minister of State for Colonial Affairs. At the beginning of the meet-ing with Perth the Tunku talked about a merger between Malaya and Singapore, but he soon expressed his 'deep-rooted suspicion of all that the present Singapore Government stands for', and proposed a merger between just Malaya, Brunei, and possibly Sarawak. 'From all that', Lord Perth concluded after the talk, 'it seems clear to me that [the Tunku] is really quite keen on getting something more to add to the Federation.'[20] This 'something' seemed to be first of all the Borneo territories. Even after the Tunku had publicly proposed the establishment of Malaysia it became clear that he would not mind excluding Singapore: in the summer of 1961 he demanded that Malaya should take over the British Borneo

---

[15] CPC(61)9. 17.4.61. PRO: CAB 134/1560. On earlier attempts at achieving closer cooperation be-tween the territories, see also Anthony J. Stockwell, 'Malaysia: The Making of a Neo-Colony?', *Jour-nal of Imperial and Commonwealth History*, 26/2 (1998), 140–1.

[16] Peter Boyce, *Malaysia and Singapore in International Diplomacy: Documents and Commen-taries* (Sydney: Sydney University Press, 1968), 8; Ongkili, *Nation-building in Malaysia*, 152.

[17] Roger Hilsman, *To Move a Nation* (Garden City, NY: Doubleday, 1967), 384; Chin, *Defence of Malaysia*, 50; Michael Leifer, *Indonesia's Foreign Policy* (London: Allen & Unwin, 1983), 76; Mackie, *Konfrontasi*, 37. For a contemporary account, see Gordon Means, 'Malaysia—A New Fed-eration in Southeast Asia', *Pacific Affairs*, 36/2 (1963), 139. Only Sopiee—after interviewing members of the 1961 Malayan cabinet—concluded that the Tunku was pursuing expansionist aims. Mohamed N. Sopiee, *From Malayan Union to Singapore Separation* (Kuala Lumpur: Penerbit Universiti Malaya, 1974), 125.

[18] Letter: Selkirk (Singapore) to Macmillan. 3.10.61. PRO: PREM 11/3422.

[19] Letter: Lord Moore of Wolvercote to author. 2.3.2002.

[20] Lord Perth's report of a conversation with the Tunku. 10.6.60. PRO: PREM 11/3418.

territories before any merger with Singapore.[21] When the negotiations on Malaysia between Malaya and Singapore reached a deadlock in May/June 1963, the Malayan government repeatedly suggested to the British that Malaysia should be created without Singapore.[22] Yet the inclusion of Singapore was essential to win British support for Malaysia. This was the price the Tunku had to pay for the Borneo territories.

In 1960 London was concentrating upon closer cooperation between the Borneo territories, and regarded Malaysia as something that could be achieved only in the distant future.[23] As a result of the Tunku's talk with Lord Perth, Malaysia was discussed by the Colonial Policy Committee in June and July 1960, which decided to adopt an attitude of 'benevolent neutrality' towards the Tunku's suggestions.[24] For Britain the Singapore military base and its role in colonial and Commonwealth defence and in contributing to the deterrent against communist expansion within SEATO was the most important issue. The Foreign Office stressed that Malaysia would be an 'excellent solution for Singapore' and that the Tunku 'must not be allowed to pick up all the plums [Borneo] leaving [Britain] to deal with the thistles [Singapore]'.[25]

The thorny issue was the strong left-wing movement in the city-state. Singapore's constitution, which allowed for internal self-government, was due to be reviewed in 1963. It was believed that full independence would have to be granted to the colony then, although there were doubts that Singapore would be a viable state on its own. Independence through merger was the official policy of Prime Minister Lee Kuan Yew's governing People's Action Party (PAP), as this would be the fastest way to achieve independence. However, Lee's position became increasingly precarious because the radical left-wing of his party challenged his leadership. One of the reasons why the Tunku began to push the Malaysia idea in 1961 was Lee's eroding power. If Lee's government fell, Malaysia could not be achieved.[26]

The British Secretary of State for Commonwealth Relations, Duncan Sandys, told the Tunku in January 1961 that, in his personal view, Malaysia was desirable.[27] However, when the Tunku informed Sir Geofroy Tory on 26 May that he would make a public proposal, the British High Commissioner in Kuala Lumpur had the feeling that the Tunku was 'perhaps faster moving ahead than we were

---

[21] CO memorandum for Macmillan. 6.7.61. PRO: PREM 11/3418.

[22] Letter: Macmillan to Selkirk (Singapore). 5.8.63. PRO: PREM 11/4188.

[23] Letter: Goode to Schönenberger. 20.9.78. Papers of Sir William Goode, Rhodes House Library, Oxford (hereafter Goode Papers): file 5, box 5. Sopiee, *From Malayan Union to Singapore Separation*, 132.

[24] Minutes: Brooke to Macmillan. 27.6.60 and 6.7.60. PRO: PREM 11/3418.

[25] Blue FO minute by Warner. 26.7.60. PRO: FO 371/152141, D1022/24. Minute: Wilford (FO) to Selwyn Lloyd. 4.7.60. Ibid. D1022/21.

[26] Letter: Selkirk (Singapore) to Macleod. 4.5.61. PRO: DO 169/25. See also Mackie, *Konfrontasi*, 37–40; and Ernest C. T. Chew and Edwin Lee, *A History of Singapore* (Oxford: Oxford University Press, 1991), 140–1.

[27] Letter: Selkirk (Singapore) to Macleod. 27.6.61. PRO: PREM 11/3418. See also Lee Kuan Yew, *The Singapore Story: Memoirs of Lee Kuan Yew* (Singapore: Times Education, 1998), 364.

prepared to go'.[28] Indeed, Harold Macmillan expressed doubts as to whether the plan for a federation of the former British colonies would work.[29] Whitehall realized that no agreed British policy yet existed. Consequently, it took Macmillan six weeks to answer a letter in which the Malayan Prime Minister had asked for the British view of 'Greater Malaysia'. Lord Selkirk complained that the British had always hinted that Malaysia was desirable but now appeared 'lethargic and indifferent', much to the Tunku's confusion.[30]

London had two reasons to proceed cautiously. First, the development of democratic institutions in the British crown colonies of North Borneo and Sarawak was still in its infancy. Political parties hardly existed, and free elections had never been held. There was a feeling in London and in the colonies that in the new federation the Malayans would just take over the British role in Borneo. In the opinion of the last British Governor of Sarawak, the 'project seemed hopelessly ill-founded and unreal'.[31] Second, Whitehall was considering the future British defence strategy in Southeast Asia. The Chiefs of Staff were discussing whether a new base would have to be established in Labuan or even Australia because of the possible loss of the Singapore base, and whether the new airborne strategy would make up for the necessary reduction in manpower east of Suez.[32] In this context concerns about the future of Britain's military facilities in Singapore after its possible merger with Malaya, particularly with regard to SEATO operations, were voiced.[33]

Concerns about the future use of the Singapore base for SEATO operations were not unfounded. Malaya had refused to join SEATO after gaining independence in 1957. The Australians blamed Duncan Sandys, then Minister of Defence, for Kuala Lumpur's anti-SEATO attitude. In Canberra's view, Sandys's public remarks about atomic weapons being available for the British forces in Southeast Asia shortly before Merdeka, Malaya's independence day, stiffened opinion against SEATO in the country.[34] Worse, in April 1959 the Kuala Lumpur government questioned for the first time the use of Commonwealth aircraft based in Malaya for SEATO exercises.[35] The stakes were raised in January 1960 when the British wanted to move a small party of Royal Engineers to Thailand. The Malayan Defence Minister, Tun Abdul Razak, informed the British High Commissioner in Kuala Lumpur that British forces stationed in Malaya under

---

[28] Telegram 382: Kuala Lumpur to CRO. 26.5.61. PRO: PREM 11/3418.
[29] Harold Macmillan, *At the End of the Day* (London: Macmillan, 1973), 249.
[30] Letter: Selkirk (Singapore) to Macmillan. 3.10.61. PRO: PREM 11/3422.
[31] Letter: Goode (North Borneo) to Allen (Singapore). 11.8.60. PRO: CO 1030/977. Letter: Goode to Sheppard. 2.10.84. Goode Papers: file 5, box 5.
[32] For an excellent discussion of British defence policy and the creation of Malaysia, see Easter, 'British Defence Policy', 38–53. See also Phillip Darby, *British Defence Policy East of Suez, 1947–1968* (London: Oxford University Press, 1973), 235–7.
[33] CO memorandum for Macmillan. 6.7.1961. PRO: PREM 11/3418.
[34] Savingram 94: EA Canberra to Washington. 5.9.57. National Archives of Australia, Canberra (hereafter AUSNA): A1838/277, file 3027/9/5.
[35] Memorandum 548: Critchley (Kuala Lumpur) to EA Canberra. 24.4.59. Ibid.

AMDA should not take part in SEATO exercises. The letter sent shock waves through the British defence establishment in Singapore. The fear was that the British Far East garrison would become a 'white elephant', particularly as it was considered unlikely that Britain would conduct major operations in Asia except under SEATO.[36] Lord Selkirk impressed on Macmillan that the other SEATO members should not gain knowledge of the Malayan government's position because Britain's prestige would 'suffer a serious blow'.[37] The Australian defence committee concluded that it would be necessary to consider the value of stationing forces in Malaya if they could not be used in SEATO exercises.[38] The British Chiefs of Staffs noted with concern that Britain had already dedicated the Commonwealth brigade to SEATO. Lord Mountbatten, the Chief of the Defence Staff, concluded that it had to be clearly understood that Britain would have to deploy its forces from Malaya in an emergency, regardless of Kuala Lumpur's objections.[39]

British attempts to arrive at a written understanding with the Malayans in the following months led London into the danger of facing even more restrictions. In the negotiations Britain insisted that AMDA was the legal basis for the freedom of movement of its forces in Malaya. Tun Razak in turn complained to the Australians that Britain's rigid interpretation of AMDA, with which Australia and New Zealand had associated themselves in 1959, had almost brought the defence agreement to grief.[40] Eventually, the Tunku gave Duncan Sandys private assurances that British forces would be allowed to go directly to Thailand for active SEATO operations. The Malayans, however, continued to object to direct participation of British troops stationed in Malaya in SEATO exercises.[41] Therefore, the British forces in Malaya had to go through Singapore as a quarantine both before and after use in SEATO exercises.[42] Naturally, it was uncertain whether Singapore's gaining of independence within the larger Federation of Malaysia would allow the continuation of this practice. The US State Department found this aspect of the Malaysia plan unsettling, and noted that Washington would be 'seriously concerned over [the] loss to [the] British of their SEATO capability'.[43]

---

[36] Letter: Tun Razak to Tory (Kuala Lumpur). 8.1.60. Telegram SEACOS 1: FEDSEC Singapore to Ministry of Defence. 12.1.60. Both in PRO: DEFE 11/273.

[37] Letter: Selkirk (Singapore) to Macmillan. 17.2.60. PRO: FO 371/152143, D1051/5.

[38] Minute: Townley (Australian Minister of Defence) to Menzies. 31.3.60. AUSNA: A1209/64, file 60/128.

[39] COS(60) 6th meeting. 26.1.60. PRO: DEFE 4/124.

[40] Telegram 2728: Shann (London) to EA Canberra. 21.6.60. AUSNA: A1209/64, file 60/128. Memorandum 1038: Critchley (Kuala Lumpur) to EA Canberra. 14.7.60. AUSNA: A1838/277, file 3027/9/5.

[41] Minute: Sandys to Macmillan. 18.10.60. PRO: PREM 11/3865. Minute: Sandys to Macmillan. 23.3.61. PRO: PREM 11/3280.

[42] Telegram 75: CO to Selkirk (Singapore). 23.2.60. PRO: DEFE 11/273. Telegram 185: Critchley (Kuala Lumpur) to EA Canberra. 13.5.60. AUSNA: A1209/64, file 60/128.

[43] Deptel 484: Rusk to Bangkok. 10.10.61. John F. Kennedy Presidential Library, Boston (hereafter JFKL): NSF, Vietnam Country Series, September–November 1961, box 194.

This uncertainty, in turn, prompted Prime Minister Macmillan to question Britain's role in SEATO. He produced a paper on 29 September 1961 on Britain's future commitments and defence policy. Macmillan put the Malaysia plan into the context of the need to reduce defence expenditure. The creation of the new federation was desirable as it would relieve Britain of the responsibility for internal security in Singapore and Borneo. With regard to SEATO, restrictions on the use of the Singapore base might be helpful to explain to the other SEATO members that Britain's role within the alliance had to be reassessed, possibly leading to the abandonment of its land contribution to SEATO operations. 'We should take advantage of that,' Macmillan wrote, 'and try to adjust our agreed role in a way that suits us best, politically as well as financially.'[44] Contrary to Easter's assertion, it remains doubtful that Macmillan was serious about abandoning Britain's obligations under the Manila treaty. Less than three weeks after circulating his own critical memorandum Macmillan wrote to Lord Selkirk that Britain should continue to play its part in SEATO.[45] A few days later, Macmillan pointed out in a directive to the Minister of Defence that, despite the need to persuade SEATO members to agree to a 'more realistic concept of SEATO land operations', Britain's primary objective in the Far East was to 'prevent Chinese Communist expansion throughout the area by support of S.E.A.T.O. and other means'.[46]

The Tunku went to London in November 1961 to discuss the Malaysia plan and readily agreed that there would be no limits to the British use of the Singapore base within Malaysia. The Malayan Prime Minister accepted the British formula on the future defence agreements: the renegotiation of AMDA was avoided and an annex merely extended the agreement to apply to all territories of the Federation of Malaysia. Macmillan stressed in his diary that he found the agreement quite satisfactory, particularly in regard to the Singapore base. In his view the Tunku had accepted Britain's demands more readily than expected.[47] Having secured the unhampered use of the Singapore base and thus having reached the envisaged defence arrangements, the British stated publicly that the creation of Malaysia was desirable.[48]

After the Anglo-Malayan agreement of November 1961 the creation of Malaysia became firm British policy, demonstrating that the Singapore base and maintaining British defence interests in the area, including Britain's SEATO membership, were paramount for the Macmillan government. From the Singapore angle, Malaysia had to be brought into being as quickly as possible because of

---

[44] Memorandum by Macmillan. 29.9.61. PRO: CAB 134/1929.

[45] Easter, 'British Defence Policy', 402. Letter: Macmillan to Selkirk (Singapore). 17.10.61. PRO: PREM 11/3737.

[46] D(61)65. 23.10.61. PRO: CAB 131/26, f. 134. The same priorities remained valid throughout the Macmillan government. See ODC(63)3: 'Policy Guidance for Commander-in-Chief'. 2.7.63. PRO: CAB 134/2302.

[47] Political diaries, 2nd Series, MSS Harold Macmillan, Bodleian Library, Oxford (hereafter: Macmillan diaries): 22.11.61, dep. d. 44, f. 34.

[48] Chin, *Defence of Malaysia*, 55.

Lee's shaky government. From the Borneo angle, the opposite was true. White-hall, and the Colonial Office especially, were aware that it was not in the Borneo territories' interest to be rushed into a federation.[49] Ultimately, however, Britain decided that the wishes of the Borneo peoples were secondary to the political in-terests of the United Kingdom. At a meeting on Malaysia chaired by the Prime Minister it was pointed out that the British 'might have to press North Borneo and Sarawak into [Malaysia] more urgently than we should ideally want. For this rea-son it was important to retain flexibility in our position with relation to the views of the local peoples and the proposed commission [to survey the views of the peo-ples of Sarawak and North Borneo on Malaysia] should not be unduly formal in its constitution'.[50] This commission was formed in January 1962 and headed by Lord Cobbold.

The Cobbold Commission's report of June 1962 concluded that the majority of the population in Borneo was in favour of Malaysia if certain safeguards were made for the indigenous peoples.[51] Allegedly the Commission was independent; in fact it was politicized. In a personal letter to Macmillan, Lord Cobbold made crystal clear that his 'yes' to Malaysia was conditional on Singapore joining in. It was his firm conviction that a federation just between Malaya and the Borneo ter-ritories had 'few attractions'. He expressed his concern that the Malayans might make a mess of the territories in the early years because 'many of the local head-hunting tribes are backward and fearless and would revert with pleasure to their former pastimes'.[52] However, in the light of his report, Malaya and Britain agreed on 1 August 1962 that Malaya, Singapore, North Borneo, Brunei, and Sarawak should form the new federation of Malaysia on 31 August 1963.[53]

The British were aware that Malaysia provided them only with an opportunity to slow down the loss of military power in Southeast Asia.[54] Yet Britain regarded its continued military presence in Southeast Asia, including its nuclear capability, as a means to influence American policy.[55] Sir Geofroy Tory, the British High Commissioner in Kuala Lumpur, therefore believed that the 'preservation of our residual interests in Southeast Asia depends on the achievement of Malaysia and . . . is [in] our own enlightened self-interest'.[56] Indeed, the Malaysia plan offered a range of opportunities for Britain. First and most importantly, the new Federa-tion of Malaysia would not infringe British rights to the use of the Singapore base for Britain's defence purposes in the area. Second, possible political disturbances in Singapore with its mainly Chinese population and well-organized trade unions

[49] CPC(60)17. July 1960. PRO: CAB 134/1559. See also Mohamed N. Sopiee, 'The Advocacy of Malaysia before 1961', *Modern Asian Studies*, 7/4 (1973), 717–32.

[50] GEN 754/2nd meeting. 15.11.61. PRO: CAB 130/179.

[51] Boyce, *Malaysia and Singapore*, 13.

[52] Letter: Cobbold to Macmillan. 21.6.62. PRO: PREM 11/3867.

[53] Lord Selkirk saw the only remaining problem as that of keeping Lee Kuan Yew in power for an-other thirteen months. Letter: Selkirk (Singapore) to Macmillan. 30.7.62. PRO: PREM 11/4146.

[54] Minute: De Zulueta to Macmillan. 15.12.61. PRO: PREM 11/4189.

[55] PM(W)(62)20: MOD brief for Anglo-American talks in Washington. 17.4.62. PRO: CAB 133/246.

[56] Telegram 404: Tory (Kuala Lumpur) to CRO. 4.7.62. PRO: PREM 11/3867.

were now considered more unlikely as Malaysia would remove the possibility of exploiting anti-colonial feelings in the city. Even if disturbances were to break out, it would not be up to the British to deal with them. Third, Britain would cease to be responsible for the internal security of its former colonies and British forces in the area could be substantially reduced. Fourth, granting independence to the remaining British colonies would improve London's standing in the eyes of the neutralist countries in Southeast Asia'.

British deliberations on the Malaysia concept highlighted the dilemma of the Macmillan government. How could Britain maintain its political influence and prestige while reducing its forces in the area? Cuts in defence expenditure were deemed necessary, yet there was no willingness to admit any weakness or to retreat from any defence commitments.[57] Macmillan's passing ideas about reassessing Britain's role in SEATO revealed that he seemed to be prepared at least to consider giving up defence obligations. However, in 1961 Macmillan envisaged a possible reassessment only if circumstances beyond Whitehall's control— the loss of the Singapore base—rendered Britain's contribution to SEATO land forces impossible. In Southeast Asia he was least committed to SEATO, an attitude that could be in part attributed to the problem the alliance had created for Britain during the Laos crisis.

CRISIS IN LAOS

While the military presence in Singapore and the membership of SEATO secured Britain's position as a world power, the Laos crisis revealed both the advantages and disadvantages of this status. On the one hand, Britain was about to be dragged into a conflict it was desperate to avoid. On the other hand, its SEATO membership and its military presence gave London more clout in the formulation of western policy in the area. However, Britain was clearly the junior partner in the Anglo-American alliance, and was ultimately reluctant to defy Washington's wishes.

In an attempt to prevent the Laotian leader Prince Souvanna Phouma from forging a national unity government that would include the communist Pathet Lao, the Americans had sponsored a right-wing coup in Laos in 1958. By the end of 1960, however, US policy in Laos lay in shambles. The pro-American regime was ousted in August. Souvanna Phouma was briefly back in power only to be violently replaced by a right-wing government under Prince Boun Oum. Souvanna's forces and the Pathet Lao fought back against the new regime. They appealed for Soviet aid and Moscow responded by shipping military equipment through North Vietnam to Laos.[58]

[57] Michael Middeke, 'Britain's Interdependence Policy and Anglo-American Cooperation on Nuclear and Conventional Force Provision, 1957–1964', Ph.D. thesis (London School of Economics, 1999), 319–24.

[58] Zhai, *China and the Vietnam Wars*, 93–6; Anderson, *Trapped by Success*, 191.

Alarmed by the possibility of a communist victory, Washington in early 1961 urged the member states of SEATO to be prepared to intervene in the conflict. SEATO's Military Planning Office (MPO) had drawn up MPO Plan 5 for this purpose. A static plan, it proposed that SEATO forces should occupy the two main Laotian cities of Vientiane and Luang Prabang and hold the main centres of communication along the Mekong river. A US brigade and the Commonwealth brigade stationed in Malaya were the chief land forces that SEATO members had agreed to allocate to such an operation, albeit without automatic commitment as the governments concerned had reserved the right to decide whether or not to send these forces if the plan were put into practice.[59]

Although London agreed that contingency planning had to go ahead, the British government looked upon the possibility of SEATO intervention in Laos with dismay. The view of British officials in the region was that the Americans themselves had brought on the crisis by insisting on arming the extreme right-wing forces in Laos.[60] When the crisis escalated in late 1960 Macmillan sent a personal telegram to President Dwight D. Eisenhower. He expressed his concern that Anglo-American policy was for the first time in many years divergent on tactics.[61] The Laos crisis brought the dangers of their military presence in Southeast Asia home to the British. While the forces in Singapore and Malaya were a political asset in peacetime, their availability within the collective framework of SEATO confronted the British government with difficult choices. Would Britain go along with a military intervention it regarded as unnecessary and potentially disastrous if the other SEATO members and particularly the United States demanded such a move? Macmillan's concerns reflected not only political but also military doubts, for the British Chiefs of Staff warned the Prime Minister on 4 January that SEATO intervention might trigger a Chinese response. They regarded the involvement in the conflict as a 'bottom-less pit in which our limited military resources would very rapidly disappear'.[62] To avoid all this, London was working for a negotiated settlement. Lord Home, the Foreign Secretary, informed the Cabinet on 6 January 1961 that the best Britain could hope for would be the revival of the International Commission, a body designed to supervise the Geneva agreements, which had been disbanded in Laos in 1959. Home thought it likely that this would lead to the reconvention of the Geneva conference.[63]

Yet Macmillan regarded the loss of Laos to the communist bloc as a major blow, which would put Thailand, Burma, Malaya, and Singapore in a dangerous—if not hopeless—position. In spite of his doubts about Washington's potentially aggressive and dangerous stance, Macmillan therefore felt that Britain could not but join the Americans if they decided to intervene in Laos. This

---

[59] Memorandum on SEATO planning for 6th meeting of SEATO council. 10.5.60. PRO: FO 371/152172, D1078/54/G.

[60] Memorandum: Home to Macmillan. 30.3.61. PRO: PREM 11/3280.

[61] Macmillan to Eisenhower. 30.12.60. PRO: PREM 11/3278.

[62] MOD memorandum for Macmillan. 4.1.61. Ibid.

[63] C(61)4. 6.1.61. PRO: CAB 129/104.

decision was made when Macmillan met Lord Home and top Foreign Office officials at Chequers on 2 January 1961.[64] The British determination to stand by its American ally was confirmed in March 1961 during Macmillan's summit with Kennedy at Key West. Kennedy stressed at a meeting on 26 March that he, contrary to Eisenhower, was working for a negotiated settlement. However, Kennedy pressed Macmillan hard for a limited military commitment in case negotiations on Laos failed. The British Prime Minister agreed that a collapse of Laos had to be prevented and that the United States could not be expected to intervene alone. 'Therefore,' he concluded, 'some degree of British military contribution must be made.'[65]

Macmillan's view that Britain was bound to assist the Americans if they decided to intervene was shared by senior members of the cabinet, among them Duncan Sandys, Selwyn Lloyd, the Chancellor of the Exchequer, and Richard A. Butler, the Home Secretary. The Minister of Defence, Harold Watkinson, pointed out that military intervention in Laos had 'always been a nonsense', but if the Americans were determined Britain could play its part because of the availability of British military forces stationed in Singapore and Malaya.[66]

On 27 March Dean Rusk and Lord Home attended the SEATO council of ministers meeting in Bangkok. It was expected that Thailand and the Philippines would demand military intervention in Laos. The British were uncertain whether the US government would support this line. Moreover, an appeal from the King of Laos for SEATO intervention seemed imminent. Rusk, however, made it clear that Washington was working for a moderate result. Therefore, the British regarded the official SEATO resolution on Laos that was issued after the meeting as satisfactory. It supported the British initiative to involve the Soviet Union in negotiations, but reaffirmed SEATO's determination not to sit idly by if negotiations failed.[67]

FROM LAOS CRISIS TO SEATO CRISIS

The Geneva conference on Laos began on 15 May 1961. Britain had achieved its objective. An escalation of the crisis was prevented and negotiations to reneutralize Laos were under way. Yet this diplomatic victory came at a price. SEATO was publicly dismissed as a paper tiger,[68] disillusionment within the

---

[64] Macmillan diaries: 2.1.61, dep. d. 41, f. 30. Note for the record of discussions held at Chequers. 3.1.61. PRO: PREM 11/3278.

[65] Note by Macmillan on conversation with Kennedy at Key West. 26.3.61. PRO: PREM 11/3280. David Kaiser also stresses Kennedy's reluctance to send US combat forces to Laos and escalate the conflict. Kaiser, *American Tragedy*, 39–43.

[66] Telegrams track 54 and 69: Watkinson to Macmillan (in Antigua). 30.3.61, and Home to Macmillan (in Jamaica). 31.3.61. Both in PRO: PREM 11/3280.

[67] Blue FO minute by Southeast Asia Department. 12.4.61. PRO: FO 371/159732, D1071/105/G.

[68] See 'Paper Tiger's Birthday', *The Guardian*, 7.9.62.

alliance became widespread, and the future of the organization uncertain.[69] Thailand, the most important Asian member, caused the most immediate internal SEATO crisis. The Thais blamed Britain and France for weakening the alliance because of their opposition to intervention. Bangkok became determined to change SEATO's voting procedures in an attempt to limit British and French influence, or even make the Europeans leave the organization altogether.[70] Although the British had pointed out to the Americans that they would have intervened in Laos if necessary, doubts about Britain's commitment to SEATO were also voiced in Washington.[71]

Thailand's exasperation with Britain and France stemmed from their reaction to a further escalation of the Laos crisis two weeks before the Geneva conference convened. A Pathet Lao offensive posed a military threat to the Mekong valley, and, in Bangkok's view, to Thailand's own integrity.[72] At the SEATO council meeting of 30 April 1961, the Americans suggested that there were three options open to the alliance: an appeal to the United Nations, the implementation of MPO Plan 5, or the establishment of a SEATO standing force in Thailand. The minimum action that was required immediately was the calling of 'Charter Yellow', bringing SEATO troops to the first stage of alert. Six of the eight SEATO members agreed to put the troops on alert.[73] Only the French were opposed and the British representative claimed that he had to contact his government for instructions.[74] The following day, Macmillan sent a message to Kennedy asking to defer discussions of 'Charter Yellow' in SEATO until 3 May to give the British cabinet time to consult. Washington agreed to the postponement because there was progress on the diplomatic front and the conflicting parties had agreed to meet on 1 May.[75] The Thai attempt to persuade the six consenting members to go to 'Charter Yellow' failed as the majority was of the opinion that such a move would not constitute SEATO action.[76]

The Thai government concluded that France and Britain should not be allowed to prevent SEATO from taking elementary precautions again. In September 1961, Thanat Khoman, the Thai Foreign Minister, proposed that major SEATO decisions be taken by a three-quarters majority. He threatened that he would either not attend the 1962 council meeting or Thailand would even withdraw from the

[69]   Embtel 274: Young (Bangkok) to State Department. Foreign Relations of the United States (hereafter FRUS): 1961–1963, xxiii, Southeast Asia, 13–16.

[70]   Memorandum: Johnson (State Department) to Rusk. 26.9.61. Ibid. 26.

[71]   Report on visit to Asia by Vice-President Johnson. 23.5.61. United States–Vietnam Relations, 1945–1967 (hereafter USVR): Book 11, 159–66. Draft memorandum: M. Bundy to Kennedy. 8.11.61. FRUS: 1961–1963, i, Vietnam 1961, 561–72.

[72]   Blue FO minute by Warner. 12.4.62. PRO: FO 371/166652, DT1015/147/G.

[73]   American troops were already at the second stage of alert, 'Charter Blue', while Thai and Filipino forces were even at 'Charter Green', and ready to go into action.

[74]   Telegram 342: Whittington (Bangkok) to FO. 30.4.61. PRO: FO 371/159733, D1071/112/G.

[75]   Telegrams 932 and 933: FO to Bangkok. 1.5.61 and 2.5.61. PRO: FO 371/159733, D1071/112/G. Macmillan diaries: 1.5.61 and 4.5.61, dep. d. 42, ff. 17–22.

[76]   Despatch 20: McDermot (Bangkok) to FO. 5.3.62. PRO: FO 371/166644, DT1011/1.

alliance if his proposal was not adopted in substance.[77] The Thai determination to change the voting procedure hung over SEATO for more than a year. None of the western members supported the abandonment of unanimity, but various attempts were made to accommodate Bangkok's demands.[78] The Australians produced a compromise proposal, which introduced the idea of abstentions. A motion would carry if by a certain target date six members had cast affirmative votes and none negative votes. The Thais flatly rejected the compromise in January 1962.[79]

The Foreign Office found the Thai proposal unacceptable, particularly as it suggested majority voting on matters involving peace and war.[80] The Australian compromise proposal was not supported by the British either. However, Lord Home preferred the United Kingdom representative to keep a low profile at SEATO meetings. Britain was not to appear obstructive. His main concern was the Geneva conference on Laos and Thailand's cooperation in reaching a settlement there was badly needed.[81] Therefore, the British were considering steps to alleviate Bangkok's concerns. Yet Frederick Warner, the head of the Southeast Asia Department in the Foreign Office, was concerned that reassurances would commit Britain more to Thailand's defence than London perhaps wanted. Lord Home, however, did not share these concerns. On the contrary, he was even thinking of prepositioning military supplies in Thailand. 'If SEATO has any purpose at all it must include the defence of Thailand', Home concluded in February 1962. 'If that goes Malaya would be badly squeezed.'[82] For the Foreign Secretary, Britain's defence obligations in SEATO and towards the Commonwealth were two sides of the same coin. SEATO helped to keep the communist threat at bay. Without the alliance's successful containment of the communists, Commonwealth defence interests would be seriously compromised.

The voting issue triggered discussions in Washington and London about the future of SEATO in general. U. Alexis Johnson, Under-Secretary of State for Political Affairs and former US ambassador to Bangkok, suggested the phasing out of the alliance. In his view, a wider Pacific Area Treaty Organization should take SEATO's place.[83] Dean Rusk himself expressed his interest in exploring the possibility of dismantling the organization and replacing it with a regional economic association. Bilateral agreements and perhaps an overall guarantee would

[77] Paper by EA Wellington for Thanat visit. 30.8.62. National Archives of New Zealand, Wellington (hereafter NZNA): PM 120/1/24/1, part 1. On the voting dispute, see also Pearson, *Paper Tiger*, 89–94, and Buszynski, *SEATO*, 85–94.

[78] Memorandum: Taylor to Kennedy. 12.1.62. FRUS: 1961–1963, xxiii, Southeast Asia, 34–6.

[79] Telegram 54: McDermot (Bangkok) to FO. 31.1.62. PRO: FO 371/166646, DT1015/26. Blue FO minute by Warner. 1.2.62. Ibid. DT1015/33.

[80] Minute by Ramsbotham (FO). 8.2.62. Minute by Shuckburgh (FO). 9.2.62. Both in PRO: FO 371/166647, DT1015/54.

[81] Minute by Home on blue FO minute by Warner. 29.1.62. PRO: FO 371/166646, DT1015/32.

[82] Minute by Home. 22.2.62. Blue FO minute by Warner. 21.2.62. Both in PRO: FO 371/166660, DT1091/10/G.

[83] Letter: Ledward (Washington) to Warner (FO). 20.3.62. PRO: FO 371/166649, DT1015/82/G.

assure the security of member states.[84] Matters came to a head in February 1962 because President Kennedy desired that the State Department make up its mind on the US position with regard to SEATO voting procedures.[85] Dean Rusk met senior State Department officials, among them U. Alexis Johnson, W. Averell Harriman, and Roger Hilsman on 13 February to discuss SEATO. It was decided not to agree to a change in voting procedures but rather to build up an American relationship with Thailand within the SEATO framework by de-emphasizing SEATO and re-emphasizing the American bilateral commitment. This commitment and the usefulness of SEATO were to be spelled out in a letter to Thanat. The Thai Foreign Minister was invited to Washington to publicize the commitment.[86] Thanat accepted Washington's invitation, and on 6 March 1962 the Rusk–Thanat communiqué was published in Washington. It pointed out that the Americans interpreted Article IV(1) of the Manila treaty as committing each nation to act individually regardless of action taken by others.[87]

The State Department rejected any suggestions of phasing out SEATO. However, it was agreed to 'phase-down' the organization by slowly decreasing the size of its headquarters and its non-military activities. The emphasis was to be put on military planning. Military exercises were to continue and maybe even increased. Interestingly, the State Department did not regard Britain's membership of SEATO as vital. The scaling down of SEATO would make it easier, it was thought, for Britain and France to withdraw from the organization 'without loss of face'.[88]

In London, British policy makers also discussed the future of SEATO. Lord Selkirk proved to be the most outspoken critic, yet the government never seriously considered withdrawal from the alliance. A few months after the beginning of the Laos conference, Lord Selkirk made his doubts about SEATO and a possible British involvement in Indochina known to Prime Minister Macmillan.[89] There was some uncertainty within the Foreign Office about the future role of Britain in the area, mainly because the situations in Laos, South Vietnam, and Malaya were still in flux.[90] However, Macmillan pointed out in his response to Selkirk in October 1961 that it was premature to abandon British security interests in the

---

[84] Memorandum: Peters (State Department) to Johnson (State Department). 19.9.61. FRUS: 1961–1963, xxiii, Southeast Asia, 25. The Policy Planning Council developed these ideas and termed the grouping Southeast Asia Independent Nations Group. Paper prepared by the Policy Planning Council. 3.11.61. Ibid. 31–3.

[85] Memorandum: Harriman to Rusk. 9.2.62. FRUS: 1961–1963, xxiii, Southeast Asia, 39–44.

[86] Memorandum for the Record by Hilsman. 13.2.62. FRUS: 1961–1963, xxiii, Southeast Asia, 45–7. Letter: Rusk to Thanat in Deptel 1230: Rusk to Bangkok. 16.2.62. Ibid. 909–11. See also memorandum: Bowles to Kennedy. 4.4.62. FRUS: 1961–1963, ii, Vietnam 1962, 299–303.

[87] EA brief for ANZUS council meeting: 'The future of SEATO'. 2.5.62. NZNA: PM 120/1/1, part 15.

[88] Memorandum for the Record by Hilsman. 13.2.62. FRUS: 1961–1963, xxiii, Southeast Asia, 45–7. Letter: Rusk to Home. 19.2.62. PRO: FO 371/166647, DT1015/59.

[89] Letter: Selkirk (Singapore) to Macmillan. 14.8.61. PRO: PREM 11/3737.

[90] Blue FO minute by Cable. 29.8.61. Minute by Peck. 20.9.61. Both in PRO: FO 371/159702, D1015/16.

Indochinese countries. Particularly South Vietnam 'was likely to require massive western support for years to come . . . to avoid political collapse', Macmillan wrote.[91]

Lord Selkirk expressed his views on SEATO still more forcefully in March 1962. He argued that the western military position would not be weakened if SEATO were dissolved. The organization had diverted Britain's attention from its primary task—the defence of the Malayan area—to Indochina, where the British were not in a strategic position to take part in military operations. 'If it is questionable policy to put an expeditionary force in Europe, it is still more questionable to launch them in Southeast Asia and in any case our forces are being reduced', Selkirk wrote to Lord Home. In the Malayan area, however, Britain could continue to play 'quite an effective role'.[92]

The British ambassador in Bangkok, Dermot McDermot, argued the opposite case. He found SEATO a valuable organization. It was the basis of Thai security and very important to the defence of Australia and New Zealand. McDermot regarded British support for the alliance as essential in order to demonstrate London's willingness to resist communism. Betraying ignorance of Washington's own doubts about SEATO, including the necessity of Britain's SEATO membership, McDermot expressed the view that the Americans valued the 'considerable' British conventional forces in the area. He argued that SEATO membership put London in the position to influence American policy. Contracting out of SEATO or evading obligations, however, would severely damage Britain's relationship with Australia and New Zealand.[93] Particularly Australia's faith in the effectiveness of the Commonwealth, the British noted, had already been shaken by the withdrawal of South Africa from the organization, and Britain's application for membership of the European Economic Community (EEC).[94] Canberra suspected Britain to disengage from its responsibilities in Asia and the Pacific.[95]

The Foreign Office sided with the ambassador in Bangkok. Indeed, nobody seemed to support Selkirk's view. 'I have no doubt in my mind that we must remain in SEATO for the present', concluded Frederick Warner of the Southeast Asia Department. Anything else would have a bad effect on Britain's relations with Washington, Canberra, and Wellington. Lord Home agreed, and so did Edward Peck, the Assistant Under-Secretary of State, who had previously been posted to Singapore and had found Lord Selkirk's grasp of Southeast Asian

---

[91] Letter: Macmillan to Selkirk (Singapore). 17.10.61. PRO: PREM 11/3737.

[92] Letter: Selkirk (Singapore) to Home. 6.3.62. PRO: FO 371/166649, DT1015/74/G.

[93] Despatch 20: McDermot (Bangkok) to Home. 5.3.62. PRO: FO 371/166644, DT1011/1.

[94] On Commonwealth concerns about the British application to join the EEC and the problems the economic links with the Commonwealth caused for the application, see N. Piers Ludlow, *Dealing with Britain: The Six and the First UK Application to the EEC* (Cambridge: Cambridge University Press, 1997), 34–5, 88, and 132–5; and John W. Young, *Britain and European Unity, 1945–1992* (Basingstoke: Macmillan, 1993), 74 and 78–82.

[95] CRO brief on Anglo-Australian relations for the visit of Under-Secretary of State Tilney. July 1963. PRO: DO 169/104.

matters wanting.[96] Peck stressed that a British move to disrupt SEATO would push the Australians and eventually the New Zealanders into a stronger alliance with the Americans. The Thais would do the same and Britain's political influence in Southeast Asia would be considerably weakened at a time when London still wished to retain a say in Southeast Asian affairs.[97]

This reasoning was in line with the British government's policy towards the creation of Malaysia. The most important benefit of the new federation was the prospect that British forces could be deployed from the Singapore base for SEATO and Commonwealth defence purposes. Having secured the Tunku's agreement to the unlimited use of the base, Britain continued to be in a position to make a credible contribution to SEATO. Backed by its military forces in Southeast Asia, the British could then retain a say in the region's affairs. It is worth pointing out that the arguments the Foreign Office put forward in support of Britain's full and active membership in SEATO revolved around one central theme: the maintenance of British political influence in Southeast Asia. Indeed, the Foreign Office did not argue that Britain's forces in the area were from a military point of view absolutely necessary to contain communism. Instead, the British military contribution to deterring communist expansion in Asia was important in political terms within the western alliance. It was designed to reassure Washington, Canberra, and Wellington that Britain was prepared to play its part in the cold war struggle. Although the British noted that the PRC's ultimate aim was to dominate Southeast Asia in the long run,[98] the immediate danger for Britain was not the loss of political influence because of communist expansion, but the loss of influence in Asia's non-communist countries and within the western alliance.

Consequently, Lord Home spelled out to Selkirk in April 1962 that Britain had no intention of dissolving SEATO. The alliance had been a successful deterrent against further communist expansion. At the same time British membership of SEATO had enabled London to prevent the alliance from issuing threats too lightly. To Home, the attitude of the Americans was all important. Britain had established a common working policy with Washington, particularly on Laos and Vietnam, and this, Home pointed out, was 'worth preserving'.[99]

MILITARY ASSISTANCE TO THAILAND

The British government showed its determination to preserve the common working policy with the Americans in the wake of the Nam Tha incident. While the Geneva conference on Laos stood adjourned in April 1962, the Americans

[96] Sir Edward Peck in interview with the author. 12.2.2002.
[97] Blue FO minute by Warner. 12.4.62. Minutes by Peck and Home. 13.4.62. All in PRO: FO 371/166652, DT1015/147/G.
[98] MOD Memorandum: 'The military position'. 7.7.60. PRO: CAB 134/1644.
[99] Letter: Home to Selkirk (Singapore). 17.4.62. PRO: FO 371/166652, DT1015/147/G.

persuaded the Thai government to induce the right-wing Laotian leader, General Phoumi Nosavan, to begin serious negotiations with the moderate Souvanna Phouma. However, before talks got under way Pathet Lao forces overran Nam Tha, Phoumi's last remaining stronghold, on 6 May 1962 and advanced within thirty miles of the Thai–Laotian border. In a cabinet meeting, Lord Home stressed that this move threatened Thai security. In keeping with the Rusk–Thanat agreement, the Americans sent the Seventh Fleet to the Gulf of Thailand, moved troops already in Thailand closer to the Laotian border, and asked other SEATO members to send token forces as well.[100]

London promptly responded to Rusk's request. Prime Minister Macmillan met Lord Home and Harold Watkinson, the Minister of Defence, on the afternoon of 15 May and decided that Britain would offer a squadron of twelve Hunter aircraft to the Thai government. The Americans were informed immediately, and the British cabinet gave 'full approval' to the decision the following day.[101] Dean Rusk expressed his delight,[102] while the British move apparently came as a surprise to the Australians. They had also agreed to make fighter aircraft available, and Prime Minister Menzies had urged his British colleague to do the same, yet the Australian Cabinet had stressed that Australian forces would go to Thailand even if Britain refused to make a contribution.[103]

Whereas Canberra seemed to underestimate Britain's determination to stand firm in Asia, the British decision to deploy Hunter aircraft to Thailand was, in fact, not at all controversial. The Chiefs of Staff stressed that sending the Hunter squadron was the easiest way to make a token contribution. The Foreign Office found Rusk's request modest and was looking for a way to 'show the flag'. To the disappointment of Whitehall, the Thais asked the British to deploy the Hunters to Chieng Mai in the north of Thailand. The Foreign Office felt that the British contribution would have been more visible in Bangkok. Yet the British ambassador in Thailand reassured the Foreign Office. He pointed out that Chieng Mai was the second biggest city in Thailand, and, as opposed to Bangkok, there was no danger that the British contribution would get lost in the larger American contingent.[104]

In the House of Commons on 17 May, Macmillan expressed the hope that the deployment of a token force in Thailand would have a stabilizing effect on the situation in Laos. He made clear that Britain's move was not a 'formal action on

[100] CC(62)33. 15.5.62. PRO: CAB 128/36. Despatch 37: McDermot to Home. 31.5.62. PRO: FO 371/166631, DS1192/60. On the Nam Tha incident, see also Edwards, *Crises and Commitments*, 240–1; Ralph B. Smith, *An International History of the Vietnam War,* ii (New York: St. Martin's Press, 1985), 61–4, and Buszynski, *SEATO*, 87–93.

[101] Minute by Peck (FO). 15.5.62. Telegram 3624: FO to Washington. 15.5.62. Both in PRO: FO 371/166629, DS1192/6/G. CC34(62)2. 17.5.62. PRO: CAB 128/36.

[102] Telegram 1386: Ormsby-Gore (Washington) to FO. 16.5.62. PRO: FO 371/166629, DS1192/5.

[103] Blue FO minute by Peck and Australian telegram 305 containing message from Menzies to Macmillan. 15.5.62. Ibid. DS1192/12/G.

[104] Blue FO minute by Warner. 15.5.62. Ibid. DS1192/6/G. Telegram 634: FO to Bangkok. 29.5.62. Telegram 239: McDermot (Bangkok) to FO. 30.5.62. Both in ibid. DS1192/39. COS(62), 36th meeting. 29.5.62. PRO: DEFE 4/145. COS(62)227. 30.5.62. PRO: DEFE 5/127.

the part of the S.E.A.T.O. Powers as a whole'.[105] In the discussions with the Americans about the British contribution London had been keen to stress the bilateral nature of the deployment. The British were relieved to discover that the Americans were thinking on similar lines.[106]

In fact, the British underwrote the Rusk–Thanat communiqué by sending troops to Thailand on a bilateral basis.[107] London had welcomed the communiqué publicly in March 1962, and had shown its approval of it in a SEATO council representatives meeting in April. Yet only the action taken in May 1962 made it evident that Britain regarded the communiqué and its stress on individual and collective obligations of SEATO members as practical policy. The Nam Tha incident had therefore provided an urgently needed opportunity to repair the fabric of collective defence in Southeast Asia, opined the British ambassador in Bangkok. 'We have now re-established an effective joint purpose in the South East Asia Treaty Organisation', the ambassador concluded, 'and we have obliged the Thais to recognize the framework under which the United States assistance to them is offered.'[108] SEATO was kept in being and the Thais were reassured, yet the principle of collective action had been undermined. It was evident that the United States and the United Kingdom preferred bilateral assistance if an ally in the region came under pressure. In this way, the control over their forces remained solely in their hands. SEATO was increasingly regarded as a useful tool to either justify military action or to fall back on if bilateral aid proved insufficient—SEATO planning for Vietnam turned out to be a case in point.

MILITARY PLANNING FOR VIETNAM

Prior to the start of the Geneva conference on Laos, SEATO's deliberations on the situation in the RVN were overshadowed by the Laos crisis. Nevertheless, the SEATO member countries were aware of the mounting insurgency. Discussions in 1960 had centred around intelligence assessments, particularly the problem of ascertaining the strength of National Liberation Front (NLF) forces.[109] The final communiqué of the SEATO council meeting of March 1961 had stressed the alliance's concern about the insurgency in South Vietnam and the 'firm resolve not to acquiesce' in the communist takeover of the RVN.[110] Once negotiations on Laos had begun, the situation in South Vietnam gained more prominence.

[105] *House of Commons Debates*, 17.5.62, Vol. 659, Col. 1533–4.

[106] Telegram 3624: FO to Washington. 15.5.62. PRO: FO 371/166629, DS1192/6/G. Telegram 1386: Ormsby-Gore (Washington) to FO. 16.5.62. Ibid. DS1192/5.

[107] Darby, *British Defence Policy*, 229.

[108] Despatch 37: McDermot (Bangkok) to Home. 31.5.62. PRO: FO 371/166631, DS1192/60.

[109] Report to NATO on SEATO meeting. 16.6.60. PRO: FO 371/152153, D1071/115. Telegram 545: Whittington (Bangkok) to FO. 7.10.60. PRO: FO 371/152741, DV1015/61. EA brief for SEATO council meeting. 1.4.63. NZNA: PM 478/4/1, part 16.

[110] Savingram 15: Whittington (Bangkok) to FO. 29.3.61. PRO: FO 371/159732, D1071/98. New Zealand Press Release SCM/61/D-9. 17.4.61. NZNA: PM 120/2/2, part 4.

Whereas Britain had seemed reluctant to support SEATO military planning for South Vietnam before the Laos conference, it readily agreed in the latter half of 1961 that SEATO should develop a counter-insurgency plan for Vietnam.

In 1960, MPO Plan 6 had been the only plan under development in SEATO's military planning office which dealt with the RVN. Plan 6 was a contingency plan to counter open North Vietnamese aggression against the South in a situation where Hanoi did not have direct Chinese assistance. Although Britain had agreed that a plan had to be drawn up for this contingency, London expressed its uneasiness about some of its provisions. Britain feared that the idea of mounting Korea-style amphibious landings in the Democratic Republic of Vietnam (DRV) to counter North Vietnamese aggression would trigger Chinese intervention. However, the British regarded an open DRV attack as highly unlikely. Objections to MPO Plan 6 were therefore seen as academic and planning went ahead, albeit at low priority.[111]

The real threat to South Vietnam was indirect aggression by subversion. In late 1960, the Australian military adviser in Bangkok proposed that SEATO should address this problem. He suggested to Admiral Harry D. Felt, the American Commander-in-Chief Pacific, that SEATO develop a counter-insurgency plan for South Vietnam. Felt signalled his support, prompting the Australian Chiefs of Staff to favour an Australian initiative in SEATO's military planning council to begin counter-insurgency planning for Vietnam. The Australian Ministry of External Affairs, however, strongly opposed this, arguing that the situation in Vietnam was not serious enough to warrant such a move. Moreover, the special American effort in Vietnam precluded the need to take collective responsibility. Therefore, Canberra felt that the US and not Australia should initiate a proposal for counter-insurgency planning.[112] With the crisis in Laos looming large, the British did not support counter-insurgency planning for Vietnam at this stage. The Foreign Office asked the Australians to postpone their intention of raising the issue in SEATO and was relieved when Canberra agreed. Yet the Foreign Office remained concerned that the Americans might introduce the idea of counter-insurgency planing for Vietnam at SEATO as it was known that Admiral Felt was favourable to such a move.[113]

Because of the continuing division between the Australian military and the Ministry of External Affairs, Canberra sought Lord Mountbatten's views on Vietnam

111 Minute by Secondé (FO). 8.3.60. PRO: FO 371/152171, D1078/34. FO brief on military planning for SEATO council meeting. 10.5.60. Ibid. D1078/46. Blue FO minute by Warner. 25.11.60. PRO: FO 371/152168, D1077/36. Memorandum by Simons (FO). 22.11.60. Letter: Warner (FO) to Peck (Singapore). 29.11.60. Both ibid. D1077/37. Letter: Warner (FO) to Peck (Singapore). 30.12.60. PRO: FO 371/152174, D1078/87/G.

112 Report 80/60 by the Joint Planning Committee. October 1960. Minute of Defence Committee, Agendum 88/1960. 27.10.60. Note for the File by Bunting (EA Canberra). 2.11.60. All in AUSNA: A1209/134, file 1961/457.

113 Minutes by Secondé (FO). 24.10.60 and 4.11.60. PRO: FO 371/152174, D1078/74. Letter: Secondé (FO) to Simons (Singapore). 1.11.60. Ibid. D1078/73/G. COS(60)69th meeting. 3.11.60. PRO: DEFE 4/130.

at an ANZAM Defence Committee meeting in February 1961. Mountbatten was cautious and stressed that Britain's position as co-chairman at the 1954 Geneva conference limited its freedom of action with regard to counter-insurgency operations in the RVN.[114] After the American administration had agreed to the British view that the Laos crisis had to be solved at the conference table, however, Foreign Office officials showed less restraint than Mountbatten, indicating Britain's concern about the deteriorating security situation in the RVN. Frederick Warner personally felt that it might become necessary to develop a plan for Vietnam similar to the MPO Plan 5 for intervention in Laos. On 17 March the Foreign Office told the Australians that it would recommend to Lord Home that Britain should agree to counter-insurgency planning for Vietnam if the suggestion was made. This undermined the argument that Britain and New Zealand would oppose planning, which External Affairs had used on 15 March to frustrate the Australian military's still more urgent demand for counter-insurgency planning.[115]

The main resistance to SEATO planning to counter the insurgency in Vietnam came from Washington. In early 1961, the State Department was opposed to any SEATO involvement because Saigon was 'capable of bolstering itself against insurgency'. The American Military Assistance Advisory Group (MAAG) had developed its own counter-insurgency plan, and the State Department feared that the discussions with Diem on the adoption and implementation of this plan would be disturbed if SEATO also started planning.[116] Moreover, the Australian and British embassies in Saigon noted that SEATO was not in the forefront of President Diem's mind. The South Vietnamese looked primarily to the Americans for help.[117]

In August 1961, Thailand circulated a proposal that SEATO should develop counter-insurgency plans for Burma, Cambodia, and the RVN. With regard to Vietnam the American military was responsive. General Taylor had already pointed out to Kennedy in July 1961 that there was no contingency plan in existence that could deal with infiltration through Laos into South Vietnam.[118] Admiral Felt again strongly favoured SEATO planning for Vietnam. In his view SEATO should no longer defer the development of a plan on the lines of MPO Plan 5. He therefore proposed that SEATO's military advisers should direct the MPO to develop such a plan as soon as possible. However, Felt's view was still not shared by the State Department. Yet to the surprise of the State Department, Felt went ahead in early October 1961 and initiated counter-insurgency planning

[114] Minute of Defence Committee meeting, Agendum No. 11/1961. 16.2.61. Minute of ANZAM Defence Committee meeting. 22.2.61. Both in AUSNA: A1209/134, file 61/317.

[115] Telegram 4970: Shann (London) to EA Canberra. 10.11.60. AUSNA: A1209/64, file 60/184, part 1. Telegram 1289: London to EA Canberra. 17.3.61. Minute of Defence Committee meeting, Agendum No. 29/1961. 15.3.61. Both in AUSNA: A1209/134, file 1961/457.

[116] Telegram 658: Washington to EA Canberra. 21.3.61. Telegram 687: Washington to EA Canberra. 23.3.61. Ibid.

[117] Savingram 58: Forsyth (Saigon) to EA Canberra. 3.6.61. AUSNA: A1838/346, file TS696/8/4, part 1.

[118] Memorandum: Taylor to Kennedy. 26.7.61. FRUS: 1961–1963, i, Vietnam 1961, 243.

for Vietnam in SEATO. Days before the meeting the ANZAM Defence Committee had decided to support counter-insurgency planning for Vietnam on military grounds. The British Chiefs of Staff showed alarm about the 'increasing Vietcong threat' and instructed Admiral David Luce, the British representative at SEATO's military advisers meeting, to make sure that counter-insurgency planning for Vietnam would not be delayed by referring the issue to SEATO council representatives. As the Foreign Office had already signalled in March that it was willing to support counter-insurgency planning, it fully supported the Chiefs of Staff's conclusions. Consequently, Britain and all other SEATO members went along with Felt's initiative.[119] Faced with this, the State Department also agreed to the drawing up of a SEATO counter-insurgency plan for South Vietnam.[120]

Within the wider debate in Washington in autumn 1961, which centred around the question whether American troops should be sent to Vietnam, SEATO intervention was also discussed. In September 1961, Walt Rostow, Kennedy's deputy national security adviser, advocated the introduction of SEATO forces to seal the border to Laos and deter further communist subversion. This undertaking would, according to a plan produced by the Vietnam Task Force, require the dispatch of 11,000 SEATO combat troops, among them the 4,400 men strong Commonwealth brigade.[121] The American Joint Chiefs of Staff, however, found this plan 'not feasible'. They also opposed the deployment of troops close to the 17th parallel, although it was not believed that this deployment would trigger an open North Vietnamese or Chinese attack on South Vietnam.[122] In mid-October 1961, Kennedy decided to dispatch General Taylor and Walt Rostow to Vietnam to find out whether sending SEATO or US forces was feasible and would accomplish anything. Moreover, they were to consult with SEATO allies 'principally with the British and the Australians, regarding SEATO actions in support of the deteriorating situation in Vietnam'.[123]

Whereas the Australians were doubtful that Britain would agree to SEATO action in Vietnam, the Americans correctly assumed that London considered South

[119] New Zealand telegram 68: Weir (Bangkok) to EA Wellington. 6.10.61. PRO: FO 371/159747, D1077/30/G. Telegram 1796: FO to Bangkok. 10.10.61. PRO: DO 169/140.

[120] Telegrams 1309, 2329, 2442, and 2509: Washington to EA Canberra. 21.8.61, 21.9.61, 3.10.61, and 10.10.61. Minute of ANZAM Defence Committee meeting. 20.9.61. All in AUSNA: A1209/134, file 1961/47. Deptel 484: Rusk to Bangkok. 10.10.61. JFKL: NSF, Vietnam Country Series, September–November 1961, box 194.

[121] Memorandum: Rostow (White House) to Johnson (State Department). 29.9.61. FRUS: 1961–1963, i, Vietnam 1961, 315. Memorandum for the record by M. Bundy (White House). 3.10.61. Ibid. 321. Vietnam Task Force Paper: 'Concept for Intervention in Viet-Nam'. Undated. JFKL: NSF, Vietnam Country Series, September–November 1961, box 194. 'Plan for Intervention in Vietnam'. Undated. USVR: Book 11, 300–10. Both papers were attached to a State Department paper of 11.10.61. FRUS: 1961–1963, i, Vietnam 1961, 337, footnote.

[122] Memorandum: Lemnitzer (JCS) to McNamara. 9.10.61. Ibid. 330–1. SNIE 10–3–61: 'Probable communist reactions to certain SEATO undertakings in South Vietnam'. 3.10.61. USVR: Book 11, 313–21.

[123] Memorandum for the record by Gilpatric (Pentagon). 11.10.61. Draft Kennedy instructions to Taylor. 11.10.61. Both in FRUS: 1961–1963, i, Vietnam 1961, 343–5. NSAM 104. 13.10.61. USVR: Book 11, 328.

Vietnam in a rather different light from Laos. At the SEATO Council of Representatives meeting on 11 October 1961, the American ambassador in Bangkok stressed the serious situation in the RVN and the possible need for a military contribution by SEATO in dealing with the insurgency. Britain made clear that it shared the American concern about Vietnam and pointed out that it had just sent a British advisory mission to Saigon to give assistance in countering the insurgency.[124] Washington eventually decided not to seek SEATO action in Vietnam, but to step up its bilateral assistance. While the British government urged the Kennedy administration to give the South Vietnamese themselves a last chance to win their own war,[125] its attitude in SEATO demonstrated that Britain was prepared to support the Americans in their attempt to ensure the survival of an independent non-communist South Vietnam. Frederick Warner even told the Australians quite categorically in January 1962 that Britain would support SEATO intervention in Vietnam if it became necessary.[126] Warner was convinced that Britain could not escape involvement in South Vietnam if the situation escalated.[127]

Consequently, Britain proved to be cooperative in developing MPO Plan 7 entitled 'A Plan to Assist the Government of South Vietnam to Counter Communist Insurgency in South Vietnam'. It was designed to assist the Saigon government to regain 'full control' of its territory. Initially, SEATO forces were to be deployed in the Saigon area to secure the capital itself and in the Tourane area close to the 17th parallel. If necessary, operations could be extended into Laos to deny the NLF forces safe havens. SEATO's aims would be first of all to release forces of the Army of the Republic of Vietnam (ARVN) for offensive operations, and then to assist ARVN to 'destroy the Viet Cong'.[128]

The British did not like the term 'destroy'. They were concerned about the potentially aggressive aspects of the plan—particularly the deployment of SEATO troops to Tourane close to the demilitarized zone between the RVN and the DRV, and also about the possibility of widening the conflict to Laos. However, the Foreign Office had no intention to appear obstructive and did not want to raise objections to the plan 'in the interest of avoiding a row in SEATO'.[129] This attitude reflected, on the one hand, that Britain wanted to demonstrate to its allies that it was committed to saving South Vietnam after having advocated a negotiated settlement to the Laos crisis. On the other hand, SEATO intervention in South Vietnam did not seem at all imminent in the wake of Kennedy's decision to step up the American aid programme in late 1961. It was, for instance, not

---

[124] Telegram 2482: Washington to EA Canberra. 6.10.61. AUSNA: A1838/285, file 2498/9. Telegram 548: Booker (Bangkok) to EA Canberra. 11.10.61. AUSNA: A1209/134, file 1961/47.

[125] Message from Home to Rusk in telegram 7945: FO to Washington. 2.11.61. PRO: PREM 11/3392, also in PREM 11/3736.

[126] Telegram 35: Shann (London) to EA Canberra. 3.1.62. AUSNA: A1209/80, file 62/482, part 1.

[127] Blue FO minute by Warner. 21.6.61. PRO: FO 371/159715, D1053/2.

[128] Memorandum: Bagley (Naval Aide) to Taylor. 23.2.62. FRUS: 1961–1963, ii, Vietnam 1962, 172–4.

[129] Letter: Secondé (FO) to Pumphrey (Singapore). 2.2.62. PRO: FO 371/166660, DT1091/5/G.

deemed necessary to keep the British embassy in Saigon closely informed about the development of MPO Plan 7. When the embassy expressed an interest in this plan and even thought about opening a sub-registry for SEATO papers in 1962, a visit to Bangkok of Cosmo Stewart, the counsellor of the Saigon embassy, damp- ened this desire. He found it interesting to know more about MPO Plan 7, yet he concluded that SEATO planning was quite 'academic', and therefore thought it unnecessary to open a sub-registry for SEATO files in Saigon.[130]

SEATO action had become only a fall-back option. As early as April 1960, the British embassy in Bangkok had pointed out that SEATO had 'little scope for playing a role in the counter-subversion field', and that in this context 'effective dealings between Governments must be bilateral'.[131] By 1962, the primary aid to the South Vietnamese government to counter the insurgency was bilateral, mainly from the Americans, but also from Britain in the form of the British Advis- ory Mission. This was exactly the way Whitehall wanted to provide assistance to Diem's regime, Sir David Ormsby-Gore, the British ambassador in Washington, made clear to the State Department in December 1961. With regard to giving aid to the RVN, he pointed out, Britain 'thought in bilateral rather than multilateral terms'.[132]

CONCLUSION

The plan to create a federation of Malaysia by merging Malaya with Singapore and the British territories in northern Borneo offered a solution to the Macmillan government's most urgent problems in Southeast Asia. Malaysia would enable London to maintain its military presence in the area and, simultaneously, make cuts in defence expenditure by reducing the number of troops without any loss of face because Malaysia would take over responsibility for internal security. When the Tunku agreed to leave the status of the Singapore base within Malaysia un- touched, the British government embraced the Malaysia scheme and the creation of the new federation became firm British policy.

Britain was certainly more committed to the SEATO alliance than previously assumed or even recognized at the time. The willingness to maintain the unre- stricted use of the Singapore base demonstrated this, as well as British policy to- wards SEATO during and after the Laos crisis. Whereas Lord Selkirk advocated that Britain should focus on the defence of its colonial and Commonwealth interests, the Macmillan government preferred Britain also to continue to play a role in SEATO. Lord Home, the Foreign Secretary, regarded Commonwealth defence and SEATO's role as a deterrent against communist expansion as closely

---

[130] Letter: Burrows (Saigon) to Williams (FO). 25.9.62. PRO: FO 371/166662, DT1091/51. Letter: Burrows (Saigon) to Williams (FO). 14.11.62. Ibid. DT1091/57/G.

[131] Memorandum by British embassy Bangkok: 'SEATO and Counter-Subversion'. 7.4.60. PRO: FO 371/152148, D1071/51.

[132] Deptel 3228: Ball to London. 13.12.61. FRUS: 1961–1963, i, Vietnam 1961, 733.

linked. If SEATO failed to prevent communist expansion into Indochina and perhaps even Thailand, the defence of Malaya would be much more difficult.

Yet it was not only the cold war and deterring communist expansion that made the British value their SEATO membership. SEATO was very important to the British with regard to their status in the western alliance. The organization was regarded as a means to stay in close touch with the American allies and influence their policy if possible. Britain also wanted to maintain the close military links with the old Commonwealth countries, Australia and New Zealand. It was realized that both countries had to look to the United States for security. Yet for the time being the special British military ties with those countries had to be maintained. Abandoning SEATO would, the British government believed, seriously undermine its relations with Australia and New Zealand, particularly at a time when other issues, like the British application to the EEC, were souring relations with Commonwealth countries. The British were therefore first and foremost worried about their loss of political influence in the area if they could not live up to their SEATO commitment.

Whereas London was certainly willing to contribute to SEATO as a deterrent, it remains difficult to imagine that Britain would have taken part in SEATO action. In the last resort, however, London might have supported the United States if Washington had decided to intervene in Indochina, be it Laos or South Vietnam, under the umbrella of SEATO. Yet Britain preferred bilateral agreements to 'collective' decision-making because the Macmillan government was in favour of arrangements that guaranteed Whitehall's control over any British military involvement. Therefore, Macmillan readily agreed to deploy a token force of Hunter aircraft to Thailand in 1962 on a bilateral basis. As the United States also favoured a bilateral approach in Vietnam, the British government was never confronted with the difficult decision to endorse SEATO intervention in that country between 1961 and 1963.

Even SEATO's contingency planning for South Vietnam remained academic. In evaluating MPO Plan 6, the plan to counter an open DRV attack, Britain showed concern about a possible escalation leading to PRC intervention. Similar doubts were voiced in London with regard to MPO Plan 7. Britain's agreement to Plan 7 in 1961, as opposed to its reservations in 1960, showed the Macmillan government's unwillingness to appear obstructive within SEATO. Britain's support for SEATO's counter-insurgency planning was partly motivated by the conviction that the deteriorating security situation in the RVN necessitated such a move. It was also an expression of Britain's willingness to demonstrate to the other members of SEATO and particularly to the Americans that Britain wanted to maintain SEATO as a credible deterrent against communist expansion. And with the assurance that the Singapore base was still available for the foreseeable future, Britain could make a valuable contribution to this deterrent.

The Macmillan government realized that Britain's declining military power in the region would in the long run result in diminished political influence. However, in the short run, London wanted to maintain its position in the area. Essentially,

Britain tried to play a role out of all proportion to its actual military and economic strength, and Britain could only play this role if it was perceived to be in a position to influence American policy. Therefore, Britain was keen to maintain its military presence in Southeast Asia and eager to show that it identified with US cold war interests in Indochina. Abandoning SEATO and concentrating merely on Commonwealth defence was out of the question. The ability to influence American decisions in Indochina and maintaining credibility in Australia and New Zealand were simply too important from London's point of view.

Frederick Warner, the head of the Foreign Office's Southeast Asia Department, observed in November 1961 that Britain was facing a dilemma because of the two connections it had with Indochina. As a member of SEATO, London was committed to take part in the defence of Laos and the RVN. Yet in its role as co-chairman of the 1954 Geneva conference Britain was obliged to act as a peace-maker. Warner regarded these possibly contradictory roles as a handicap.[133] However, the political goal of the British government was to support the Kennedy administration in its attempt to prevent the fall of the non-communist regime in Saigon. Ultimately, there was no difficulty in reconciling this with the role as co-chairman of the Geneva conference. Quite the opposite, the co-chairmanship offered Britain the opportunity to 'fight' the war in South Vietnam on the diplomatic front.

[133] Blue FO minute by Warner. 1.11.61. PRO: FO 371/159722, D10113/9.

2

The Diplomatic Front:
Britain and the International
Control Commission in Vietnam

THE INTERNATIONAL COMMISSION for Supervision and Control (ICC) in
Vietnam was one of the concrete achievements of the 1954 Geneva agreements on
Indochina. It lasted until 1973 when it was replaced by a new Commission pur-
suant to the Paris Accords.[1] The ICC was to inform the members of the Geneva
conference of the failure of any party to implement the agreement.[2] Since in practice the members of the Geneva conference were taken to mean the co-chairmen
of that conference, the ICC addressed its reports to Britain and the Soviet Union.[3]
Britain felt a moral obligation to show interest in the preservation of a peace
London had sponsored, and proved willing to accept its continued responsibility
as co-chairman.

The composition of the ICC followed the cold war pattern. The Commission
comprised three delegations, one each from Canada, India, and Poland, with the
non-aligned Indians presiding. So far, the major academic writing has focused on
the Canadian role in the Commission.[4] British and Canadian documents show,
however, that, while not being as closely involved in the Commission's day-to-
day work as Canada, Britain was trying to influence the Commission's decisions
in the background. The Americans described the ICC as a 'troika' of India,
Canada, and Poland that was supervised by a 'condominium'—Britain and the
Soviet Union.[5]

[1] Ramesh Chandra Thakur, *Peacekeeping in Vietnam: Canada, India, Poland, and the International Commission* (Edmonton: University of Alberta Press, 1984), 58.
[2] Article 43 of the Vietnam CFA. The agreements are in FRUS: 1952–1954, xvi, The Geneva Conference, 1521–39. See also the appendix of Douglas A. Ross, *In the Interests of Peace: Canada and
Vietnam* (Toronto: Toronto University Press, 1984), 389–403.
[3] Thakur, *Peacekeeping in Vietnam*, 72.
[4] Four books on Canada's role in the Commission were published in the 1980s. James Eayrs, *In
Defence of Canada. Indochina: Roots of Complicity* (Toronto: Toronto University Press, 1983) cov-
ers, with the exception of a detailed account on the Seaborn mission in 1964–5, the period from 1954
to 1957 only. A detailed analysis of the Commission's voting record is given by Thakur, *Peacekeeping
in Vietnam*. Ross, *Interests of Peace*, stresses the importance of India's position. Victor Levant, *Quiet
Complicity: Canadian Involvement in the Vietnamese War* (Toronto: Between the Lines, 1986) tends
to oversimplify the Commission's procedures in order to prove Canada's complicity in 'America's
war'. All four books rely on official publications or American documents (such as the Pentagon
Papers), and they virtually ignore British policy towards the ICC.
[5] Memorandum: Wood to M. Bundy. 8.11.61. USNA: RG 59, Central Files, 751k.00/11-861.

As the receiver of the ICC's reports, London had a keen interest in the way these reports were drafted. Therefore, the Foreign Office tried to remain well informed about what was going on in the Commission and developed an extensive pattern of how to contact the different governments involved in the ICC's decision-making process. To keep in close contact with the Canadians there were frequent exchanges between the Foreign Office and Canada House in London. Moreover, the British ambassador in Saigon was in close touch with the Canadian and Indian commissioners, and sometimes even with their Polish colleague. The British High Commission in New Delhi repeatedly called on the Indian Commonwealth Secretary to promote the British view on ICC matters. If necessary, the United States administration was directly approached in Washington. The South Vietnamese were encouraged to send copies of all their complaints, which were addressed to the ICC, to Britain as well. The British Consulate General in Hanoi monitored the DRV's attitude towards the ICC and received the commissioners on their visits to Hanoi. Through the British embassy in Moscow, ICC matters were discussed with the Soviet co-chairman.

This chapter will determine how Britain used its role as co-chairman, particularly in the run-up to the ICC's special report of June 1962, the most important statement the Commission issued with regard to the insurrection in the RVN. Did Britain try to work for an end to the hostilities? Did the Macmillan government attempt to prevent the American military build-up that Kennedy authorized in November 1961? In short, did Britain play the role of a peacemaker?

THE LEGAL FRAMEWORK

The end of the first Indochina war between the French and the Vietminh was negotiated at the Geneva conference which met from 8 May to 21 July 1954. The three ceasefire agreements (CFA) for Laos, Cambodia, and Vietnam were signed on 20 July 1954, and the Final Declaration of the Geneva Conference on the next day. The gist of the agreements provided for an armistice, a regrouping of French and Vietminh forces on either side of a demarcation line along the 17th parallel that was to divide Vietnam temporarily, and regulations against the introduction of foreign military personnel and war material. Not all of the nine governments present at Geneva gave unambiguous verbal assent to the Final Declaration of the Conference.[6] The US representative Walter Bedell Smith refused to associate the US government with the agreement. The United States would only 'take note' of the ceasefire agreements and the Final Declaration and pledged to 'refrain from the threat or the use of force to disturb them'.[7]

---

[6] The participants of the Geneva conference were the United States, Britain, France, the Soviet Union, the People's Republic of China, the Democratic Republic of Vietnam, the State of Vietnam, Laos, and Cambodia. The Final Declaration was published in Cmnd. 9239, Miscellaneous No. 20: *Further Documents Relating to the Discussion of Korea and Indochina at the Geneva Conference* (London: HMSO, 1954).

[7] Ross, *Interests of Peace*, 81.

On 11 August 1954 representatives of India, Poland, and Canada held the con-
stitutional meeting of the ICC in Hanoi. Separate commissions in Cambodia and
Laos were set up simultaneously. The CFA left the organization of the ICC headquarters by and large undefined. Therefore, the Commission itself decided to set
up four committees which were to report to the three commissioners: an operations committee that dealt with military matters, a freedoms committee to deal
with petitions, an administration committee, and a legal committee.[8]

Chapter six of the Vietnam CFA listed some of the tasks of the ICC. It was to
be responsible for 'supervising the proper execution by the parties of the provisions of the Agreement'. In particular, it was to control the movement of the
armed forces of the two parties, supervise the demarcation line, and also the ports
and airfields along all frontiers of Vietnam to monitor the introduction into the
country of military personnel and 'all kinds of arms, munitions and war material'.[9] To this end, the ICC had to set up mobile inspection teams as required and
fourteen fixed teams, seven in South and seven in North Vietnam.[10] These
inspection teams would undertake the necessary investigations either on the
Commission's own initiative or at the request of one of the parties or the Joint
Commission. The Joint Commission, also defined in Chapter six of the Vietnam
CFA, comprised members of the Vietminh and the French High Command, and
was to ensure the execution of the provisions concerning the ceasefire, the re-
groupment and demarcation line, and the demilitarized zone.[11] Until 1956 the
ICC tried to minimize its role by not questioning the competence of the Joint
Commission. However, the CFA provided for referral to the ICC of any disputes
on which the Joint Commission failed to agree. Furthermore, the French High
Command withdrew completely in June 1956, and after that date the Joint Commission did not resume its functions. The RVN did not agree to participate in the
Joint Commission arguing that it was not a signatory to the CFA. All matters that
should have been dealt with by the Joint Commission were after this referred to
the ICC.[12]

The main thrust of the Geneva agreements was the principle that military
strengths were to be frozen at existing levels. To achieve this, the two sides were
denied any increase in their military potential, while being permitted to replace
men and material. Articles 16 to 20 of the CFA addressed these problems. They
prohibited troop reinforcements outside of a 'man-to-man' rotation (Article 16),
the introduction of war material beyond a 'piece-for-piece' replacement (Article
17), new military bases, the transfer of existing bases to foreign control, the ad-
herence to any military alliance, and the use of a zone for the resumption of hostilities (Articles 18 and 19). Fourteen points of entry for the rotation of personnel
and replacement of material which were identical with the location of the fixed

---

[8] Thakur, *Peacekeeping in Vietnam*, 58–61.   [9] Vietnam CFA, Article 36.
[10] Vietnam CFA, Article 35. Fixed teams were to be set up in North Vietnam at Loo Cay, Lang Son,
Tien Yen, Haiphong, Vinh, Dong Hoi, and Muong Sen; in South Vietnam at Tourane (Da Nang), Qui
Nhon, Nha Trang, Ba Ngoi, Saigon, Cap St. Jacques (Vung Tau), and Tan Chau.
[11] Vietnam CFA, Articles 33 and 37.   [12] Thakur, *Peacekeeping in Vietnam*, 59.

inspection teams were listed in Article 20. These articles became, together with Article 24 which prohibited the parties from undertaking any 'operation against the other party', the main basis for complaints to the ICC. However, the ICC had no power to enforce the CFA. The mandate of the ICC was supervisory. Execution of the CFA rested 'with the parties'.[13]

The tenure of the Commission was nowhere specified. As for decisional procedures, general recommendations of the ICC could be made by majority vote. Decisions on questions dealing with the violation by the armed forces of one of the parties of the zone of the other required unanimity. If the ICC failed to reach the unanimous decision which was in certain cases required, it was to submit a majority report and one or more minority reports.[14]

MORE AMERICAN ADVISERS

Between 1954 and 1961 the ICC in Vietnam drafted eleven so-called 'Interim Reports' in which violations of the CFA by both parties were brought to the attention of the co-chairmen. After 1962 the ICC issued 'Special Reports'. These consisted of a majority report approved by India and either Canada or Poland and a Canadian or Polish minority statement. According to some scholars the decision-making within the ICC between 1959 and 1962 was marked by an Indo-Canadian collusion.[15] The most important decisions in this period were indeed taken by an Indo-Canadian majority vote. However, it would be exaggerated to say that the Indian and Canadian commissioners worked closely together. Time and again the Canadians complained about the Indians' overly legalistic attitude and their 'weakness' in the face of Polish delaying tactics. In late 1960 and early 1961, relations were strained to the breaking point over the Indian resistance to pressuring Hanoi to allow a team investigation at Gia Lam Airport.[16] At this airport forty to fifty Soviet planes arrived daily with war material destined for Laos. The Foreign Ministry in Ottawa had to restrain the overly excited Canadian commissioner Charles Woodsworth, pointing out that the Gia Lam issue was not important enough to damage the relations with the Indians in the Commission permanently.[17]

The British, too, often regarded the Indian attitude as tiresome. They were aware that the overall record of the Commission's findings before 1959 was overwhelmingly in favour of the DRV.[18] Having this in mind, the British as well as the

---

[13] Vietnam CFA, Article 28.   [14] Vietnam CFA, Articles 41, 42, and 43.
[15] Ross, *Interests of Peace*, 223.
[16] Letter: Woodsworth (ICC Saigon) to EA Ottawa. 2.2.61. National Archives of Canada, Ottawa (hereafter CNA): RG 25, Vol. 4637, File 50052-A-40, part 36.
[17] Letter: Robertson (EA Ottawa) to Woodsworth (ICC Saigon). 2.2.61. Ibid.
[18] Nevertheless, Whitehall thought it necessary to keep the ICC in Vietnam in operation, whereas it supported the abolition of the commissions in Laos and Cambodia (GEN 682/12. 12.3.59. PRO: FO 371/143772, D10710/4). Having undertaken by oral agreement a continuing responsibility for organizing the finances of the ICC (Blue FO minute by Cable. 29.10.65. PRO: FO 371/180214, D1071/4),

Canadians were shocked when they learned in late 1959 that the Americans planned to increase the strength of their Military Assistance Advisory Group (MAAG) in Saigon from 342 members, which was the hitherto agreed ceiling, to 682.[19] The MAAG was formed in 1950 as a supply-support group for the French war effort. After the French withdrawal, the MAAG had been transformed into the organizer and instructor of the Army of the Republic of Vietnam (ARVN).[20]

The Americans argued that even the enlarged MAAG would not exceed the number of foreign advisers in Saigon in 1954. At the time of the armistice 888 American *and* French advisers had been stationed in South Vietnam.[21] In private, London and Ottawa did not accept this argument. If one was to agree to this reasoning, the Americans would be allowed to replace the 150,000 French troops that had been in Vietnam in 1954 as well. They regarded the American move as a clear breach of the CFA.[22] However, the British had no intention to do anything about this. They pointed out to the Canadians that they were not prepared to try to dissuade the Americans from augmenting the MAAG. The United States would go ahead with the increase anyway. Therefore, there was no reason to use up British credits in Washington on this issue.[23]

In February 1960, the American ambassador in London raised the issue with Foreign Secretary Selwyn Lloyd and asked for London's help in persuading the Indians to go along with the increased number of US advisers. Selwyn Lloyd refused to commit the British in any way, yet he agreed to see what the British could do in New Delhi.[24] In the event, the British High Commissioner in Delhi did not have to do anything. The US ambassador in New Delhi spoke to Foreign Minister Manilal J. Desai in late February, and Desai readily accepted the American argument that the CFA allowed the Saigon government to invite up to 888 foreign military advisers.[25] This Indian view came as a complete surprise to London and Ottawa.[26] Hanoi reacted sharply to the ICC's Indian-Canadian majority decision of April 1960 to allow the increase in the MAAG. Conveniently forgetting the views of their own legal advisers, the British brushed off General Vo Nguyen Giap's argument, which they had themselves accepted in private, namely that the Commission's ruling was against the spirit of the CFA by accepting an argument

the British and the Soviets agreed to press the ICC to achieve savings which led to the abolition of four fixed teams (for details of the Anglo-Soviet talks, see PRO: FO 371/152177–80). By 1961, however, the British were against further reductions because of the deteriorating situation in Vietnam (Minute by Secondé (FO). 6.10.61. PRO: FO 371/160136, DV1071/58).

[19] Minute by Butler (FO). 4.1.60. PRO: FO 371/152780, DV1203/1.

[20] Levant, *Quiet Complicity*, 148.

[21] Department of State Instruction 499. 5.2.60. USNA: RG 59, Central Files, 751k.5-msp/2-560.

[22] Minute by Butler (FO). 7.1.60. PRO: FO 371/152780, DV1203/1. Airgram G-92: Ottawa to State Department. 13.1.60. USNA: RG 59, Central Files, 751k.5-msp/1-1360.

[23] Telegram 544: London to EA Ottawa. 24.2.60. CNA: RG 25, Vol. 4637, File 50052-A-40, part 35.

[24] Letter: Lloyd to Parkes (Saigon). 26.2.60. PRO: FO 371/152780, DV1203/6.

[25] Embtel 2830: Bunker (New Delhi) to State Department. 25.2.60. USNA: RG 59, Central Files, 751k.5-msp/2-2560. Telegram 616: London to EA Ottawa. 2.3.60. CNA: RG 25, Vol. 4637, File 50052-A-40, part 35.

[26] Minute by Butler (FO). 2.3.60. PRO: FO 371/152780, DV1203/13.

which ultimately could justify the introduction of 150,000 American troops into South Vietnam.[27]

NORTH VIETNAMESE SUBVERSION

The American intention to increase the military effort in Vietnam to an extent that, in the British view, was not compatible with the CFA did not make the Foreign Office look for ways to restrain the Americans. Instead, London began to focus on how to justify possible further US intervention. Arguing that Hanoi had broken the CFA first by instigating and directing communist subversion in the RVN seemed to be the only way to justify American actions. Subversion was an 'old' issue in the Vietnam Commission. The ICC had been receiving a continuing flow of letters over the past five years from the South Vietnamese Liaison Office, alleging that the subversive activities carried out in the RVN were actually directed from Hanoi. These letters were referred to the Commission's legal committee in order to decide whether they attracted any of the articles of the Geneva agreement. On 13 January 1956 the committee reported that the alleged activities would go against the spirit of the CFA. The Indian and Canadian commissioners accepted the report and instructed the legal committee to examine the South Vietnamese letters. The Canadians, however, had been unsuccessful during the previous years in obtaining consideration of these letters by the committee because of Polish obstructionist tactics, more or less connived at by the Indians.[28]

In early 1960, the British came to the conclusion that the time had come to press the Indians on the issue of subversion. The problem was, of course, to prove that the DRV was really behind the subversive activities in the RVN. The British received copies of the South Vietnamese letters to the ICC complaining about subversion, and were generally not impressed by the evidence produced.[29] However, this was no reason not to pursue the issue, as Cosmo Stewart of the British embassy in Saigon stated bluntly: 'We are not concerned . . . to try to reach the truth behind this welter of allegations.' Instead, something had to be done about 'the exaggerated Indian preoccupation with impartiality and legalism'. Stewart concluded that 'a much firmer grip' needed to be taken by the Commission by a 'more ruthless Chairman than the Indians seem able to provide'.[30] Put simply, Hanoi had to be found guilty, with or without evidence.

In April 1960, the Indians sided with the Canadians not only on the MAAG issue but also on the issue of Law 10/59.[31] In communist diplomatic circles it was

[27] Blue FO minute by Warner. 23.6.60. PRO: FO 371/152782, DV1203/42.

[28] Memorandum by Grondin (EA Ottawa): 'International Commission For Vietnam'. 22.4.61. CNA: RG 25, Vol. 4637, File 50052-A-40, part 36.

[29] Letter: Chancery Saigon to South East Asia Department. 17.5.60. PRO: FO 371/152760, DV1071/23.

[30] Letter: Stewart (Saigon) to Warner (FO). 18.2.60. PRO: FO 371/152179, D10710/20.

[31] This South Vietnamese law set up military tribunals and provided for special penalties to deal with the so-called subversive elements (in other words communists) in the RVN. The DRV complained

noted with concern that there seemed to be a change in the Indian attitude, which was now described as 'negative'.[32] In the West, the 'surprisingly co-operative' Indian stance did not go unnoticed either. In May, not only the British but the United States, too, thought that the time was ripe to tackle the Indians on subversion.[33] At the end of April, the Canadians had already secured Indian agreement that the legal committee would, if necessary, meet every day and look into the South Vietnamese charges of subversion.[34] However, the British noted with dismay that the Canadians were in favour of proceeding slowly, and therefore hoped for a more aggressive approach by the new Canadian commissioner Charles Woodsworth.[35]

In June, London grew impatient. The Foreign Office doubted whether the Canadian tactics were correct because of the danger of the subversion issue getting bogged down in the legal committee again. Moreover, there was the possibility that the 'south Vietnamese may well fail to produce sufficient evidence'. To get things moving, the Foreign Office proposed an alternative way. The Indians and Canadians were to be persuaded to send a letter to Hanoi asking them to declare that the DRV had nothing to do with the subversion in South Vietnam. This move was intended to put Hanoi in an awkward position, and to satisfy Saigon by showing that the ICC had finally done something regarding the matter.[36] The Canadians, however, were afraid that this exercise could well turn out to be counter-productive: the DRV would be given a platform to state that the peasantry had to defend itself against the terrorist Saigon regime. This argument convinced London, and it was decided to go along with the Canadian approach to move step by step, the first step being a concerted Anglo-Canadian approach to the Indians.[37] However, the Indians were not very forthcoming, and the Canadians only secured a promise from India in August 1960 that the Commission would issue, if necessary by an Indian-Canadian majority vote, a statement affirming the relevance of subversion, sabotage, and espionage to the Geneva agreements, and the competence of the ICC in this field. There, matters rested for more than half a year.[38]

The Canadian commissioner Woodsworth, as the British had hoped for, turned out to be quite aggressive, but in Gopala Menon he did not face the 'ruth-

---

about this law, arguing it violated Article 14(c) of the CFA which prohibited reprisals against persons 'on account of their activities during the hostilities'.

[32] Minute (Vermerk) 86/60 by Claudius (Hanoi). 15.4.60. Archiv des Ministeriums für Auswärtige Angelegenheiten der Deutschen Demokratischen Republik, Berlin (hereafter MfAA): A8570.

[33] Letter: Stewart (Saigon) to Warner (FO). 13.5.60. PRO: FO 371/152760, DV1071/22.

[34] Canadian telegram 94: Saigon to EA Ottawa. 23.4.60. Ibid. DV1071/18.

[35] Letter: Stewart (Saigon) to Warner (FO). 13.5.60. Ibid. DV1071/22.

[36] Letter: Butler (FO) to Stewart (Saigon). 8.6.60. Ibid. Telegram 1736: London to EA Ottawa. 8.6.60. CNA: RG 25, Vol. 4637, File 50052-A-40, part 35.

[37] Letter: Warner (FO) to Stewart (Saigon). 21.6.60. PRO: FO 371/152760, DV1071/22. Letter: Stewart (Saigon) to Butler (FO). 25.6.60. Ibid. DV1071/25.

[38] Letter: Stewart (Saigon) to Warner (FO). 8.7.60. Ibid. Memorandum by Grondin (EA Ottawa): 'International Commission for Vietnam'. 22.4.61. CNA: RG 25, Vol. 4637, File 50052-A40, part 36.

less' Indian chairman the Foreign Office was calling for. On the contrary, Menon, Woodsworth complained,

is not a man of any great strength of character or conviction and he is also a poor administrator. [His] primary aim seems to be to achieve some kind of compromise or agreement among the three Delegations on all issues, regardless of the nature of these issues. . . . His subsequent efforts to achieve unanimity at all costs have resulted—as might be expected— in the bogging down of practically all Commission business, and in the creation of an atmosphere of irritation, suspicion and frustration.[39]

The Canadians, facing deadlock in the Commission, decided to press the Indian government in New Delhi to get the ICC on record as having the competence and duty to investigate complaints about subversion. Indeed, this approach proved to be promising. In March 1961, the Indian Commonwealth Secretary Yezdezard Gundevia reassured the Canadians that Menon had been given instructions to adopt the statement on subversion. Yet with or without instructions, Menon had still not given his approval to adopting the statement by the beginning of June.[40]

Meanwhile, the need to put the blame on Hanoi for the deteriorating security situation in South Vietnam became more and more urgent. The anticipated American build-up in the wake of Vice-President Lyndon B. Johnson's visit to Vietnam in May 1961 put the British and Canadians on full alert. After having heard from the French that a further increase to the MAAG was in the offing, the immediate worry was that Washington might even contemplate sending US troops to Vietnam.[41] Soon, however, Washington assured the Canadians that there was 'no intention of sending USA troops into Vietnam', and the British were informed that the United States was only thinking about a further increase to the MAAG of one hundred advisers.[42] When the British embassy in Saigon subsequently suggested that Washington could 'quietly increase' the MAAG by one hundred men, the American ambassador in Vietnam reported to the State Department that the British appeared to be under a 'misconception as to [the] order of magnitude of [the] required MAAG augmentation'. President Diem had asked for an additional one thousand advisers, the MAAG itself had requested an increase of 561 plus 1,400 US logistical and support personnel, and Kennedy had actually authorized the sending of up to 4,385.[43]

---

[39]   Letter: Woodsworth (ICC Saigon) to EA Ottawa. 2.2.61. Ibid.

[40]   Letter: Ward (New Delhi) to Fair (CRO). 9.2.61. PRO: FO 371/160134, DV1071/9. Telegram Y-72: EA Ottawa to Saigon. 10.3.61. Telegram 232: Ronning (New Delhi) to Saigon. 25.3.61. Telegram Y-317: EA Ottawa to Woodsworth (ICC Saigon). 29.5.61. All in CNA: RG 25, Vol. 4637, File 50052-A-40, part 36.

[41]   Telegram 252: Dixon (Paris) to FO. 10.5.61. PRO: FO 371/160135, DV1071/21. Letter: Ledward (Saigon) to Peterson (FO). 12.5.61. Ibid. DV1071/22.

[42]   Telegram 120: Saigon to EA Ottawa. 20.5.61. CNA: RG 25, Vol. 4637, File 50052-A-40, part 36.

[43]   Embtel 1842: Nolting (Saigon) to State Department. 3.6.61. JFKL: NSF, Vietnam Country Series, box 193. Memorandum: Cottrell (State Department) to Rusk. 24.5.61. USNA: RG 59, Central Files, 751k.5-msp/5-2461. The paper of the Vietnam task force on 'Points to save Vietnam' of 1.5.61, which Kennedy approved in NSAM 52, envisaged the augmentation of the MAAG by two groups of 1,600 advisers each. FRUS: 1961–1963, i, Vietnam 1961, 92–115.

The British then learned that the United States did not only plan to introduce more than one hundred additional MAAG personnel into Vietnam, but were planning to declare that Washington did not regard Articles 16 and 17 of the CFA as applicable anymore. Britain strongly opposed this, arguing that such a step would endanger the Laos conference in Geneva and would have a detrimental effect on the Indians. Since the United States was not a party to the CFA, the British argued, there was no reason for Washington to repudiate the articles. London agreed that an increase to the MAAG was necessary, yet as they did not know about the possible extent of the increase, they told the Canadians that they saw no need 'to handle the issue in such a dramatic fashion'.[44]

In early June, the State Department informed the British embassy in Washington that an additional reason for not observing Articles 16 and 17 was that the DRV had violated Article 24, which prohibited the parties from undertaking any operation against the other party. Frederick Warner, the head of the Southeast Asia Department in the Foreign Office, stressed in a subsequent conversation with the US embassy in London that all this seemed to indicate an American 'intention to conduct military operations in North Vietnam'.[45] Privately, the Foreign Office thought that it made sense to send 'agents and bands of guerrillas . . . to operate in North Vietnam', yet it was fundamental not to take any responsibility for these operations. The State Department demonstrated that these were exactly Washington's sentiments and flatly denied that the United States was planning covert action against the DRV. Instead, the State Department expressed its irritation at Warner's suggestion that the US had any such intentions. Simultaneously, the British embassy in Washington was told that there must have been a 'misunderstanding' about the planned increase to the MAAG. The Americans claimed that they had made it plain to the British that the sending of one hundred men was only a 'first instalment' and that further increases had to be made. But the British were still not told the exact number.[46] Clearly, the Americans were less than frank with the British about their intentions. Kennedy had approved Ranger raids and 'similar military action' in the DRV in May 1961 with his approval of the recommendation of the task force Vietnam through NSAM 52.[47] Raids started soon after, and Hanoi claimed in August 1961 that it had captured four RVN commandos.[48] DRV officials informed the East German embassy that they estimated that the RVN was trying to infiltrate 800 men, particularly into North Vietnam's Catholic areas.[49]

[44] Telegram 1805: Washington to EA Ottawa. 6.6.61. CNA: RG 25, Vol. 4637, File 50052-A-40, part 37.
[45] Deptel 5820: Rusk to London. 13.6.61. USNA: RG 59, Central Files, 751k.5-msp/6-1361. Embtel 5006: Bruce (London) to State Department. 8.6.61. Ibid. 751k.5-msp/6-861.
[46] Telegram 3876: FO to Washington. 6.6.61. Telegram 1444: Caccia (Washington) to FO. 13.6.61. Both in PRO: FO 371/160157, DV1202/14/G.
[47] 'Points to save Vietnam'. Paper prepared by Vietnam task force. 1.5.61. FRUS: 1961–63, i, Vietnam 1961, 111. NSAM 52. 11.5.61. Ibid. 132–4.
[48] Minute by McGhie (FO). 14.8.61. PRO: FO 371/160123, DV1016/26.
[49] Letter: Witt (Hanoi) to Schütz (Berlin). 28.11.61. Bundesarchiv—Militärarchiv, Freiburg (hereafter BArchMA): VA-01/6426, Bd. 1.

It was not only Washington's eagerness to increase its military effort, which made Whitehall regard the issue of subversion as even more crucial. In May, the Foreign Office considered what the British themselves could do to assist the South Vietnamese counter-insurgency effort. These considerations later led to the sending of the British Advisory Mission to Saigon. In view of these plans in Washington and London, the Foreign Office concluded that 'it would make all the difference in the world to our legal position as one of the Co-Chairmen if we were enabled to pin charges of direction of the subversion directly to the D.R.V.'[50] It was therefore decided to approach the Indians again on the matter. 'This won't have any effect,' mused the pessimistic Frederick Warner, 'but let's try it'.[51]

Yet a further approach to the Indians turned out to be unnecessary. The Canadians had also stepped up their pressure on the Indians in May after President Kennedy personally had raised the issue with John Diefenbaker, the Canadian Prime Minister. Again, it was realized that the problem was not the Indian government but that Gopala Menon in Saigon was 'the main stumbling block'. The Canadian delegation to the ICC in Saigon informed Ottawa on 17 June that this problem had finally been overcome.[52] By an Indian-Canadian majority decision the ICC adopted a statement on 24 June 1961 declaring that it was in its competence to investigate South Vietnamese complaints about subversion.[53]

The Foreign Office noted with relief that it was now unlikely that Washington would repudiate Articles 16 and 17.[54] Indeed, the Americans concluded that the ICC majority decision on subversion had made it an 'unpropitious time' for the United States and the RVN to denounce publicly 'important' articles of the Geneva accords.[55] Moreover, the United States decided to keep quiet about the introduction of most of the additional men and material into South Vietnam. The Indian chargé d'affaires in Washington was informed on 30 June that the United States would increase the MAAG by only one hundred, which would still keep its size below the ceiling of 888. It was not mentioned that this would be just the 'first instalment'. Washington also told the Indians that this move was a reaction to the violation of the CFA by the DRV, but it did not mean that the United States would cease to respect the Geneva agreements or intended to 'push aside' any part of the CFA, including Articles 16 and 17. Privately, however, Washington did not rule out that these articles would have to be repudiated at some point,

[50] Draft letter: Peck (FO) to Pritchard (New Delhi). 30.5.61. PRO: FO 371/160135, DV1071/24.

[51] Minute by Warner (FO). 30.5.61. Ibid.

[52] Minute by McGhie (FO). 12.6.61. Ibid. Memorandum by Teakles (EA Ottawa). 19.5.61. Telegram Y-317: EA Ottawa to Woodsworth (ICC Saigon). 29.5.61. Both in CNA: RG 25, Vol. 4637, File 50052-A-40, part 36.

[53] Telegram 387: Stewart (Saigon) to FO. 29.6.61. PRO: FO 371/160135, DV1071/27.

[54] Minute by McGhie (FO). 3.7.61. Ibid.

[55] Embtel 17: Nolting (Saigon) to State Department. 5.7.61. USNA: RG 59, Central Files, 751k.5/7-561.

particularly as two months later, in September 1961, the strength of the MAAG was to rise to over 939.[56]

The immediate problem for London was to justify the Commission's decision on subversion vis-à-vis the Soviet Union. In mid-July Hanoi addressed a note to the British calling upon the co-chairmen to instruct the ICC to reverse its decision on subversion. As usual, London did not undertake to react to Hanoi's note as long as Moscow refrained from raising the North Vietnamese complaints with the British. London expected such an approach soon as Hanoi's *démarche* was 'more than usually hysterical in tone'.[57] The problem remained that there was no convincing evidence against the DRV. 'I can not see that we have any real proof that the trouble in S[outh] Vietnam is directed from N[orth] Vietnam', James Cable of the Foreign Office concluded.[58] In Saigon, Cosmo Stewart echoed this view: 'The difficulty is that so far, although many assertions have been made, inter alia to the International Commission by the South Vietnamese Liaison mission, that such a connection [between the insurgents and the DRV] exists, no really worthwhile evidence, either documentary or human, has yet been produced for an examination.'[59]

To counter the anticipated Soviet approach, Britain considered it important to make the South Vietnamese produce a well-documented riposte. Therefore, the British handed an *aide mémoire* to the South Vietnamese asking them to draft a riposte, which should not be propagandist in tone but should link the specific complaints to the relevant articles of the CFA.[60] As the RVN 'never had managed so far to prepare cases well enough documented to satisfy the somewhat legal approach of the commission', the British offered their help and suggested some amendments to the 'comprehensive review' Saigon had produced on Britain's request.[61] This review was finally addressed in a letter to the British co-chairman with an appeal to ensure that 'appropriate instructions be sent by the two co-chairmen to the . . . International Control Commission to give full effect to the Commission's decision of June 24, 1961'.[62] Although the publishing of the letter achieved little publicity in London in September, the Foreign Office still considered the whole operation worthwhile, and was happy to make use of it to answer a Soviet note of 9 October which referred to the North Vietnamese earlier protests.[63] The Americans, too, welcomed the exercise and congratulated the

[56] Depcirctel 2084: Rusk to New Delhi, London, Paris, Saigon, Ottawa. 1.7.61. Ibid. 751k.5/7-161. Deptel 102: Rusk to Saigon. 20.7.61. Ibid. 751k.5-msp/7-2061. Telegram Y-392: EA Ottawa to Saigon. 7.7.61. CNA: RG 25, Vol. 4637, File 50052-A-40, part 37. Minutes of meeting of Vietnam task force. 26.6.61. JFKL: NSF, Vietnam Country Series, box 193.

[57] Minute by McGhie (FO). 14.7.61. PRO: FO 371/160135, DV 1071/31.

[58] Minute by Cable (FO). 19.6.61. PRO: FO 371/160112, DV 1015/83.

[59] Letter: Stewart (Saigon) to Warner (FO). 23.6.61. PRO: FO 371/160157, DV 1202/21.

[60] British *aide mémoire*. 22.7.61. PRO: FO 371/160135, DV 1071/39.

[61] Telegram 439: Hohler (Saigon) to FO. 24.7.61. Telegram 537: Hohler (Saigon) to FO. 8.8.61. Both in ibid. DV 1071/34. Embtel 209: Nolting (Saigon) to State Department. 10.8.61. USNA: RG 59, Central Files, 751k.00/8-1061.

[62] Savingram 1021: FO to Moscow. 31.8.61. PRO: FO 371/160136, DV 1071/46.

[63] Letter: South East Asia Department to Chancery Saigon. 26.9.61. Ibid. DV 1071/50. Savingram 1345: FO to Moscow. 20.10.61. Ibid. DV 1071/52.

Saigon government on the 'excellent letter to the British Co-Chairman'.[64] The State Department was, however, very disappointed that it had received no mentioning in the British press.[65]

THE NAM CASE

Far more useful in providing the evidence against Hanoi than the British-initiated South Vietnamese letter proved to be the kidnapping and murder of the chief of the RVN's Liaison Office to the ICC, Colonel Hoang Thuy Nam. On 1 October 1961 an armed band captured Nam near Saigon. The kidnappers first tortured and then executed him. His body was found on 16 October. Two days later, the Canadian commissioner was able to obtain a unanimous decision of the ICC to send a letter of condolence to the Saigon regime. More importantly, the Polish commissioner reluctantly agreed to the sending of another letter to the South Vietnamese Liaison Office asking for substantiation of the claim that communist insurgents were responsible for the murder. It was indicated that the ICC would consider taking the case further, which it indeed agreed to do on 23 November.[66]

In the interim, however, London and Ottawa worked hard to defuse a major crisis that threatened to blow up the Commission. The RVN refused to permit the Polish ICC delegation to take part along with the other delegations at Colonel Nam's funeral. At the cemetery gates, a large crowd demonstrated against the ICC, displaying banners reading 'ICC must pay for Colonel Nam's death' and 'Polish Delegation should go home'.[67] On 25 October 1961 all South Vietnamese domestic labour and motor drivers were withdrawn from the Polish ICC delegation. The Canadians suspected that the RVN wanted to bring about the withdrawal of the Commission because Saigon was hoping for more American military aid.[68] Ottawa immediately consulted the Foreign Office, and the British promised to make strong representations in Saigon 'pointing out ... how very desirable it was for the ICC to remain in South Vietnam'.[69]

When the Canadian commissioner warned South Vietnam's Foreign Minister Vu Van Mau that the Poles might withdraw from the Commission because of Saigon's harassment, Mau replied that he would write immediately to the ICC 'formally requesting them to consider moving to Hanoi'.[70] The Indian government

---

[64] Deptel 279: Rusk to Saigon. 7.9.61. USNA: RG 59, Central Files, 751k.00/8-2561.

[65] Telegram 2333: Washington to EA Canberra. 21.9.61. AUSNA: A1209/134, file 1961/127, part 1. Embtel 1210: Jones (London) to State Department. 22.9.61. USNA: RG 59, Central Files, 751k.00/9-2261.

[66] Minutes of the 636th meeting of the ICC. 28.11.61. CNA: RG 25, Vol. 4661, File 50052-A-12-40, part 48. Telegram 770: Hohler (Saigon) to FO. 23.11.61. PRO: FO 371/160139, DV1071/108.

[67] State Department memorandum 'ICSC—Vietnam'. 2.11.61. USNA: RG 59, Central Files, 751k.00/11-261.

[68] Telegram 662: Hohler (Saigon) to FO. 26.10.61. PRO: FO 371/160137, DV1071/62.

[69] Telegram 3859: London to EA Ottawa. 26.10.61. CNA: RG 25, Vol. 4637, File 50052-A-40, part 37.

[70] Telegram 209: Woodsworth (ICC Saigon) to EA Ottawa. 1.11.61. Ibid.

regarded such a move as 'fatal', and insisted that the RVN restore the services to the Polish delegation.[71] Facing South Vietnamese intransigence, the Canadian Foreign Minister Howard Green instructed the embassy in Washington to talk urgently to the State Department because the Americans alone were 'in a position to influence the Republic of Vietnam'.[72]

Ottawa assumed that the United States wanted the ICC to continue its work whereas the British were not entirely convinced that this was Washington's purpose.[73] Frederick Warner of the Foreign Office thought it necessary to consider carefully whether the Commission should remain in Saigon if the Americans decided to send combat troops to South Vietnam. Yet for the time being the British wanted the ICC to stay, and Warner suggested inviting the Americans 'to join us in getting the Vietnamese to hold their hand'.[74]

Washington was not behind Saigon's agitation against the ICC. Quite the contrary. Before the RVN started the campaign, US ambassador Nolting had urged the South Vietnamese to exploit the Commission's initiative to investigate the murder of Colonel Nam, which he regarded as an 'unprecedented opportunity' and a 'real breakthrough'.[75] Although Washington complained about the ineffectiveness of the ICC, it was thought that the Commission still performed a 'useful function by somewhat restraining the overtness of Communist aggression'.[76] Consequently, on 3 November Nolting readily joined his British colleague Henry Hohler in pressing Saigon to end the discriminatory treatment of the Polish delegation, emphasizing the necessity for the Commission to remain in Saigon.[77] Hohler followed this up the next day, handing a British note to Vu Van Mau that reminded Saigon of its responsibility for the protection of the lives and property of the Commission's members. The South Vietnamese finally responded and restored services to the Polish delegation on 8 November. London proudly informed the Indians of its part in this.[78] Yet Saigon's campaign against the Commission showed that however closely London and Ottawa cooperated in putting pressure on the RVN, it was finally Washington's attitude that counted.

[71] Embtel 1304: Timmons (New Delhi) to State Department. 4.11.61. USNA: RG 59, Central Files, 751k.00/11-461.

[72] Telegram: Green to Washington. 1.11.61. CNA, RG 25, Vol. 4638, File 50052-A-40, part 38.

[73] Minute by Warner (FO). 31.10.61. PRO: FO 371/160138, DV1071/84.

[74] Blue FO minute by Warner. 2.11.61. PRO: FO 371/160137, DV1071/79.

[75] Deptel 507: Nolting (Saigon) to State Department. 18.10.61. FRUS: 1961–1963, i, Vietnam 1961, 393–4.

[76] Memorandum: Wood to M. Bundy. 8.11.61. USNA: RG 59, Central Files, 751k.00/11-861.

[77] Canadian telegram 240: Saigon to EA Ottawa. 3.11.61. PRO: FO 371/160137, DV1071/80.

[78] Telegram 702: Hohler (Saigon) to FO. 4.11.61. Ibid. DV1071/74. Telegram 3528: CRO to New Delhi. 8.11.61. Ibid. DV1071/80.

THE US MILITARY BUILD-UP

In spite of the counter-insurgency methods that President Kennedy had decided to introduce in South Vietnam in early 1961, the increase to the MAAG, the augmentation of ARVN, and the sending of four hundred Green Berets in the summer, by September the Diem regime was in far deeper trouble than ever before. The insurgents, since February 1961 organized as the People's Liberation Armed Forces (PLAF), had tripled their attacks and consolidated their position in many villages. Kennedy was troubled by the conflicting viewpoints of his advisers as to how the United States should react. He therefore decided to dispatch General Maxwell Taylor, his military representative, and Walt Rostow of the White House staff to South Vietnam to study the situation at first hand. The result was a report which recommended a substantial increase in the American military presence and even the sending of combat forces.[79]

In Washington plans were drawn up to prepare the ground diplomatically and politically for such a move. It was recommended that the British, Canadians, and Indians should be informed of the US plans before any public announcement was made. The President himself was to discuss Vietnam with India's Prime Minister Jawaharlal Nehru who was expected to visit the United States in November 1961. As far as the ICC was concerned, the United States and South Vietnam would prepare a note stating that Saigon could no longer observe Articles 16 and 17 of the CFA as it had requested American help in defending the country against the insurgency directed by Hanoi. This note would be submitted privately in Saigon to the ICC and to the British embassy. Thereafter the note was to be published.[80]

Kennedy eventually authorized a large increase in American advisers rather than the introduction of combat troops, and he agreed to the dispatch of American helicopter units, mine sweepers, and air reconnaissance aircraft.[81] As far as the political and diplomatic handling of the increase was concerned, the Americans followed the above-mentioned recommendations. In November the British and Canadians were informed that the United States was to increase its military presence in Vietnam.[82] The Macmillan government was pleased that the United States would not send combat troops, generally regarded the new measures as potentially useful and promised to give the United States full support. But the Foreign Office urged Washington to be discreet about the build-up.[83] Foreign Secretary Lord

[79] Memorandum: Taylor to Kennedy. 3.11.61. FRUS: 1961–1963, i, Vietnam 1961, 479–503. Lawrence J. Bassett and Stephen E. Pelz, 'The Failed Search for Victory', in Thomas G. Paterson (ed.), *Kennedy's Quest for Victory: American Foreign Policy, 1961–1963* (New York: Oxford University Press, 1989), 144. Herring, *America's Longest War*, 83–4.

[80] 'Position Paper Vietnam' for Prime Minister Nehru's visit. Undated. JFKL: POF, Country File Vietnam, box 128a. Memorandum: Wood to Johnson. 25.10.61. FRUS: 1961–1963, i, Vietnam 1961, 436–9.

[81] NSAM 111. 22.11.61. Ibid. 656–7.

[82] Telegram 3514: Heeney (Washington) to EA Ottawa. 17.11.61. Telegram 4205: London to EA Ottawa. 23.11.61. Both in CNA: RG 25, Vol. 4638, File 50052-A-40, part 38.

[83] Telegram 4205: London to EA Ottawa. 23.11.61. Ibid.

Home instructed the ambassador in Washington to send a personal message to US Foreign Secretary Dean Rusk in order to 'dissuade the Americans from making an official announcement about the measures'.[84] In response Rusk, rather vaguely, stressed that the United States would avoid any publicity which would be 'needlessly provocative'.[85]

Yet one aim of the American decision to increase its aid was to boost the RVN's morale, and that could not be done in secrecy. Not surprisingly, London was alarmed about abundant evidence of the American build-up. On 8 December 1961 the Foreign Office noted with concern that 'contrary to all the advice which we have given' the United States had reverted to the idea of publicly announcing that Washington and Saigon were not bound by the Geneva CFA anymore.[86] Henry Hohler pointed out on the same day that the ICC was bound to ask for details, and that the CFA therefore would be stretched to the breaking point. Still hoping that publicity could be avoided, Hohler told US ambassador Nolting that 'the wisest course for the US was to deny that they were sending troops and material . . . beyond the Geneva limits'.[87] At this point, however, Washington had already made its decision. The State Department had instructed the US embassy in Saigon on 5 December that the US military build-up was to be presented as a legitimate defensive measure. The DRV had committed 'acts of aggression in flagrant violation of [the] Geneva Accords', and consequently Saigon had asked the United States for additional advisers and military equipment. These 'measures of US support' would be terminated as soon as the DRV resumed its observance of the CFA. Two days later, the US ambassador presented this position to the South Vietnamese, who agreed to send a note containing this justification to the ICC.[88]

On 10 December 1961 the South Vietnamese Government delivered the note regarding US military assistance first to the Canadians and then to the Indians in Saigon.[89] The note closely followed the wording of the State Department's instructions of 5 December. It stressed Saigon's right to self-defence and informed the ICC that the RVN had requested Washington to intensify its aid in personnel and material. These measures would end as soon as the DRV ceased the 'acts of aggression' and respected the Geneva CFA.[90] The next day, the USS *Core* arrived

[84] Message: Home to Rusk in telegram 8377: FO to Washington. 16.11.61. PRO: PREM 11/3736. Minute by Secondé (FO). 20.11.61. PRO: FO 371/160139, DV1071/105/G. Embtel 2063: Bruce (London) to State Department. 22.11.61. USNA: RG 59, Central Files, 751k.00/11-2261.

[85] Message: Rusk to Ormsby-Gore. 25.11.61, transmitted to London in telegram 3199: Ormsby-Gore (Washington) to FO. 27.11.61. PRO: FO 371/160129, DV103145/21. The text of the message is also in FRUS: 1961–1963, i, Vietnam 1961, 668–9.

[86] Supplementary FO brief for Home for four-power NATO ministerial meeting in Paris (11–15 December 1961). 8.12.61. PRO: FO 371/160130, DV103145/47. Telegram 9179: FO to Washington. 8.12.61. Minute by McGhie (FO). 8.12.61. Both ibid. DV103145/33.

[87] Telegram 835: Hohler (Saigon) to FO. 8.12.61. PRO: FO 371/160140, DV1071/122/G.

[88] Deptel 729: Rusk to Saigon. 5.12.61. USNA: RG 59, Central Files, 751k.00/11-1261. Embtel 770: Nolting (Saigon) to State Department. 7.12.61. Ibid. 751k.5/12-761.

[89] Telegram 253: Hooton (ICC Saigon) to EA Ottawa. 11.12.61. CNA: RG 25, Vol. 4638, File 50052-A-40, part 39.

[90] Telegram 840: Hohler (Saigon) to FO. 11.12.61. PRO: FO 371/160140, DV1071/123.

with forty helicopters and four hundred technicians at Saigon.[91] G. Parthasarathi, the new Indian chairman of the ICC, called on the British and complained that the 'Commission was now placed in an impossible position'. The DRV would present the South Vietnamese note coupled with the undisguised arrival of US men and material as an open repudiation of the CFA.[92] The Americans told the British and Australians that Parthasarathi had recommended to his government that it should forward the South Vietnamese note to the co-chairmen. To the delight of the Americans, however, the Indian government instructed him not to take any initiative unless the DRV brought the issue to the attention of the ICC.[93]

While still supporting the American build-up, the Foreign Office concluded that the British as co-chairman 'will have a difficult time defending US policy, since it will be hard for the ICC in Saigon to ignore the massive US assistance'.[94] Lord Home, who was due to meet Dean Rusk in Paris, was advised to point out that the breakdown of the Geneva machinery had to be avoided since this could lead to a demand for an international conference. Therefore, the Americans should stress that Saigon had not repudiated the whole Geneva agreement but considered itself temporarily not bound to certain limitations of the CFA. As the Indian attitude in the ICC was regarded as crucial, the Americans should moreover refrain from further public announcements about the nature of their aid.[95]

Washington, of course, was aware of the importance of the Indian position. Kennedy met Nehru in November, and although the United States did not get any assurances that New Delhi would acquiesce in the new military measures, the Americans felt that the Indians had a better understanding of the situation in the RVN and the American problem there.[96] Before Nehru had met Kennedy on Rhode Island, the British had talked to him as well. Duncan Sandys, the Secretary of State for Commonwealth Relations, impressed on the Indian Prime Minister that the ICC should work more effectively. With regard to the meeting between Nehru and Kennedy, the British thought that Kennedy's remarks on Vietnam had made an impression on Nehru.[97] Lord Mountbatten, the Chief of the Defence Staff, also met Nehru in Washington and reported that Nehru seemed to have

[91] Telegram Y-662: EA Ottawa to Washington. 11.12.61. CNA: RG 25, Vol. 4638, File 50052-A-40, part 39. Deptel 2499: Jones (London) to State Department. 4.1.62. JFKL: NSF, Vietnam Country Series, box 195.

[92] Telegram 841: Hohler (Saigon) to FO. 11.12.61. PRO: FO 371/160140, DV1071/123.

[93] Telegram 3077: Washington to EA Canberra. 13.12.61. AUSNA: A1209/134, file 61/127, part 2. Telegram 2221: New Delhi to CRO. 12.12.61. PRO: FO 371/160140, DV1071/123.

[94] FO brief for Prime Minister's talks with President Kennedy at Bermuda. December 1961. PRO: CAB 133/299.

[95] Telegram 4753: FO to Home in Paris. 12.12.61. PRO: FO 371/160140, DV1071/123.

[96] Telegram 3534: Heeney (Washington) to EA Ottawa. 20.11.61. CNA: RG 25, Vol. 4638, File 50052-A-40, part 38. Letter: Rusk to Stevenson (UN representative). 21.11.61. USNA: RG 59, Central Files, 751k.00/11-1061. Telegram 331: Woodberry (Saigon) to EA Canberra. 16.11.61. AUSNA: A1209/138, file 1961/818, part 1.

[97] Minute: Sandys to Macmillan. 4.11.61. PRO: PREM 11/3392. Letter: Lansdowne (FO) to Bowles (State Department). 24.11.61. PRO: FO 371/160129, DV103145/27.

taken an 'instant liking' to Kennedy.[98] That Kennedy, indeed, had made an impression was proven by Nehru himself immediately after the undisguised arrival of US helicopters in the RVN in December. Talking to the US ambassador in New Delhi, the Indian Prime Minister expressed his conviction that the United States had no aggressive intentions and that the DRV had to cease supporting the dissident elements in the South. 'This is a most encouraging development', noted the desk officer of the Foreign Office's Southeast Asia Department in London. 'This Indian reaction will come as a severe shock to the North Vietnamese.'[99]

There were other signs of an increasingly pro-western Indian attitude. The new Indian commissioner Parthasarathi was a high calibre diplomat. He had been on the Vietnam and Laos Commissions in the mid-1950s, and before he became chairman of the ICC in Vietnam again, he had been the Indian ambassador in Beijing. Western diplomats regarded Parthasarathi's appointment as evidence of Nehru's concern over Vietnam, and the special attention the Indian Prime Minister afforded ICC matters.[100] The new chairman made a good first impression with the Canadians, too. He not only regarded the Nam murder as a convincing case but was, according to the Canadian commissioner, 'both intelligent and competent and prepared to cast his mind beyond the detail of [the] commission'.[101] Put another way, he could turn out to be the 'ruthless' Indian commissioner the British had been waiting for since early 1960.

However ruthless a commissioner Parthasarathi was, even the United States admitted that the ICC had to address the increased American assistance. W. Averell Harriman, newly appointed Under-Secretary of States for Far Eastern Affairs, explained to the Canadians that they should press in the Commission for 'parallel and related consideration' of the issues of subversion and the American build-up. The United States would meet Ottawa's and London's concerns by reaffirming that except for Articles 16 and 17 Washington regarded the CFA as continuing in force, and that the ultimate US objective was a resumption of the full observance of the CFA.[102] Ottawa did not accept the US view that Articles 16 and 17 should be regarded as inapplicable for the time being as they were the principal articles of the CFA and the Indians would not like this approach. Yet the Canadians agreed to press the ICC for the parallel consideration of increased US aid

[98] Letter: Mountbatten to Home. 10.11.61. Ibid. DV103145/23. Contrary to Mountbatten's observation, Brands and McMahon have stressed that the meeting between Nehru and Kennedy in November did not go well. See H. W. Brands, *India and the United States: The Cold Peace* (Boston: Twayne Publishers, 1990), 105–6; and Robert J. McMahon, *The Cold War on the Periphery: The United States, India and Pakistan* (New York: Columbia University Press, 1994), 280–1.

[99] Telegram 2226: New Delhi to CRO. 12.12.61. Minute by McGhie (FO). 14.12.61. Both in PRO: FO 371/166728, DV1071/2.

[100] Telegram 618: New Delhi to EA Canberra. 16.11.61. AUSNA: A1209/134, file 61/127, part 2. Report No. 2016 by Duckwitz (New Delhi). 21.11.61. Politisches Archiv des Auswärtigen Amtes, Bonn (hereafter PA): Abt. 7, Ref. 710, Bd. 1665. Letter: Powles (New Delhi) to Holyoake. 25.11.61. NZNA: PM 478/4/1, part 13.

[101] Telegram 246: Hooton (ICC Saigon) to EA Ottawa. 4.12.61. CNA: RG 25, Vol. 4638, File 50052-A-40, part 39.

[102] Telegram 3790: Heeney (Washington) to EA Ottawa. 15.12.61. Ibid.

and DRV subversion. To be able to do this successfully, they urged Washington, as the British had done, to underplay the US build-up by avoiding 'explicit demonstration that [the] articles of [the] CFA are being evaded'.[103] Like London, Ottawa had nothing against the American military build-up beyond the Geneva levels as long as it was done secretly. Although the American military build-up could not be concealed and some details of the US measures were leaked to the press, Washington tried to be more discreet and agreed with the British that it should refrain from notifying the ICC about the arrival of new men and material.[104] President Kennedy backed this policy throughout the first half of 1962. He maintained that the Americans should not be convicted 'out of their own mouths'.[105]

Initially, the Canadians were sceptical as to whether the Indians would agree to deal with the US build-up and DRV subversion simultaneously. It was regarded as encouraging that in late January the legal committee, which was dealing with the Nam case, was about to produce a 'very strong and effective report on subversion', but the Canadians suspected that Parthasarathi 'felt so strongly about the blatant unloading of helicopters in front of the Hotel Majestic that he might be inclined to deal with violations of the Agreement in respect of American equipment before the subversion and Colonel Nam issues, and not to follow a chronological sequence'.[106] The Indian attitude remained ambiguous for over a month, mainly because Nehru was busy electioneering and Foreign Minister Desai was ill, leaving Commonwealth Secretary Gundevia in charge.[107]

According to the Indian chairman of the legal committee who supported the Canadian stance, Gundevia represented a 'source of great weakness'.[108] In Gundevia's view the United States was committing 'daylight robbery' in Vietnam, whereas Hanoi managed to conceal its violations of the CFA. As the ICC could not ignore what was openly taking place, Gundevia told the Americans that he 'saw little chance that [a] simultaneous citation could be achieved'.[109] There were, however, indications of a different Indian attitude. The Canadians were assured by junior officials of the Indian Ministry of External Affairs that simultaneous citations might be possible.[110] The British ambassador in Saigon got the impression that the Indian commissioner was under instructions to hold a fair balance between the DRV and the RVN.[111]

[103] Telegram Y-11: EA Ottawa to Washington. 5.1.62. Ibid.

[104] Letter: Chancery Saigon to South East Asia Department (FO). 20.12.61. PRO: FO 371/160130, DV103145/55. Letter: Peck (FO) to Ledward (Washington). 9.2.62. PRO: FO 371/166718, DV103145/34/G.

[105] Letter: Hohler (Saigon) to Warner (FO). 23.8.62. PRO: FO 371/166734, DV1071/140.

[106] Letter: Chancery Saigon to South East Asia Department (FO). 24.1.62. PRO: FO 371/166728, DV1071/8.

[107] Embtel 2474: Timmons (New Delhi) to State Department. 14.2.62. FRUS: 1961–1963, ii, Vietnam 1962, 126–7.

[108] Telegram 1: Hooton (ICC Saigon) to New Delhi. 26.2.62. CNA: RG 25, Vol. 4638, File 50052-A-40, part 40. Telegram 39: Saigon to EA Canberra. 2.2.62. AUSNA: A1209/80, file 1962/624, part 1.

[109] Embtel 2474: Timmons (New Delhi) to State Department. 14.2.62. FRUS: 1961–1963, ii, Vietnam 1962, 126–7.

[110] Minute by McGhie (FO). 9.2.62. PRO: FO 371/166728, DV1071/14.

[111] Letter: Hohler (Saigon) to Warner (FO). 1.2.62. Ibid. DV1071/13.

In March, the legal committee finally signed an Indian-Canadian majority report accusing the DRV of supporting and organizing hostile activities in the
South. Encouraged by this development the Foreign Office desired more, and
London instructed ambassador Hohler to find out if the Indians would agree to
the ICC sending a special report on these lines to the co-chairmen without mentioning US military aid. In view of the British request, Parthasarathi pointed out
that he was under firm and clear instructions to work for simultaneous citations
of North and South Vietnam. The Canadians were told the same.[112] As Ottawa
had been working for simultaneous citations since January, the British concluded
that the Canadians were 'on the right track' and that 'they should make the running'.[113]

NO NEGOTIATIONS ON VIETNAM

In April it became clear that it would still take the ICC several weeks to draft a report.[114] London was not particularly anxious to hasten its production as it was
worried that it would lead to fresh demands for an international conference.[115]
The Foreign Office had made its opposition to a conference on Vietnam clear to
the Americans in November 1961, when the acting Indian Secretary for Commonwealth Relations had broached the idea with the Americans and British.
London argued that a conference on Vietnam would endanger the ongoing talks
on Laos, and, quite simply, there was nothing to negotiate in Vietnam. The DRV
would agree to the unification of the country on its terms alone, and only when
the PLAF had been pushed out of the RVN might it eventually be feasible to hold
a conference.[116]

The British government indeed appeared more united in its opposition against
a negotiated settlement in Vietnam than the Kennedy administration. US ambassador John Galbraith in New Delhi, W. Averell Harriman, and Chester Bowles,
the President's Special Representative in the State Department, argued that
a Laos-like settlement should be sought in Vietnam.[117] In November 1961,
Harriman informed Malcolm MacDonald, the head of the British delegation at
the Geneva conference on Laos, that he had recommended to Kennedy that he

---

[112] Savingram 65: FO to Saigon. 8.3.62. Telegram 208: Hohler (Saigon) to FO. 15.3.62. Both in
PRO: FO 371/166729, DV1071/24. Canadian telegram 48: Hooton (ICC Saigon) to EA Ottawa.
22.3.62. Ibid. DV1071/33.
[113] Minute by McGhie (FO). 8.3.62. Ibid. DV1071/24. Minute by McGhie (FO). 16.3.62. Ibid.
DV1071/28.
[114] Letter: Jackson (Saigon) to McGhie (FO). 11.4.62. PRO: FO 371/166730, DV1071/45.
[115] Brief for Parliamentary Question by Warner (FO). 13.4.62. Ibid. DV1071/46.
[116] Embtel 1304: Timmons (New Delhi) to State Department. 4.11.61. USNA: RG 59, Central
Files, 751k.00/11-461. Embtel 1913: Jones (London) to State Department. 9.11.61. Ibid. 751k.
00/11-9-61. Blue FO minute by Warner. 7.11.61. PRO: FO 371/160118, DV1015/206.
[117] Chester Bowles, *Promises to Keep: My Years in Public Life 1941–1969* (New York: Harper &
Row, 1971), 408–10.

discuss Vietnam in the same manner as Laos. MacDonald expressed his considerable reserve about such a policy.[118]

In January 1962, the British ambassador in Saigon strongly opposed Harriman's inclination to support a Vietnam conference, too. In Hohler's view the tendency to treat Laos and Vietnam as identical problems should be discouraged. As opposed to Laos, a neutralist solution was not possible for Vietnam. '[A]ny solution of the Vietnam problem', Hohler argued, 'that does not crush and eradicate the Viet Cong will simply hand over South Vietnam to the Communists.' He added that the consequences of the fall of the RVN would be 'disastrous to British interest and investment in South East Asia and seriously damaging to the prospects of the Free World containing the Communist threat'.[119] The Foreign Office echoed these views. The British aim was to divert international attention away from British and American actions in Vietnam 'while we get on with the task of defeating the Viet Cong'. A conference could not achieve anything useful until the insurgency was mastered and negotiations on an equal footing between the RVN and the DRV were possible.[120] After a visit to Vietnam in January 1962, Edward Peck, Assistant Under-Secretary of State in the Foreign Office, warned that the communists might alter their tactics to a peace offensive and the internationalization of the conflict because of the increased American military involvement in Vietnam and the more effective help provided by the British advisers in Saigon.[121]

Following the creation of the American Military Assistance Command Vietnam (MACV) in early February 1962, London's concerns proved well-founded as Hanoi and Beijing called publicly for an international conference.[122] The Foreign Office was disappointed that it had not been informed of the creation of the MACV in advance. Yet London made clear that it continued to support the strongest measures against the insurgents.[123] However, the increased pressure for a conference made ambassador Hohler soften his position on negotiations. In mid-February he introduced the idea of bilateral talks between the British and Soviet co-chairmen, but the Foreign Office flatly turned down any such proposal.[124] Nonetheless, Hohler repeated his views—also the Foreign Office's opposition to them—in the presence of Joseph Mendenhall, the counsellor at the US embassy in Saigon, and the Indian commissioner Parthasarathi in April, which led the American counsellor to believe that there were certain circles within the British

---

[118] Savingram: MacDonald (Geneva) to FO. 20.11.61. PRO: FO 371/160128, DV103145/18.

[119] Despatch 2: Hohler (Saigon) to Home. 3.1.62. PRO: FO 371/166698, DV1015/6/G.

[120] FO brief for Lord Privy Seal's visit to Canada. 16.1.62. PRO: FO 371/166698, DV1015/20.

[121] Report on visit to South East Asia by Peck (FO). 30.1.62. PRO: FO 371/166359, D1051/9. This view was shared by the British ambassador in Saigon. Despatch 14: Hohler (Saigon) to Home. 28.2.62. PRO: FO 371/166701, DV1015/64/G.

[122] Minute by Oliver (FO). 20.9.63. PRO: FO 371/170153, DV2231/1.

[123] Embtel 2953: Bruce (London) to State Department. 9.2.62. USNA: RG 59, Central Files, 751k.00/2-962. Letter: Scott (London) to EA Wellington. NZNA: PM 478/4/1, part 14.

[124] Letter: Hohler (Saigon) to Peck (FO). 15.2.62. Minute by McGhie (FO). 27.2.62. Both in PRO: FO 371/166728, DV1071/14.

government that would support a conference on Vietnam.[125] Similar suspicions about British wavering were voiced in Canberra. External Affairs closely monitored British statements on a possible Vietnam conference, and noted that although London certainly did not want negotiations at the moment, it was worrying that talks were not ruled out completely. While the British pointed out to the Australians again in early April that negotiations on Vietnam were not desirable, Australian suspicions grew in mid-April when the first secretary of the British High Commission mentioned that international pressure for a conference might become so strong that talks on Vietnam would have to be held.[126]

In fact, British opposition to a conference was very firm. The Foreign Office spelled out this policy in a long dispatch to its Washington embassy after Hanoi had called for international consultations. Britain shared the American view that there should be no bargaining on Vietnam, the dispatch stressed, and three reasons for this attitude were given. First, the Laos negotiations would be disturbed by a Vietnam conference. Second, the west would not gain from negotiations until the authority of the Saigon regime had been restored and the PLAF 'considerably discomfited'. With US support the ARVN still had the overall military superiority and was now ready for a 'real trial of strength'. In London's view, this advantage should not be bargained away. Third, at a conference the west would be confronted with unacceptable demands for the withdrawal of American advisers and the neutralization of the RVN. The DRV, however, would remain a communist state. As calls for negotiations would fall on fertile ground in neutral countries, the Foreign Office concluded that the aim of British and American policy was to do nothing to encourage the demand for international discussions. While the 'maximum amount of suitable military support' had to be given to the RVN, this had to be done 'in as unobtrusive a way as possible', and London and Washington had to 'keep many of our activities secret'.[127]

Moreover, the west should handle the ICC carefully and avoid creating difficulties for it. The main purpose was to keep the Commission in existence, 'since by its very existence it provides a shield against demands for other international actions'. If the Commission were to cease its work, it would be, in London's view, much more difficult to resist demands for the reconvening of the Geneva conference. Although the British regarded the condemnation of the DRV for its subversive activities as an 'important objective', the Foreign Office dispatch demonstrated that keeping the ICC in being in order to prevent negotiations had gained priority in the Foreign Office's thinking.[128]

---

[125] Despatch 427: Mendenhall (Saigon) to State Department. 13.4.62. USNA: RG 59, Central Files, 751k.00/4-1362.

[126] EA memorandum 'South Vietnam: British views'. 22.3.62. AUSNA: A1838/2, file 3014/9/7, part 1. Savingram 53: London to Canberra. 5.4.62. Record of conversation between Anderson (EA Canberra) and Molyneux (British High Commission). 19.4.62. Both in AUSNA: A1838/334, file 3014/11/51, part 1.

[127] Despatch 110: FO to Ormsby-Gore (Washington). 20.3.62. PRO: FO 371/166702, DV1015/83/G.

[128] Ibid.

The DRV repeated its request for international consultations in two notes to the British in March. Washington agreed with London that the demands for a conference should be strongly resisted, at least as long as the military situation was unfavourable to the west. In the event, Moscow did not press for a conference, much to the Foreign Office's relief.[129] That a conference on Vietnam was anathema to the Foreign Office was also made clear to the Canadian Commissioner Jeffrey Hooton. When he visited London in May 1962 he was told that the British were 'above all . . . anxious to avoid an international conference on Vietnam until the situation had been restored and . . . should therefore prefer, if possible, that the [special] report would not call for direct action by the Co-Chairmen which might stimulate demands for a conference'.[130]

It is conceivable that a different British attitude towards negotiations might have made an impact on the events in Vietnam in that it would have strengthened those forces in Washington and Hanoi that were advocating a Laos-like conference on Vietnam. Not only did the DRV call for talks in February and March, but Hanoi also informed East German diplomats in strict confidence in June that it was preparing a strong delegation for Geneva in order to convert the Laos conference, following its successful conclusion, into a conference on Vietnam. Although the North Vietnamese pointed out to the East German embassy that the central committee of the Lao Dong, the DRV's ruling communist party, had not yet approved this policy, Hanoi was clearly reluctant to escalate the armed conflict. There was indeed a brief encounter between the Americans and the DRV delegation in Geneva in July, but apart from American reluctance to negotiate in the first place, the United States doubted the seriousness of the North Vietnamese, mainly because DRV breaches of the 1962 Laos agreement were already apparent.[131]

The East German chargé d'affaires in the DRV did not only blame the Americans for the failure to get negotiations started. He pointed to London, stressing that the 'bad attitude of the English government' was the reason as to why there had not been a proper exchange of views between the conflicting parties in Vietnam. Although the chargé admitted that the British supported US Vietnam policy and the military campaign against the PLAF, he was still hopeful that Britain would eventually look for a peaceful solution.[132] This view was too optimistic. London remained steadfast in its opposition to negotiations in the months to come, and regarded it as vital that the west did not become 'tired first' in Vietnam.[133]

---

[129] Minute by Oliver (FO). 20.9.63. PRO: FO 371/170153, DV2231/1.

[130] Letter: Peck (FO) to Hohler (Saigon). 16.5.62. PRO: FO 371/166731, DV1071/65.

[131] Minute (Vermerk) 197/62 by Ramm (Hanoi). 23.6.62. MfAA: A8570. See also William J. Duiker, *Sacred War: Nationalism and Revolution in a Divided Vietnam* (New York: McGraw-Hill, 1995), 154–6. William J. Duiker, *The Communist Road to Power in Vietnam* (Boulder, Colo.: Westview Press, 1981), 206–8. Bassett and Pelz, 'The Failed Search for Victory', 240. Alan E. Goodman, *The Lost Peace: America's Search for a Negotiated Settlement* (Stanford, Calif.: Hoover Institution Press, 1978), 12–14.

[132] Minute (Vermerk) 207/62 by Dreßler (Hanoi). 18.7.62. MfAA: A8570.

[133] Minute by Peck (FO). 28.1.63. PRO: FO 371/170131, DV1201/20.

THE 1962 SPECIAL REPORT

In May 1962, Parthasarathi gave the Indian draft Special Report to the Canadian commissioner Hooton. The Indian chairman stressed that Nehru had approved it word by word. Hooton was delighted, praised the draft as an 'exceptionally useful document' and pointed out that the Indian government was 'well aware that [the] position they are taking . . . will be interpreted, correctly, as a turning point in Indian foreign policy in direction of greatly increased firmness in dealing with the communist bloc'.[134] The Canadians passed the draft report to the British. Equally delighted, the Foreign Office advised the Canadians to concur with it as it was 'firmer in condemnation of [the] North than was expected'.[135]

At a formal Commission meeting on 2 June 1962 the Indian draft Special Report was adopted by an Indian-Canadian majority vote.[136] The principal conclusions of this report were that in specific instances there was 'evidence to show that armed and unarmed personnel, arms, munitions and other supplies had been sent [from the DRV to the South] with the object of supporting, organizing and carrying out hostile activities, including armed attacks . . . in violation of Articles 10, 19, 24 and 27' of the CFA. As for the RVN, it was stated that it had violated the Articles 16 and 17 of the CFA 'in receiving increased military aid from the United States of America'. Moreover, the establishment of the American MACV in February 1962 and the introduction of US military personnel beyond the strength of the MAAG 'amounted to a factual military alliance prohibited under Article 19' of the CFA. The Polish delegation did not concur with these conclusions and issued a minority statement. In this the Poles criticized the report for placing on the same level 'doubtful and legally unfounded allegations . . . and grave and undeniable violations'.[137]

The Indians had resisted Canadian attempts to establish more clearly a cause and effect relationship between the two sets of allegations in the report.[138] Yet it was essential for the west to make crystal clear that the American measures were merely a reaction to the DRV's violations of the CFA. Britain was reluctant to play up the report publicly, but hoped other western countries would do so.[139] Indeed, Canada, the United States, and South Vietnam made statements on the release of the report, pointing out the cause and effect nature of the North

---

[134] Canadian telegram 84: Hooton (ICC Saigon) to EA Ottawa. 19.5.62. PRO: FO 371/166731, DV1071/65.

[135] Savingram 2725: FO to Washington. 23.5.62. Ibid. DV1071/65.

[136] Minutes of the 652nd meeting of the ICC. 2.6.62. CNA: RG 25, Vol. 4662, File 50052-A-12-40, part 50.

[137] Cmnd. 1755, Vietnam No. 1: Special Report to the Co-Chairmen of the Geneva Conference on Indo-China, 2 June 1962 (London: HMSO, 1962).

[138] Report of Activities of the ICC Vietnam. 19.6.62. CNA: RG 25, Vol. 4638, File 50052-A-40, part 40.

[139] Telegram 2914: London to EA Canberra. 20.6.62. AUSNA: A1209/80, file 1962/624, part 1.

Vietnamese 'attack' and the increased US help.[140] Britain did the same in its communications with the Soviet Union. As the Foreign Office wanted to take action on the report before the Soviet co-chairman could do so, a note to Moscow was prepared at the end of May. The note established the cause and effect relationship emphasizing that 'the complaints of Northern subversion [were] of long standing . . . [whereas] the intensification in US assistance . . . [began] long after the threat from North Vietnam had developed'.[141] London proposed in this note to publish the report, and as the Soviets did not react to this, Britain circulated it unilaterally on 25 June 1962.[142]

The Special Report represented a major propaganda victory for the west. 'The recognition by an impartial authority of North Vietnam's responsibility in the terrorist campaign in the South', New Zealand's Prime Minister Keith Holyoake told the press, 'should appreciably strengthen the international position of South Vietnam and its allies'.[143] The Americans noted with satisfaction that the DRV regarded the report as a serious blow to its prestige.[144] Indeed, North Vietnam reacted furiously, charging that the report 'deliberately put forward untruths'.[145] The primary target of Hanoi's propaganda campaign was the Indian delegation. The North Vietnamese press charged that the Indian delegate was not worthy of being the chairman of the ICC, and that he was misrepresenting the South Vietnamese patriotic struggle as subversive activities.[146] The Soviet Union avoided any direct criticism of New Delhi for its role in the Special Report, and the North Vietnamese admitted during a confidential press conference for socialist journalists held at the DRV's foreign ministry in early July 1962 that the initial tactic of harshly criticizing India had been a mistake. In the future, only objective and accurate reports with regard to India would be issued.[147] In any case, it was all too obvious that the ICC had issued, as an East German diplomat put it, a

---

[140] Status Report prepared by Southeast Asia task force. 27.6.62. FRUS: 1961–1963, ii, Vietnam 1962, 480–1. For the Canadians it was consistent with their long-standing policy to stress in public the defensive character of US activities in Vietnam. See Canadian House of Commons Debates, 8.3.61, 1602.

[141] Savingram 29937: FO to Washington. 31.5.62. PRO: FO 371/166731, DV1071/75. The note was finally handed to the Soviets on 14.6.62.

[142] Letter: Warner (FO) to Wright (Paris). 18.6.62. FO guidance telegram 250 to certain posts. 25.6.62. Both in PRO: FO 371/166732, DV1071/97.

[143] Press statement by Holyoake. 27.6.62. NZNA: PM 478/4/4, part 6. The Australians took the same line. EA Canberra's press release on Special Report. 25.6.62. AUSNA: A1209/80, file 1962/624, part 1.

[144] Airgram A-20: Barbour (Saigon) to State Department. 10.7.62. USNA: RG 59, Central Files, 751k.00/7-1062.

[145] The quote is from a letter of 15 June 1962 addressed to the ICC by Vo Nguyen Giap. It was handed to the British as co-chairman by the Soviets and was transmitted to the FO in telegram 1143: Roberts (Moscow) to FO. 21.6.62. PRO: FO 371/166732, DV1071/100.

[146] Report of Activities of the ICC Vietnam. 19.6.62. CNA: RG 25, Vol. 4638, File 50052-A-40, part 40.

[147] Minute (Vermerk) 207/62 by Dreßler. 18.7.62. MfAA: A8570. Memorandum by Schütz (military attaché) on a confidential press conference of the DRV Ministry of External Affairs on 5 July 1962. 6.7.62. BArchMA: VA-01/6427.

'damaging report'.[148] Moreover, as a result of India's support for the Special Report, the DRV gave up its neutral stance towards the Sino-Indian dispute and increasingly supported the Chinese position. This helped those forces within the DRV polit bureau that preferred to follow a pro-Chinese line in the Sino-Soviet dispute. Indeed, relations between Hanoi and Beijing became increasingly close from mid-1962 onwards.[149]

The obvious weakness of the Special Report was that the ICC did not undertake an investigation of its own but treated Saigon's allegations as fact.[150] It is not surprising that the Canadians acted this way, but it is more difficult to explain the Indian attitude. One reason for the Indian stance might have been the increasingly strained relations with Beijing.[151] The DRV's ambassador in East Berlin gave three other reasons for India's policy towards Vietnam in his conversation with the East Germans in June 1961. First, New Delhi was afraid of the revolutionary movement in Vietnam. Second, the Indians needed American dollars to finance their latest five-year plan. Third, a reunification of North and South Vietnam was not in the interest of India.[152]

US financial assistance might well have played a role, as the US aid programme to India reached record levels between 1960 and 1964.[153] In April 1961 the Kennedy administration pledged to provide India with one billion dollars in economic aid over the next two years. Nehru warmly welcomed US aid and expressed deep gratitude.[154] Moreover, India and the United States had begun in the 1950s to coordinate their covert action against Chinese communist influence in the Himalayas.[155] But whatever the wider Indian foreign policy interests, it rather appears that there was among the Indians a genuine belief that the DRV was behind the insurrection in the South. Even Commonwealth Secretary Gundevia, who did not support the Indian line concerning the Special Report, was of this opinion.[156] In the end, it did not matter if there was convincing proof as to whether the insurgency was directed by Hanoi or not, for the Indians perceived it this way, as did the Canadians and the British. Time and again Britain complained about the flimsy evidence the South Vietnamese provided. Canadian, British, and American

---

[148] Minute (Vermerk) 197/62 by Ramm (Hanoi). 23.6.62. MfAA: A8570.

[149] Zhai, *China and the Vietnam Wars*, 91 and 116.   [150] See: Levant, *Quiet Complicity*, 167.

[151] CIA memorandum: 'Indian Role in Vietnam'. 27.7.61. JFKL: NSF, Vietnam Country Series, box 193.

[152] Minute (Aktenvermerk) by Stude (MfAA) on a conversation between ambassador Thuan and deputy minister Stibi. 16.6.62. MfAA: C1065/73.

[153] A. Appadorai and M. S. Rajan, *India's Foreign Policy and Relations* (New Delhi: South Asian Publishers, 1985), 252–3.

[154] Brands, *India and the United States*, 100–1; McMahon, *Cold War on the Periphery*, 276–7. The PRC might have perceived the increase in US economic aid to India as a threat because of the resulting improvement of US–Indian relations, and US aid therefore might have played a role in Beijing's decision to attack India in the autumn of 1962. See Yaacov I. Vertzberger, *Misperceptions in Foreign Policymaking: The Sino-Indian Conflict, 1959–1962* (Boulder, Colo.: Westview Press, 1984), 95.

[155] See S. Mahmud Ali, *Cold War in the High Himalayas: The USA, China and South Asia in the 1950s* (New York: St. Martin's Press, 1999).

[156] Embtel 2474: Timmons (New Delhi) to State Department. 14.2.62. FRUS: 1961–1963, ii, Vietnam 1962, 126–7.

military experts even had evidence that contradicted the general perception. They observed in late 1961 that, while there were a few North Vietnamese cadres, the PLAF consisted of ethnic South Vietnamese and were armed with captured American and French weapons.[157] Similarly, the British embassy in Laos sought to destroy the American thesis that the insurgents made wide use of Southern Laos to infiltrate men and material. The embassy dismissed South Vietnamese evidence of the existence of the Ho-Chi-Minh trail, and denied the possibility of sending army units through Laos to Vietnam. If at all, only some communist cadres could use this route.[158] These arguments, however, did not change the general perception in London, Ottawa, and, needless to say, Washington that a communist insurrection in the RVN had to be directed by Hanoi.[159]

The United States went ahead with its military build-up without knowing what India's reaction would be. Clearly, Washington would have preferred a positive Indian and therefore ICC attitude, but even a hostile ICC would not have deterred the Americans. Otherwise they would have proceeded more cautiously. Canada and Britain had to deal with the ICC. The months prior to the publishing of the Special Report marked the climax of Anglo-Canadian cooperation with regard to Vietnam. Both Ottawa and London supported the military build-up, but tried to convince the United States to be more 'discreet' about it, and even deceive and mislead the ICC if necessary. They both put pressure on the Indians, and the Foreign Office believed that this had kept the Indian Commissioner 'on the rails on several occasions'.[160]

MASTERLY INACTIVITY

In its Special Report the ICC had promised a further report on subversion. And, indeed, the Indian and Canadian members of the legal committee immediately started to work on it. As the Polish delegate refused to take part, they went to New Delhi to draft it there. Britain was not optimistic that the report would emerge quickly, as the British embassy summed up in August 1962:

During the past nine months we have gone from the low point of Colonel Nam's murder to a boom in the I.C.C.'s shares (in South Viet Nam at least) following the publication of the Special Report. The long-awaited further report on subversion by the Legal Committee may keep the shares fairly high for a period, but the current signs are that we may be heading for another recession.[161]

[157] Memorandum for the Commissioner by Major Kierans (ICC Saigon). 21.10.61. CNA: RG 25, Vol. 4637, File 50052-A-40, part 37.

[158] Despatch 39: Addis (Vientiane) to Home, enclosing report by Toy (military attaché). 2.11.61. PRO: FO 371/160118, DV1015/203/G.

[159] Larry E. Cable, *Conflicts and Myths: The Development of American Counter-insurgency Doctrine and the Vietnam War* (New York: New York University Press, 1986) considered different explanations and argued that the NLF campaign was an indigenous South Vietnamese insurrection in reaction to Diem's repressive regime.

[160] Letter: Peck (FO) to Hohler (Saigon). 16.5.62. PRO: FO 371/166731, DV1071/65.

[161] Letter: Burrows (Saigon) to FO. 22.8.62. PRO: FO 371/166735, DV1071/141.

The feeling was that with the Special Report the Indians had gone 'as far as they dare—perhaps rather further' and that it was in the Indian character to look for a counter-balance.[162] In October the draft report of the legal committee was finally handed to India's Ministry of External Affairs, which had to decide the next step. It was two thousand pages long and the Canadians expected that the editing would take the Indians some time.[163] The British embassy in Saigon proposed to send a letter from the British co-chairman to New Delhi congratulating the Indians on the Special Report, and asking for another report on the same lines. The Foreign Office strongly opposed this proposal because it was determined to preserve at least the appearance of Britain's support for the Geneva accords. Congratulating the Indians for the Special Report would be a departure from the 'impartial role' of the co-chairman, the Foreign Office argued, and was therefore out of the question. Moreover, such a letter might have been counter-productive because the Indians, in London's view, were 'still trembling from the shock of publishing the original report and would resent pressure from us to follow it up'.[164]

While the legal committee's report was bogged down in New Delhi, relations between the Indian and Canadian delegations deteriorated at an alarming rate. The British put the blame on the Canadian commissioner Gordon Cox who took up his post in November 1962. The British ambassador complained that Cox had arrived in a 'crusading spirit' trying to prosecute the cold war in the Commission, but was quickly frustrated by the inactivity of the ICC.[165] Because he was, as Hohler's successor Gordon Etherington-Smith put it, 'unduly emotional and mercurial' he had several head-on collisions with his Indian colleague. This was, the British ambassador pointed out, regrettable and avoidable.[166]

At the same time the Canadian and British positions began to drift apart. Whereas Cox was pressing for action, London favoured the 'masterly inactivity' of the ICC, championed by the new Indian chairman Ramchundur Goburdhan. The Foreign Office was certain that any other approach would be worse for the west: 'The hard fact is that for the Commission to attempt to do what it is supposed to do would blacken the free world more than the communist, while to wind it up would require the consent of the 1954 signatories in a way which [would] almost certainly precipitate a conference or [at] least [an] accusation that the West is trying to cover up its crimes.'[167]

[162] Telegram 4044: FO to Washington. 1.6.62. PRO: FO 371/166732, DV1071/81. Letter: Petrie (New Delhi) to Fair (CRO). 28.8.62. PRO: FO 371/166735, DV1071/143.

[163] Telegram 1555: New Delhi to CRO. 9.10.62. Ibid. DV1071/150.

[164] Telegram 735: Hohler (Saigon) to FO. 5.10.62. Telegram 793: FO to Saigon. 11.10.62. Both ibid.

[165] Letter: Canadian Delegation (ICC Saigon) to EA Ottawa. 17.11.62. CNA: RG 25, Vol. 4638, File 50052-A-40, part 40. Letter: Hohler (Saigon) to Peck (FO). 17.1.63. PRO: FO 371/170118, DV1071/3.

[166] Letter: Etherington-Smith (Saigon) to Peck (FO). 25.6.64. PRO: FO 371/175512, DV1071/25/G.

[167] Minute by Williams (FO). 19.1.62. PRO: FO 371/170118, DV1071/3.

Still, London was more worried about a possible conference than about an ineffective Commission. The Canadians were told that it would be wrong to try to force Goburdhan's hand, as there was 'little doubt that his present policy of inactivity favours the West, and is meant to do so'.[168] Inactivity did not only suit Whitehall. By August 1963, even the Polish delegation was in favour of a policy of 'masterly inactivity'. The Polish commissioner, Mieczyslaw Maneli, pointed out to the British that his government did not want 'any trouble with the Commission', and he implied that the main reason for this was that the Poles and the Soviets could not longer be sure of 'controlling their Chinese friends'. Therefore Maneli favoured a 'minimum of further action' on the issues of communist subversion and American intervention. Naturally, he also opposed the publication of the legal committee's report. Even the Saigon government had, to the surprise of the British embassy, lost interest in this report. This was all the more reason for the Indians to maintain their policy of 'masterly inactivity'.[169]

CONCLUSION

Because of Anthony Eden's role as peacemaker at Geneva the British could not turn a blind eye to the developments in Indochina after 1954. London did not want to lose its credibility, especially among neutral and Commonwealth countries. It has been shown, however, that Britain's main interest between 1961 and 1963 was not to make the Geneva agreements work. Britain had no intention to play the role of a peacemaker again. The aim was to interpret the CFA in such a way that the American military intervention in the RVN could be justified. The communists were blamed for the resumption of hostilities and an attempt was made to explore every possible way of portraying the American intervention as a defensive measure. Like Canada, Britain pretended that it still honoured the Geneva framework and that it was searching for a peaceful settlement of the conflict, yet Whitehall privately ruled out negotiations, advised the Americans to conceal their military build-up and tried to make sure that the ICC put the blame on the DRV for the breakdown of the peace in Vietnam.

Britain supported the American policy in Vietnam wholeheartedly. The British only wanted to 'sell' this policy in a different, less confrontational way. The aim was not to antagonize world public opinion, particularly in the non-aligned countries. There were three main reasons for Britain's support of US policy. First, the British did not disagree with the general American assessment that a pro-western government in Saigon had to be supported. The loss of the RVN to the communists would be first of all 'disastrous' for British interests in Southeast Asia, the British ambassador in Saigon pointed out. Moreover, the defeat of the RVN regime would 'seriously damage' western efforts at containing communism

---

[168] Letter: Burrows (Saigon) to Williams. 31.3.63. Ibid.
[169] Letter: Burrows (Saigon) to Warner. 13.8.63. PRO: FO 371/170119, DV1071/24.

in the region. Interestingly the ambassador betrayed less concern about western cold war interests and more about Britain's national interest.[170] Second, it was unlikely that the United States would change its Vietnam policy if the British objected to it. Consequently, there was no reason to use up British credits in Washington even if London had disagreed, as Frederick Warner of the Foreign Office put it.[171] Third, the British were well-equipped in the diplomatic field to prove to the Americans that they were a useful ally. Britain was keen to continue to play its role as co-chairman of the Geneva conference and to represent western interests vis-à-vis the Soviet Union. Two of the three ICC members were Commonwealth countries, and the British could make use of their special diplomatic ties with Canada and India to look after western interests in Indochina.

Britain therefore fought the Vietnam War for the Americans on the diplomatic front. In this role, the British were in a position to give advice to Washington and impress their way of 'selling' the US military build-up to the world. It was the general perception at the time that the communist regime in the DRV was the instigator of the communist insurgency in the RVN, and it was up to Britain and the ICC to turn this perception into a public statement, even if the British themselves complained about the less than convincing evidence for this perception.

The ICC was certainly an ineffective body as far as the supervision of the CFA was concerned. It had no executive power, and it is no surprise that its findings had nothing more than propaganda value. As the west badly needed a propaganda victory, the ICC's findings provided such useful propaganda in 1962, and the Commission's work was therefore highly regarded in the west. That the ICC could not deter Washington was obvious. It could only make the justification of American action either easier or more difficult. After the Special Report of 1962 Britain quickly became resigned to the fact that further reports of the ICC were not very likely to favour the west. Washington's and Saigon's violations of the CFA were just too obvious. London therefore had nothing against India's policy of 'masterly inactivity'.

The British government was opposed to the idea of reconvening the Geneva conference to solve the Vietnam conflict. A different British attitude between 1961 and 1963 might have strengthened the position of people like Averell Harriman in Washington who lobbied for a Laos-like conference on Vietnam. In this way British support for a conference might have changed the course of the conflict in Vietnam, particularly as Hanoi seemed reluctant to bring about an escalation of the war in 1962. What is more, the DRV's public calls for negotiations, it appears from East German records, were meant quite seriously. London's refusal to sponsor another peace deal in Vietnam was best demonstrated by Britain's strong resistance to the reconvention of the Geneva conference. The mere existence of the ICC was regarded as the perfect shield against demands for such a conference. It provided a useful propaganda tool against domestic and international demands

---

[170] Despatch 2: Hohler (Saigon) to Home. 3.1.62. PRO: FO 371/166698, DV1015/6/G.
[171] Telegram 544: London to EA Ottawa. 24.2.60. CNA: RG 25, Vol. 4637, File 50052-A-40, part 35.

that Britain should do something to promote peace in Vietnam. The publicly dis-
played willingness to uphold the co-chairmanship and to support the continued
existence of the ICC was to demonstrate Britain's continued interest in a peaceful
settlement of the Vietnam conflict based on the Geneva agreements of 1954. Yet
between 1961 and 1963 the co-chairmanship cloaked London's real objectives in
Vietnam, which were identical with Washington's policy. The communist insurgency in the RVN had to be defeated militarily. Frederick Warner, the head of the
Foreign Office's Southeast Asia Department, assured Averell Harriman in July
1962—just after the meeting between US and DRV representatives had come to
nothing—that London would continue to hold off communist attempts to hold a
conference. Warner also pointed out that Britain was 'entirely in agreement with
the United States on seeking a military solution in Vietnam'.[172] What is more, the
Macmillan government proved that it not only agreed with American policy but
was also prepared to send British counter-insurgency experts to Saigon in order to
assist the RVN in its struggle against the communists.

[172] Record by Warner (FO) on his talk with Harriman. 22.7.62. PRO: FO 371/166354, DV1015/25.

3

Proving an Active Ally:
The Origins of the
British Advisory Mission

ON 15 FEBRUARY 1960 a South Vietnamese airforce plane departed from
Saigon's Tan Son Nhut airport. On board was President Ngo Dinh Diem accompanied by a party of thirteen, among them Vu Van Mau, the Foreign Minister.
After a short flight the aircraft landed in Kuala Lumpur where the Malayan King,
the Yang di-Pertuan Agong, greeted Diem. Later on Diem was welcomed by
Tunku Abdul Rahman, the Malayan Prime Minister. The Tunku had hoped that
Diem's state visit would enable him to secure South Vietnam's support for his
idea of a Southeast Asia Friendship and Economic Treaty (SEAFET). Diem, however, had not made the trip to Kuala Lumpur to encourage the Tunku's vague
scheme for regional cooperation. He had come because he was eager to learn
more about anti-guerrilla warfare.[1]

Diem was therefore grateful when Tun Razak, the Malayan Deputy Prime
Minister and Minister of Defence, personally briefed him on the special military
measures the Malayans and British had developed in order to fight communist
guerrillas in the jungles.[2] During his state visit Diem was also introduced to
Robert Thompson, Malaya's Permanent Secretary of Defence. Nothing at the
time suggested, however, that Diem would offer Thompson a job as his personal
adviser a couple of months later.[3] The Tunku was happy to share Malaya's expertise with the South Vietnamese, while Diem was suitably impressed by what
he was told about counter-subversion techniques. Consequently, the two Southeast Asian leaders pledged in their final communiqué that both countries would
examine the possibilities of expanding still further their cooperation in order to
fight communist subversion.[4]

---

[1] Despatch 219: Purnell (Kuala Lumpur) to State Department. 29.2.60. USNA: RG 59, Central
Files, 751k.11/2-2960. Telegram 49: Forsyth (Saigon) to EA Canberra. 15.2.60. Memorandum 357:
Hall (Kuala Lumpur) to EA Canberra. Both in AUSNA: A1838/333, file 3006/10/1, part 1.

[2] Telegram 428: Byington (Kuala Lumpur) to State Department. 15.2.60. USNA: RG 59, Central
Files, 751k.11/2-1560. The text of the communiqué is also in AUSNA: A1838/333, file 3006/10/1, part
1.

[3] Robert Thompson, *Make for the Hills: Memories of Far Eastern Wars* (London: Leo Cooper,
1989), 122.

[4] Telegram 94: Kuala Lumpur to CRO. 19.2.60. PRO: FO 371/152758, DV1061/1. Telegram 75:
Forsyth (Saigon) to EA Canberra. 24.2.60. AUSNA: A1838/333, file 3006/10/1, part 1.

Diem lost no time in following up this pledge. Just one day after his return from Kuala Lumpur he invited Roderick Parkes, the British ambassador, to the Presidential Palace. Praising Britain's achievements in Malaya, especially in combating terrorism, he asked if an expert from Malaya could come to Saigon to explain in more detail what tactics the British had used against the communists. The British ambassador was non-committal and pointed out that the South Vietnamese would have to address the Malayans directly, but he promised Diem to inform Kuala Lumpur of his request in advance.[5]

In Diem's visit to Malaya in early 1960 and his interest in British-Malayan advice lay the roots of the British Advisory Mission (BRIAM) to Vietnam. Yet the path to establishing the mission was neither smooth nor was it straightforward. As the security situation in the RVN deteriorated, the British came to the conclusion that they had to play a more active role in Vietnam. Not surprisingly, Malaya was the prism through which the British in Southeast Asia and in London saw the renewed conflict in South Vietnam. The Malayan emergency had been, after all, a prime example of successfully overcoming a communist insurgency in a Southeast Asian country. Yet it took the British one and a half years to convince their allies, the South Vietnamese and the Americans, of the merits of British advice. Given in later years the American pressure on its allies to 'show the flag' in Vietnam, it is striking that there was considerable US opposition—mainly from the US military—to have British advisers in Saigon. By focusing on the eighteen months between Diem's state visit to Malaya and the establishment of BRIAM in September 1961, this chapter will therefore explore two questions: why was London so determined to play a more prominent role in the fight against the Vietnamese communists? And how did the British finally achieve their aim of establishing BRIAM?

APPLYING THE LESSONS OF MALAYA

In March 1960, ambassador Parkes regarded Diem's request for a visit of an expert from Malaya with scepticism. He feared that Diem might eventually ask for direct British assistance, a move that he regarded as highly undesirable. In his view, the British government was not prepared to provide a complete training mission of a size that could do any good. Even if London decided to send only one officer, his presence would create difficulties with the American military advisers. Moreover, Parkes was certain that if assistance was to be provided, Britain would run into serious trouble under the Geneva agreements.[6] Nobody in London, however, seemed to share Parkes's anxieties. His doubts were indeed quickly forgotten when Henry Hohler—a diplomat of the 'old school' with a patrician and

---

[5] Letter: Parkes (Saigon) to Tory (Kuala Lumpur). 24.2.60. PRO: FO 371/152780, DV1203/11. The British in Kuala Lumpur kept the Australians well informed about this development. Memorandum 461: Hall (Kuala Lumpur) to EA Canberra. 17.3.60. AUSNA: A1838/333, file 3006/10/1, part 1.

[6] Letter: Parkes (Saigon) to Allen (Singapore). 25.2.60. PRO: FO 371/152780, DV1203/12.

largely military family background[7]—became the new British ambassador in Saigon a few weeks after Diem's request. Instead, British diplomats in Saigon and Malaya as well as the relevant departments in the Foreign Office and Commonwealth Relations Office (CRO) increasingly believed that the British and Malayans had to play a more active role in South Vietnam.

This belief was based on the view that the Americans had trained the ARVN for a conventional, Korean-type conflict and therefore simply for the wrong war.[8] Worse still, the Americans seemed to lack the necessary experience to remedy the situation and to provide the 'right' training. The British, on the other hand, knew all that was required to fight guerrillas because of their experience gained in Malaya.[9] They confronted their American colleagues in Saigon with this quite frequently, and not without a sense of satisfaction.[10]

In London, Diem's request for a visit from Malaya to discuss anti-subversion measures therefore fell on fertile ground. Prior to the ICC decision of early 1960 that allowed an increase to the MAAG, the Foreign Office had thought that the Geneva agreements prevented Britain from sending military personnel to Vietnam. The new Indian attitude in the ICC, it was felt, might change this and Diem's approach was described as a promising 'starter'.[11] The CRO was equally pleased with this development and British diplomats in Malaya especially were eager to help. They 'stimulated' the Malayan Ministry of Defence to call a meeting in order to consider what Kuala Lumpur could do to assist the administration in Saigon.[12] This meeting in late March 1960 was chaired by Robert Thompson who had already been designated to lead a three-men mission to South Vietnam the following month in response to Diem's request. The meeting made the broad recommendation that Malaya could provide assistance in repressing the insurgency by training the South Vietnamese military, police, and administration.[13]

It is striking how eager the British were to see the 'lessons' of the Malayan emergency being applied against the insurgents. Robert Thompson was not the only one who was to spell out the usefulness of British anti-guerrilla techniques to the Vietnamese. In March 1960, Colonel L. H. Lee, a member of staff of the Director of Operations in Kuala Lumpur, had given a course in counter-insurgency for sûreté officers in Saigon. Before he returned to Kuala Lumpur, he met President Diem and impressed on him the necessity to create a single intelli-

---

[7] Letter: Reginald Burrows to author. 21.2.2002.

[8] Despatch: Parkes (Saigon) to Home. 4.2.60. PRO: FO 371/152738, DV1015/3. Letter: Moss (FO) to de la Mare (Washington). 17.3.60. PRO: FO 371/152773, DV11345/1. See also Cable, *Conflict of Myths*,186.

[9] Telegram 47: Parkes (Saigon) to FO. 27.2.60. PRO: FO 371/152780, DV1202/8.

[10] Letter: Parkes (Saigon) to Allen (Singapore). 16.2.60. Ibid. DV1202/3.

[11] Minute by Butler (FO) on 'Malayan assistance to Laos and South Viet-Nam'. 3.3.60. PRO: FO 371/152138, D10113/4.

[12] Letter: Crombie (Kuala Lumpur) to Smith (CRO). 4.4.60. PRO: DO 35/10009.

[13] Record of a meeting held in the Secretary of State's Office (Kuala Lumpur). 24.3.60. Ibid. Telegram 80: Saigon to Singapore. 20.3.60. PRO: FO 371/152739, DV1015/26.

gence agency in South Vietnam, to consider defending the agrovilles[14] and to pursue a 'clear and hold' strategy. The ARVN should establish absolutely complete control in selected areas and remain there for twelve to eighteen months so as to re-establish lost confidence in the Diem government. One week later, all these measures that had been applied successfully in Malaya were again put to Diem by Admiral Gerald Gladstone, the British Commander-in-Chief Far Eastern Station. Diem's reaction to these suggestions was quite perceptive and showed that Diem was well aware of the shortcomings inherent in the attempt to apply Malayan methods in the RVN. Raising most of the weaknesses analysts would later list as the reason for the failure of the strategic hamlet programme, he pointed out that the situation in Vietnam was quite different from Malaya. First, it was more difficult to identify the insurgents because they were not, as in Malaya, ethnic Chinese. Second, the Vietnamese peasant preferred to live in the midst of his own paddy and would resent having to stay in defended new villages. Third, a 'food denial policy' which was successfully applied in Malaya could not work in Vietnam because of the abundance of rice and fish available everywhere in that country.[15]

Despite these early indications of Diem's reservations about British-Malayan counter-insurgency methods, the British continued to pursue their Malayan approach to the conflict in Vietnam. Following Colonel Lee and General Gladstone, Robert Thompson was the next in line to impress the lessons of Malaya upon Diem. Accompanied by C. C. Too, head of the Malayan Psychological Warfare Section, and Inche Salleh bin Ismail, the Malayan Deputy Commissioner of

---

[14] In 1959 President Diem endorsed the idea of resettling peasants in agrovilles that offered housing for up to 10,000 peasants, and construction of some of them began in 1960. The aim was to provide more security, to facilitate an extension of government social services, and to accelerate economic development. Peasants who lived too far away to be moved into an agroville were to move into 'agglomerated hamlets' that had up to 1,500 inhabitants (Despatch 426: Durbrow to State Department. 6.6.60. USNA: Central Files, 751k.00/6-660). The British embraced the scheme because it reminded them of the measures taken in Malaya (Despatch 1: Parkes to Home. 27.1.60. PRO: FO 371/152737, DV1011/1). Although convinced that the resettlement would antagonize some peasants, the British found the RVN's approach 'less ruthless' than that of the British in Malaya (Letter: Stewart to FO. 3.6.60. PRO: FO 371/152740, DV1015/40). In September 1960 the British noted with regret that Diem had to curtail the programme because of its unpopularity (Despatch 43: Hohler to Home. 22.9.60. PRO: FO 371/152741, DV1015/57).

[15] Despatch 17: Hohler (Saigon) to Home. 5.4.60. PRO: FO 371/152748, DV1017/1. Record of conversation between Admiral Gladstone and Diem. 5.4.60. PRO: FO 371/152739, DV1015/36. Telegram 142: Forsyth (Saigon) to EA Canberra. 8.4.60. AUSNA: A1838/333, file 3006/10/1, part 1. Many scholars have since made the same points as Diem. They usually add that the main difference with the situation in Malaya was that the insurgents in the RVN had outside assistance, that the insurgency in Malaya was on a smaller scale and that the British—as opposed to the United States in Vietnam—had ultimate control over the conduct of the anti-guerrilla struggle. See e.g. Richard A. Hunt, *Pacification: The American Struggle for Vietnam's Hearts and Minds* (Boulder, Colo.: Westview Press, 1995), 35–6; Donald. W. Hamilton, *The Art of Insurgency: American Military Policy and the Failure of Strategy in Southeast Asia* (Westport, Conn.: Praeger, 1998), 146–7; Robert W. Komer, *The Malayan Emergency in Retrospect: Organizing of a Successful Counterinsurgency Effort* (Santa Monica, Calif.: RAND, 1972), 78–9 and 85; Khong, *Analogies at War*, 94; D. Michael Shafer, *Deadly Paradigms: The Failure of U.S. Counterinsurgency Policy* (Princeton: Princeton University Press, 1988), 267–8.

Police and Chief Police Officer in Perak, Thompson toured South Vietnam at the beginning of April 1960. He met high-ranking ARVN generals, members of the Saigon government, and province chiefs. Thompson also got first-hand experience of Diem's tendency to bore his visitors with long monologues when the South Vietnamese President received him in Saigon.[16]

The report Thompson sent to Diem on 13 April 1960 suggested that the RVN should organize its counter-insurgency effort on the lines of the Emergency Operations Council and the Executive Committees in Malaya's states and districts.[17] Thompson recommended moreover that Diem establish one single intelligence agency, improve the communication system in general and wireless cover in particular, and pay more attention to psychological warfare. Only one of Thompson's main proposals reflected that he had actually visited the country and had taken note of the geographical conditions: he advised Diem to make increased use of boats on the extensive network of waterways, especially in the region of the Mekong delta.[18] Thompson's first visit to South Vietnam revealed that he believed the Vietnam War and the Malayan emergency to be very similar conflicts. Consequently, the same methods of fighting communist insurgents had to be applied.

Thompson's report seems to have impressed the South Vietnamese. In May 1960, the South Vietnamese chargé d'affaires in Kuala Lumpur approached Thompson and asked him whether he was willing to come to Saigon for one or two years with a team of Malayan officers. Thompson declined and stressed that he did not want to go as a 'freelancer'. Although his April visit showed that he saw himself as a somehow independent adviser—he refused to send a copy of his report to the Foreign Office as this would be a breach of obligation to Diem— Thompson nevertheless insisted that he would serve in Vietnam only under official auspices of either the United Nations or Britain.[19]

[16] Thompson, *Make for the Hills*, 122. Memorandum 557: Critchley (Kuala Lumpur) to EA Canberra. 8.4.60. AUSNA: A1838/333, file 3006/10/1, part 1.

[17] On Briggs's and Templer's administrative arrangements in Malaya and the responsibilities of these committees, see Komer, *The Malayan Emergency*, 78–9; John Coates, *Suppressing Insurgency: An Analysis of the Malayan Emergency, 1948–1954* (Boulder, Colo.: Westview Press, 1992), 84–5 and 116–19. Richard Stubbs, *Hearts and Minds in Guerrilla Warfare: The Malayan Emergency, 1948–1960* (Singapore: Oxford University Press, 1989), 98–100; Anthony Short, *Communist Insurrection in Malaya* (London: Muller, 1975), 322 ff. and 378–85.

[18] Telegram 342: Kuala Lumpur to CRO. 26.5.60. PRO: FO 371/152740, DV1015/40.

[19] Letter: Tory (Kuala Lumpur) to Pritchard (CRO). 25.4.61. Telegram 316: Kuala Lumpur to CRO. 25.4.61. Both in PRO: DO 169/109. No copy of the report was found in the FO files. Diem passed the report to the Americans. The three-page summary of the report made by the Americans has not yet been released by the National Archives in Washington. See memorandum: Wood to Cottrell. 1.7.61. FRUS: 1961–1963, i, Vietnam 1961, 196.

DIEM'S OPPOSITION TO BRITAIN'S INVOLVEMENT

Diem's visit to Malaya in February, his request for an expert to give more detailed advice and his offer to Thompson in May showed the keen Vietnamese interest in British-Malayan advice. This attitude prompted the British ambassador in Saigon to note that 'the Vietnamese are inclined, to an almost embarrassing extent, to compare the way in which we conducted our affairs in Malaya with the French record in Indo China'.[20] He was, however, confused about the changed South Vietnamese attitude when General Richard Hull, the Commander-in-Chief British Land Forces Far East in Singapore, visited Saigon in July 1960. His trip was designed as a follow-up to Thompson's visit, as during Thompson's stay the South Vietnamese had expressed an interest in discussing the insurgency with a military expert. As none was available from Malaya, the British decided to arrange for General Hull to go to Saigon. Although Hull was received in a friendly manner, he was kept 'at arm's length': neither Diem nor high-ranking generals were prepared to exchange views with him.[21] Nevertheless Hull offered to send an advisory mission to Saigon that consisted of experienced counter-insurgency officers.[22] Ambassador Hohler was confronted with further evidence that the South Vietnamese had changed their minds when he inquired whether there was any interest in such an advisory mission led by Thompson. He regarded the RVN's reply as a polite way of saying 'no'. The South Vietnamese, contrary to the British, expressed their concern that an advisory mission might embarrass Britain as co-chairman of the Geneva conference.[23] Hohler did not know why Diem had apparently lost interest in British advice. He speculated that the South Vietnamese President was afraid of criticism from the ARVN if he invited British-Malayan experts to the country.[24]

Although Diem's interest in British advice had decreased, it did not disappear. When the President learned that Field Marshal Templer, the British High Commissioner to Malaya from 1952 to 1954, was touring Malaya in October 1960, he asked him to visit Saigon too. Templer had not planned to include Saigon in his tour and was reluctant to accept Diem's invitation. The British embassy in Saigon and the Foreign Office, however, begged the Field Marshal to go. Ambassador Hohler urged Templer 'most strongly' to reconsider his decision.[25] Frederick Hoyer-Millar, Permanent Under-Secretary in the Foreign Office, pointed out that Diem's invitation provided too good an opportunity to be missed. 'I know', Hoyer-Millar wrote to Templer, 'that a visit from you would flatter President

[20] Letter: Hohler (Saigon) to Tory (Kuala Lumpur). 23.6.60. PRO: FO 371/152740, DV1631/2.

[21] Despatch 34: Hohler (Saigon) to Home. 5.8.60. PRO: FO 371/152790, DV1631/4. Memorandum 557: Critchley (Kuala Lumpur) to EA Canberra. 8.4.60. AUSNA: A1838/333, file 3006/10/1, part 1.

[22] Letter: v. Wendland to Auswärtiges Amt. 22.8.60. PA: Ref. 710, Bd. 1656.

[23] Telegram 255: Stewart (Saigon) to FO. 14.5.61. PRO: DO 169/109.

[24] Despatch 34: Hohler (Saigon) to Home. 5.8.60. PRO: FO 371/152790, DV1631/4.

[25] Letter: Tory (Kuala Lumpur) to Templer. 18.10.60. Papers of Field Marshal Sir Gerald Templer. National Army Museum, London (hereafter: Templer Papers).

Diem and what you might say to him would therefore produce important results in checking a deteriorating situation.'[26]

Hoyer-Millar's reasoning persuaded the Field Marshal. He rearranged his programme and arrived in Saigon on 25 October 1960. Accompanied by ambassador Hohler he drove to the Presidential Palace. Aware of Diem's tendency not to stop speaking once he had started, Templer himself took the initiative and began lecturing Diem on counter-insurgency methods right away. This tactic proved successful. Diem listened attentively for forty minutes and even took notes, something unheard of in Saigon's diplomatic circles.[27]

Like Thompson, Templer urged Diem to take the lessons of Malaya into consideration. Above all, he tried to make Diem understand that a guerrilla war was about winning the hearts and minds of the people. Therefore, the RVN should pay particular attention to the training of those junior military and police officers who came into contact with the population. He also pointed out that it was necessary to keep a detailed record of all incidents in order to enable the government to concentrate the security forces in the right places. As Thompson had done in his report, Templer stressed the importance of a reliable intelligence network and a good communication system, and he recommended the establishment of combined civil, military, and police intelligence committees at each administrative centre and at every level. In the course of the conversation Diem seemed especially interested in Malaya's resettlement policy and wanted to know to what extent villagers were helped with food. Templer replied that little help had been given in the form of food, but that the government had provided materials for housing and later on had built hospitals and schools. Diem's interest in British resettlement policy foreshadowed his later decision to introduce a Vietnamese version of a resettlement scheme, better known as the strategic hamlet programme.[28]

Ambassador Hohler was pleased that Templer had found a way to put his views to Diem. In his report to the Foreign Office he expressed his deep satisfaction with the way Templer's visit had gone. This feeling was underscored when Hohler learned that Diem had discussed Templer's recommendations with his brother Nhu immediately after the talk. In the ambassador's view there was a fairly good chance that the South Vietnamese would implement Templer's advice: 'I should expect [Diem] after a period to come out with a good many of the Field Marshal's ideas as his own and then to push them through with great doggedness and tenacity. At least he has now had the benefit of the best advice and experience that we can give him in this difficult field.'[29] This optimistic view was echoed in the Foreign Office. Hoyer-Millar thanked Templer for going to

---

[26] Letter: Hoyer-Millar to Templer. 17.10.60. Templer Papers. The Australians also knew about Templer's reluctance to visit Saigon. Memorandum 1748: Critchley (Kuala Lumpur) to EA Canberra. 2.11.60. AUSNA: A1838/333, file 3006/10/1, part 1.

[27] Despatch 56: Hohler to Home. 5.11.60. PRO: FO 371/152790, DV1631/5. Savingram 76: Saigon to EA Canberra. 27.10.60. AUSNA: A1838/282, file 3014/2/1, part 14.

[28] Despatch 56: Hohler to Home. 5.11.60. PRO: FO 371/152790, DV1631/5.   [29] Ibid.

Saigon and stressed that there was 'a real possibility that the excellent advice which you offered to [Diem] will produce practical results'.[30]

However well Templer's recommendations might have been received in Saigon, Diem still had no intention of welcoming a more permanent British advisory mission. Like General Hull, Templer had also raised this issue and asked whether it might be helpful to Diem if the British were to lend him an experienced officer or a civilian of middle rank for six months. Diem, however, chose not to react to this.[31] This reserved attitude on Diem's part was certainly not what the British had hoped for.

At the end of 1960, it was abundantly clear that Britain was concerned about the situation in the RVN and eager to help. Ambassador Hohler concluded in October 1960 that the time had come for Britain to 'play a more active part',[32] and his colleagues in London and Malaya agreed. They were increasingly convinced that British advice and deeper involvement in the conflict might turn out to be crucial to tip the balance in favour of Diem. Their conviction was based on the strong belief that the experience gained in the Malayan emergency could be of enormous value in the RVN. It also reflected the view that the Americans had failed to establish a viable regime in Saigon that was capable of defending itself effectively against terrorism and armed insurrection. The British found that the American training of the ARVN left much to be desired as it was 'wrongly directed in that too much stress was laid on preparation for outside aggression and not enough on internal security operations'.[33]

The string of British experts on counter-insurgency who travelled, usually from Malaya, to Saigon during the year certainly helped to put British-Malayan views across to the South Vietnamese, but, although interested, the Saigon government showed no willingness to accept the British offer of a more permanent advisory mission. Whitehall, being unable to make headway in Saigon, chose therefore to change its strategy. As all the British lobbying in Saigon had not led to any tangible results, London decided to concentrate on Washington instead. First, the British began to push for a meeting with the Americans in Washington where they wanted to discuss Vietnam. Washington agreed to hold talks in February 1961. Then, in a preliminary discussion with the State Department three days before this meeting, John B. Denson, first secretary at the British embassy, went over all the points that Field Marshal Templer had made to President Diem. Robert Cleveland, the acting Deputy Director of the State Department's Office of Southeast Asian Affairs and Chalmers B. Wood, the officer in charge of Vietnamese affairs, told him that the Americans had put forward a comprehensive counter-insurgency plan, which covered many of the points made by Templer. Denson then broached the idea of a more active British role in Vietnam

30 Letter: Hoyer-Millar to Templer. 17.11.60. Templer Papers.
31 Despatch 56: Hohler to Home. 5.11.60. PRO: FO 371/152790, DV1631/5.
32 Telegram 296: Hohler to FO. 3.10.60. PRO: FO 371/152741, DV1015/69.
33 Letter: Moss (FO) to de la Mare (Washington). 17.3.60. PRO: FO 371/152773, DV11345/1.

to the State Department.[34] The British counsellor was speaking on the lines of a brief prepared by the Foreign Office. The paper stressed that the United Kingdom was 'very willing' to join with the United States in any action in which the Americans thought British assistance helpful.[35]

Lord Hood, the minister at the British embassy, officially offered British assistance to the Americans on 21 February 1961. In the absence of Foy D. Kohler, the Assistant Secretary of State for European Affairs, Hood met Ivan B. White, Kohler's deputy. Lord Hood welcomed the American counter-insurgency plan, especially as it seemed to be in line with Field Marshal Templer's proposals. He went on to ask if London might be given as much information about the plan as possible 'in order that [the British] could give early thought to ways in which [they] might cooperate with the Americans and make full use of [their] experience in Malaya'.[36]

A 'SPECIAL RELATIONSHIP' IN ASIA?

Making a valuable contribution to the fight for the survival of the pro-western regime in Saigon was certainly not the only motivation for pursuing so persistently the idea of establishing an advisory mission in Vietnam. It was very much on the minds of the decision-makers in London that British support for America's stand in Vietnam might turn out to be beneficial for Anglo-American relations.

Indeed, the state of the 'special relationship' deeply worried Harold Macmillan, the British Prime Minister. When John F. Kennedy was elected President in November 1960, the Prime Minister's mind was occupied with finding the best way of establishing as close a relationship with Kennedy as he had had with the outgoing President Eisenhower.[37] Immediately after the election in the United States, Macmillan himself drafted a message to the President-elect. He wanted to establish contact early on and prove that, despite his age, he was a man of fresh and new ideas.[38] This first draft letter was never sent, but it triggered a lengthy process of drafting and re-drafting a possible message to Kennedy, involving all relevant government departments. The eventual product was a long, detailed statement on world affairs and on the state of Anglo-American relations.[39] Macmillan did not 'greatly care' for this draft, however. Moreover, the Foreign

---

[34] Letter: Denson (Washington) to Petersen (FO). 20.2.61. PRO: FO 371/160108, DV1015/10.

[35] FO brief on South Vietnam for discussions between Caccia and Rusk in Washington. 14.2.61. PRO: FO 371/159673, ZP14/40.

[36] Savingram 118: Caccia (Washington) to FO. 22.2.61. PRO: FO 371/159674, ZP14/55. Memorandum of Conversation between Lord Hood and White. 21.2.61. FRUS: 1961–1963, i, Vietnam 1961, 35–6.

[37] Macmillan diaries: 11.11.60, dep. d. 40, f. 98.

[38] Minute: Macmillan to Home with draft message to Kennedy attached. 9.11.60. PRO: FO 371/152107, ZP8/31/G.

[39] Revised draft memorandum on letter to Kennedy: Cabinet Office to Macmillan. 25.11.60. Ibid. ZP8/42/G.

States and that we can be used to exert the same sort of pressure on the United States Government as we have on Laos'.[55]

The British ambassador in Washington stressed in the summer of 1961 that if the British were to take the same line on Vietnam as they had done on Laos, they would not 'escape accusations of softness, particularly from those Americans who sublimate their resentment at the lack of belligerence on the part of the President beneath their resentment against ourselves as allies'. Instead, by showing its resolve in Vietnam Britain would regain American trust. The United States would then be inclined to take the British into their confidence and perhaps be more willing to listen to London's views on Southeast Asia.[56] This strategy was based on the belief that the Americans would embrace the idea of a more active British role in South Vietnam. It soon became clear, however, that this was not the case.

OPPOSITION FROM THE US MILITARY

The Foreign Office regarded the Anglo-American talks on Vietnam as 'most useful'.[57] However, cooperation between the two countries remained almost non-existent. Washington continued to be slow in producing the information the British were looking for. The counter-insurgency plan was an example. The American record of the meeting between Lord Hood and White contained Washington's promise to provide a copy of the plan. However, the British had to wait seven weeks before they received a copy. The record also gave an early indication of US reservations about the British offer as it only noted the offer without expressing any American views on it.[58]

Given in later years the American 'more flags campaign' and Lyndon B. Johnson's repeated requests for a token British force in Vietnam, it is surprising that the Kennedy administration did not embrace the British offer right away. From a diplomatic point of view, London's willingness to share America's cold war burden in Vietnam was certainly welcomed. Therefore, the State Department was inclined to support the British offer, and it immediately informed the American embassy in Saigon about Lord Hood's overture.[59] This was followed up a week later. Stressing that the defence of the RVN was among the highest of American foreign policy aims, the State Department argued that the training of the Vietnamese in counter-insurgency techniques had to be hastened. In this context, the State Department welcomed possible British assistance. It suggested that the MAAG in Vietnam should find a way to incorporate British and Malayan

[55] Blue FO minute by Warner. 16.10.61. PRO: FO 371/160174, DV1961/2.
[56] Despatch 132: Caccia (Washington) to Home. 10.7.61. PRO: FO 371/159712, DV103145/13.
[57] Letter: Warner (FO) to Ledward (Washington). 7.3.61. PRO: FO 371/160108, DV1015/11.
[58] Telegram 553: Caccia (Washington) to FO. 6.3.61. Ibid. DV1015/14/G. Deptel 1270: Rusk to Saigon. 12.4.61. USNA: RG 59, Central Files, 751k.5-msp/4-1361.
[59] Deptel 1106: Rusk to Saigon. 24.2.61. Ibid. 751k.00/2-2461.

advisers into a 'well defined part' of the anti-guerrilla training of the ARVN and the civil guard.[60] However, the American military establishment in Saigon as well as the Commander-in-Chief Pacific were convinced that they could handle the situation without any third country aid. They had no intention of letting the British in.[61]

Apparently without the knowledge of the State Department, opposition against British involvement in South Vietnam had been voiced by the MAAG as early as March 1960. General Williams, head of the MAAG, expressed his dismay at the British embassy's interfering to Edward Lansdale, a good friend of Diem's who was at that point Deputy Assistant for Special Operations in the Pentagon. 'Believe it or not', he wrote, 'even the British Ambassador was giving [the government of South Vietnam] advice on reorganization and tactics.'[62] Lansdale agreed with Williams. He was adamantly against any foreign expert giving advice on what to do with American financial aid in Vietnam. Although Lansdale thought that visits of counter-guerrilla experts from Malaya, Burma, or the Philippines might be useful, such visits were 'far different from asking them to come in to do a U.S. military task'.[63]

Lansdale's reaction to Thompson's visit in April 1960 was equally hostile. With glee he noticed that the Vietnamese seemed to be hesitant in adopting Thompson's recommendations. Probably referring to Colonel Lee's talk with Diem, he pointed out that the South Vietnamese knew that the situation in Vietnam was quite different from Malaya. Moreover, he detected Vietnamese suspicion about Thompson's promise that his measures would show results within two years. After all, it had taken the British twelve years to win in Malaya.[64]

Personal ambition certainly played a part in Lansdale's opposition. He believed that he was a brilliant counter-insurgency expert and would have liked to advise Diem himself. The American embassy, however, strongly opposed a visit from Lansdale, and US ambassador Durbrow even doubted his expertise in anti-guerrilla warfare.[65] However, Lansdale's views and his communication with General Williams underscored that the MAAG's negative reaction to the British offer in March 1961 was based on a long-standing and deep-rooted suspicion of British involvement in an essentially American effort.

The State Department was not sympathetic to the less than cooperative attitude of the American representatives in Saigon. It urged the embassy and the military to reconsider their positions, pointing out that US manoeuvrability would not be infringed as British-Malayan or other 'Free Asian' advisers would

[60] Deptel 1115: Rusk to Saigon. 1.3.61. FRUS: Vietnam 1961–1963, i, Vietnam 1961, 40–2.
[61] Deptel 1218: Bowles to Saigon. 16.3.61. USNA: RG 59, Central Files, 751k.5-msp/3-21-61.
[62] Signal 62: Williams (MAAG) to Lansdale (Pentagon). 25.3.60. FRUS: 1958–1960, i, Vietnam, 348–9.
[63] Memorandum: Lansdale to Williams. 14.4.60. Ibid. 386–7.
[64] Memorandum: Lansdale to Bonesteel (Secretary to General Staff of the Army). 25.4.60. Ibid. 410–1.
[65] Embtel 3013: Durbrow (Saigon) to State Department. 22.4.60. Ibid. 409.

be placed *under* US command. Moreover, the State Department betrayed ignorance about the Foreign Office's policy by stating that the British, in spite of their offer, might not accept because of their role as co-chairman of the Geneva conference.[66]

While the American administration debated whether or not to accept British aid in the first place, the British waited confidently for the US approval of their overtures. 'We now look forward to joint action when the Americans think the time is right', noted Frederick Warner, the head of the Southeast Asia Department in the Foreign Office, in early March 1961.[67] At this stage, the British seemed to have been completely unaware of the MAAG's opposition to their plans. It certainly did not help that the British in Saigon continued to point to the failures of the MAAG's strategy. Consequently, an Anglo-American meeting at the British embassy in Saigon on April fool's day 1961 turned out to be an unhappy occasion. US ambassador Durbrow had requested this meeting because Lord Home had shown Secretary of State Rusk a British map of the insurgency situation in the RVN at the SEATO council meeting in Bangkok in late March. Home had produced this map to demonstrate that the situation was rather more serious than the Americans in Saigon admitted. Now, Rusk wanted his ambassador in Saigon to report on the British views.

Durbrow was accompanied by a CIA representative and General Ruggles, the deputy head of the MAAG. In the US ambassador's view, the situation had not changed dramatically since 1959 and he, therefore, stated that he was 'at a loss to know why the [Foreign Office] had become so agitated about it'. General Ruggles pointed out that certain areas marked as occupied on the British map were of no value to anybody. Moreover, the ARVN had proved that they were capable of smashing any large concentration of NLF forces. The areas the Americans described as of no value were, in the view of the British, clearly the bases from which the insurgents operated, but the British officials chose not to comment on this at the meeting. With regard to the second point, however, the British stressed that it was accepted policy of guerrilla warfare not to concentrate in the face of regular troops. But even if the British estimate was too pessimistic, it was obvious that the situation was not improving. And if it continued, the British pointed out, it was bound to have a fatal effect in the long run. Commenting on the meeting, ambassador Hohler cabled to the Foreign Office that the Americans were not too optimistic that Diem would implement the right measures but they could not think of any fresh means of exercising pressure on him.[68]

The British embassy in Saigon continued to send alarming reports about the situation in Vietnam to the Foreign Office.[69] Although the Laos crisis was at its height at this time, Dermot McDermot, Assistant Under-Secretary of State at the Foreign Office, concluded that 'S[outh] Vietnam is a more dangerous problem

[66] Deptel 1218: Bowles to Saigon. 16.3.61. USNA: RG 59, Central Files, 751k.5-msp/3-21-61.
[67] Letter: Warner (FO) to Ledward (Washington). 7.3.61. PRO: FO 371/160108, DV1015/11.
[68] Telegram 161: Hohler (Saigon) to FO. 1.4.61. PRO: FO 371/160109, DV1015/24/G.
[69] Blue FO minute by Petersen. 7.4.61. Ibid. DV1015/31.

than Laos'.[70] Britain's appreciation of the situation was well founded. Hanoi informed the East German embassy in March 1961 that the NLF was in a better position than the Vietminh had been in 1954. The NLF controlled most of the countryside and Diem's power was limited to the cities. Therefore, the DRV described the situation in South Vietnam as very promising.[71]

The Foreign Office assumed that neither the US embassy nor the MAAG would like to admit, even to themselves, that they had not been particularly successful.[72] Frederick Warner quite bluntly minuted that if Diem was to implement the US counter-insurgency plan, the extent of the problem would be revealed 'even to the stupidest M.A.A.G. officer'.[73] The need for British advice in Vietnam therefore seemed, at least to the British themselves, to become more and more urgent. Colonel H. C. B. Cook, the British military attaché in Saigon, believed that the best hope for Vietnam was to make 'full use' of British expertise. In his view the Americans just could not cope with the insurgency: 'I have not yet met an American officer here who really seemed to understand what the real problem is. The trouble is they have absolutely no experience of dealing with widespread insurgency. They tend to see the problem as all out war or all out peace, whereas it is something in between.'[74]

This critical attitude did not make the British more popular with the MAAG. Sensing possible American reluctance to accept the British offer, Frederick Warner approached the US embassy in London. In the coming weeks Warner was one of the main Foreign Office officials who pushed the idea of a British advisory mission vis-à-vis the Americans.[75] In mid-April he reassured the Americans of Malaya's desire for cooperation with regard to the envisaged use of jungle warfare schools in Malaya for the training of Vietnamese officers.[76] The British embassy in Washington also reminded the State Department of Britain's own offer to help and asked whether it was likely that any of the suggestions for the mission of British experts would be taken up. The State Department replied that the issue was 'under active consideration'.[77] Although the Foreign Office tried to keep the issue of British assistance on the agenda, no movement could be detected on the American side.

---

[70] Minute by McDermot (FO). 7.4.61. Ibid.

[71] Record of conversation between Phan Hien (press secretary of DRV Ministry of External Affairs) and Kitzing (Hanoi). 14.3.61. MfAA: A8570.

[72] Minute by Evans. 14.4.61. PRO: FO 371/160109, DV1015/24/G.

[73] Minute by Warner. 15.4.61. Ibid.

[74] Letter: Colonel Cook (Saigon) to Colonel Innes (WO). 22.4.61. PRO: FO 371/160156, DV1201/5/G.

[75] Letter: Sir Edward Peck to author. 25.2.2002.

[76] Embtel 1426: Barbour (London) to State Department. 12.4.61. USNA: RG 59, Central Files, 751k.5/4-1261.

[77] Telegram 1101: Caccia (Washington) to FO. 28.4.61. PRO: DO 169/109.

THE TUNKU'S INITIATIVE

New life was pumped into the British offer in late April. Again, Malaya and the Tunku played a crucial role. On 19 April 1961, the Malayan Prime Minister suggested to his 'dear friend' Duncan Sandys, the British Secretary of State for the Commonwealth and the Colonies, that Robert Thompson should be sent to Vietnam to help in the counter-insurgency effort. He declared his willingness to put this idea to Diem on his planned state visit to South Vietnam in June.[78]

After his distinguished career in the Malayan civil service Robert Thompson was looking for a new job, and he sent a number of applications to several organizations.[79] It is quite likely that it was in his interest to boost the attractions of a British advisory mission to Vietnam, possibly through the channel of the Tunku and his senior advisers.[80] However, the official British version was that the Tunku made his suggestion to send Thompson to Vietnam 'spontaneously'.[81] This is in line with Robert Thompson's printed recollection of events. In his memoirs *Make for the Hills*, Thompson noted that on the day he was to leave Malaya to return to Britain for good, he went to the Tunku to say good-bye. The Malayan Prime Minister was worried about Thompson's future and he remarked 'out of the blue' that it was silly for Thompson to go home and become secretary to some association or other. Instead, he said to Thompson: 'You must go to Vietnam and help hold my front line' and promised to write to Macmillan and Diem about it.[82] The Tunku lived up to his promise, although he wrote to Sandys and not to Macmillan, and delayed his approach to Diem until May.

Even if the Tunku's proposal was as unexpected as the British official record and Thompson himself claimed, it reflected the general mood of the British-Malayan elite at the time. Since the emergency had been declared to be over in 1960, all the well-trained and experienced officers of the Malayan Civil Service, like Thompson, had become superfluous. It was certainly in their interest to find a place in the world where their expertise could be applied. The RVN seemed ideal. The most experienced anti-guerrilla experts would be able to go on a permanent mission to Saigon. The Malayan jungle warfare schools were conveniently located to take in officers from their South Vietnamese neighbours for crash courses, thus securing the jobs of the lower ranked counter-insurgency specialists. Denis Allen, the Deputy High Commissioner for Singapore, expressed precisely this view. 'Like yourself,' he wrote to Geofroy Tory in Kuala Lumpur after he had heard about the Tunku's suggestion, 'we here have . . . long been keen

---

[78] Letter: Tunku Abdul Rahman to Sandys. 19.4.61. Ibid.

[79] Isabel Oliphant, Robert Thompson's daughter, who is in possession of his papers, in interview with the author. 13.2.2002.

[80] Letter: Reginald Burrows to author. 21.2.2002.

[81] Minute: Sandys to Selwyn Lloyd. 25.7.61. PRO: PREM 11/3736. Telegram 2996: FO to Washington. 1.5.61. PRO: DO 169/109.

[82] Thompson, *Make for the Hills*, 121.

that use should be made of experienced Malayan Civil Service Officers in this part of the World.'[83]

The Tunku's initiative provided a convenient opening for the Foreign Office to pursue the idea of a British mission in Saigon more forcefully. During the first three weeks of May the British approached the Americans at least five times. Hiding behind the Tunku's initiative, they stressed that a reply to the Tunku's letter to Sandys had to be made soon. Therefore, an American decision was urgently required.[84]

THE DEBATE IN WASHINGTON

London's future role in Vietnam was only of minor importance to the American administration's overall deliberations on how to save the Saigon government. In the spring of 1961, major decisions had to be taken. The main issues were a further increase to the number of American advisers in the MAAG, and the financing of an additional 20,000 ARVN troops. Although the issue of third country aid to Vietnam was on the agenda, it was only one of many points. In principle, third country aid was not controversial. With the sanction of the Department of Defense, it was welcomed in the first report of the newly formed Presidential Task Force Vietnam. This report became the basis for Kennedy's Vietnam decisions of May 1961.[85]

However, a controversy arose between the State Department and the American military about possible British involvement in training the South Vietnamese army. Faced with the repeated British representations of early May, the State Department revealed that it was in favour of a British mission, and that Kennedy had been advised accordingly. Nevertheless, the British learned that 'certain sections' in the Pentagon still wanted the Americans to carry out all counter-insurgency training on their own. Therefore, a Presidential decision on third country aid was needed, and only then could detailed discussions between the American and British ambassadors in Saigon about Britain's future role in Vietnam begin. The National Security Council was to discuss third country aid in early May, and the British were informed of the State Department's hope that a favourable decision would be reached.[86]

While the British impatiently awaited Kennedy's decision, the wrangling behind the scenes continued in Washington. The Presidential Task Force Vietnam convened for its second meeting on 4 May 1961. When the members of the task force turned to Britain's possible role in counter-insurgency training, the American

[83] Letter: Allen (Singapore) to Tory (Kuala Lumpur). 5.5.61. PRO: DO 169/109.

[84] Telegram 1996: FO to Washington. 1.5.61. Telegram 2322: FO to Washington. 10.5.61. Both in ibid.

[85] Memorandum: Gilpatric (Pentagon) to Kennedy. 3.5.61. Attachment: paper of the Vietnam Task force on 'Points to save Vietnam' of 1.5.61. FRUS: 1961–1963, i, Vietnam 1961, 92–115.

[86] Telegram 1127: Caccia (Washington) to FO. 2.5.61. PRO: DO 169/109.

military voiced its doubts. Haydn Williams of the Department of Defense's Office of International Security Affairs pointed out that neither the MAAG in Saigon nor Admiral Felt, the Commander-in-Chief Pacific, wanted to divide the responsibility for training the South Vietnamese. General Bonesteel, representing the Joint Chiefs of Staff, expressed his concern about the possible role of the British, too. In his view Britain might use a mission in Saigon to exercise control over American freedom of action. Moreover, the British might dilute the American intention to show military strength. The State Department representatives doubted this and stressed that the British mission would not be big enough to warrant a voice in policy formation. Although Robert Cleveland of the State Department expressed his belief that the British were anxious to come in, Walt W. Rostow, Kennedy's Deputy Special Assistant for National Security, emphasized the problem of getting the British committed in Vietnam and not how to prevent their involvement. No agreement was reached at the meeting.[87]

The task force's discussion revealed that the Americans did not realize how eager London was to make a commitment to South Vietnam's survival. The military's opposition to a more prominent British role continued, but in Walt W. Rostow the State Department had found a powerful ally in the White House. Moreover, the Pentagon itself did not speak with one voice. Roswell Gilpatric, the Deputy Secretary of Defense, did not share his generals' misgivings. He welcomed British involvement in Vietnam for political reasons and made this view known in a memorandum to President Kennedy.[88] Therefore, it is not surprising that Kennedy endorsed National Security Action Memorandum 52 in the meeting of the National Security Council on 11 May 1961. NSAM 52 enabled the administration to ask third countries for help in counter-insurgency training.[89]

The British had not been informed of this decision when *The Times* reported on 12 May 1961 that Britain was to be invited to assist in training and helping the RVN to defend itself against communist guerrillas.[90] Surprised by this report, the British embassy in Washington approached the State Department again. However, it turned out that Kennedy's decision to welcome third country aid had not automatically cleared the way for a British advisory mission in Saigon. The Americans stressed that no concrete plans concerning British involvement had yet been made.[91]

This was not the kind of answer the British had hoped for, and therefore Richard Ledward, the counsellor at the British embassy in Washington, presented the British case again to the Americans on 15 May. He made clear that

---

[87] Draft memorandum of conversation of the second meeting of the Presidential Task Force on Vietnam at the Pentagon. 4.5.61. FRUS: 1961–1963, i, Vietnam 1961, 115–23.

[88] Memorandum: Gilpatric to Kennedy. 3.5.61. Ibid. 92–115.

[89] NSAM 52. 11.5.61. Ibid. 132–4.

[90] 'Britain to join the anti-guerrilla measure'. *The Times*. 12.5.61, p. 16. Telegram 251: FO to Washington. 12.5.61. PRO: DO 169/109. Airgram G–1465: Bruce (London) to Department of State. 16.5.61. USNA: RG 59: Central Files 751k.5/5-1661.

[91] Telegram 1239: Caccia (Washington) to FO. 13.5.61. PRO: DO 169/109.

London had not been too happy about the press leak and really needed a definite answer soon in order to draft a letter to the Tunku and to secure Robert Thompson's services in the first place.[92] Still, this approach was not sufficient. Only after the British embassy had informed the Americans that the Tunku was about to visit Saigon and propose the Thompson mission directly to Diem, did Washington finally authorize the US embassy in Saigon to start discussions with the British ambassador on the possible role of the Thompson mission. What the British did not tell the Americans was that they themselves had prompted the Tunku to make this direct proposition to Diem.[93] In the event, the Tunku did not even visit Saigon. However, he wrote to Diem asking if he wanted to 're-engage' Thompson for service in Vietnam.[94] When the State Department learned about this letter, it noted that the Tunku had made this proposition as a Malayan offer.[95]

ANGLO-AMERICAN NEGOTIATIONS IN SAIGON

British lobbying had finally borne fruit. At the end of May, three months after the official British offer had been made, the American and British embassies in Saigon started discussing the possible role of the Thompson mission. As British ambassador Henry Hohler was on home leave his deputy Charles Stewart met US ambassador Nolting.[96] It is hardly conceivable that these discussions would have ever been started without the constant British reminders of their offer. London's pressure had been essential to clear the lines in Washington. The State Department had welcomed the British offer and President Kennedy had supported third country aid in principle,[97] but the administration had at no point made a clear-cut decision in favour of a British mission. Surprisingly, the important question of what a British mission was supposed to do in Saigon, with all the potential political consequences, was not settled in Washington. A carefully worded State Department telegram to Saigon of 22 May merely shifted the problem from Washington to Saigon.[98] Knowing very well that the toughest opposition to the British mission was centred around the MAAG, it was convenient for the policy makers in Washington to leave it to the Americans in Saigon to tackle this difficult and divisive issue.

---

[92] Memorandum of conversation: 'The introduction of additional Military Personnel into South Vietnam'. 15.5.61. USNA: RG 59: Central Files 751g.00/5-16-61.

[93] Telegram 859: CRO to Kuala Lumpur. 19.5.61. PRO: DO 169/109.

[94] Telegram 384: Kuala Lumpur to CRO. 26.5.61. Ibid.

[95] Deptel 1475: Rusk to Saigon. 30.5.61. USNA: RG 59: Central Files 751k.5-msp/5-2661.

[96] Telegram 286: Stewart (Saigon) to FO. 30.5.61. PRO: DO 169/109. Letter: Stewart (Saigon) to Peterson (FO). 29.5.61. PRO: FO 371/160111, DV1015/77.

[97] Deptel 1423: Bowles to Saigon transmitting the Presidential Programme for Vietnam. 20.5.61. FRUS: 1961–1963, i, Vietnam 1961, 141.

[98] Deptel 1429: Rusk to Saigon. 22.5.61. USNA: RG 59, Central Files, 751k.5-msp/5-1361.

Indeed, the wrangling continued into June. The men on the spot, Stewart and Nolting, met on 29 May, and the US ambassador pointed out that the MAAG was very suspicious of British intentions.[99] Shortly after this first Anglo-American meeting, General Lionel McGarr, Chief of the MAAG in South Vietnam, spelled out his opposition to a British role in military matters in a message to General Lyman Lemnitzer, the Chairman of the JCS. McGarr complained about the State Department's increasing pressure to bring in British-Malayan training officers. He was convinced that it would cause confusion if different counter-insurgency concepts and methods were to be introduced. For McGarr the involvement of third countries constituted a blow to American prestige, and he insisted that the British furnish concrete anti-guerrilla material for American evaluation in order to prove the qualifications of the 'Thompson group'. However, McGarr had no objection to British involvement outside the field of the MAAG, stressing that this should be sufficient to 'show the flag'.[100]

It was up to the American task force in Saigon to find suitable fields for British assistance, and the Americans had no difficulty determining plenty of areas outside the MAAG's activities: Thompson was to devote his attention to administrative support, advice on police and security matters as well as propaganda and intelligence. All these fields were set out in a letter by ambassador Nolting, and the British could readily agree to these.[101] However, the longest paragraph in the letter was about what the British should not do. Under the heading 'military', the British were warned off MAAG territory. The MAAG had, the British were told, 'intimate relations' with the ARVN and had developed a 'particular doctrine'. This doctrine was based on an 'extensive survey of the problems of anti-guerrilla warfare' that had even taken Thompson's report of May 1960 into consideration. As the South Vietnamese had already given their assent to this doctrine, Nolting made very clear that British assistance in the military field was not wanted: 'It would appear to me to be somewhat disruptive at this date to insert possibly different techniques and ideas for counterinsurgency on the military side. Thus I suggest that the military not be a field of particular British effort at this time, although such facilities as the jungle warfare school in Malaya may well be utilized.'[102]

Robert Thompson had no intention of agreeing to this limitation. The Foreign Office invited him to participate in an interdepartmental meeting that considered Nolting's letter. Thompson was adamant that he should be empowered to give advice in all fields because military, political, and social action had to be coordinated. If he was appointed—and there was no other candidate[103]—Thompson

[99] Telegram 287: Stewart (Saigon) to FO. 30.5.61. PRO: DO 169/109.

[100] Telegram SGN 376: McGarr (Saigon) to Lemnitzer (JCS). 7.6.61. FRUS: 1961–1963, i, Vietnam 1961, 166–7.

[101] Embtel 1864: Nolting to Department of State. 10.6.61. USNA: RG 59, Central Files, 751k.5-msp/6-1061. Embtel 1876: Nolting to Department of State. 14.6.61. FRUS: 1961–1963, i, Vietnam 1961, 175–6. Telegrams 327, 328, and 329: Stewart (Saigon) to FO. 12.6.61. All in PRO: DO 169/109.

[102] Letter: Nolting to Stewart. 12.6.61. Enclosure to despatch 579: Mendenhall (Saigon) to Department of State. 16.6.61. USNA: RG 59, Central Files, 641.51k/6-1661.

[103] Sir Edward Peck in interview with the author. 12.02.2002.

thought it was essential to get inside the 'American machine'. He even professed that he would be prepared 'to become an American for this purpose if necessary'.[104]

Ambassador Henry Hohler, who also attended the meeting, supported Thompson's position. It was decided to inform ambassador Nolting that Thompson not only expected to range over the whole field of counter-insurgency but also wanted to have some say in policy formulation. However, the participants of the meeting were under no illusion that the Americans were prepared to accept this position. Therefore, the idea was introduced that Thompson should go to Washington to work out 'some unwritten understanding with the Americans'. All were agreed that the first and foremost aim was to establish a mission in Vietnam as soon as possible.[105] With this priority in mind, the Foreign Office proceeded cautiously and refrained from bluntly conveying Thompson's views to the Americans. Although it was decided in a subsequent meeting at the Foreign Office to 'have another go at the US Embassy', Thompson's position was watered down by stressing that the Americans should at least keep Thompson informed of US military plans. Moreover, it was thought best not to obtain a rigid definition of Thompson's functions, since this might only limit his activities.[106]

Accordingly, the British letter in reply to Nolting's suggestions seemed to show obedience to American wishes. London stressed its delight that Anglo-American ideas coincided over so wide a field. The letter even conceded that the Thompson mission would not regard military policy as part of its function. However, it emphasized that coordination of the military and civilian effort was essential.[107] Stressing this was clearly an attempt at obtaining at least some influence on the formulation of military policy. The British then tried to sneak into the MAAG's domain through the back door. When Charles Stewart again explained London's position on 5 July 1961, this time to Francis Cunningham, the counsellor-general at the US embassy in Saigon, he also stressed that Thompson really would have to know something about military activity in advance. He therefore suggested to have a 'joint country team'. Thompson would be on this team as well as MAAG and United States Operations Mission (USOM) representatives. Stewart reported back to the Foreign Office that Cunningham seemed to accept this idea.[108] Even if Stewart's impression was correct, the American military flatly rejected any notion of giving the British the status of an allied country in Vietnam. The Commander-in-Chief Pacific cabled Rusk that anything that would amount to a joint British role in administering the military assistance programme was completely unacceptable. The American intention should be to continue the 'clearly

---

[104] Record of a meeting held at the Foreign Office on UK assistance to Vietnam. 13.6.61. PRO: DO 169/109.
[105] Ibid.
[106] Record of a meeting held at the Foreign Office on UK assistance to Vietnam. 15.6.61. PRO: DO 169/109.
[107] Telegram 446: FO to Saigon. 21.6.61. Ibid.
[108] Telegram 394: Stewart (Saigon) to FO. 5.7.61. Ibid.

unilateral' relations with South Vietnam in the security field. The US military commitment should 'in no way be exposed to British influence'.[109]

The main British aim was to establish a mission in Saigon, and therefore London preferred not to press the issue. After his return to the RVN in August 1961 ambassador Hohler agreed to Nolting's suggestion that no attempt should be made to delimit Thompson's responsibilities more precisely as set out in his letter or to lay down fixed channels of communication. The ambassadors agreed to leave it to the good senses of the men on the spot to find the best way of working together informally. In Hohler's view the British mission would be, broadly speaking, responsible for civilian and intelligence matters, and the MAAG for the operational side.[110] This informal understanding was acceptable to the Foreign Office. Accordingly, the terms of reference for the Thompson mission were kept fairly general. It did not seem advantageous to lay down 'rigid rules' in London.[111]

As the Americans were not to be moved from their previous position, a vague and flexible understanding with regard to relations between the MAAG and the Thompson mission appeared to be the best deal the British could get at this point in time. To be sure, 'flexibility' almost guaranteed an early clash between the MAAG and Thompson, especially as the latter had at no point indicated his willingness to leave the military field exclusively to the Americans. Similarly, the scepticism of the MAAG had not been overcome. Shortly before Thompson's arrival in Saigon, General McGarr again made his reservations clear. In his first annual report as Chief of the MAAG on 1 September 1961 he showed his willingness to cooperate with the British mission in principle. However, he pointed to the limits of Thompson's mandate by stressing that the British ambassador had agreed with the MAAG that the Thompson mission 'will not participate in the military field in either operational or advisory matters'.[112]

THE ADVISORY MISSION IS BORN

London had achieved its first and foremost aim, the establishment of an advisory mission in Saigon—even if the agreement that had been reached with the Americans was rather vague. The Foreign Office's new strategy of 1961 had thus proved to be right. Instead of trying to come to an understanding with the South Vietnamese, an Anglo-American agreement on the issue had been sought. It is indeed striking that the Saigon government was not at all involved in defining the

---

[109] Navy message 120127Z: Commander-in-Chief Pacific to Rusk. 13.7.61. USNA: RG 59, Central Files, 751j.5/7-1261.
[110] Telegram 474: Hohler (Saigon) to FO. 8.8.61. PRO: DO 169/109.
[111] Letter: Secondé (FO) to Stewart (Saigon). 15.8.61. Ibid.
[112] First Twelve Month Report of Chief of MAAG, Vietnam: McGarr to Commander-in-Chief, Pacific. 1.9.61. JFKL: NSF, Vietnam Country Series, box 194. The report is also in Hoover Institution on War, Revolution and Peace, Palo Alto. General Edward G. Lansdale Papers (hereafter HI: Lansdale Papers): folder 1: Vietnam, General 1961–63, box 49.

scope of the British mission. What is more, Vietnamese views were neither sought nor considered important. This is all the more remarkable as the British mission was designed to advise the South Vietnamese government. In the Foreign Office's view the RVN would accept the British mission once American agreement had been secured. And there was some reason to believe that this was indeed the case. In particular, Vice-President Johnson's visit to Saigon in May left the British with the impression that Diem was inclined to accept British assistance. Johnson and Diem discussed the possibility of 'foreign aid' and announced that the 'assistance of other free governments to the Government of the Republic of Vietnam in its battle against Communist guerrilla forces would be welcome'.[113] At a subsequent SEATO meeting the Americans made it clear that the RVN would indeed require 'technical assistance' and encouraged SEATO members to provide that kind of aid.[114] It was during the Laos conference at Geneva in late May 1961, that Vu Van Mau, the South Vietnamese Foreign Secretary, received word that the Americans and British were discussing the Thompson mission. He approached Lord Home who had the impression that Mau had taken up the idea 'with alacrity'.[115]

Diem himself expressed different feelings when he talked to the American military. He assured General McGarr in June that the help of third countries was not wanted in the counter-insurgency field.[116] The South Vietnamese President either chose to say whatever would please the American general, or he was still 'blowing hot and cold' on the idea of a British mission, just as he had done in late 1960. This attitude, again, proved that the Foreign Office was right to seek an agreement with the Americans to achieve its aims. Indeed, after the Anglo-American understanding was reached in late July, the State Department instructed its Saigon embassy to advise Diem's government to accept the British mission.[117] It came therefore as no surprise that Diem approved the official British offer on 8 August 1961, only three days after it had been made.[118]

Within the British government there was a broad consensus as to the usefulness of this undertaking. The Foreign Office, backed by the CRO, easily got the Treasury's approval for the necessary funds, even at a time when major efforts were being made to reduce expenditure overseas.[119] Prime Minister Macmillan's involvement in the sending of the mission was minimal. He knew about the envisaged

[113] Extract from US/South-Vietnamese communiqué in telegram 251: Stewart (Saigon) to FO. PRO: DO 169/109.
[114] Embtel 2111: Young (Bangkok) to State Department. 22.5.61. FRUS: 1961–1963, i, Vietnam 1961, 147–9.
[115] Telegram 3617: FO to Washington. 26.5.61. PRO: DO 169/109. The New Zealanders were informed about this exchange several weeks later. Telegram 1339: London to EA Wellington. 28.6.61. NZNA: PM 478/4/1, part 13.
[116] Telegram SGN376: McGarr (MAAG) to Lemnitzer (JCS). 7.6.61. FRUS: 1961–1963, i, Vietnam 1961, 166–8.
[117] Deptel 114: Rusk to Saigon. 26.7.61. USNA: RG 59, Central Files, 751k.5-msp/7-861.
[118] Telegram 472: Hohler to FO. 5.8.61. Telegram 473: Hohler (Saigon) to FO. 8.8.61. Both in PRO: DO 169/109.
[119] Minute: Lloyd to Home. 27.7.61. PRO: PREM 11/3736.

British advisory role, endorsed the appointment of Robert Thompson, and asked to be kept informed about the decisions made by the Treasury and the Foreign Office.[120] Foreign Secretary Home put a very persuasive case to the Treasury. He reasoned that the situation in the RVN had seriously deteriorated. The Americans would not tolerate the victory of the communist insurgents, and because of its commitment to SEATO Britain would be involved if the conflict escalated. Therefore, the British should do something to remedy the situation, especially as the Americans seemed to be incapable of coping with the insurgency on their own. He concluded that the sending of a British advisory mission to Vietnam would cure many a problem and considerably improve London's standing in Southeast Asia: 'Such a scheme would hearten the Vietnamese and please the Americans, fulfil our SEATO obligations and to that extent encourage the Thais and Filipinos, as well as commending itself to the Malayans, Australians and New Zealanders. Above all it might just tip the balance against a very expensive war in which we should all get involved.'[121]

Duncan Sandys also argued that the British advisory effort in Vietnam had to be put into the context of London's interests in Southeast Asia. He described the mission as a 'timely reminder' that Britain was ready to play a helpful role in the region. This was all the more useful and necessary as Australia, New Zealand, and Pakistan had criticized London for not being sufficiently interested in the problems of Southeast Asia.[122]

The British kept the Australians and New Zealanders informed about their general plans for an advisory mission. Canberra appeared slightly better informed; it knew about the Tunku's letter to Diem and encouraged the Malayan Prime Minister to visit Vietnam when they heard about his plans to cancel the trip.[123] The New Zealanders, on the other hand, described it as 'unforeseen' when Lord Selkirk informed them and the Australians in late June 1961 that Britain was to send an advisory mission to Vietnam. Selkirk mentioned London's plans at the meeting of the British Defence Co-ordinating Committee in the Far East, and both the Australian and New Zealand representatives on that committee remained silent. The New Zealanders in London were briefed in more detail a couple of days after this meeting, but although both Commonwealth countries welcomed the mission in general, they privately voiced doubts about the envisaged training programme in the Malayan federation about which the British in Singapore kept them well-informed.[124] External Affairs in Wellington thought

120 Letter: Bligh (Admiralty House) to Hubback (Treasury). 24.7.61. Ibid. Telegram 3329: Ormsby-Gore (Washington) to FO. 28.10.63. PRO: FO 371/170102, DV1017/46.

121 Minute: Home to Lloyd. 21.7.61. PRO: PREM 11/3736.

122 Minute: Sandys to Lloyd. 25.7.61. PRO: DO 169/109.

123 Telegram 2016: London to EA Canberra. 28.4.61. AUSNA: 1209/134, file 1961/127, part 1. Memorandum 714: Critchley (Kuala Lumpur) to EA Canberra. 17.6.61. Memorandum 547: Blakeney (EA Canberra) to Kuala Lumpur. 28.6.61. Both in AUSNA: A1838/333, file 3006/10/1, part 1. The British embassy in Saigon also informed the Australians in detail about the Anglo-American talks on the British advisory mission. Memorandum 798: Forsyth (Saigon) to EA Canberra. 26.7.61. AUSNA: 1838/334, file 3014/11/51, part 1.

124 Letter: Singapore to EA Wellington. 24.6.61. Letter: McIntosh (EA Wellington) to London. 14.6.61. Letter: Shepherd (Canberra) to EA Wellington. 22.6.61. Telegram 1339: London to

that training the South Vietnamese just in Malaya was more efficacious than sending trainers to the RVN. The Australians, on the other hand, doubted that it was useful to train ARVN officers in Malaya. Instead, training should be provided 'on the spot'. Neither of them made these views known to the British, and both Canberra and Wellington were apprehensive that Britain might ask them to contribute to the costs of the mission.[125] No such suggestion was ever made, yet the reluctance in Australia and New Zealand to make financial contributions to the British plans shows that Britain was at this point not only more concerned about the situation in the RVN than its Commonwealth allies, the British government was also more willing to become involved in the anti-guerrilla struggle in Vietnam.

In August 1961 the stage was set for the sending of a British advisory mission to Saigon. The Americans and the South Vietnamese had accepted the British offer, the Treasury had agreed to provide up to £100,000 per annum, and with Robert Thompson a suitable head of the mission had been found. The mission's budget was to be £40,000, the rest would be used to finance the enlarged training programme for ARVN officers and the civil guard in Malaya.[126]

Readers of *The Times* learned on 18 September 1961 that Robert Thompson had left for Saigon to establish a British advisory mission 'on police and administrative matters'.[127] The article was largely based on the Foreign Office briefing of the previous day. The announcement was deliberately vague in order not to give the impression that any breach of the provisions of the Geneva agreements was afoot.[128] The British, however, feared that it may be impossible to 'conceal the real nature of the mission for long' and that the DRV might react by closing the British Consulate General in Hanoi.[129] Although the Macmillan government had no intention of revealing the full scope of the mission to the British public, it widely publicized the mission among its allies. The New Zealanders were told in September 1961 that the mission's purpose was to demonstrate Britain's willingness to help Saigon at a time when the Foreign Office's overall expenditure was being cut by more than 5 per cent.[130] The British informed the members of SEATO about the mission at a council meeting in early September, stressing London's hope that the mission would supplement the US effort in the RVN.[131]

Wellington. 28.6.61. All in NZNA: PM 478/4/1, part 13. Memorandum 1004: Ryan (Singapore) to EA Canberra. 6.7.61. Note by Woodberry (Saigon). 6.7.61. Both in AUSNA: A4531/6, file 221/5/10, part 1.

[125] Letter: Shepherd (Canberra) to EA Wellington. 14.8.61. All in NZNA: PM 478/4/1, part 13.
[126] Telegram 1949: London to EA Wellington. 14.9.61. Ibid.
[127] 'British Mission to South Vietnam', *The Times*. 18.9.61, p. 9.
[128] Telegram 619: FO to Saigon. 5.9.61. PRO: DO 169/110. Telegram 620: FO to Saigon. 5.9.61. PRO: PREM 11/3736. Telegram 1912: CRO to Ottawa. 8.9.61. PRO: DO 169/110. Telegram 185: London to EA Ottawa. 19.9.61. CNA: RG 25, Vol. 4637, File 50052-A-40, part 37.
[129] Telegram 197: FO to Hanoi. 30.8.61. PRO: DO 169/110.
[130] Telegram 1949: London to EA Wellington. 14.9.61. NZNA: PM 478/4/1, part 13.
[131] Telegram 1632: FO to Bangkok. 8.9.61. Telegram 2966: CRO to New Delhi. 8.9.61. Both in PRO: DO 169/110.

CONCLUSION

Robert Thompson arrived in Saigon in late September 1961 and took up his post as head of BRIAM, the British Advisory Mission to Vietnam. Neither American nor South Vietnamese pressure was behind the establishment of BRIAM. Not only was there no pressure from the governments of these two countries, Washington and Saigon had to be persuaded to agree to BRIAM. It is true that President Diem asked for British-Malayan advice in early 1960, but the South Vietnamese subsequently turned down two British offers of sending an advisory mission to Saigon. From February 1961 London changed the approach and tried to gain Washington's approval for sending BRIAM. Although the State Department supported the British offer, the American military made its opposition to BRIAM abundantly clear. It would have been very easy for the British government to abandon the whole idea and wash its hands of the counter-insurgency business in Vietnam. Nobody in Washington or Saigon could have blamed the British for this. But London chose the opposite path.

The British did not find it advisable to appear too keen on sending a British mission to Vietnam and preferred to put subtle if constant pressure on the American administration. In order to conceal that the establishment of the mission was in Britain's own interest, it was portrayed as a major concession, almost a sacrifice, on Britain's part. The British also tried to hide behind the Tunku and his April 1961 suggestion to send Thompson as head of an advisory mission to Vietnam. As soon as this strategy had proved successful, the British played down the Tunku's role. Indeed, when the State Department expressed the view that Malaya should play a more prominent role in the mission, the Foreign Office quickly told the Americans that the Tunku seemed to have lost interest in supporting the South Vietnamese.[132] There was no evidence for this,[133] and the Tunku proved the contrary when he readily agreed to offer more training facilities for South Vietnamese officers in August 1961.[134] Clearly, London wanted the mission to be a recognizable British effort to help the South Vietnamese.

BRIAM, then, was the result of Whitehall's decision to play a more prominent role in Saigon's fight against the communist insurgency. One important reason behind this decision was certainly the view that British advice could be of real value in the RVN. However, London was by no means certain that BRIAM could achieve anything in the military field. It was therefore not crucial to define BRIAM's tasks precisely. The first and foremost objective was to show a British presence in Saigon. To understand London's eagerness to establish BRIAM, the decision has to seen against the background of Britain's Southeast Asia policy. Four points have to be made in this context.

[132] Embtel 453: Jones (London) to State Department. 31.7.61. USNA: RG 59, Central Files, 751k.5-msp/7-3161.
[133] Embtel 505: Baldwin (Kuala Lumpur) to State Department. 1.8.61. Ibid. 751k.5-msp/7-161.
[134] Telegram 566: Kuala Lumpur to CRO. 3.8.61. PRO: DO 169/109.

First, Prime Minister Macmillan was worried about the state of the 'special relationship'. Although the British government might have ultimately supported American intervention in Laos, the Laos crisis had put strain on relations with the United States, Britain's major ally in Southeast Asia. The Foreign Office was desperate to regain American trust. To prove that Britain was 'with the United States' in South Vietnam did indeed help and the Americans gladly noted that the British attitude on Vietnam was quite different from that on Laos.[135] Second, even if Thompson was unable to influence the outcome of the struggle in the RVN, the British expected that his presence would guarantee them far more information about American policy in South Vietnam. With the benefit of this knowledge, it was hoped, London would be in a position to influence US decisions on Vietnam. Third, BRIAM was not only designed to reassure the Americans. It was to show to the Soviet Union that Britain was not prepared to promote negotiations on South Vietnam, and in fact quite the contrary. With the establishment of BRIAM the British made it clear that they, as co-chairman of the Geneva conference, would turn a 'blind eye' on American and 'possibly on some British activities' in South Vietnam.[136] Fourth, Britain had substantial interests in Southeast Asia, mainly in Malaya and Singapore, and London wanted to show that it was still able and willing to safeguard these interests. An additional commitment to the survival of the anti-communist regime in Vietnam was designed to improve Britain's standing in the eyes of its allies in the region. Australia and New Zealand were kept well-informed about British plans, although the latter to a lesser extent. Interestingly, both these countries that decided in 1965 to send troops to Vietnam seemed at this stage reluctant to be associated with the increased British involvement.

When Robert Thompson left for Southeast Asia in September 1961, it was uncertain whether BRIAM could fulfil all the hopes the mission had evoked in London. What did seem certain, however, was that the first few months would be difficult, that the MAAG would be very suspicious of British activities, and that a lot depended on whether Thompson was able to establish good personal relationships with his American and South Vietnamese counterparts.

---

[135] Embtel 370: Bruce (London) to State Department. 25.7.61. USNA: RG 59, Central Files, 751k.00/7-2561.

[136] Minute: Peck (FO) to Hoyer-Millar (FO). 18.10.61. PRO: FO 371/160136, DV1071/52.

4
Winning the Shooting War: BRIAM and the Strategic Hamlet Programme

On 4 April 1963 David Ormsby-Gore, the British ambassador in Washington, accompanied Robert Thompson to meet President John F. Kennedy. The only other American present in the Oval Office was Chalmers B. Wood, the Director of the Working Group on Vietnam.[1] The private meeting with the President lasted twenty minutes and marked the peak of Thompson's influence as head of the British Advisory Mission, one and a half years after taking up the post. It was an expression of the intimate relationship he had formed with the Americans. He had worked closely with the American embassy in Saigon and the Military Assistance Command Vietnam (MACV) and was highly respected by them.[2] To explain why it would be useful for the President to meet Thompson, William Brubeck, the Special Assistant to the Secretary of State and Executive Secretary, summarized Washington's view on Thompson's achievements: 'Mr. Thompson's deep involvement in the Vietnamese war has coincided with the period of our expanded assistance. His long experience in countering guerrilla warfare, his influential relationship with President Diem, and his position as a knowledgeable observer outside our own organizations should make his views on the progress of the war of value to the President.'[3]

In April 1963, Thompson was convinced that progress had been made in Vietnam. He painted a rosy picture for the American President: the morale of the South Vietnamese and their western advisers was high, the American helicopters had proved useful and the surrender policy—one of Thompson's projects—was on sound lines. Above all, Thompson praised the strategic hamlet programme, stressing that it had gone better than anyone had expected and that it provided a degree of security which the French had never been able to achieve.[4]

---

[1] Memorandum: Brubeck to M. Bundy. 3.4.63. JFKL: NSF, Country Series Vietnam, box 199. Memorandum of Conversation. 4.4.63. FRUS: 1961–1963, iii, Vietnam 1963, 198.
[2] Biographical data sheet on Thompson. Attachment to memo: Brubeck to M. Bundy. 19.3.63. USNA: RG 59, Central Files, POL 27–10 S.VIET.
[3] Draft memorandum: Brubeck to M. Bundy. 15.3.63. Attachment to memorandum: Brubeck to M. Bundy. 19.3.63. Ibid.
[4] Memorandum of Conversation between Kennedy and Thompson. 4.4.63. FRUS: 1961–1963, iii, Vietnam 1963, 198–200. In his memoirs, Thompson mentioned his meeting with Kennedy but omitted

In Thompson's view the future looked bright. He told Kennedy that, if progress continued to be made at the present rate, one or two areas could be cleared of NLF forces and declared 'white' by the summer. Furthermore, Washington should make an announcement by the end of 1963 that it was reducing the number of American military advisers by approximately one thousand if confidence of success continued to grow.[5] Such a move, Thompson argued, would reaffirm the honesty of US intentions and would weaken the communist's propaganda that Saigon was a satellite and the conflict an American war. Most importantly, it would show that 'we are winning'.[6] President Kennedy liked what the head of BRIAM had to say, and he 'warmly congratulated Bob [Thompson] on his presentation and on his very fine work in Viet-Nam'.[7]

Robert Thompson believed the strategic hamlet programme to be the right approach to defeat the insurgency. Because of the similarities between this programme and the methods employed by the British to defeat communist guerrillas in the Malayan insurgency, it is widely believed that Robert Thompson was the brain behind the strategic hamlet programme. However, this chapter will demonstrate that the programme itself was not Thompson's conception. It will show that Thompson strove to influence the programme as best he could after realizing that his own strategy—the delta plan—would not be adopted by Ngo Dinh Diem's Saigon government. Interestingly, in the process of going along with the strategic hamlet programme, Thompson, like many Americans, increasingly believed that progress was being made in suppressing the insurgency, and that victory was imminent.

The optimism Thompson showed in his meeting with Kennedy is striking, as is his access to the highest quarters of the American administration. Indeed, Thompson's ability to gain American trust was exactly what the British government had hoped for by sending the advisory mission to Vietnam. This chapter explores how Thompson managed to establish good relations with US officials. It will become clear that Thompson had to tread very carefully with the Americans, particularly in the first few weeks after his arrival in Saigon.[8]

PROMOTING THOMPSON IN WASHINGTON

Robert Thompson left London as the newly appointed head of the British Advisory Mission to Vietnam on 17 September 1961. Instead of directly flying to East

---

details of the optimistic assessment he gave the President. Instead, he stressed that he found Kennedy 'a great disappointment' and 'a bit of a dilettante' (Thompson, *Make for the Hills*, 137).

[5] Memorandum of Conversation between Kennedy and Thompson. 4.4.63. FRUS: 1961–1963, iii, Vietnam 1963, 200. Thompson also told Secretary of Defense McNamara that the withdrawal of 1,000 US advisers might be possible at the end of the year. Memorandum of Conversation between Harriman and Thompson. 4.4.61. Ibid. 193.

[6] Memorandum of Conversation between Kennedy and Thompson. 4.4.63. Ibid. 200.

[7] Letter: Wood to Nolting (Saigon). 4.4.63. Ibid. 205.

[8] Reginald Burrows confirmed this view in his letter to the author of 21.2.2002.

Asia he boarded a Britannia flight and travelled via New York to Washington. The Foreign Office wanted Thompson to make himself known to high-ranking officials of the Kennedy administration.[9] Thompson himself knew full well how crucial it was to establish a good rapport with the Americans.[10] In August, Field Marshal Templer had agreed to send a letter of introduction for Thompson to General Maxwell Taylor, Kennedy's military representative. This opened doors in Washington. Thompson did not only meet General Taylor and Walt Rostow in the White House offices, but also General Lyman Lemnitzer, the Chairman of the JCS.[11]

As usual, Thompson advanced the ideas that had been applied in Malaya for controlling the insurgents in Vietnam. The State Department deemed two of them, an amnesty plan to encourage NLF surrenders and the denial of food supplies, important enough to report them to the Saigon embassy.[12] As the Foreign Office had hoped, Thompson immediately became a useful source of information on American thinking and planning in Vietnam. He confirmed the Foreign Office's suspicion that there was serious talk of putting American troops into Vietnam in September 1961 if the situation further deteriorated.[13]

However, the content of the talks was not what really mattered from a British point of view. Thompson, the figurehead of the British effort to save Vietnam, had to be advertised and marketed. He had to be propelled from an unknown entity to nothing less than the most experienced counter-insurgency expert in South Vietnam. Thompson's trip to Washington in September 1961 turned out to be the first step in this direction. He himself felt that he was 'well received'.[14] The State Department expressed the hope that Diem's government may be persuaded to accept some of Thompson's advice because of his 'Malayan experience', employing the very term the British were busily promoting.[15] In turn, the Foreign Office stressed that Britain was as 'thoroughly committed' as the United States to the defence of South Vietnam and thanked the Americans for the 'full cooperation and the cordial treatment' that had been given to Thompson in Washington.[16]

Robert Thompson was the kind of Briton who was bound to impress the Americans. After joining the Colonial Service in 1938, he had spent most of his life in Southeast Asia. During the war he had distinguished himself in the Burma campaigns. His service in Burma did not only make him familiar with guerrilla tactics and jungle warfare, he also got used to working closely with the American

[9] Telegram: London to EA Ottawa. 19.9.61. CNA: RG 25, Vol. 4637, File 50052-A-40, Part 37. See also Thompson, *Make for the Hills*, 124.

[10] William Trueheart Oral History I, 13. Lyndon B. Johnson Presidential Library, Austin, Texas (hereafter LBJL): Oral History Collection.

[11] Editorial Note. FRUS: 1961–1963, i, Vietnam 1961, 301. No detailed records of these conversations have been found in the American or British archives.

[12] Deptel 351: Bowles to Saigon. 28.9.61. USNA: RG 59, Central Files, 751k.00/9-2861.

[13] Letter: Hohler (Saigon) to Peck (FO). 7.10.61. PRO: FO 371/160156, DV1201/10/G.

[14] Thompson, *Make for the Hills*, 124.

[15] Deptel 351: Bowles to Saigon. 28.9.61. USNA: RG 59, Central Files, 751k.00/9-2861.

[16] Embtel 1738: Bruce (London) to State Department. 27.10.61. Ibid. 751k.00/10-2761.

allies in the field. Moreover, Thompson had been sent on a public relations tour to the United States in 1943. He gave lectures and talks on his Burma experience in order to convince the US public that Britain, too, was fighting World War II in Europe *and* Asia.[17] The public relations message Thompson brought to Washington almost twenty years later was remarkably similar.

Thompson returned to Malaya after the war and rose quickly through the ranks of the Malayan Civil Service. He also met his future wife, Merry Newboult, the daughter of Sir Alec Newboult who was the acting High Commissioner in Malaya after the assassination of Sir Edward Gent. During the emergency Thompson was preoccupied with administrative tasks, first as Assistant Commissioner for Labour in Perak, then as Deputy Commissioner for Labour and Chinese Affairs in Johore and finally as Secretary to the Member for Home Affairs in Kuala Lumpur. The Ministry for Home Affairs was responsible for propaganda, psychological warfare, the issuing of identity cards, and all intelligence relating to the emergency.[18] In 1955 Thompson moved on to the post of Co-ordination Officer Security in the Ministry of Defence. After Malaya's independence in 1957 Thompson was promoted to Malaya's Permanent Secretary of Defence under Tun Razak as Minister.[19]

Yet not only his professional success commended the 45-year-old Thompson to his new post as head of BRIAM. He was also a sociable person with the right education (Marlborough and Cambridge) and appropriate pastimes. Thompson liked horses, played tennis and golf, and enjoyed the odd glass of whisky—he converted one of the rooms in his Saigon office into a store where he kept stocks of drinks, mainly whisky and French wines.[20] From the perspective of the British embassy in Saigon, Thompson and his colleagues led the life of 'temporary bachelors' in Saigon. For Thompson, whose professional experience had thus far been largely limited to Malaya, BRIAM offered the opportunity to expand his views.[21] He was particularly keen to get on well with the Americans, especially with high-ranking officials, and, as Reginald Burrows of the British embassy put it in retrospect, 'his sights were always on the White House'.[22] The occasional diplomatic drink party or playing golf with his American counterparts certainly helped to gain the confidence and sometimes even friendship of the US representatives in Vietnam. For example, William Trueheart, US ambassador Nolting's deputy in Saigon, came to regard Thompson as a 'very close personal friend',[23] who even became the godfather of one of Trueheart's children.[24]

---

[17] Thompson, *Make for the Hills*, 19–40.   [18] Ibid. 77–108.   [19] Ibid. 108–10.
[20] Ibid. 125.   [21] Reginald Burrows in interview with the author. 14.2.2002.
[22] Letter: Reginald Burrows to author. 21.2.2002.
[23] William Trueheart Oral History I, 13. LBJL: Oral History Collection.
[24] Isabel Oliphant, Sir Robert Thompson's daughter, in interview with the author. 13.2.2002.

THE DELTA PLAN

In late 1961, however, Trueheart would have hardly dared to describe Thompson in such an affectionate way. After his stay in Washington and a brief stop in Kuala Lumpur where he met the Tunku and Tun Razak, Thompson arrived in Saigon's Hotel Majestic on 29 September.[25] Here Dennis Duncanson, Jock Hindmarsh, and Desmond Palmer joined him. They all had worked in the Malayan civil service. Duncanson was an expert in psychological warfare, Hindmarsh had been responsible for police training in Malaya, and Palmer had worked in intelligence.[26] The Britons set up their temporary offices in the hotel before BRIAM found its permanent home in a French villa on Boulevard Cong Ly. They immediately started to tour the country in order to survey the situation in Vietnam.[27] Desmond Palmer, the typical 'colonial administrator',[28] almost always accompanied Thompson on his frequent tours of Vietnam during his time as head of BRIAM. Mostly the Americans flew them to the countryside by helicopter. Quite often, however, Thompson and his team took their own black Citroen and drove without any escort to villages and hamlets in the vicinity of Saigon.[29]

Given the suspicions of the Americans in Saigon, and the long-standing opposition to British involvement by the MAAG in particular, Thompson was bound to have a difficult start. The Foreign Office hoped that Thompson would exercise the greatest care in not crossing wires or even swords with the MAAG.[30] Thompson, however, did not proceed very carefully in the beginning. The main problem turned out to be his first initiative, an initiative that was to shape BRIAM's entire activity in South Vietnam, the delta plan. After barely a month in the RVN, Thompson produced a paper entitled 'Appreciation of Vietnam, November 1961–April 1962'.[31] In this report Thompson concluded that a campaign on Malayan lines in the whole area of the Mekong delta south and west of Saigon would bring success, possibly within six months. He had toured the area for five days and found it to be most promising for the measures he had in mind, mainly because conditions were very similar to those in Malaya.[32]

Thompson's proposals centred around four main ideas. First, on the organizational level, he called for what he termed a super state war executive committee. This would serve as a combined military and civil headquarters to direct and

[25] Telegram 713: Kuala Lumpur to CRO. 28.9.61. PRO: DO 169/110.

[26] Ian Beckett, 'Robert Thompson and the British Advisory Mission to South Vietnam 1961–65', *Small Wars and Insurgencies*, 8/2 (1997), 45.

[27] Thompson, *Make for the Hills*, 125.

[28] Reginald Burrows in interview with the author. 14.2.2002.

[29] Isabel Oliphant in interview with the author. 13.2.2002.

[30] Telegram 1949: London to EA Wellington. 14.9.61. NZNA: PM 478/4/1, part 13.

[31] Embtel 597: Nolting (Saigon) to State Department. 5.11.61. JFKL: NSF, Country Series Vietnam, box 194 and USNA: RG 59, Central Files, 751k.00/11-561.

[32] Telegram 708: Hohler (Saigon) to FO. 6.11.61. PRO: PREM 11/3736.

coordinate all emergency plans and measures. Second, strategic hamlets were to provide security for the population and deprive the NLF of their base of support. While General Taylor recommended in his November 1961 report to use a recent flooding disaster in the Mekong valley as a cover to introduce US combat forces, Thompson argued that advantage could be taken of this situation in a different way. The floods would facilitate the regrouping of villages along the Cambodian border and the fringes of the Mangrove areas that were controlled by the NLF. It was therefore essential to build properly defended villages in these areas. Fortifying existing villages and hamlets in the remainder of the delta was deemed sufficient. In addition, the introduction of curfews and controls on all roads and waterways should disrupt the NLF courier system and help support a limited programme of food control. Third, Thompson regarded the already existing self-defence corps as the key to the success of the programme. Their advantage was that the members of this corps lived in the hamlets. If properly trained, equipped, and supported by the civil guard and the army in case of a large-scale attack, they could play a decisive part in the defeat of the NLF. Fourth, all these measures were designed to induce the communist insurgents to react and attack the hamlets. This would provide the main opportunity for 'killing terrorists'. The population's reward for their cooperation was to be the same as during the Malayan emergency. As soon as areas were cleared of NLF forces and declared 'white', social improvements would follow together with the relaxing of controls.[33]

The Foreign Office welcomed Thompson's proposals, which became known as the delta plan. Thompson put forward the plan at a time when the Kennedy administration was making important decisions on Vietnam. On his fact-finding tour to Vietnam in October 1961 General Taylor met with Robert Thompson and showed an interest in the British adviser's views.[34] London was aware of the various proposals before the President and hoped that Kennedy would not decide to send combat troops. Lord Home urged his American colleague Rusk in a letter of 2 November 1961 to give the South Vietnamese a last chance to 'fight it out' themselves.[35] However, David Ormsby-Gore concluded after a meeting with Dean Rusk on 8 November that the US decision on combat troops would be a 'close run thing'.[36] Therefore, the Foreign Office instructed Ormsby-Gore to pass Thompson's paper to General Taylor and other members of the administration in the hope that the Americans would consider the plan seriously as an alternative to a 'massive injection of US personnel'.[37] London's instructions were not necessary, as Ormsby-Gore had already delivered a copy of Thompson's report together with Lord Home's letter of 2 November.[38]

[33] Telegram 708: Hohler (Saigon) to FO. 6.11.61. PRO: PREM 11/3736.
[34] Deptel 717: Taylor (White House) to Nolting (Saigon). 1.12.61. USNA: RG 59, Central Files, 751k.00/11-3061.
[35] Telegram 7945: Home to Rusk. 2.11.61. PRO: PREM 11/3392.
[36] Telegram 2984: Ormsby-Gore (Washington) to FO. 8.11.61. PRO: PREM 11/3736.
[37] Telegram 8169: FO to Washington. 9.11.61. Ibid.
[38] Memorandum of Conversation between Ormsby-Gore and Ball (State Department). 3.11.61. USNA: RG 59, Central Files, 751k.00/11-361.

The delta plan could be regarded as an alternative to the sending of American soldiers because very little additional manpower was required to implement it. Only additional material equipment was an urgent necessity: coastal and river patrol boats, radios for the civil guards, better clothing and carbines for the self-defence corps, helicopters to fly out the wounded, and large quantities of barbed wire to fortify the villages and hamlets.[39] Although the RVN did not have the necessary resources to provide this equipment, the Foreign Office stressed that it had the necessary manpower. Consequently, US troops were not required.[40]

CROSSING SWORDS WITH THE AMERICANS .

Thompson's recommendations clearly went beyond the original remit of his mission, which had been agreed between the British and American embassies in Saigon. Therefore ambassador Nolting was not amused when he received Thompson's report on 5 November. He noted angrily that Thompson had made 'sweeping recommendations' even on the size, training, and equipment of the military forces. Thompson's emphasis on developing the civil side of the struggle at the expense of the military was not in accord with American policy. A sharp change like this could undermine the progress already made and bring, in Nolting's view, 'disastrous confusion'. He also resented Thompson's opposition to sending foreign troops to Vietnam, especially as the US ambassador regarded an American military presence as essential.[41]

Yet it was not only the contents of Thompson's plan that irritated the ambassador, it was also his conduct vis-à-vis the South Vietnamese. Without consulting the US embassy or the MAAG, Thompson sent the report to President Diem on 11 November.[42] Two weeks later Diem received Thompson in the Presidential Palace. Thompson did not speak French, and President Diem's English was poor. Therefore, Dennis Duncanson, who knew several languages and was a fluent French speaker, always accompanied Thompson to the Presidential Palace as his interpreter.[43] The meeting in late November 1961 lasted more than three hours, giving Thompson the opportunity to explain the delta plan in detail. Diem readily agreed that major battles would take place in the villages and espoused the vague idea of granting some form of autonomy to villages and hamlets. Diem complained at length about the Americans: their lack of comprehension of the situation in Vietnam, the unhelpfulness of USOM, and, above all, the conditions

[39] Telegram 708: Hohler (Saigon) to FO. 6.11.61. PRO: PREM 11/3736.
[40] Telegram 8169: FO to Washington. 9.11.61. Ibid. Telegram 701: Hohler (Saigon) to FO. 4.11.61. PRO: FO 371/160128, DV103145/7.
[41] Embtel 597: Nolting (Saigon) to State Department. 5.11.61. USNA: RG 59, Central Files, 751k.00/11-561.
[42] Letter: Thompson (BRIAM) to Diem. 11.11.61. USVR: Book 11, 345–58.
[43] Reginald Burrows in interview with the author. 14.2.2002. Isabel Oliphant, Sir Robert Thompson's daughter, in interview with the author. 13.2.2002.

the US attached to granting more aid. Thompson concluded that Diem's criticism of the United States partly accounted for the 'warm manner' in which Diem received him and for the trust he was apparently prepared to place in British advice.[44]

Kennedy decided against sending combat troops to the RVN in late 1961. It appears doubtful that Thompson's delta plan had any influence on American thinking at this stage. The Foreign Office, however, believed that Lord Home's letter of 2 November had made some impact and noted that the British suggestion to give the South Vietnamese a last chance to win their own war was now US policy.[45] Yet this American policy was in line with the recommendations made by General Taylor. He stressed in his report that the 'present war cannot be won by direct U.S. action; it must be won by the Vietnamese'.[46] Lord Home's letter of 2 November therefore merely re-emphasized a position the Americans had reached independently of British advice.

In the wake of the Taylor report, the Kennedy administration set out to tackle both the military and political shortcomings of the Saigon regime. The US position was that the expansion of military aid was to go hand in hand with Diem's acceptance of political advisers at all levels of his government. While Diem welcomed military aid, he resented American political interference.[47] US ambassador Nolting was all too well aware of this. Thompson's initiative did not facilitate Nolting's task of persuading Diem to allow American political advisers into his administration. Indeed, Diem appeared to be keen to play off the British and Americans against each other. He let the United States know on 30 November that he accepted Thompson's plan and asked the MAAG if they had any comments on it.[48]

This was the last straw for Nolting. He summoned Thompson and ambassador Hohler to the American embassy and bluntly informed them of his disapproval of Thompson's actions. In his view the difficulties with BRIAM were procedural *and* substantive. Thompson had submitted his recommendations to Diem without prior consultations with the United States. Nolting had reminded Hohler several times that Thompson was not to give advice on military matters, and Hohler had accepted all this. Nevertheless, Thompson had chosen to disregard the Anglo-American understanding that had been reached prior to his arrival in Saigon.[49]

---

[44] Letter: Thompson (BRIAM) to McGhie (FO). 27.11.61. PRO: FO 371/160119, DV1015/258. Letter: Thompson (BRIAM) to McGhie (FO). 27.11.61. Ibid. DV1015/259.

[45] Telegram 3038: Ormsby-Gore (Washington) to FO. 13.11.61. PRO: PREM 11/3736. Despatch 110: Home to Ormsby-Gore (Washington). 20.3.62. PRO: FO 371/166702, DV1015/83/G.

[46] Evaluation Prepared by Members of the Taylor Mission. Paper attached to memorandum: Taylor to Kennedy. 3.11.61. FRUS: 1961–1963, i, Vietnam 1961, 491.

[47] Bassett and Pelz, 'The Failed Search for Victory', 239.

[48] Embtel 737: Nolting (Saigon) to State Department. 30.11.61. FRUS: 1961–1963, i, Vietnam 1961, 698–700.

[49] Ibid.

To defend Thompson, the British stressed that General Taylor had specifically asked for Thompson's views without limitations to the subject matter when the two had met in October. On being informed of this, Taylor maintained that he had only expressed a personal interest in Thompson's views. He had been surprised to receive Thompson's report in early November and was disturbed that Thompson was using him 'as a screen for his out-of-channels operations in Saigon'.[50] Taylor asked Nolting to tell the British that Thompson must have misunderstood his request.[51]

There was more to Nolting's anger than just Thompson's 'out-of-channels' approach. Although the US ambassador admitted that the delta plan was 'an admirable paper from the standpoint of presentation and as a statement of concept of anti-guerrilla operations', two of the proposed measures directly contravened American policy. First, the MAAG did not agree with Thompson that the clearance of the delta provinces should have first priority. The American military regarded the area north of Saigon as more important and Nolting pointed out that Thompson had not surveyed this area when he submitted his report. Second, Thompson's idea of a super state war executive committee would allow Diem to bypass the field command and give him effective operational control in the delta area. Nolting speculated that this was one of the reasons why Diem liked Thompson's plan.[52]

He also noted that for more than six months the Americans had urged Diem to set up a proper military command structure headed by a field command and to delegate authority to it. Although Diem had accepted this in principle, he continued to give direct orders to ARVN units without involving the field command. Nolting was convinced that effective counter-insurgency operations would be impossible unless Diem agreed to delegate authority. Thompson's recommendations, therefore, struck a 'hard blow' at this effort. Nolting also told Hohler and Thompson that the delta plan would not facilitate his negotiations with Diem. If Diem were to raise the plan in these talks, he would have to inform him that the United States did not agree with the command arrangements.[53]

On 30 November Nolting did not repeat his earlier view that Thompson's emphasis on developing the civil side of the conflict would cause disastrous confusion. The US ambassador was aware that criticizing this emphasis would have fallen on deaf ears in Washington as Kennedy had decided, against Nolting's advice, not to send US combat troops to Vietnam. The US ambassador clearly saw the writing on the wall: military aid was to be dramatically increased, but Washington had become more and more amenable to measures that stressed the political as well as the military side of the conflict.

---

[50] Memorandum: Taylor (White House) to Johnson (State Department). 1.12.61. USNA: RG 59, Central Files, 751k.00/12-161.

[51] Deptel 717: Taylor (White House) to Nolting (Saigon). 1.12.61. Ibid. 751k.00/11-3061.

[52] Embtel 737: Nolting (Saigon) to State Department. 30.11.61. FRUS: 1961–1963, i, Vietnam 1961, 698–700.

[53] Ibid.

At the conclusion of the meeting, Nolting got the impression that Thompson was 'thoroughly annoyed'. Nonetheless, Hohler and Thompson seemed to have accepted Nolting's views 'with good grace'. They stressed that they wanted to cooperate closely with the United States. Nolting noted with satisfaction that this implied their acceptance of playing a junior role in the advisory effort in Vietnam.[54]

A 'SPECIAL' ANGLO-AMERICAN RELATIONSHIP IN VIETNAM?

Indeed, Thompson tried to retrieve the situation. He indicated in a subsequent meeting with Nolting that he would revise the delta plan in order to preserve a unified military command structure. Thompson maintained, however, that the delta area should have first priority. The Americans admitted that this area was better suited for Thompson's Malaya-type measures. However, they still considered it necessary to strike as quickly as possible in the area north of Saigon. While this would not clear the NLF forces from the region permanently, it would provide quick military victories, which were deemed essential to bolster Vietnamese morale. Thompson, on the other hand, did not promise speedy victories. His delta plan would not show concrete results for months. In spite of different opinions on where to strike first, Nolting stressed in a report to Washington on 12 December that Thompson was now getting on well with the MAAG.[55]

So merely two weeks after Nolting had found BRIAM 'badly off rails',[56] he reported to Washington that Thompson was working 'closely and amicably' with the MAAG.[57] It is difficult to determine whether the Foreign Office put pressure on Thompson to improve his relations with the Americans.[58] Although aware of Anglo-American difficulties in South Vietnam, the Foreign Office did not appear to know exactly what was going on. It was not before mid-December, three weeks after the clash between Nolting and the British, that the Foreign Office had clear indications that there were Anglo-American disagreements over priority areas.[59] How serious, then, was the conflict between Nolting and BRIAM? In Washington, W. Averell Harriman, Assistant Secretary for Far Eastern Affairs, tried to play it down. He told ambassador Ormsby-Gore that the United States

---

[54] Embtel 737: Nolting (Saigon) to State Department. 30.11.61. FRUS: 1961–1963, i, Vietnam 1961, 698–700.

[55] Embtel 794: Nolting (Saigon) to State Department. 12.12.61. USNA: RG 59, Central Files, 751k.00/12-1261.

[56] Embtel 737: Nolting (Saigon) to State Department. 30.11.61. FRUS: 1961–1963, i, Vietnam 1961, 698–700.

[57] Embtel 794: Nolting (Saigon) to State Department. 12.12.61. USNA: RG 59, Central Files, 751k.00/12-1261.

[58] No British record of the meeting described in Embtel 737 has been found in the available British material.

[59] Despatch 74: Hohler (Saigon) to Home. 14.12.61. Minute on this despatch by McGhie. 20.12.61. PRO: FO 371/160163, DV1632/5.

wanted BRIAM to continue. 'Such minor differences that occurred', Harriman said, 'could be straightened out in Saigon.'[60] However 'minor' these differences were, the Americans felt the need to reassure the British and tell them that they preferred BRIAM's continuation.

As previously shown, the United States had in May begun to look for other pro-western countries to share the burden in the RVN. Most were reluctant. Even the Australian Prime Minister, Sir Robert Menzies, usually a staunch supporter of the American fight against communism in the area, explained that he could not make a commitment because of the forthcoming Australian national elections in December 1961.[61] Therefore, the continuation of the Thompson mission, which had originally been established against resistance from the US military, became all the more important for Washington. Despite all British protestations to the contrary, memories of London's Laos policy were still fresh and doubts about British steadfastness in Southeast Asia remained. Washington considered it possible that London might go back on its policy of firm support for the RVN. Prior to the Bermuda meeting with Prime Minister Macmillan in December 1961, President Kennedy was briefed that the British might threaten to withdraw BRIAM if the United States made a move which Britain strongly opposed, for instance using Chinese Nationalist personnel in Vietnam.[62]

There is nothing, however, in the British record to suggest that London was even considering the withdrawal of BRIAM. Three weeks after the confrontation with Nolting, the British ambassador even thought about expanding the mission. The background to this was Harriman's request to Ormsby-Gore on 11 December for Britain's views with regard to sending additional aid and the drawing up of a 'shopping list' for Colombo plan aid by the Saigon government. Ambassador Hohler, however, was not interested in granting Colombo plan aid to assist the Saigon regime. Instead, he stressed that Britain 'should concentrate on squeezing every penny [it] can to support the Thompson mission, since it is here that our one major chance of helping Vietnam must lie'.[63] The Foreign Office was more cautious, pointing out that there could be no large-scale expansion of the mission. All that they envisaged was maybe supplying two or three additional officers for assisting in the training programme.[64] The Americans were informed accordingly.[65]

The clash with the Americans in Saigon left Robert Thompson unbruised. In fact, his mission was not at all compromised. The ideas contained in the delta

[60] Memorandum of conversation between Ormsby-Gore and Harriman. 7.12.61. USNA: RG 59, Central Files, 751k.oo/12-761.

[61] Telegram 1925: Menzies to Beale (Washington), containing message from Menzies to Rusk. 26.11.61. AUSNA: A1209/138, file 1961/818, part 1. Deptel 846: Rusk to Saigon. 4.1.62. USNA: RG 59, Central Files, 751k.5/12-3061.

[62] Position Paper for the Bermuda meeting with Macmillan: 'The Viet-Nam Situation'. 16.12.61. USNA: RG 59, Lot 65D134, Folder: Deputy Assistant Secretary for Politico-Military Affairs subject files, 1961–1963, Macmillan Visit (1962).

[63] Letter: Hohler (Saigon) to Warner (FO). 20.12.61. PRO: FO 371/160153, DV1151/5.

[64] Telegram: FO to Washington. 28.12.61. PRO: FO 371/160130, DV103145/44.

[65] Deptel 805: Rusk to Saigon. 22.12.61. USNA: RG 59, Central Files, 751k.5/12-2261.

plan were put firmly on the agenda. The South Vietnamese press began to devote much attention to the 'lessons' of the Malayan emergency. In early January 1962 the *Times of Vietnam* published a long report entitled 'How Malaya defeats communism'. Brian Hill, the Australian Ambassador in Saigon, saw this as evidence of the interest that BRIAM had stimulated in adapting the measures that had been taken in Malaya to the insurgency situation in Vietnam.[66]

From December 1961 Thompson went out of his way to keep the Americans informed of his activity, and so did the other members of his mission.[67] This looked like a concession. However, Thompson had professed that he was willing to 'become an American' if need be before he went to Saigon. He thought it was not a sacrifice but more of a blessing that he was asked to coordinate his activities with the MAAG and to work as closely as possible with it, for in this manner Thompson could gain valuable insights into US thinking and, at the same time, work for the adoption of his own ideas.

From early January 1962, Thompson's star was rising quickly. It was a great advantage that he had come to Vietnam with clear ideas about what an insurgency was and how it could be defeated.[68] Americans, British, and Vietnamese alike appreciated his experience and his ability to write concise and convincing reports. U. Alexis Johnson, Deputy Under-Secretary of State for Political Affairs, praised the 'reasonableness' of Thompson's advice.[69] Reginald Burrows, counsellor in the British embassy in Saigon, found his approach 'refreshingly down-to-earth', and the Foreign Office, too, liked the 'good stuff' Thompson was producing.[70]

By mid-January 1962 US ambassador Nolting believed that the initial problems between the Americans and BRIAM had been overcome. When in Washington for consultations, he told David Ormsby-Gore that he found Thompson's delta plan very impressive. Moreover, Nolting accepted that Thompson was to give advice on all aspects of the security situation, including the military. With regard to priority areas, Nolting took a compromising stance as well, expressing the hope that operations in both areas, the delta and north of Saigon could be carried out simul-

---

[66] Memorandum 28: Hill (Saigon) to EA Canberra. 9.1.62. Attached were press clippings. The quoted article was published in the *Times of Vietnam* on 4 January 1962. AUSNA: A1838/333, file 3006/10/1, part 1.

[67] Letter: Burrows (Saigon) to Warner (FO). 17.1.62. PRO: FO 371/166699, DV1015/25. Letter: Trueheart (Saigon) to Cottrell (Vietnam Task Force, Washington). 12.2.62. FRUS: 1961–1963, ii, Vietnam 1962, 120.

[68] Thompson had developed a clear concept of the nature of an insurgency. He distinguished three phases: first, subversion; second, insurgency, and finally the climax of the guerrilla phase at which point the insurgency strategy is either continued, the rural discontent is transferred into the cities, or the military tactic is switched from guerrilla to conventional warfare (Robert Thompson, *Defeating Communist Insurgency: Experiences from Malaya and Vietnam* (London: Chatto & Windus, 1966), 29 ff.).

[69] Letter: Johnson (State Department) to Taylor (White House). 18.1.62. FRUS: 1961–1963, ii, Vietnam 1962, 50.

[70] Letter: Burrows (Saigon) to Warner (FO). 17.1.62. PRO: FO 371/166699, DV1015/25. Minute by Everard (FO). 22.8.63. PRO: FO 371/170135, DV1201/89.

taneously.[71] Whatever Nolting's views, the lower ranks in the American military remained more reserved. This was not only the impression of the Australians,[72] but Edward Lansdale also received reports from Vietnam later in the year that pointed out that the US military 'resented' Thompson because he had time to think whereas the Americans were bogged down with paperwork. Although it was better to have Thompson's plans 'than none at all', Thompson's ideas were still regarded as not exactly fitting the situation in Vietnam as Thompson was 'trying to cast the solution to the Vietnamese problem in the mould he learned in Malaya'. When Thompson 'dabble[d] in military tactics', the US military even found him counter-productive because he was not regarded as an expert in this field.[73]

Unaware of any of these feelings among the US military, the Foreign Office gladly noted after Nolting's talk with Ormsby-Gore that Thompson had established close relations with the Americans and that the initial conflict about tactical priorities in dealing with the insurgency appeared to have been resolved.[74] After his return to Saigon Nolting again paid tribute to the influence of Thompson's views on American strategy. Thompson was advocating a long-haul concept, stressing that it would take at least five years to defeat the NLF forces. Nolting informed ambassador Hohler that the Americans had come round to this view and agreed that Vietnam had to be cleared area by area. The MAAG and Nolting welcomed this new policy and gave much of the credit for this change of attitude to BRIAM. Thompson's 'clear and realistic advice', Nolting stressed to Hohler on 16 January 1962, had made a 'great impression both in Washington and . . . in Honolulu'.[75]

Ambassador Hohler, in turn, praised BRIAM's influence on the state of Anglo-American relations. In an enthusiastic dispatch he noted that a new relationship between the Americans and British was developing in Saigon because they were cooperating in a common enterprise. Although the United States had still not volunteered information on their policy, British requests for information were increasingly met. Hohler was certain that US confidence in the British would grow further if they continued to give visible and sound advice. He concluded that a 'special relationship' was developing in Vietnam, quite against the overall trend in the region.[76]

[71] Letter: Denson (Washington) to FO. 10.1.62. PRO: FO 371/166728, DV1071/41/G.

[72] Record of Conversation between Loomes (EA Canberra) and Colonel Serong. 15.5.62. AUSNA: A1838/346, file TS696/8/4, part 1.

[73] Letter: United States Army Concept Team Vietnam to Lansdale. 30.11.62. HI: Lansdale Papers, folder: Vietnam, Correspondence, box 49.

[74] FO brief for Lord Privy Seal's visit to Canada. 16.1.61. PRO: FO 371/166698, DV1015/20.

[75] Letter: Burrows (Saigon) to Warner. 24.1.62. PRO: FO 371/166717, DV103145/20.

[76] Despatch 7: Hohler (Saigon) to FO. 16.1.62. Ibid. DV103145/14.

HILSMAN'S STRATEGIC CONCEPT FOR VIETNAM

Roger Hilsman, Director of the State Department's Bureau of Intelligence and Research, made Thompson's concepts even more widely known in Washington. Because of his experience as an Office of Strategic Services (OSS) guerrilla leader in Burma in World War II, Hilsman regarded himself as a counter-insurgency expert. Under his direction the Bureau of Intelligence and Research looked into the history of anti-guerrilla campaigns, among them the Malayan emergency. At President Kennedy's request Hilsman attended the second conference on Vietnam at Honolulu on 15 January. From there he went on to Saigon. It was his first visit to Vietnam. He stayed for five days, toured the country, and met key American advisers as well as Thompson.[77] On his return to Washington he briefed President Kennedy and General Taylor. Kennedy asked Hilsman to draft his own recommendations for coping with the insurgency in South Vietnam.[78] Although the Foreign Office was worried that too many plans for Vietnam were being drawn up, leaving 'too many hands at the tiller', Hilsman's 'Strategic Concept for South Vietnam' was regarded as another tribute to Thompson's work.[79] Indeed, Hilsman mentioned Thompson in a footnote of his plan, pointing out that the 'basic approach followed in this plan was developed by Mr. R. G. K. Thompson, who played a major role in directing counter-insurgency operations in Malaya and who is now a Special Advisor attached to the British Embassy in Saigon'.[80]

Three elements formed the core of Hilsman's concept: strategic hamlets, the adoption of guerrilla tactics by ARVN, and civic action. According to Hilsman, the basic problem in Vietnam was political not military and the key to victory over the NLF forces lay in the villages. Hilsman suggested defeating the insurgency in three phases, each requiring a combination of military, political, and social measures. In phase one, zones of strategic villages were to be established. ARVN would have to adopt the strategy and tactics of the insurgents in order to clear the selected regions and keep the NLF forces under pressure. The self-defence corps would protect the villages and the civil guard the area between them. This system was very similar to Thompson's concept, but Hilsman was more ambitious. In his view, priority should be given not only to the delta, but to the area around Hué as well. Another significant difference was the envisaged role of civic action teams. Hilsman wanted to attach Americans and nationals of other friendly countries to these teams and leave the administration of the villages to them rather than to leave it to the ARVN or paramilitary forces.[81]

---

[77]   Hilsman, *To Move a Nation*, 425–30.

[78]   Letter: Denson (Washington) to Secondé (FO). 9.2.62. PRO: FO 371/166700, DV1015/43/G. According to Kennedy's log, Hilsman and Taylor met Kennedy on 29 January 1962. FRUS: 1961–1963, ii, Vietnam 1962, 113 (footnote). Hilsman, *To Move a Nation*, 438–9.

[79]   Minute by McGhie (FO). 15.2.62. PRO: FO 371/166700, DV1015/43/G.

[80]   'A Strategic Concept for South Vietnam'. Paper prepared by Hilsman. 2.2.62. FRUS: 1961–1963, ii, Vietnam 1962, 82.

[81]   Ibid. 82–7.

In the second phase, the zones of strategic hamlets would be extended to cover the remaining densely populated areas. More economic aid would flow into the villages. In addition, the Montagnard tribesmen in the border area contiguous to Laos would be targeted. As this area was sparsely populated, strategic villages could not be established. Borrowing from Britain's Malayan experience, Hilsman suggested the need to control the availability of food in the area. Rice would be bought up, stored in a secure place and closely controlled rations would then be given to the Montagnards once a week. Lastly, the aim of phase three was to seal off the whole border by resettling 'suitably hardy, loyal and tough villagers' along it in permanently defended, strategic villages.[82]

The British embassy in Washington received an outline of Hilsman's ideas shortly after the drawing up of his plan. Hilsman himself told the British that Kennedy's reaction had been enthusiastic. The British, however, took Hilsman's information with a pinch of salt. In their view Hilsman was inclined to 'over-rate his own abilities and possibly his influence'.[83] Indeed, Hilsman did not mention that the US military resented Hilsman's concept, especially as it conveyed the impression that the US military in Vietnam had so far not been effective, helpful, imaginative, and resourceful.[84]

Thompson claimed in his report on the 'strategic concept' that he found himself in broad agreement with Hilsman. Naturally, he supported the establishment of strategic hamlets. By February 1962, Thompson had even come round to the view that a start could be made in two areas simultaneously and had informed the South Vietnamese accordingly. Because he did not regard political reforms as being of major importance, Thompson stressed that Hilsman had used the word 'political' in their meeting as meaning not just political but also administrative. The lack of administration was in Thompson's view the fundamental and most pressing problem, as it made the implementation of any coordinated civil and military plan impossible.[85]

Thompson, however, disapproved of Hilsman's emphasis on civic action. Although he himself had included it in his own plan, Thompson was coming increasingly to the conclusion that the civic action teams were a menace. They confused the civil chains of command and their inexperienced members irritated the villagers. Thompson was particularly critical of Ngo Trong Hieu, the Vietnamese Minister for Civic Action, who seemed to use the civic action teams to create a private army for himself on the Hitler youth model. Accordingly, Thompson felt that it was not at all desirable to attach foreigners to these teams. He warned that there should not be 'too many enthusiastic foreign amateurs

---

[82] Ibid. 87–8.

[83] Letter: Denson (Washington) to Secondé (FO). 9.2.62. PRO: FO 371/166700, DV1015/43/G.

[84] Memorandum on the Substance of Discussion at a State Department–Joint Chiefs of Staff Meeting. 9.2.62. FRUS: 1961–1963, ii, Vietnam 1962, 113–16. Memorandum: Cottrell (Vietnam Task Force) to Harriman (State Department). 17.2.62. Ibid. 142.

[85] Letter: Thompson (BRIAM) to Denson (Washington). 26.2.62. PRO: FO 371/166700, DV1015/43/G.

swanning about in the villages unless they have something very definite and practical to offer'.[86] Thompson's negative reaction to the idea of attaching foreigners to the civic action teams might have been even more outspoken had he known that Hilsman's concept provided for the attachment of one hundred British/Malayan advisers to them.[87] Hilsman worked hard to make his concept widely known in Washington. He talked to Robert Kennedy, the JCS, and the heads of CIA and the Agency for International Development (AID). In these meetings he admitted that British thinking had influenced his concept, thereby promoting Thompson's status as a counter-insurgency expert.[88]

BRIAM AND THE COMMONWEALTH ALLIES

Hilsman was only one in a long row of distinguished visitors who wanted to hear Thompson's views when touring Vietnam. A call on Thompson became almost standard practice for anybody desiring information on the state of the insurgency. Apart from the Americans and, naturally, British officials like Lieutenant-General Nigel Poett, the Commander-in-Chief Far East Land Forces,[89] other pro-western representatives became aware of Thompson's influence. BRIAM was an important source of information for the West Germans.[90] The French described Britain's decision to send Thompson to Vietnam as an 'excellent move'.[91] The Malayan Prime Minister, increasingly worried about the situation in Vietnam, agreed to provide more facilities for the training of South Vietnamese. The Tunku met Diem in October 1961, repeated BRIAM's recommendations and advised him to regard Thompson as one of his own officers.[92]

BRIAM also had a significant effect on Britain's relations with its other major western allies in the region, Australia and New Zealand. In the 1950s Australia had come to regard Southeast Asia as vital for its forward defence strategy. Prime

[86] Letter: Thompson (BRIAM) to Denson (Washington). 26.2.62. PRO: FO 371/166700, DV1015/43/G.

[87] 'A Strategic Concept for South Vietnam'. Paper prepared by Hilsman. 2.2.62. FRUS: 1961–1963, ii, Vietnam 1962, 90.

[88] Memorandum on the Substance of Discussion at a State Department–Joint Chiefs of Staff Meeting. 9.2.62. FRUS: 1961–1963, ii, Vietnam 1962, 113–16. Hilsman, *To Move a Nation*, 439.

[89] Poett consulted Thompson for the first time in Saigon in December 1961 and agreed with Thompson's delta plan. Despatch 74: Hohler (Saigon) to FO. 14.12.61. PRO: FO 371/160163, DV1632/5. The general visited Saigon regularly, always spoke with Diem and was also fully briefed by General Harkins of the MACV. Nigel Poett, *The Memoirs of General Sir Nigel Poett* (London: Leo Cooper, 1991), 140–1.

[90] Memorandum 247/62 by v. Wendland (Saigon). 14.5.62; Report 13/62: 'Sicherheitslage in Südvietnam (Security situation in South Vietnam)' by Herrmann (Bangkok) to Bundesminister der Verteidigung (Minister of Defence). 17.4.62. Both in PA: Ref. 710 (IB5), Band 1665.

[91] Telegram 179: Paris to EA Wellington. 27.10.61. NZNA: PM 478/4/1, part 13.

[92] Despatch 9: Tory (Kuala Lumpur) to CRO. 13.11.61. PRO: FO 371/159704, D1022/26. Despatch 65: Hohler (Saigon) to FO. 14.11.61. PRO: FO 371/160163, DV1632/4. See also Frederick Nolting, *From Trust to Tragedy: The Political Memoirs of Frederick Nolting, Kennedy's Ambassador to Diem's Vietnam* (New York: Praeger, 1988), 37–8.

Minister Robert Menzies therefore supported American 'nation building' in Vietnam, and he warmly welcomed Diem when he visited Australia in 1957.[93] Canberra argued for a fierce anti-communist policy in Indochina. Its interest was to see that the United States did not 'lightly pass over its obligations to South Vietnam'.[94] Australia also supported US plans to intervene in Laos in early 1961. Faced with British reluctance the Australian cabinet made, in complete secrecy, an unprecedented decision: Australia would fight alongside the United States in Laos, even if Britain did not send its own forces.[95]

One of Lord Home's reasons for sending the Thompson mission had been to reassure particularly the Australians of Britain's continued interest in Southeast Asia. In December 1961, the Commonwealth Relations Office was anxious to demonstrate to the Australians that Britain and the United State were 'pulling together' in Vietnam, and that the increased American aid was complementary to BRIAM's recommendations.[96] The Foreign Office agreed that it was not useful to draw Canberra's attention to the Anglo-American differences over tactical priorities that still existed at the beginning of January 1962. As long as BRIAM's position vis-à-vis the Americans was not entirely secure, there was no desire to see Australian involvement in Vietnam.[97] Therefore, the Foreign Office refrained from providing detailed information about Thompson's activities to the Australians and simply reassured them of the Anglo-American agreement to hold the line in the RVN.[98] The Australians eventually got hold of the delta plan, but the Americans rather than the British passed it to them.[99] The New Zealanders, too, complained that Whitehall was very 'cagey' about BRIAM.[100] It certainly did not help New Zealand that its High Commission enquired in London about rumours that US and South Vietnamese irregulars were undertaking covert operations in North Vietnam. Edward Peck of the Foreign Office refused to comment on these rumours and urged the New Zealanders not to ask further questions.[101] The British apparently knew much more about these covert operations in North Vietnam than they were willing to admit.[102]

By mid-January 1962 ambassador Hohler was certain that Thompson had secured a prominent place as *the* counter-insurgency expert in Saigon, and that

[93] Edwards, *Crises and Commitments*, 194–7.

[94] Memorandum by Griffith (Prime Minister's Department). 17.11.61. AUSNA: A1209/138, file 1961/818, part 1.

[95] Edwards, *Crises and Commitments*, 220.

[96] Letter: Fair (FO) to McGhie (FO). 20.12.61. PRO: FO 371/160130, DV103145/52.

[97] Letter: McGhie (FO) to Fair (CRO). 4.1.62. Ibid.

[98] Telegram 35: Shann (London) to EA Canberra. 3.1.62. AUSNA: A1209/80, file 62/482, part 1.

[99] Telegram 4: Saigon to EA Canberra. 4.1.62. AUSNA: A1209/138, file 1961/818, part 1. Memorandum: Shepherd (Canberra) to EA Wellington. 26.1.62. NZNA: PM 478/4/6, part 1.

[100] Telegram 2686: London to EA Wellington. 7.12.61. NZNA: PM 478/4/1, part 14.

[101] Memorandum: Scott (London) to EA Wellington. 16.1.62. Ibid.

[102] To what extent the British were informed about covert activities or if they were even involved is impossible to determine. Reports of the Joint Intelligence Committee on Vietnam are still retained, and so are several FO files that might touch on this issue. Similarly, the National Archives in College Park have withdrawn a number of telegrams from the US embassy in London that, according to references in other telegrams, deal with Vietnam.

contributions to the struggle against the NLF by other countries would not endanger Thompson's status.[103] While the British had volunteered to send the mission, the Australians had to be prompted to make a similar contribution. The RVN complained to Brian Hill, the Australian ambassador in Saigon, about the slowness of Australian aid, especially in comparison with Britain and its advisory mission.[104] This complaint seemed unfair as Canberra had been very generous in providing economic assistance through SEATO. However, BRIAM had now eclipsed Australia's material aid.[105]

As Thompson's position did not seem to be threatened by increased Australian involvement, the Australians were taken into closer confidence. Copies of Foreign Office telegrams describing the initial differences between the British and Americans in Saigon were given to them, and Australia and New Zealand were informed of Britain's police training plans in Malaya.[106] Furthermore, the Americans helped to elevate Thompson's position in Australian and New Zealand eyes. The State Department informed the Australian and New Zealand ambassadors in February 1962 that the United States was pleased about the notable contribution BRIAM was making in Vietnam.[107] At the same time Thompson tried to assert his influence on the Australian aid programme to Vietnam. He told the Australians that they could help by providing large quantities of barbed wire for strategic hamlets.[108]

In March, Thompson travelled to Canberra and met the Australian Chiefs of Staff and officials from the Department of External Affairs. He repeated his request for Australian material aid. In addition to barbed wire he listed corrugated iron for roofing houses, generators, fire fighting equipment, mobile medical facilities, and portable audio and motion picture units for propaganda purposes.[109] Moreover, Thompson elaborated on his view of the situation in South Vietnam. The Vietnamese peasants were basically anti-communist, the NLF forces had targeted the villages and the delta plan was designed to counter this effort. The

---

[103] Despatch 7: Hohler (Saigon) to FO. 16.1.62. PRO: FO 371/166717, DV103145/14.

[104] Telegram 23: Hill (Saigon) to EA Canberra. 24.1.62. AUSNA: A1838/333, file 3996/10/1, part 1.

[105] Australian economic assistance for SEATO defence began in 1956. Australia was the only SEATO member providing this kind of aid. It mainly went to Thailand and Vietnam. The cabinet decided in March 1961 to allow the Minister for External Affairs to commit a further one million Australian pounds to this (Cabinet Decision No. 1270 on Submission No. 1035. 21.3.61. AUSNA: A4940/1, file C3127). The South Vietnamese civil guard received 200,000 Australian pounds (almost $500,000) in civilian aid from Canberra in 1961. Memorandum of Conversation between Dexter (Australian embassy) and Spurgin (Vietnam Task Force). 28.9.61. USNA: RG 59, Central Files, 751k.5/9-2861.

[106] Letter: Allen (Singapore) to Ramsbotham (FO). 17.1.62. PRO: FO 371/166983, WP18/3/G. Hohler's telegrams 868 and 869 of 19.12.61 are in AUSNA: A1209/80, file 62/482, part 1.

[107] Telegram 357: Beale (Washington) to EA Canberra. 16.2.62. AUSNA: A1209/138, file 1961/818, part 1. Memorandum: Laking (Washington) to EA Wellington. 6.3.62. NZNA: PM 478/4/1, part 14.

[108] Telegram: Hill (Saigon) to EA Canberra. 12.1.62. AUSNA: A1209/38, file 1961/818, part 1.

[109] Note for the file by Deschamps. Undated, probably March 1962. AUSNA: A1838/284, file 2481/5/12. Note by Herde on Cabinet submission 159: 'Australian Participation in Counter-communist activity in Southeast Asia'. 27.4.62. AUSNA: A4940/1, file C4642.

essence of his plan would be the creation of an 'auto defence unit' in each village, the self-defence corps. While the Americans had trained the ARVN well, there was need for training in jungle warfare for both the army and the civil guard. Although the British and Malays provided some training, more would be useful and Thompson suggested that the Australians might help in this respect.[110]

Thompson's approach had the desired effect. The Australian cabinet promptly endorsed a further increase to the funds available for counter-subversion aid in Southeast Asia. The Australians continued to seek Thompson's advice, which he gladly gave. Thompson believed that the best places to concentrate the initial delivery of Australian barbed wire were the provinces of Vinh Long and Vinh Binh. Not surprisingly, these provinces formed the southern flank of the delta plan where the South Vietnamese seemed inclined to begin the implementation of the plan. BRIAM had already done some field work in Vinh Long, had found the province chief able and energetic and concluded that thirty-six defended villages were needed. Subsequently, the Australian ambassador in Saigon sought and got American approval for Thompson's recommendations. The Australian government went along with Thompson's view as well, and the first coils of Australian barbed wire arrived in Vinh Long in July 1962.[111]

In the wake of Thompson's visit in March the Australians also considered but rejected the possibility of sending Australian personnel to Vietnam. In May, however, Dean Rusk spelled out to his Australian colleague Sir Garfield Barwick that material aid was not enough.[112] At a subsequent ANZUS meeting in Canberra the Americans pressed the Australians and New Zealanders still further to show their flags in the RVN and told them that the United States would like to see up to two hundred experienced military advisers from Australia and up to twenty from New Zealand.[113] Whereas New Zealand only succumbed to US pressure a year later, the Australian cabinet immediately obliged and agreed to the sending of Australian advisers if the Saigon government requested them.[114]

Far from weakening Thompson's position, the increased Australian involvement strengthened Britain's Malayan approach to the insurgency in Vietnam. The Australians, themselves experienced in counter-guerrilla warfare in Malaya,

---

[110] Summary record of talks between Thompson and various Australian authorities by British High Commission Canberra. Passed to Australia as enclosure to a letter: Molyneux (UK High Commission) to Griffith (Prime Minister's Department). 16.4.62. AUSNA: A1209/110, file 62/399.

[111] Savingram 37: Hill (Saigon) to EA Canberra. 27.4.62. Telegram 147: Hill to EA Canberra. 2.5.62. Savingram 38: Hill to EA Canberra. 2.5.62. All in AUSNA: A1838/280, file 3014/15/1, part 2. EA memorandum for Senator Gorton. 11.5.62. AUSNA: A1838/287, file 1481/5, part 4. Memorandum: Cooper (Manila Treaty Branch, EA Canberra) to Waller (Division I, EA Canberra). 22.8.63. AUSNA: A1838/280, file 3014/10/15, part 3.

[112] Record of conversation between Barwick and Rusk in Washington. 9.5.62. AUSNA: A1209/80, file 1962/708.

[113] COS(62)M19. Chiefs of Staff meeting. 11.5.62. NZNA: PM 478/4/6, part 1. See also Report 247/62 by v. Wendland (Saigon) to Auswärtiges Amt. 14.5.62. PA: Ref. 710 (IB5), Band 1665.

[114] Cabinet Decision No. 241. 15.5.62. AUSNA: A5819/2, volume 5, agendum 164. On New Zealand's Vietnam policy, see Roberto Rabel 'Vietnam and the Collapse of the Foreign Policy Consensus', in Malcolm McKinnon (ed.), *New Zealand in World Affairs, 1957–1972* (Wellington: New Zealand Institute of International Affairs, 1991), 40–63.

agreed with the measures Thompson recommended and were prepared to listen to his advice on what kind of aid they should provide. Moreover, BRIAM fulfilled the desired effect of demonstrating to the Australians that London was committed to containing communism in Southeast Asia. Thompson remained highly respected by the Australians and therefore influential. When Barwick came to Vietnam in May 1962, he asked Thompson where in his opinion Australian advisers would be most useful. The South Vietnamese wanted the Australians to establish a jungle warfare school in Quang Ngai. Thompson accompanied Barwick on a flight in the Presidential Dakota over this area and explained that he generally agreed with the South Vietnamese proposal. Although he would have preferred the deployment of Australian advisers in the delta, the advantage of Quang Ngai would be that it would allow the setting up of a separate Australian unit.[115] The American military in Saigon, however, preferred the integration of the Australians into the existing MAAG establishment. Another clearly visible mission of independent foreign experts like BRIAM was certainly not what the US military in Saigon wanted. Canberra eventually went along with the American wishes.[116]

In August a thirty-strong Australian Army Training Team Vietnam (AATTV) arrived in Vietnam.[117] The British embassy generally maintained good relations with the Australians and gave them what help and advice it could offer from its greater resources.[118] When the AATTV landed in Saigon, the British helped with the publicity for the team and made sure that the correspondents of *Reuters* and *The Times* witnessed the disembarkation of the Australian soldiers at Tan Son Nuth airport.[119] The AATTV was led by Colonel F. P. Serong. He was an experienced anti-guerrilla war expert and the founder of the Australian Jungle Training Centre in Canungra. Canungra-trained forces had previously fought in Malaya during the emergency.[120] Serong was to become the 'Australian Thompson', but with a more junior status. The MAAG had learned from its experience with BRIAM and insisted that Serong worked under the MAAG and not independently.[121] After a shaky start, Serong and his team developed good relations with the United States. Although more numerous, the AATTV did not overshadow BRIAM's team of five experts because the Australians became 'too merged' with

---

[115] Letter: Barwick to Townley (Minister of Defence). 1.6.62. AUSNA: A1838/280, file 3014/10/15/2. Telegram 211: Saigon to EA Canberra. 2.6.62. AUSNA: A1838/287, file 2481/5, part 4.

[116] Telegram 213: Saigon to EA Canberra. 4.6.62. AUSNA: A1838/280, file 3014/15/1, part 2. Letter: Brennan (EA Canberra) to Hill (Saigon). 13.7.62. AUSNA: A4531/11, file 221/1/4/1/5, part 1.

[117] On the AATTV, see Ian McNeill, *Australian Army Advisers in Vietnam, 1962–1972* (Canberra: Australian War Memorial, 1984), and by the same author: *To Long Tan: The Australian Army and the Vietnam War, 1950–1966* (St. Leonards: Allen & Unwin, 1993).

[118] Reginald Burrows in interview with the author. 14.2.2002.

[119] Minute: Woodberry (Saigon) to Neylan (Saigon). 31.7.62. AUSNA: A4531/11, file 221/1/4/5, part 1.

[120] Australian embassy press release. March 1963. AUSNA: A4531/11, file 221/1/4/1/5, part 2.

[121] Telegram 241: Saigon to EA Canberra. 14.6.62. Telegram 258: Hill (Saigon) to EA Canberra. 27.6.62. Both in AUSNA: A1838/280, file 3014/10/15/2. Letter: Harkins (MAAG) to Hill. 26.6.62. AUSNA: A4531/11, file 221/1/4/1/5, part 1.

the American advisers, as the British military attaché noted in September 1962. It was therefore difficult to identify their contribution as Australian.[122]

THOMPSON'S SECOND VISIT TO WASHINGTON

Thompson's visit to Australia in late March was only one of several stops on his way back to Britain, where he wanted to spend his leave with his wife and children in Exmoor. From Canberra he flew to Honolulu for talks with Admiral Felt, the US Commander-in-Chief Pacific. To the delight of the Foreign Office the Americans had invited Thompson to visit Washington, too.[123] This suited the British because the American military build-up, the formation of the new Military Assistance Command Vietnam under General Paul D. Harkins, and the attempted assassination of President Diem by two pilots of the South Vietnamese air force in February 1962 had changed the situation considerably. Therefore, the Foreign Office was very interested in having high-level Anglo-American talks on Vietnam.[124]

Roger Hilsman was eager to make Thompson feel welcome in Washington. Shortly after his arrival at Washington's Friendship airport on 2 April 1962, Thompson was chauffeured to *Le Bistro* on M Street, where Hilsman had invited him for lunch. The following four days in Washington demonstrated Thompson's growing influence with the Americans, at least with those interested in counterinsurgency. He met General Taylor in the White House Offices, W. Averell Harriman and U. Alexis Johnson in the State Department, General Curtis LeMay, the Air Force chief, in the Pentagon, and D. Fitzgerald at the CIA. Thompson also attended a Vietnam task force meeting. Edward Lansdale, who had been so critical of Thompson's involvement in 1960, was so worried about Thompson's frequent meetings with American officials outside the defence establishment that he organized at short notice a lunch for him in the Pentagon's Blue Room. Not surprisingly, Thompson found the visit to Washington exhausting and, according to his memoirs, became bored with explaining his concepts time and again.[125]

Nonetheless, Thompson created a very good impression. The New Zealand ambassador in Washington, who also met Thompson, characterized him as a 'man of excellent judgement and common sense'.[126] The Americans were equally impressed. Clarifying the problems in Vietnam and outlining the best means of approaching them revealed Thompson, in the words of a member of the US

[122] Letter: Lee (Saigon) to Jones (WO). 13.9.62. PRO: FO 371/166750, DV1201/64.
[123] Letter: Secondé to Denson. 19.2.62. PRO: FO 371/166700, DV1015/43/G. Letter: Thompson to McGhie (FO). 21.2.62. PRO: DO 169/110. Thompson, *Make for the Hills*, 133.
[124] Despatch 110: Warner (FO) to Ormsby-Gore (Washington). 20.3.62. Minute by Peck (FO). 20.3.62. Both in PRO: FO 371/166702, DV1015/83/G.
[125] Memorandum: Lansdale to Admiral Griffin and Generals Krulak, Burchinal, Rossom, Buse. 23.3.62. Itinerary for R. G. K. Thompson. Undated. Both in HI: Lansdale Papers, folder: Biographical Sketches, box 45. Thompson, *Make for the Hills*, 133–4.
[126] Memorandum: Laking (Washington) to EA Wellington. 6.4.62. NZNA: PM 478/4/1, part 15.

Vietnam task force, to be a 'man of high professional ability'.[127] Roger Hilsman believed that US confidence in Thompson and his qualities had increased even more because of his visit. On Hilsman's prompting and with the full support of W. Averell Harriman,[128] Dean Rusk expressed his personal appreciation of Thompson's 'outstanding' assistance in a letter to Lord Home. The use of 'our best resources of experience and talent,' Rusk wrote, 'is vital to the pursuit of our common aims'.[129] The US Secretary of State repeated the appreciation of British assistance in Vietnam orally at the Anglo-American summit in Washington at the end of April 1962.[130] President Kennedy also mentioned Thompson in a meeting with Prime Minister Macmillan and praised the very good work BRIAM had done in Vietnam.[131]

Apart from Thompson's personality and professionalism, his success in Washington was certainly due to his strategy of combining measured criticism of US methods with praise for the American effort. Roger Hilsman, for instance, must have been glad that Thompson stressed, more than ever, that the Vietnamese village was the key to defeating the insurgency. Again echoing Hilsman's concept, he claimed that the villages were anti-communist, but not necessarily pro-Diem. He went even so far as to say that, compared with the Malayan emergency, the strength and the vigour of the village was a favourable factor in Vietnam. However, he made his disapproval of the current civic action teams, one of the pillars of Hilsman's concept, abundantly clear. As in his correspondence with the Foreign Office he said that the teams had a 'touch' of the Hitler youth. Talking about air power, Thompson criticized indiscriminate attacks, but pointed out that these had become less frequent. Moreover, he praised the effectiveness of US helicopters and attack planes. Because of this new equipment and increased American military assistance in general, Thompson came to the conclusion that the Saigon government was not losing the war anymore, even if it was not yet winning. In addition, Thompson impressed on the Americans that not every so-called 'Vietcong' was a communist. Many were fighting a nationalistic war against foreign domination. Therefore, the NLF forces would like to get the United States more committed in combat. This had to be resisted and foreign assistance had to be played down. Repeating Lord Home's plea of November 1961, Thompson stressed that neither the United States nor other pro-western countries should therefore participate in large numbers in the fighting. In short, 'only the Vietnamese should shoot Vietnamese'.[132] Thompson

---

127 Telegram 1053: Washington to EA Canberra. 26.4.62. AUSNA: A1209/80, file 62/482, part 1.
128 Memorandum: Hilsman to Rusk. 25.4.62. USNA: RG 59, Central Files, 751k.00/4-2562.
129 Letter: Rusk to Home. 26.4.62. Ibid. 751k.00/4-2662.
130 Note of Conversation at Luncheon at the State Department. 28.4.62. PRO: CAB 133/300.
131 Record of a meeting held at the White House. 28.4.62. PRO: CAB 133/300.
132 Memorandum: Cottrell (Vietnam Task Force) to Harriman (State Department). 6.4.62. FRUS: 1961–1963, ii, Vietnam 1962, 311–15. Memorandum: Bagley (Naval Aide) to Taylor (White House). 5.4.62. FRUS: 1961–1963, ii, Vietnam 1962, 307–8. Memorandum: Laking (Washington) to EA Wellington. 6.4.62. NZNA: PM 478/4/1, part 15. Letter: Warner (FO) to Butler (Paris). 13.4.62. PRO: FO 371/166702, DV1015/94. A decade later, Thompson repeated his conviction that the Vietnam war could have been won by the RVN with US assistance but not by the US forces themselves, in Robert Thompson, *Peace Is Not at Hand* (London: Chatto & Windus, 1974), 59.

1. President Ngo Dinh Diem, as always dressed in white, arrives for the beginning of the National Day Parade in Saigon on 26 October 1962.

2. Prime Minister Macmillan was eager to establish a good relationship with the new US President. After their first meeting in Key West they continued the talks in Washington in April 1961. From left to right: Secretary of State Rusk, Macmillan, Kennedy, Foreign Secretary Lord Home.

3. The Malaysia plan was often discussed at informal meetings. From left to right: Singaporean Prime Minister Lee Kuan Yew, Dato Ismail, Malayan minister and friend of the Tunku, Lord Selkirk, and Singapore's Finance Minister Goh Keng Suree.

4. Between 1960 and 1963, Lord Selkirk, British Commissioner-General for Southeast Asia, travelled regularly to Vietnam and met President Diem. Reginald Burrows (right) of the British embassy accompanied him on this occasion.

5. Indian Prime Minister Nehru visited the United States in November 1961. Kennedy took the opportunity to explain why he wanted to increase military aid to Vietnam.

6. Secretary of Defense Robert McNamara (left), and General Maxwell Taylor, Kennedy's military representative, discussing with the President in the White House on 25 January 1963.

7. Ambassador David Ormsby-Gore (right) chatting with John F. Kennedy in April 1962. After the Anglo-American meetings, the Prime Minister noted in his diary that the British ambassador was in a unique position because he was 'very close' to the President, and an intimate friend of his brother.

8. April 1960: The first meeting in Saigon between Robert Thompson (left), then still Malaya's Permanent Secretary of Defence, and the South Vietnamese President.

9. Roger Hilsman of the State Department being interviewed by a Japanese journalist in June 1963. Hilsman developed a 'Strategic Concept' for Vietnam that was in part based on Robert Thompson's ideas.

10. Desmond Palmer (left), the deputy head of BRIAM, accompanied Thompson (right) on most of his tours through Vietnam between 1961 and 1964.

11. Robert Thompson with Jock Hindmarsh (centre) who was BRIAM's expert on police training.

12. Sharpened bamboo stakes placed in moats were often used as a protective barrier against PLAF attacks. Here soldiers of the ARVN's 7th Division place the stakes in a moat around an outpost in January 1963.

13. Bamboo fence around a strategic hamlet

14. 'Volunteer workers' pile up barbed wire and steel fence posts in July 1961, shortly after the inauguration of the strategic hamlet programme.

15. Strategic hamlet in the delta province of Long An in January 1963. Many hamlets were poorly built, and, as the British military attaché put it, 'more suited to fencing the cattle in than the Vietcong out'.

16. The strategic hamlet of Buon Chay, 24 miles north of Dalat. More than 400 Montagnards were resettled here in January 1963.

17. Particularly in his first two years in Vietnam Robert Thompson (left) never got tired of explaining his concepts to ARVN officers.

18. A young trainee of the self defence force signs for his equipment at a training camp in Thua Thien Province in July 1963.

19. Robert Thompson talking to members of the Village Committee at a strategic hamlet in the delta province of Phuoc Tuy in August 1962.

20. South Vietnamese soldier aboard an American CH-21 helicopter prior to going into combat in the delta provinces in February 1963.

21. Edward Peck (centre) of the Foreign Office visiting Vietnam. The US army took him and Thompson to Go Cong Province and showed them villages that had recently been recaptured from the PLAF.

22. Ngo Dinh Nhu (left), President Diem's powerful and ruthless brother, welcomes Robert Kennedy at Tan Son Nhut Airport. Also present: William Trueheart (right) of the US embassy who became Robert Thompson's close friend.

23. Enthusiastic citizens of Saigon surround a victorious tank after the army coup against Ngo Dinh Diem in November 1963.

24. Ambassador Gordon Etherington-Smith (centre) with General Duong Van Minh (to his right), the first of many military leaders after the coup against Diem. Left of the ambassador is his military attaché, Colonel Lee.

also repeated his complaints about the administrative weaknesses of the RVN but expressed hope that he might be able to influence the Saigon government to adopt reforms. It would be, however, a mistake to press forward with too many reforms at one time. The priority had to be the establishment of a security system for the villages, the rest could come later.

Thompson's visit to Washington demonstrated the remarkable closeness of Anglo-American relations with regard to Vietnam. Counter-insurgency had become a widely accepted concept in Washington, not least because it fit perfectly into Kennedy's new military doctrine of flexible response.[133] Therefore, Thompson's advice on Malayan lines was welcome. After initial problems, the British and Americans coordinated their advice to the RVN government. Increasingly Thompson's problem was not American resistance to his suggestions, but South Vietnamese. This, in turn, strengthened Anglo-American cooperation as the foreign advisers in Saigon had to deal with the same difficulty: Diem would appear to accept their advice, but then either fail to implement it or alter it and do it the Vietnamese way.

THE RVN'S STRATEGIC HAMLET PROGRAMME

Indeed, the British soon realized that the Diem regime was not inclined to adopt all aspects of the delta plan. In late 1961 the South Vietnamese had appeared to welcome Thompson's ideas. Diem had indicated his interest in Thompson's concept for the clearing of the delta in November, and a few weeks later Diem's brother Ngo Dinh Nhu and Nguyen Dinh Thuan, the Secretary at the Presidency, had expressed their support for BRIAM and praised the 'excellent advice' the British were giving.[134] Consequently, Thompson drafted a policy directive of the delta plan for the South Vietnamese President in January. Having gained American approval, it was put to the South Vietnamese in February.[135] The directive combined all the aspects of anti-guerrilla warfare that Thompson had previously put forward in the delta plan, including strategic hamlets, civic action, clearly defined roles for the self-defence corps, the civil guard and ARVN, a limited programme of food denial, and the introduction of identity cards, curfews, and prohibited zones. Above all, the plan called for the complete coordination of all civil and military action. These measures were to start in several priority areas within the delta and were designed to control, protect, and win over the Vietnamese peasants, gain the necessary intelligence to isolate the NLF forces from the population and break its organization

---

[133] John L. Gaddis, *Strategies of Containment: A Critical Appraisal of U.S. National Security Policy* (New York: Oxford University Press, 1987), 237–50.

[134] Minute by McGhie (FO). 25.1.62. PRO: FO 371/166699, DV1015/26. Record of meeting with Thuan by Burrows (Saigon) 30.1.62. Ibid. DV1015/36.

[135] Telegram 288: White (London) to Wellington. 8.2.62. NZNA: PM 478/4/1, part 14. Despatch 14: Hohler (Saigon) to FO. 28.2.62. PRO: FO 371/166701, DV1015/64/G. Embtel 1159: Trueheart (Saigon) to State Department. 9.3.62. USNA: RG 59, Central Files, 751k.5/3-962. Despatch 431: Mendenhall (Saigon) to State Department. 16.4.62. Ibid. 751k.5/4-1662.

within rural communities. The overall aim was to establish and maintain 'white' areas clear of NLF forces.[136]

Simultaneously, the Americans in Vietnam had developed a concept called the 'Outline Plan for Counterinsurgency Operations', which was considered to be consonant with the delta pacification plan. Yet only BRIAM's plan was submitted to the South Vietnamese government. The Americans feared that it would hamper the implementation of the approved Anglo-American counterinsurgency concepts if the Saigon government was confronted with too many plans simultaneously.[137] The Americans did not foresee, however, that the South Vietnamese themselves would take the initiative.

On 3 February 1962 Diem signed a decree establishing an inter-ministerial committee for strategic hamlets. The task of this body was to develop a national plan for securing the villages in Vietnam.[138] The decree took the British by surprise and the little they knew about the new policy caused concern. Although the South Vietnamese seemed to have incorporated some key features of Thompson's ideas, the ambitious aim of starting the programme all over Vietnam worried the British embassy. Thompson found the administrative arrangements of the strategic hamlet programme disturbing. He went to see Thuan at the presidency and told him that the planned inter-ministerial committee would only lead to eternal wrangles over policy. Instead, one ministry should be in charge of making political decisions and a committee should implement this policy.[139]

By the end of February, ambassador Hohler expressed his alarm about the developments in the RVN in a long dispatch to the Foreign Office. He pointed out that the South Vietnamese were pressing ahead with the creation of strategic hamlets without any effective coordination. By establishing hamlets at a great rate lacking any interdependent basis and often in areas where they could not be defended, their whole object was being compromised and they were becoming worse than useless. Hohler believed that his American colleague was worried about the situation, too, particularly about the ascendancy of Diem's brother Nhu within the framework of the strategic hamlet programme. Ngo Dinh Nhu was Diem's closest adviser, and western observers regarded him as a sinister and brutal man. While ostensibly accepting the delta plan, Nhu's intention to reform the social, economic, and administrative structure of South Vietnam was in Hohler's view incompatible with Anglo-American advice.[140] Frederick Warner echoed the ambassador's worries and even questioned Nhu's mental sanity. Nhu believed that his idea of promoting a new ideology of 'personalism' in the villages

---

[136] Draft Paper by the Head of the British Advisory Mission (Thompson). Undated. FRUS: 1961–1963, ii, Vietnam 1962, 102–9.

[137] Despatch 429: Mendenhall (Saigon) to State Department. 16.4.62. USNA: RG 59, Central Files, 751k.5/4-1662.

[138] Review of Status of Civic Action in Vietnam. Enclosure 1 to a paper prepared by the Special Group (CI). 7.3.62. FRUS: 1961–1963, ii, Vietnam 1962, 205. Military Attaché's summary report for February/March 1962 by Colonel Lee. 25.4.62. PRO: FO 371/1667474, DV1201/15/G.

[139] Letter: Burrows (Saigon) to Secondé (FO). 14.2.62. PRO: FO 371/166700, DV1015/44.

[140] Despatch 14: Hohler (Saigon) to FO. 28.2.62. PRO: FO 371/166701, DV1015/64/G.

would overcome the attraction of communism. This proved in Warner's view that he was 'slightly round the bend'.[141]

In mid-March ambassador Hohler requested a meeting with Diem. He stressed that he was anxious to see the delta plan put into operation and declared that it would be a very positive thing if a beginning were made by clearing one province, so that it could be declared 'white'. This would be very helpful to the Americans in Saigon as they were under heavy pressure from Washington to achieve results. Diem remained non-committal and warned, ominously but without going into details, that some people drew false deductions from the Malayan emergency, mainly about the length of such an operation. In contrast to previous meetings with the British he did not criticize the Americans. Instead, he referred in very warm terms to US aid and advice.[142] The South Vietnamese had no intention of rejecting British advice openly, but Diem's positive attitude to Thompson's ideas of late 1961 appears to have evaporated as soon as the South Vietnamese President was confronted with concrete British proposals. The Foreign Office concluded with disappointment that Diem continued to follow his own ideas and chose either to ignore Anglo-American advice completely, or to select only the elements that pleased him.[143]

Yet it was typical of the South Vietnamese not to allow western advisers to become completely disillusioned. Just two days after Hohler's meeting with Diem, the South Vietnamese president approved the delta plan, albeit with some changes. For the most part Diem followed BRIAM's draft directive in his 'Special Instruction on the Plan to Restore Security in the Third Tactical Zone', the official South Vietnamese title of the delta plan. However, very important aspects of Thompson's draft were omitted. Thompson had put emphasis on three factors for the successful pacification of the delta area: first, the complete coordination of all civil and military action; second, the prompt payment of compensation for damage to property or loss of life, and third, a clear chain of command. None of these three factors was mentioned in Diem's version of the delta plan. What is more, in Thompson's concept the ARVN was to keep the NLF forces off-balance and under pressure, yet the South Vietnamese wanted the army also to carry out sweeping actions, something Thompson regarded as completely useless.[144] It became clear that the nationwide strategic hamlet programme was Diem's first priority. Article one of Diem's 'Special Instruction' pointed out that the decree merely established a priority plan within the framework of national pacification. The last paragraph therefore stressed the need to remain vigilant in other parts of the country.[145]

---

[141] Telegram 1917: Shann (London) to EA Canberra. 3.5.62. AUSNA: A1209/80, file 62/482, part 1.

[142] Note by Hohler on his conversation with Diem. 14.3.62. PRO: FO 371/166702, DV1015/84.

[143] 'Recent developments in Southeast Asia'. Blue FO minute for Lord Lansdowne. 21.3.62. PRO: FO 371/166353, D1015/10.

[144] For Thompson's views on military sweeps, see Thompson, Make for the Hills, 124.

[145] Diem's decree, dated 16 March 1962, and entitled 'Special Instructions on the Plan to Restore Security in the Third Tactical Zone' was transmitted to Washington as an enclosure to despatch 431: Mendenhall (Saigon) to State Department. 16.4.62. USNA: RG 59, Central Files, 751k.5/4-1662. The

Despite these changes the British ambassador welcomed Diem's limited approval of the delta plan and hoped that its implementation would start soon.[146] Thompson was also encouraged by this development. Accompanying a party of Vietnamese civilian and military officials headed by Diem's brother Nhu he inspected newly constructed strategic hamlets north of Saigon on 19 March 1962. Thompson later conveniently forgot this encounter with Nhu and claimed that he had never met him.[147] At the time, however, he told the Australian ambassador that he found the journey north with Nhu a heartening experience, not only because the strategic hamlets were well constructed but because Nhu spoke throughout the day as if he had understood all elements of the delta plan and realized the importance of applying all these elements comprehensively.[148] Thompson was still hoping that the strategic hamlet programme would be integrated into the delta plan, but he was aware that Diem's approval of his plan was just the first step. While Diem had signed the South Vietnamese version of BRIAM's draft instruction, he had not approved the additional implementing instructions of the plan that Thompson had also drafted. During his stay in Washington in April, Thompson expressed his concern about the possibility that the Saigon government would modify these instructions and water down his concept still further.[149]

The British embassy in Saigon shared Thompson's worries. In April and May 1962, when Thompson was first in Washington and then on leave in England, ambassador Hohler and his team became convinced that the South Vietnamese had no intention of implementing BRIAM's concepts. One reason for this was that President Diem decided to make Colonel Hoang Van Lac responsible for the implementation of the delta plan. According to Colonel L. H. Lee, the British military attaché in Saigon, this was an unfortunate appointment because Lac was not 'overburdened with brains'.[150] The Australian ambassador, too, was critical of Lac. He had met him in his earlier post as province chief in Rach Gia and had witnessed him letting his deputy 'take the roasting' from visiting Vietnamese parliamentarians for maladministration of flood relief in the province.[151] After his appointment as special commissioner for delta pacification Lac remained 'singularly elusive' and, despite much telephoning by BRIAM, he managed to evade meeting members of the British mission for weeks.[152] The Americans had more luck. They met Lac twice in early April and Nolting's deputy Trueheart even got the impression that Lac was intelligent and straightforward. However, True-

---

decree without the covering despatch is printed in FRUS: 1961–1963, ii, Vietnam 1962, 238–44. For BRIAM's original plan, see ibid. 102–9.

[146] Letter: Hohler (Saigon) to Peck (FO). 29.3.62. PRO: FO 371/166702, DV1015/91/G.
[147] Thompson, *Make for the Hills,* 135.
[148] Savingram 25: Hill (Saigon) to EA Canberra. 22.3.62. AUSNA: A1838/346, file TS696/8/4, part 1.
[149] Memorandum: Cottrell (Vietnam Task Force) to Harriman. 6.4.62. FRUS: 1961–1963, ii, Vietnam 1962, 311–15.
[150] Letter: Lee (Saigon) to Jones (WO). 12.4.62. PRO: FO 371/166747, DV1201/12.
[151] Savingram 36: Hill (Saigon) to EA Canberra. 1.5.62. AUSNA: A1838/287, file 2481/5, part 4.
[152] Letter: Lee (Saigon) to Jones (WO). 12.4.62. PRO: FO 371/166747, DV1201/12.

heart realized that it would take Lac a lot of time to assemble his staff. Thus, the implementation of the delta plan did not seem imminent.[153]

In April 1962 the strategic hamlet programme received more and more attention and publicity, making it the order of the day. With suspicion the British noticed that Diem's brother Nhu was asserting himself increasingly as the driving force behind the programme.[154] In London, the Southeast Asia department of the Foreign Office noted that the signs of Nhu's malignant influence on the programme were all too apparent. It was feared that British advice would be misapplied to fit Nhu's ideas of a social revolution and therefore for the wrong motives, producing a further crumbling of the social fabric of the South Vietnamese villages.[155] BRIAM maintained that there was no ideological problem in the RVN if the peasants were given security. The real danger was that strategic hamlets were mushrooming around the country with little regard for proper siting or defence. Nhu's approach was bound to leave the counter-insurgency effort dispersed and discredited over the whole country with mediocre or worse results.[156] Still in England, Thompson also criticized Diem's handling of the strategic hamlet programme. In his view, it showed the weakness of the regime, which tended to seize on Diem's pet project at any one time to the exclusion of other important policies, and, when it no longer occupied the centre of stage, it would be dropped. This could happen to the strategic hamlet programme because hamlets were being proclaimed all over the country at once, and the failure to work slowly outwards from a secure area could only lead to defeat and disillusionment.[157]

Naturally, the British were worried that BRIAM would get the blame when things started to go wrong. 'Operation Sunrise', the attempt to clear a corridor to the north of Saigon which was considered a key NLF communication route, was a case in point. With 'Sunrise' the strategic hamlet programme was inaugurated. The operation was of purely American origin and owed nothing to BRIAM's advice. It got off to a bad start because it was launched in NLF-controlled areas. One aim was to resettle the population in newly created secure villages, but the male population had disappeared before they could be rounded up into the new hamlets. The Foreign Office noted with some concern that the *New York Times* was linking this operation with BRIAM, although Thompson had been opposed to it.[158] Lord Home was briefed prior to his departure for talks in Washington in April that it was particularly alarming that the NLF forces, after having suffered reverses in early 1962, seemed to have now regained the initiative. Although British advice was apparently accepted by Diem, the delta plan, Home was informed, seemed to

---

[153] Embtel 1289: Nolting (Saigon) to State Department. 10.4.62. FRUS: 1961–1963, ii, Vietnam 1962, 318–20.

[154] Minute by McGhie (FO). 3.4.62. PRO: FO 371/166702, DV1015/88. Report for April 1962 by Hopton (Service Attaché, Saigon). 1.5.62. AUSNA: A1838/283, file 3014/12/4, part 1.

[155] Minute by McGhie (FO). 10.4.62. PRO: FO 371/166702, DV1015/100.

[156] Savingram 36: Hill (Saigon) to EA Canberra. 1.5.62. AUSNA: A1838/287, file 2481/5, part 4.

[157] Memorandum: Jermyn (London) to EA Wellington. 8.5.62. NZNA: PM 478/4/1, part 15.

[158] *New York Times*, 27.3.62. Minute by McGhie (FO). 10.4.62. PRO: FO 371/166702, DV 1015/100.

have been shelved in favour of a scheme for the creation of hundreds of strategic hamlets devised by the 'unpopular and powerful' Ngo Dinh Nhu.[159]

By mid-May, ambassador Hohler was completely disillusioned. He found the security situation in the RVN to be worse than ever. Nhu was pressing ahead with the strategic hamlet programme and the Americans, desperate for immediate success, were planning and executing military operations, like 'Sunrise', to supplement the programme. On 7 May a further American-inspired operation codenamed 'Sea Swallow' was launched, which Hohler at least considered a better concept. The main reason for Hohler's disillusionment was that there was no room for the implementation of the delta plan because of the prominence of the strategic hamlet programme and the American preoccupation with operations 'Sunrise' and 'Sea Swallow'. All that could be hoped for was the application of BRIAM's concepts in one or two small areas. Nonetheless, Hohler wanted BRIAM to continue its work. It had been a political asset and had greatly strengthened British influence with the United States and the Vietnamese. He hoped that BRIAM's expertise could be used in other ways and that its experience would be most valuable when applied to the improvement of strategic hamlets.[160]

The absence of Thompson made it very difficult for the British to maintain their influence with the South Vietnamese. Ambassador Hohler eventually managed to ask Thuan about the relation between the delta plan and the strategic hamlet programme. The reply was discouraging. Thuan told Hohler that the Vietnamese National Security Council had decided to incorporate the delta plan into the strategic hamlet programme. This information led Hohler to postpone his leave and make a last attempt at rescuing the plan by asking the Americans for help. The British embassy in Washington also approached the State Department on 21 May and informed it about the difficulties over the delta plan. Apparently Washington was not aware of these difficulties. The State Department cabled to Saigon that it would be concerned if the delta plan had indeed been shelved and instructed the US embassy to encourage the South Vietnamese 'very strongly' to stick with the delta plan, and to support ambassador Hohler's attempts to keep the Saigon government on track.[161]

The Americans in Saigon immediately replied and mentioned that the British had also approached them. Nolting reported the US embassy had already discussed the delta plan with Colonel Lac and had discovered that his organizational concept for counter-insurgency operations in the delta had not been accepted yet. This was most discouraging and the Americans therefore sought an interview with Thuan to try to determine the South Vietnamese position.[162] William Trueheart subsequently met Thuan on 24 May. Thuan confirmed that the strategic hamlet programme would go forward throughout the country and

---

[159] FO brief for Washington talks. 19.4.62. PRO: FO 371/166353, D1015/8.
[160] Despatch 25: Hohler (Saigon) to FO. 16.5.62. PRO: FO 371/166704, DV1015/129.
[161] Deptel 1367: Rusk to Saigon. 22.5.62. FRUS: 1961–1963, ii, Vietnam 1962, 414–15.
[162] Embtel 1504: Nolting (Saigon) to State Department. 23.5.62. Ibid. 426–7.

that the delta plan would not have first priority. Instead, it had been decided to make Colonel Lac a member of the strategic hamlets coordinating committee and to give him responsibility for the construction of strategic hamlets in the delta area. Thuan could see nothing inconsistent between the delta plan and the strategic hamlet programme. After all, he claimed, the delta plan was a plan to establish strategic hamlets in the delta. Trueheart told Thuan that he found this development disturbing for two reasons. First, the delta plan called not only for the construction of strategic hamlets but also for the closest coordination between civil and military authorities at every level. No such coordination was apparent. Second, without focusing on geographical priority areas it would be almost impossible to plan American support for counter-insurgency operations. Thuan did not seem to accept this criticism and asked Trueheart if he did not think that 'things were going well'. Trueheart agreed that there was 'real momentum' behind the strategic hamlet programme. Nonetheless he expressed his fear that many of the newly constructed strategic hamlets in exposed areas were in danger of being overrun. At the end of the conversation Thuan stressed that he recognized the importance of priorities and coordination, and he asked Trueheart not to despair. 'I said I never dispaired [*sic*],' Trueheart closed his record of the conversation.[163]

Yet the British ambassador in Saigon did despair. In another bleak dispatch he described Diem's authoritarian and uncompromising nature and his dislike of the Americans. He pointed out that those who wielded the real power over the RVN regarded the British with mistrust as well. Hohler continued:

Even if we were to help Vietnam on a far larger scale than at present, there would be little real confidence in us. Such assistance as we are able to give is used in a characteristically Vietnamese way: President Diem has formally ratified proposals for the conduct of war put forward by the highly experienced Advisory mission (BRIAM); those elements in these proposals which suit his book are being adopted; the rest is quietly being discarded. President Diem's attitude to Mr. Thompson is courteous, and he often sings BRIAM's praises; but at the same time he has already decided on the areas to which he will give priority and the general strategy he will follow.[164]

Hohler's new deputy, Reginald Burrows, shared this view. He complained that the strategic hamlet programme was full of unrealistic proposals and showed the confused state of mind of the Saigon government in regard to counter-insurgency. In his view the strategic hamlet programme did reflect BRIAM's ideas but merely on a selective basis and with alterations that considerably weakened them. 'It would be dangerous to attribute to BRIAM the paternity of a child that may yet go astray', Burrows concluded.[165]

---

[163] Memorandum of a conversation between Thuan and Trueheart. 24.5.62. Ibid. 428–30. Trueheart's concerns about the lack of coordination between civil and military authorities and the absence of priority areas were cabled to the State Department in Embtel 1550: Nolting (Saigon) to State Department. 4.6.62. Ibid. 434–7.

[164] Despatch 30: Hohler (Saigon) to FO. 5.6.62. PRO: FO 371/166704, DV1015/143.

[165] Letter: Burrows (Saigon) to Secondé (FO). 30.5.62. PRO: FO 371/166748, DV1201/24.

Not only did the strategic hamlet programme turn out to be a failure in late 1963, but many also regarded it as a British-Malayan concept. Strategic hamlets had been built during the Malayan emergency, they played a prominent role in the delta plan, and therefore many observers, and scholars, pointed to Robert Thompson as the originator of this programme—and even the recent studies by David Kaiser and Lawrence Freedman underscore this myth.[166] Thompson did advocate the construction of strategic hamlets, it is true, but in a different framework. In fact, the South Vietnamese government cleverly used the introduction of the term 'strategic hamlet' by BRIAM for its own long-standing desire to control the rural population. The Saigon government had made some attempts at resettling peasants before Thompson entered the scene, and some province chiefs had established some defended hamlets on their own initiative well before BRIAM took up its work.

The ill-fated agroville programme of 1959–60 had demonstrated the South Vietnamese government's eagerness to extend its direct control in the countryside well before the Thompson mission drafted the delta plan. The curtailment of the agroville scheme did not mean that President Diem and his brother Nhu had buried the idea of resettling the peasants. Diem showed this as early as November 1960 when he asked Field Marshal Templer about details of the Malayan new villages. Although the strategic hamlet programme was publicly announced as late as February 1962, the Saigon government had indicated much earlier, even before the Thompson mission had been approved, that it was hoping to revive the idea of extending its presence down to the hamlet level and improving the physical security of the rural population. In July 1961 Nhu informed ambassador Hohler that the agroville scheme was being resumed with some modifications.[167] Nhu did not elaborate on this and it remained unclear what this revival would be about. But clearly the RVN was actively, and without the encouragement of British advisers, thinking about ways to extend its influence in the countryside. Further proof was that Diem readily agreed that the villages would be the major battlefields in countering the insurgency when he talked with Thompson in November 1961.[168]

According to the Americans in Saigon the strategic hamlet programme was a South Vietnamese initiative. Neither ambassador Nolting nor his colleagues thought that the British had inspired the programme.[169] An American paper prepared in February 1962 attempted to trace the origins of the programme. It did not

[166] Kaiser, *American Tragedy*, 167–8. Lawrence Freedman, *Kennedy's Wars: Berlin, Cuba, Laos, and Vietnam* (New York: Oxford University Press, 2000), 336. See also Larry Cable, *Conflict of Myths*, 197–8; Leslie Gelb and Richard K. Betts, *The Irony of Vietnam: The System Worked* (Washington, DC: Brookings Institution, 1979), 85; Hamilton, *Art of Insurgency*, 142; Herring, *America's Longest War*, 85; Hunt, *Pacification*, 21; Khong, *Analogies at War*, 92; Douglas Kinnard, *The Certain Trumpet: Maxwell Taylor and the American Experience in Vietnam* (Washington, DC: Brassey's, 1991), 108–9; Harry G. Summers, *On Strategy: A Critical Analysis of the Vietnam War* (Novato, Calif.: Presidio Press, 1984), 101.

[167] Letter: Hohler (Saigon) to Warner (FO). 29.7.61. PRO: FO 371/160125, DV1022/2.

[168] Letter: Thompson (BRIAM) to McGhie (FO). 27.11.61. PRO: FO 371/160119, DV1015/258.

[169] Frederick Nolting Oral History, 57. JFKL: John F. Kennedy Oral History Program.

mention the British, nor did the Americans in Saigon see a link between the South Vietnamese programme and the Malayan emergency. Instead, the US view was that some South Vietnamese province administrations had started with the construction of defended hamlets in early 1961, apparently as a 'truly spontaneous' reaction to communist attacks.[170] Similarly, the Australian service attaché also noted the growing emphasis on the construction of strategic villages throughout the country between September and December 1961, before BRIAM could have had any impact. In Binh Dinh province alone eighteen villages were established.[171]

Ung Van Khiem, Foreign Minister of the DRV, also began to be concerned about the establishment of strategic hamlets before Thompson and his team could make their recommendations. Khiem informed the ambassadors of other socialist countries in October 1961 that the ARVN had proved unable to establish permanent positions in NLF strongholds despite its ability to undertake military sweeps there. Hanoi believed that the regrouping of peasants in strategic hamlets was Saigon's reaction to this military failure.[172] The NLF's immediate reaction to both, the RVN's attempts to concentrate the peasant population and the increased American involvement in the wake of the Taylor mission, was to avoid a further escalation of the conflict. Therefore, the NLF forces were in early 1962 ordered not to expand the area under their control—roughly three-quarters of the RVN according to Hanoi—but to consolidate it. Instead of mounting further attacks and provoke a more massive American reaction, the NLF forces were to regroup and wait for the right moment to resume their activities.[173]

The Americans noted that following Thompson's return from home leave in June the British embassy appeared 'less bearish' about the situation in the RVN than it had been.[174] Thompson was still hoping that his personal influence on Diem might lead to the implementation of the delta plan within the framework of the strategic hamlet programme, which clearly had become the Saigon government's top priority during his absence.[175] Colonel Lac had finally started his work in May and produced an organization chart for the coordination of pacification.[176] Thompson's first priority was to persuade the Vietnamese to accept

[170] Despatch 334: Barbour (Saigon) to State Department. 12.2.62. USNA: RG 59, Central Files, 751k.00/2-1262. Ken Post noted in his study of counter-insurgency in the RVN that the origins of the strategic hamlet programme were unclear (Post, *Revolution, Socialism and Nationalism in Vietnam*, iv. *The Failure of Counter-Insurgency in the South* (Aldershot: Dartmouth, 1990), 119).

[171] Report for September and October 1961 by Hopton (Service Attaché, Saigon). 14.11.61. Report for November and December 1961 by Hopton. 11.1.62. Both in AUSNA: A1838/283, file 3014/12/4, part 1.

[172] Minute 248/61 by Nohr (Hanoi). 28.10.61. MfAA: A8570, ff. 101–7. Note for the record by Wenning (Hanoi). 30.10.61. Ibid.: ff. 108–13.

[173] 'Information' by Pommerening (Hanoi). 23.11.61. Note for the record by Hegen (Beijing). 5.1.62. Minute 39/62 by Nohr (Hanoi). 30.1.62. All in MfAA: A8570, ff. 114–15, 123, 133–7.

[174] Embtel 1574: Nolting (Saigon) to State Department. 7.6.62. USNA: RG 59, Central Files, 751k.00/6-762.

[175] In his memoirs Thompson stressed that his delta plan got lost in the strategic hamlet programme. Thompson, *Make for the Hills*, 129.

[176] The chart is attached to despatch 431: Mendenhall (Saigon) to State Department. 28.5.62. USNA: RG 59, Central Files, 751k.5/5-2862.

some changes to these administrative arrangements and he started discussions with Thuan. These talks proved productive and Diem accepted on 9 June the changes proposed by Thompson. Colonel Lac was made executive secretary of a more powerful strategic hamlets committee, with the divisional commanders to become chairmen of coordinating committees in each area of operations. The British and Americans were to work with Colonel Lac in drawing up a list of priority areas. US ambassador Nolting believed that this organizational change improved the prospects for the systematic clearing of the delta considerably.[177] Thompson met Diem on 11 June, and the President himself confirmed this encouraging development.[178]

THE 'PACIFICATION PLAN'

After touring the delta provinces Thompson submitted a revised version of the delta plan in July. In the covering letter he let the South Vietnamese know that the strategic hamlet programme had impressed him. He praised the improved morale of ARVN and the achievements of the self-defence force in particular.[179] In the paper itself, which was simply entitled 'Pacification Plan', Thompson repeated the major points he had made in the delta plan. He began by stressing that a violent reaction by the NLF forces was to be expected. Therefore, the strategic hamlets had to form a solid block of mutually supporting settlements, which could be rescued by the civil guard or ARVN if under heavy attack.[180]

He argued that in order to gain the support of the rural population it was important that not more than 20 to 25 per cent of the peasants were regrouped. Again, Thompson made it clear that the envisaged security framework could not be established simultaneously throughout the country because government resources were limited. Moreover, priority areas had to be selected in order to achieve an early success in one major area. This would inspire confidence in the successful outcome of the war throughout the country. Thompson conceded that limited advances could be made with the resources available in the narrow coastal strips of the provinces in tactical zones I and II. Moreover, the Montagnard tribesmen in the High Plateau had to be supported. However, Thompson still maintained that the major advance could only be achieved in the delta as it was here that the final aim of establishing and maintaining 'white areas' could be

---

[177] Embtel 1574: Nolting (Saigon) to State Department. 7.6.62. USNA: RG 59, Central Files, 751k.00/6-762. Embtel 1614: Nolting (Saigon) to State Department. 15.6.62. Ibid. 751k.00/6-1562.

[178] Letter: Burrows (Saigon) to Warner (FO). 12.6.62. PRO: FO 371/166748, DV1201/30.

[179] Letter: Thompson (BRIAM) to Thuan (Secretary at the Presidency). 18.7.62. Ibid. DV1201/40. The letter indicated that Thompson submitted 20 copies of his paper to the South Vietnamese in French. The paper itself has not been found in the British record.

[180] 'Pacification Plan' by Thompson (BRIAM). Undated. HI: Lansdale Papers, folder: US Embassy Saigon, Senior Liaison Office, Subject File: British Advisory Mission, box 60. The references to the contents and certain paragraphs made in Thompson's letter of 18 July show that it was this paper that he submitted to the South Vietnamese in July.

realized first. 'The declaration of such areas', Thompson stated, '... will raise the morale of all the rural population, even in bad areas, because people everywhere will immediately realize that the Government is winning and that the final defeat of the Vietcong is only a matter of time.' He concluded rather ominously:

Only by a systematic and methodical approach to the whole problem with careful planning, well-judged timing and great attention to all detail will it be possible by a cumulative effect to get the ball rolling so that SUCCESS leads to KILLS, KILLS to CONFIDENCE, CONFIDENCE to better INTELLIGENCE and INTELLIGENCE to greater SUCCESSES and more KILLS [emphases in the original].[181]

Thompson's paper showed that he had become resigned to the fact that BRIAM had to give its advice within the framework of the strategic hamlet programme. Nothing could be done about the South Vietnamese determination to construct strategic hamlets throughout the country. Nonetheless, Thompson continued to work for a systematic approach, which was to start in the delta. In that he was not alone. Just two days before Thompson submitted his pacification plan, the Vietnam working group in the State Department expressed its concern that the Saigon government's failure to decide on any priority areas for the strategic hamlet programme might prove fatal, and was wondering what Thompson's views were on this.[182]

The US embassy in Saigon reassured Washington that, with regard to priority areas, considerable progress had been made. President Diem raised the question of priorities himself in a meeting with the Americans on 19 July. Diem's views were strikingly similar to Thompson's recommendations, almost as if he had read the Pacification Plan just prior to the meeting. He readily agreed that in general the programme should be started in the more secure areas and extended from there. The richest and most heavily populated parts of the delta, roughly the provinces mentioned in the delta plan, were to be tackled first. As an exception to this overall approach, priority was also to be given to the coastal plains of central Vietnam in tactical zones I and II. Here the NLF forces were particularly strong, perhaps strong enough to cut the RVN eventually into halves.[183]

The US embassy also believed that it had found a way to influence Saigon's choice of priority areas directly. Through the newly established American-owned Piaster fund the resources under US control were to be concentrated on areas which were considered most important in order to accelerate the pacification there. It was not regarded as a problem that this was unlikely to slow down the construction of strategic hamlets in non-priority areas. The Americans had come to the conclusion that the strategic hamlets were causing the communist problems, even if they were spread out too thinly in NLF-controlled parts of the country. This, the Americans in Saigon stressed, was also Thompson's view.[184]

[181] 'Pacification Plan' by Thompson (BRIAM). Ibid.
[182] Deptel 61: Rusk to Saigon. 16.7.62. USNA: RG 59, Central Files, 751k.5/7-1661.
[183] Embtel 84: Nolting (Saigon) to State Department. 20.7.62. FRUS: 1961–1963, ii, Vietnam 1962, 539–40.
[184] Ibid. See also Kaiser, *American Tragedy*, 172–3.

BRITISH AND AMERICAN OPTIMISM

Against the background of organizational changes and the more direct American influence on the selection of priority areas, the military situation was, in the eyes of western observers, rapidly improving. Ambassador Nolting found the progress of the strategic hamlet programme so encouraging that he informed Secretary of Defense McNamara accordingly at the Honolulu conference of 27 July.[185] Intelligence reports underscored this trend. From July 1962 the MACV's weekly and monthly intelligence estimates were passed to the British. Colonel L. H. Lee, the British military attaché, based his assessments largely on this information and he came to the conclusion that the NLF forces had lost in August 'on points'. He pointed out that two campaigns in the delta had been successful, that the South Vietnamese had now decided on the right priority areas and that of the two hundred strategic hamlets that had come under large-scale attacks only one had been overrun.[186]

In the light of this information, the British ambassador also moved away from his pessimistic assessments of April and May. He admitted in a talk with Ngo Dinh Nhu that the South Vietnamese had done well and that the strategic hamlet programme was developing much better than anticipated.[187] Faced with Nolting's growing optimism—the US ambassador even praised Nhu for his energetic approach to the strategic hamlet programme—Hohler thought it best to be encouraging and to refrain from showing doubts until the security situation 'clarifies one way or the other'.[188] Consequently, the Americans reported to Washington in late August 1962 that the British, like the US embassy, were much encouraged by the situation in Vietnam.[189]

In September, Hohler became even more optimistic, although he noted that there was still no progress towards the coordination of the military and civilian effort, that the psychological warfare continued to be chaotic, and that the standards of strategic hamlets varied from the impressive to the pitiful. However, Hohler believed that there was now a fair hope of ultimate military success for the Saigon government.[190] The British ambassador even went so far as to inform the Australian ambassador Hill that it seemed to be a distinct possibility that the prospect of a military victory would become a reality in the first half of 1963. Hill found this assessment 'rather optimistic'.[191] Hill's Australian colleague in London also noted that the Foreign Office had become much more optimistic about the struggle in Vietnam although there was no great deal of evidence for Whitehall's

---

[185] Letter: Hohler (Saigon) to Warner. 31.7.62. PRO: FO 371/166706, DV1015/165/G.

[186] Report for August 1962 by Colonel Lee (Saigon). 20.9.62. PRO: FO 371/166750, DV1201/69.

[187] Letter: Hohler (Saigon) to Warner. 1.8.62. PRO: FO 371/166706, DV1015/166/G.

[188] Letter: Hohler (Saigon) to Warner. 15.8.62. Ibid. DV1015/170/G.

[189] Embtel 210: Nolting (Saigon) to State Department. 28.8.62. USNA: RG 59, Central Files, 751k.00/8-2862.

[190] Despatch 45: Hohler (Saigon) to FO. 12.9.62. PRO: FO 371/166707, DV1015/187/G.

[191] Savingram 66: Hill (Saigon) to EA Canberra. 19.9.62. AUSNA: A4531/6, file 221/5/10, part 1.

positive assessment.[192] The Australian Joint Intelligence Committee supported Hill's cautious assessment. While it agreed that the capability of the South Vietnamese security forces had significantly improved and that the prospects of the strategic hamlet programme were encouraging, it was too early to believe that 1963 would show whether the insurgency could be overcome or not.[193]

Yet this is exactly what Robert Thompson claimed. In a conversation with Steven Weir, the newly appointed New Zealand ambassador to Saigon, in November he stressed that the eventual outcome of the war would become apparent in the spring of 1963. He also showed how much he himself had begun to identify with the struggle. Weir found it peculiar that Thompson was not talking about the South Vietnamese or Americans but stated that 'we' had stopped losing in Vietnam. Over the next six months there would be, in Thompson's view, a good chance of finding out if 'we' could win.[194]

Thompson's optimism of late 1962 seemed well founded. The DRV embassy in East Berlin admitted as early as June 1962 that the changed tactics of the South Vietnamese forces had caused several setbacks.[195] In July, the Foreign Ministry in Hanoi informed the East Germans that Diem's military forces were still superior. They had regained the initiative and the prospect of the NLF's military victory had become very remote.[196] In November, the East German military attaché in Hanoi reported his concern about the impact of the strategic hamlet programme on the Vietnamese peasants to the International Department of the Ministry for National Defence in East Berlin. He was convinced that at least a part of the peasants led a better and more comfortable life in the new settlements.[197] The situation became more difficult still when the PRC temporarily stopped its aid to the DRV because of its own economic problems. By December, Hanoi deemed a military victory impossible. The North Vietnamese were considering but eventually rejected the option of working for a reconvention of the Geneva conference until the military position of the NLF forces was stronger. Hanoi had no intention of negotiating from a position of weakness, and prepared for a long conflict.[198]

In late 1962 the British ambassador in Saigon, however, began to retreat from his earlier position of cautious optimism.[199] Hohler's stance reflected the view of

192 Telegram 4860: London to EA Canberra. 2.10.62. AUSNA: A1209/80, file 62/482, part 1.
193 JIC(Aust)(62)85 Revise. November 1962. AUSNA: A1209/80, file 62/482, part 1.
194 Memorandum: Weir (Bangkok) to EA Wellington. 19.11.62. NZNA: PM 478/4/1, part 15.
195 Minute 13/62 by Kittler (MfAA, Berlin). 5.6.62. MfAA: C1065/73.
196 Minutes 207/62 and 208/62 by Dreßler (Hanoi). 18.7.62 and 23.7.62. MfAA: A8570, f. 189–92.
197 Memorandum: Witt (Hanoi) to Auslandsabteilung des Ministeriums für Nationale Verteidigung (International Department of the Ministry of National Defence). 13.11.62. BArchMA: VA-01, 6462 Band 2.
198 'Information' on US Intervention to all socialist ambassadors. 27.9.62. Report by Nohr (Hanoi). 10.12.62. Both in MfAA: G17331. Reports based upon captured NLF documents in early 1963 support the evidence from the GDR archives. These documents showed that the new South Vietnamese tactics had dispelled hopes of a quick NLF victory and that negotiations had to be considered. See Report on SEATO Council Representatives restricted session on 23 January 1963. 4.2.62. NZNA: PM 478/4/1, part 16.
199 Savingram 10: Hohler (Saigon) to FO. 30.10.62. PRO: FO 371/166751, DV1201/84.

his military attaché, whose assessments had become less sanguine. Colonel Lee complained about the lack of unification of military and civil action and pointed out that in one week in October only one of eleven attacks on strategic hamlets had been beaten off. In December he spoke of a 'new phase' in South Vietnam as more and more hamlets came under attack, and noted that some had even surrendered without an attempt at resistance.[200] Ambassador Hohler concluded in his annual report for 1962 that victory for the NLF seemed to be ruled out as long as the lavish US support was maintained, and that the strategic hamlet programme, if properly applied, could lead to the eradication of the insurgents. However, he stressed that the overall strength of NLF forces had increased, and that President Diem had still a very long way to go to win the hearts and minds of his people.[201]

While Thompson remained satisfied with the progress in Vietnam, the Foreign Office became alarmed when they received news about the series of reverses the ARVN suffered in the first week of 1963, including the widely publicized military defeat at Ap Bac.[202] With regard to the military aspect ambassador Hohler did not share London's concerns. In his view the more immediate threat to the Diem government lay in the political field. Diem had never been a popular leader, the power base of his regime was very narrow, and he relied on the tight grip his security forces maintained in the country. The Eisenhower administration had tried to persuade Diem to introduce reforms in its last year in power, and so had Kennedy in late 1961, but Diem had not responded. Increasingly, the American press focused on the political shortcomings of Diem's repressive regime. Against this background the British ambassador found Diem's handling of the US press and the public relations aspect of the military setbacks in early 1963 simply deplorable. The danger was in his view that the US Congress would stop further appropriations for Vietnam if Diem did not manage to improve his relations with the American press.[203]

Hohler did not remain alone in his doubts about the significance of the political weaknesses of the Diem regime. Roger Hilsman shared these concerns, although he generally expressed agreement with the State Department's satisfaction about the progress in Vietnam. Most observers, however, concentrated on the military side of the conflict. The Pentagon concluded in March 1963 that the military situation had significantly improved over the previous six

[200] Letter: Lee (Saigon) to Jones (WO). 20.11.62. PRO: FO 371/166752, DV1201/91. Minute by Everard (FO). 7.12.61. Ibid. DV1201/87. Letter: Lee (Saigon) to Jones (WO). 12.12.62. Ibid. DV1201/99.

[201] Despatch 1: Hohler (Saigon) to FO. 2.1.63. PRO: FO 371/170088, DV1011/1. See also telegram 1: Hohler (Saigon) to FO. 3.1.63. PRO: FO 371/170131, DV1201/4. This despatch was also passed to the Australians in April 1963. See AUSNA: A1209/80, file 62/482, part 1.

[202] Memorandum: Jermyn (London) to EA Wellington. 9.1.63. NZNA: PM 478/4/1, part 16. See on Ap Bac: Kahin, *Intervention*, 142–3; Kaiser, *American Tragedy*, 180–5.

[203] Letter: Hohler (Saigon) to Warner (FO). 16.1.63. PRO: FO 371/170131, DV1201/4.

months.[204] The Australians and New Zealanders also believed that slow but steady progress was being made.[205]

'WE ARE NOW WINNING THE SHOOTING WAR'

Robert Thompson was the most optimistic of all observers. He had predicted in late 1962 that it would be possible in the spring of 1963 to determine whether the South Vietnamese could master the insurgency or not. And this is exactly what he did after a visit to the delta provinces in March 1963. Thompson forecast Diem's victory.[206] If the right pattern and direction of strategic hamlets were maintained, if BRIAM's surrender policy was exploited, and if a 'white area' was achieved by August, then, Thompson concluded, the RVN 'should be able to regain control of all the areas under V[iet]C[ong] control . . . by the end of the year or at the latest by the end of the next dry season'.[207]

Thompson did not only submit this report to President Diem. He was determined to spread his optimism among western observers and thereby create an atmosphere of confidence in the certainty of eventual victory. Shortly before Thompson left for Washington in late March, he told the Australians that the time had come to lay greater stress on social and economic benefits in the hamlets, and advised them to make changes to their provisions of material aid accordingly.[208] He sent a copy of his report to Australian ambassador Hill, and stressed in the covering letter that 'we are now winning the shooting war . . . The immediate need', he continued, 'is greater confidence both here and in the free world.'[209]

With this message of confidence Thompson travelled to Washington, and it was this optimism that he presented to President Kennedy on 4 April 1963. Thompson was well aware that there were many long-term problems, which had to be solved to establish a stable RVN. He saw four main dangers: the nature of the Diem regime, overt infiltration from the DRV, NLF subversion of strategic hamlets, and the South Vietnamese desire to build strategic hamlets too rapidly. The fourth was, in his view, the most dangerous point. While Thompson recognized that the narrow political support of the Diem regime did not make for long-term stability, he saw no alternative to Diem and believed the President's and Nhu's approach would achieve the right results in the short term.[210] Overall,

---

[204] Telegrams 282 and 648: Washington to EA Canberra. 29.1.63 and 11.3.63. Both in AUSNA: A1209/80, file 62/80, part 1.

[205] Memorandum: Shepherd (Canberra) to EA Wellington. 4.3.63. NZNA: PM 478/4/1, part 16.

[206] Memorandum on 'The Situation in South Vietnam' by Thompson (BRIAM) for Warner (FO). 11.3.63. PRO: FO 371/170100, DV1017/17.

[207] Memorandum 293: Hill (Saigon) to EA Canberra. 20.3.63. AUSNA: A4531/11, file 201/2/7A, part 4.

[208] Savingram 23: Hill (Saigon) to EA Canberra. 19.3.63. AUSNA: A1838/280, file 3014/10/15, part 3.

[209] Letter: Thompson (BRIAM) to Hill (Saigon). 18.3.63. AUSNA: A4531/11, file 201/2/7A, part 4.

[210] Memorandum on 'The Situation in South Vietnam' by Thompson (BRIAM) for Warner (FO). 11.3.63. PRO: FO 371/170100, DV1017/17.

Thompson was certain that progress had been made. Although he still harboured some doubts, he believed it was the right tactical approach to spread his 'we are winning' message. In a letter to the British High Commissioner in New Zealand he explained why he took such an optimistic stance:

The key to the present situation is confidence. The peasants are not going to stick their necks out unless they think they will be on the winning side. Naturally therefore I have to be optimistic if I am to influence events. You must play as if you are going to win. Anyone can sit back and send gloomy reports. We are I think in for a very slow year requiring a lot of hard foundation work before any real tangible or manifest improvement will show. Both the Americans and Viets [sic] are bad at this and all the time are seeking quick results which are generally quite meaningless minor local victories. We have to regain control and restore Government authority in the populated areas with our basic infrastructure secure. Then, given better organisation and coordinated action, you can eradicate the Vietcong cell organisation. It's as long a process getting all this across as doing it.[211]

Ambassador Hohler was obviously one of those who preferred to sit back and write more gloomy reports. He placed his agreement with Thompson's assessment in the region of 90 per cent. Yet his conclusions were quite different. The reason for his more reserved judgement, Hohler claimed, was that the embassy staff had to take into account the full flow of political and military information from all sources. Whereas BRIAM and the Americans had few, if any contacts with the French in Vietnam, the British embassy's sources included also the French embassy as well French colons who retained a wide range of contacts throughout the RVN.[212] Based on this information, Hohler believed that it was premature to claim that the shooting war was being won. He did not deny that the situation had improved, but all encouraging signs were offset by the steadily growing numerical strength of the NLF forces despite the enormous casualties which the Saigon government claimed to have inflicted on them.[213] According to SEATO estimates the number of communist insurgents rose from between 18,000 to 20,000 in August 1962 to between 22,000 to 24,000 in February 1963.[214] Moreover, Hohler was worried about the political weaknesses of the Diem government: corruption was widespread and inept officers were still appointed senior commanders on grounds of political reliability. Hohler repeated his conviction that the Diem government would fall within weeks if the United States withdrew its support. Although there was no immediate danger of this, it was not altogether unlikely in the medium term because of the bad handling of the American pressmen by the South Vietnamese and the personal vendetta of Ngo Dinh

[211] Extract from letter by Thompson (BRIAM). Undated. Enclosure to letter: Williams (Official Secretary, Government House) to McIntosh (EA Wellington). 27.5.63. NZNA: PM 478/4/1, part 16.
[212] Letter: Reginald Burrows to the author. 21.2.2002.
[213] Letter: Hohler (Saigon) to Peck (FO). 20.3.63. PRO: FO 371/170100, DV1017/17. See also memorandum 324: Hill (Saigon) to EA Canberra. 29.3.63. AUSNA: A4531/11, file 201/2/7A, part 4.
[214] EA Wellington brief for the SEATO Council meeting in Paris in April 1963. 1.4.63. NZNA: PM 478/4/1, part 16.

Nhu's wife against the US press.[215] As President Diem himself was not married, the beautiful and outspoken Madame Nhu played the role of the RVN's first lady. She had no understanding for the majority of the Vietnamese and ran an anti-vice campaign in Saigon, banning among other things public dancing.[216]

The Foreign Office noted with some concern that it was receiving contradictory reports on the situation in Vietnam. Frederick Warner, the head of the Southeast Asia Department, brought the different assessments of Thompson and Hohler to the attention of Lord Home. Warner attempted to strike a balance between BRIAM and the British embassy. He came to the conclusion that, although progress had been made, there was a long struggle ahead. He recognized the danger that the American public might lose patience with the Saigon government and expressed his hope that US aid would continue. As for the British, Warner thought it best if London continued with its policy and quietly gave advice and assistance through BRIAM.[217] Lord Home supported this and reiterated his support for the American stance in Vietnam. He minuted on Warner's submission: 'I hope the Americans can hold on.'[218]

While Thompson was on leave in April and May 1963, the British embassy continued to send pessimistic reports to London. Hohler pointed out that the highest number ever of 'Vietcong incidents' had been reported in March. He was also convinced that the strategic hamlet programme was going ahead too rapidly.[219] In May it became clear that there was no hope of declaring a 'white area' in the delta provinces of Vinh Long and Vinh Binh by the summer as Thompson had hoped.[220] The British military attaché underscored Hohler's criticism of the hamlet programme. In April 1963 the South Vietnamese announced that 5,917 of 11,143 planned strategic hamlets had been built. Many of these hamlets, Colonel Lee complained, had only flimsy and inadequate defences and were 'more suited to fencing the cattle in than the Vietcong out'.[221]

When Robert Thompson returned from his leave on 12 June, he did not only have to face his increasingly grim colleagues at the British embassy, for with the outbreak of the Buddhist crisis in May 1963, the political situation had dramatically changed. Before he left Saigon in March, Thompson had discounted the possibility of a *coup d'état*. Now he had to deal with a situation that would ultimately lead to the fall of Diem and his brother Nhu.[222]

---

[215] Memorandum 324: Hill (Saigon) to EA Canberra. 29.3.63. AUSNA: A4531/11, file 201/2/7A, part 4.

[216] Thompson, *Make for the Hills*, 136.

[217] Blue FO minute by Warner. 3.4.63. PRO: FO 371/170110, DV103145/19/G.

[218] Minute by Lord Home. 7.4.63. Ibid.

[219] Savingram 24: Hohler (Saigon) to FO. 4.4.63. PRO: FO 371/170133, DV1201/44.

[220] Letter: Palmer (BRIAM) to Warner (FO). 7.5.63. PRO: FO 371/170101, DV1017/22. Savingram 31: Hohler (Saigon) to FO. 8.5.63. PRO: FO 371/170133, DV1201/54.

[221] Summary report for April 1963 by Lee (Saigon). 14.5.63. PRO: FO 371/170134, DV1201/62.

[222] Memorandum by Thompson (BRIAM) for Warner (FO). 11.3.63. PRO: FO 371/170100, DV1017/17.

CONCLUSION

From a British point of view, BRIAM was a success story. Robert Thompson enjoyed a privileged relationship with the South Vietnamese President, although Diem did not follow his advice as closely as the British would have liked, and even pursued at times different policies behind Thompson's back. Yet the difficulties of the British ambassador in getting his views across to the Vietnamese when Thompson was on leave in the spring of 1962 demonstrate how important Thompson had become for the British.

Above all, the establishment of BRIAM helped, after initial problems, to improve Anglo-American relations in Vietnam. The Americans were more inclined to take the British into their confidence and, from July 1962, they shared their intelligence assessments with them. In Washington, the Kennedy administration became aware of Thompson's 'good work', and he was elevated to the status of most important 'independent' adviser, whose views were frequently sought. Indeed, the British tended to regard BRIAM mainly as a political asset that had strengthened British influence with the United States. Even when ambassador Hohler voiced doubts in May and June 1962 that BRIAM would have a useful impact on the security situation because of South Vietnamese reluctance to adopt the delta plan, he wanted BRIAM to continue its work as it had improved Anglo-American relations. It was also important that BRIAM continued to be a recognizable British effort, and it was therefore not surprising that the British embassy and BRIAM remained physically separate. When the embassy moved in the summer of 1962 into a new spacious building that had adequate room for Thompson and his team as well as all the modern amenities of the day, BRIAM remained in its French villa on Boulevard Cong Ly.[223]

With regard to Britain's allies in the region, Australia and New Zealand in particular, BRIAM sent out the intended message: Britain did care about Southeast Asia and it was doing what it could to prevent the fall of the Saigon government. It quickly became clear that Britain's decision to send the advisory mission before the massive influx of American aid and personnel put Thompson in an advantageous position. As other western countries, particularly Australia, looked for ways to expand their aid to the RVN, Thompson found himself in the position of influencing these aid programmes. His advice was not only sought by high-ranking British and American government officials, but the Australians and New Zealanders were also keen to get his assessment of the situation.

The strategic hamlet programme was a South Vietnamese initiative and its origins can be traced back to long before the British advisers arrived in Saigon. It was not based on Thompson's ideas, as is so widely believed. Yet Thompson certainly had an impact on the development of this programme. First, his delta plan made

---

[223] Memorandum 685: Woodberry (Saigon) to EA Canberra. 24.7.62. AUSNA: A4531/6, file 221/5/10, part 1.

the concept of strategic and defended hamlets more widely known and more acceptable, especially to the Americans. Second, even when it was clear that his
original concept for the delta would not be implemented, Thompson tried to
influence the strategic hamlet programme as best he could. With the help of
the Americans, the delta became one of the priority areas of the strategic hamlet
programme.

This development greatly encouraged Thompson. He began to identify with the
South Vietnamese and American war effort and claimed in March 1963 that victory was in sight. As evidence from East German archives suggests, the influx of US
material aid and personnel and the changed military tactics, including the building
of strategic hamlets, did indeed cause problems for the NLF forces. To predict
Saigon's victory, however, was obviously premature. Even if, as Thompson stated
in private, he had to be optimistic in order to influence events in Vietnam, he certainly did not have to go as far as he did and stake his credibility on the success of
the counter-insurgency effort. It seems rather as if Thompson had started down the
path so many Americans had already gone and would continue to go down in
Vietnam. Thompson decided, at least in the short run, to turn a blind eye to the de-
ficiencies of the Saigon government. He was satisfied with the partial implementation of his concepts, if only progress of some kind was being made. Although his
concept of counter-insurgency was based on the principle of cutting the link between the insurgents and their popular support among the peasants, he regarded
the insurgency as mainly a military struggle, and erroneously believed that the
Vietnamese peasants would reject communism.

The British embassy in Saigon took a slightly different stance. It was enthusiastic about the impact of BRIAM in Saigon and Washington, and ambassador
Hohler shared Thompson's belief in a Malayan approach to the problems in
Vietnam. However, the embassy did not lose sight of the political aspect of the
war, and neither the ambassador nor the military attaché were fooled by the stat-
istics of completed hamlets. In stressing the weaknesses of the Diem regime, the
embassy shared a belief that became increasingly prominent in the American
State Department: ultimate success could not be achieved with the unpopular
and ineffective Ngos in power.

Thompson's more sanguine assessment did at times influence the British ambassador, especially in the summer and autumn of 1962. However, from early
1963 the differences between Hohler's and Thompson's assessments started to
grow. There is no evidence in the records that there were personal differences between the two, and the Australian ambassador noted in March 1963 that Hohler
and Thompson continued to get on 'extremely well'.[224] However, Hohler's
deputy admitted that it was awkward for the embassy to have another body in
Saigon that the Foreign Office was listening to.[225] Increasingly, the two British

[224] Memorandum 324: Hill (Saigon) to EA Canberra. 29.3.63. AUSNA: A4531/11, file 201/2/7A,
part 4.
[225] Reginald Burrows in interview with the author. 14.2.2002.

missions focused on different problems. Thompson was preoccupied with the strategic hamlet programme in the delta and his surrender policy. Hohler was worried about the political weaknesses of the Saigon government, the bad press it received in the United States, and the devastating impact of the vast American aid on South Vietnam's economy.

The Foreign Office was at times concerned about the differing assessments it received from Saigon. However, it did nothing to arrive at an agreed British assessment of the situation. London was pleased with the political benefits of sending BRIAM. There was no reason to complain about Thompson's achievements. Yet the Foreign Office, like ambassador Hohler, did not lose sight of the political aspect of the war in Vietnam and was prepared to take Hohler's views into account. This political aspect was soon to be propelled to the fore: the Buddhist crisis began on 8 May, and escalated with the first self-immolation of a Buddhist monk in June. A political crisis had erupted that would lead to a major turning point of the war in Vietnam, the fall of Ngo Dinh Diem.

5

The Coup: Britain and the Fall of Ngo Dinh Diem

NGO DINH DIEM died in the back of an amphibious armoured personnel carrier on 2 November 1963. ARVN bullets killed his brother Nhu as well. On 3 November 1963, the Foreign Office received information from a 'reliable' source that Diem and Nhu were indeed dead. The source was Diem's niece, a certain Mrs Smith, former typist with the British Council Office in Saigon and married to a British Council lecturer. The new South Vietnamese authorities had asked the Smiths to identify their relatives. They were driven to the St Paul Hospital, saw the bodies, and confirmed that a single shot in the neck had killed Diem. His brother Nhu had been repeatedly shot in the back.[1] The coup and the death of Diem and Nhu sparked a wave of relief and rejoicing in Saigon. ARVN had never been so popular before. Young Vietnamese women garlanded South Vietnamese soldiers with fragrant flowers. 'The town was literally en fête', Robert Thompson noted.[2] The smiles had returned to the faces of Saigon's inhabitants, if only for a short period. After more than nine years the dark Diem era was over.

Given the authoritarian nature of his regime, it was no surprise that Diem never became a popular leader. With luck and American assistance he fought off serious challenges to his position in 1954 and 1955. Most of the plots against him in the following years were discovered early and thwarted. In November 1960, a coup led by junior officers almost succeeded. Twenty months later, in February 1962, Diem narrowly escaped an assassination attempt by two Vietnamese Air Force pilots who bombed the Presidential Palace. A further twenty months on, Diem's time was up. In the wake of the Buddhist crisis his popularity sank to an all-time low. He lost Washington's support. He lost control of some of the most loyal generals of the ARVN. When the Gia Long Palace was surrounded by hostile troops, Diem and Nhu tried to escape. Realizing the hopelessness of their situation, they surrendered in front of the Chinese Catholic Church of Saint Xavier in Cholon. The armoured personnel carrier was waiting for them.

---

[1] Telegram 646: Etherington-Smith (Saigon) to FO. 3.11.63. Telegram 655: Etherington-Smith (Saigon) to FO. 4.11.63. Both in PRO: FO 371/170094, DV1015/109. Despatch 66: Etherington-Smith (Saigon) to FO. 20.11.63. PRO: FO 371/170095, DV1015/127.

[2] Letter: Thompson (BRIAM) to Peck (FO). 5.11.63. PRO: FO 371/170102, DV1017/49/G. Letter: Etherington-Smith (Saigon) to FO. 13.11.63. PRO: FO 371/170095, DV1015/122. See also David Halberstam, *The Best and the Brightest*, 4th edn. (New York: Ballantine Books, 1993), 290–1; and Kahin, *Intervention*, 180.

Almost instantly the American public was informed about Diem's ouster. CBS News broadcast pictures from Saigon only twenty-four hours after the event. David Halberstam's article in *The New York Times* was particularly well informed and contained the chronology of the coup.[3] Since then, numerous scholars have subjected the events that led to the overthrow of Ngo Dinh Diem to close scrutiny. Not only has this shed light on the American knowledge of and involvement in the coup; it has also shown the divisions within the Kennedy administration. The Pentagon and the higher echelons of the CIA supported Diem. State Department and White House officials were keen to see his removal. This split was also reflected in Saigon. Henry Cabot Lodge, the new US ambassador in Vietnam from August 1963, agreed with the State Department's anti-Diem line. His military counter-part, General Paul Harkins, opposed the idea of supporting a putsch.[4]

In the months prior to Diem's ouster a split similar to that in the American administration emerged among the British. The embassy in Saigon and the Foreign Office were very critical of Diem while BRIAM tended to support his regime. Indeed, the Foreign Office prevented Robert Thompson making his pro-Diem views known to President Kennedy at a time when the US administration was still debating the removal of Diem. Confronted with the political turmoil in Saigon in the wake of the Buddhist crisis, the British had no intention of getting more deeply involved in the dangerous situation in the RVN. The Macmillan government was preoccupied with Indonesia's opposition to the formation of Malaysia and therefore preferred to leave the messy Vietnam conflict to the Americans.

The British were never enthusiastic supporters of Ngo Dinh Diem. However, as Diem consolidated his position in 1955 and became President of the newly formed Republic of Vietnam, the British concluded that there was no alternative to Diem.[5] The policy of the British government towards Diem after the beginning of the communist insurgency in South Vietnam has remained obscure. Serious doubts about Diem and particularly about his brother Nhu were voiced in London as early as 1960. The British came close to discussing the removal of Diem with Washington in the following years. Before focusing on the Buddhist crisis and the fall of Diem, the views that the Saigon embassy and the Foreign Office had formed in previous years will be explored in the first part of this chapter.

---

[3] William Prochnau, *Once upon a Distant War: David Halberstam, Neil Sheehan, Peter Arnett: Young War Correspondents and their Early Vietnam Battles* (New York: Vintage Books, 1996), 482.

[4] See Anne E. Blair, *Lodge in Vietnam: A Patriot Abroad* (New Haven: Yale University Press, 1995), 24–70. Herring, *America's Longest War*, 95–107. Young, *The Vietnam Wars*, 89–105. Halberstam, *The Best and the Brightest*, 282–90. Kahin, *Intervention*, 153–81. Geoffrey Warner, 'The United States and the Fall of Diem', Part I: 'The Coup That Never Was', *Australian Outlook*, 28/3 (1974), 245–58.

[5] On Britain's initial assessment of Diem, see Combs, 'The Path Not Taken', 33–57.

BRITISH ATTITUDES TOWARDS THE NGO DINH DIEM

Born in 1900, Ngo Dinh Diem grew up in central Vietnam. He was one of nine children of a minister at the imperial court in Annan and was brought up in the mandarin tradition. A devout Catholic, Diem hated communism and delighted the French when he prevented a communist-inspired uprising as a village supervisor in 1929. The colonial regime rewarded him with the post of minister of the interior. After differences with Emperor Bao Dai and the French about reforms he had proposed, Diem resigned from the imperial service in 1933. In the following years he lived as a scholar-recluse and refused various offers from the Japanese, Vietminh, and Bao Dai to rejoin the government. He developed a bitter hatred for the Vietminh who imprisoned him for six months in 1945 and killed his brother Khoi. Diem went to the United States after World War II, settled at a Maryknoll seminary and gave talks on his vision of an independent non-communist Vietnam.[6]

Emperor Bao Dai appointed Diem as Prime Minister of the State of Vietnam in June 1954. The circumstances of this appointment, particularly the role of the French in it, are still unclear.[7] After surviving the first two difficult years in power in Saigon, Diem's brother Ngo Dinh Nhu established himself as his unofficial adviser. With the help of the semi-secret Can Lao party Nhu controlled the political life in the RVN and brutally suppressed any form of opposition. Diem and Nhu ran the country through a close-knit family oligarchy. Their younger brother Ngo Dinh Can remained at the family seat in Hué and controlled the whole of central Vietnam. Ngo Dinh Thuc, the eldest brother, was first bishop in Vinh Long province and later archbishop of Hué. He worked for the regime's interest within the Catholic Church and was allegedly involved in illegal real estate deals. The ambassador in London, Ngo Dinh Luyen, was the youngest of the Ngo brothers. The father of Diem's sister-in-law, Madame Nhu, was the RVN's ambassador in Washington.[8]

Ambassador Hohler's predecessor, Roderick Parkes, represented Britain in Saigon between 1957 and 1960. During his term lavish American economic and military support for South Vietnam seemed to have created a viable new state. The Republic of Vietnam became the showpiece of US nation-building in the Third World and western politicians courted the South Vietnamese leader. President Eisenhower met Diem during his elaborately staged state visit to the United States in May 1957. The visit was a public relations success. *Life* magazine portrayed

[6] Despatch 64: Etherington-Smith (Saigon) to FO. 13.11.63. PRO: FO 371/170095, DV1015/126. Herring, *America's Longest War,* 48–9. Anderson, *Trapped by Success,* 47–8. McMaster, *Dereliction of Duty,* 35–7.

[7] Anderson, *Trapped by Success,* 52–8.

[8] Despatch 64: Etherington-Smith (Saigon) to FO. 13.11.63. PRO: FO 371/170095, DV1015/126. Herring, *America's Longest War,* 48–9. Anderson, *Trapped by Success,* 47–8. McMaster, *Dereliction of Duty,* 35–7.

Diem as the 'tough miracle man of South Vietnam'.[9] Equally successful was his tour of Australia in September 1957, when Prime Minister Menzies welcomed Diem as the first foreign head of state to visit the country.[10] By the time ambassador Parkes prepared to leave Saigon in the spring of 1960, however, the tale of the 'miracle man' had turned stale. Diem's inability to cope with the rising tide of rebellion in the countryside exposed the weaknesses of his regime. Summing up his Vietnam experience, outgoing ambassador Parkes pointed out that Confucianism was at the heart of Diem's regime. The South Vietnamese president could not rein in his 'baneful brothers' because the family was the essential plank of Confucianism. Ambassador Parkes described the Vietnamese as jealous, sadist, and ruthless backbiters; yet he was certain that the United States and the Free World would never let down the RVN, 'this courageous, if expensive, little country'.[11]

As the security situation in South Vietnam in the spring of 1960 worsened, the Foreign Office became worried about the weaknesses of Diem's regime and its narrow power base. Diem seemed to be growing more repressive in the face of widespread discontent with the regime.[12] The middle-class opposition also became more outspoken. On 26 April 1960, eighteen prominent South Vietnamese anti-communists, who called themselves the 'group of patriots', issued a letter after a meeting at the Hotel Caravelle. The statement, which became known as the Caravelle Manifesto, sternly criticized Diem. It charged the government and the army with corruption, and particularly deplored the malign influence of Tran Kim Tuyen, the head of the Can Lao party's secret police force.[13] Unreported in the South Vietnamese press, the group received wide publicity in Britain.[14] Yet the Foreign Office refused to use the emergence of a more vocal opposition to press Diem for a more popular government and rebuffed the idea of French ambassador Roger Lalouette to make concerted though separate representations to Diem. Similarly, Henry Hohler, the new British ambassador, was worried that Elbridge Durbrow, his US colleague, was overdoing his remonstrance with Diem. Durbrow had informed Hohler that he was in Diem's 'dog house' after having raised the weaknesses of the regime several times in April and May 1960.[15]

The American embassy singled out the Can Lao party as the major source of difficulty because it dominated political life in the RVN and was Ngo Dinh Nhu's principle means of repression. As Diem proved unwilling to rein in this semi-secret party, Durbrow wanted to take 'drastic action' in May 1960 and suggested

---

[9] Anderson, *Trapped by Success*, 161–2.   [10] Edwards, *Crises and Commitments*, 194–5.
[11] Despatch 11: Parkes (Saigon) to FO. 23.2.60. PRO: FO 371/152738, DV1015/6.
[12] Despatch 13: Stewart (Saigon) to FO. 10.3.60. Minute by Butler (FO). 16.3.60. Both ibid. DV1015/10.
[13] The American embassy was handed a copy of the manifesto almost two weeks before it was issued. See Embtel 2981: Durbrow (Saigon) to State Department. 19.11.60. FRUS: 1958–1960, i, Vietnam, 404. For a text of the manifesto, see Bernard Fall, *The Two Vietnams* (New York: Frederick A. Praeger, 1963), 432–8. See also Kahin, *Intervention*, 122.
[14] Minute by Butler (FO). 3.5.60. PRO: FO 371/152739, DV1015/32.
[15] Letter: Warner (FO) to Hohler (Saigon). 9.5.60. Ibid. DV1015/35. Record of conversation between Hohler and Forsyth (Australian ambassador). 7.6.60. AUSNA: A1838/277, file 3014/12, part 1. Letter: Hohler (Saigon) to Warner. 24.6.60. PRO: FO 371/152753, DV10345/2.

to threaten the withdrawal of American aid if Diem did not change his ways.[16] This initiative met with stern and successful opposition from the Pentagon, especially from Edward Lansdale. He feared that Durbrow wanted to start scolding Diem rather than make constructive proposals.[17] In late August 1960, British and American diplomats noted that civil discontent with the Saigon government was still growing.[18] London's regional labour attaché visited the country in September and concluded that, due to his repressive policies, Diem had completely lost the support of the representatives of organized labour.[19] While Durbrow saw no alternative to Diem for the time being, he wanted Diem to rid himself of Ngo Dinh Nhu's malign influence and to sack Tuyen.[20] Edward Lansdale was again vehemently opposed to Durbrow's suggestion. He likened the transfer of Nhu to a post abroad to the 'traumatic surgery of removing President Diem's "right arm"'.[21] This time Lansdale, however, could not prevent Durbrow's drastic action.[22]

Independently of Durbrow, ambassador Hohler reached similar conclusions. Henry Hohler had taken up his post at the small British embassy in Saigon when it was coming to be recognized of growing importance. The ambassador came from a rich family, and he was a diplomat for whom social background and personal connections were of key importance. In the day-to-day business of the embassy he remained somewhat aloof, cool, and self-contained.[23] Following his cautious stance during his first months as British ambassador in Saigon, Hohler began to voice his views more forcefully in early October. Diem's regime, he found, was characterized by a 'steady rot'. However, there was nobody in sight of comparable calibre to Diem. Therefore, a 'sharp rejuvenating shock' was needed in Vietnam to dispel the growing malaise and to 'electrify popular imagination'. This shock could be the removal of Nhu, whom Hohler described as a 'man of great intelligence, matched unfortunately with a great perversity of imagination'.[24]

[16] Embtel 3095: Durbrow (Saigon) to State Department. 3.5.60. FRUS: 1958–1960, i, Vietnam, 433–7.

[17] Memorandum prepared in the Department of Defense and attached note by Colonel Edwin F. Black (Military Assistant to James Douglas, Deputy Secretary of Defense). 4.5.60. Ibid. 439–41. Deptel 2037: Herter to Saigon. 9.5.60. Ibid. 448–9.

[18] Airgram G-79: Durbrow (Saigon) to State Department. 25.8.60. USNA: RG 59, Central Files, 751k.00/8-2560. Embtel 538: Durbrow (Saigon) to State Department. 5.9.60. FRUS: 1958–1960, i, Vietnam, 560–3. Despatch 41: Hohler (Saigon) to FO. 31.8.60. PRO: FO 371/152741, DV1015/51. Telegram: London to EA Ottawa. 8.9.60. CNA: RG 25, Vol. 4637, File 50051-A-40, part 35.

[19] Letter: Priddle (Singapore) to Wallis (Ministry of Labour). 27.9.60. PRO: FO 371/152798, DV1901/5.

[20] Embtel 624: Durbrow (Saigon) to State Department. 16.9.60. FRUS: 1958–1960, i, Vietnam, 575–9.

[21] Memorandum by Lansdale (Pentagon). 20.9.60. Ibid. 579–85.

[22] Deptel 581: Dillon to Saigon. 7.9.60. Ibid. 591–4.

[23] Letter: Reginald Burrows to author. 21.2.2002.

[24] Letter: Hohler (Saigon) to McDermot (FO). 8.10.60. PRO: FO 371/152742, DV1015/64. Savingram 5: Hohler (Saigon) to FO. 8.10.60. Ibid. DV1015/62.

US ambassador Durbrow went to see Diem on 14 October and raised 'as a friend and most reluctantly' the issue of Ngo Dinh Nhu and Tran Kim Tuyen.[25] The US ambassador informed Hohler and his Australian colleague of this *démarche* the following day. The American ambassador was adamant that the French should not learn of his remarks on Nhu.[26] The Foreign Office expressed delight about Durbrow's *démarche*. Frederick Warner spoke of a 'very sensible and honest effort'. 'We could do with more Durbrows', concluded Lord Lansdowne, and Michael Butler of the Southeast Asia department noted that 'Mr. Durbrow seems to me to have spoken extremely, and unexpectedly well . . . I think we can now await further developments. Mr. Hohler already has discretion to act when he considers it appropriate.'[27]

In October 1960 the British and Americans agreed that public discontent with the Diem regime had reached dangerous levels, and that the president should not only introduce badly needed reforms but also rid himself of his sinister brother. London clearly preferred to leave it to the Americans to make the running, but the Foreign Office was prepared to put pressure on Diem as well. Yet from a British point of view it would have been tactically unwise to criticize Diem's government in late October. Just two weeks after Durbrow's *démarche*, Field Marshal Templer visited Saigon to promote a Malaya-style approach to the insurgency. The impact of Templer's advice would certainly have evaporated if Hohler had raised the political weaknesses of the regime or even Nhu with President Diem. Therefore, British criticism of Nhu and Diem's government remained unexpressed.

THE FAILED COUP OF 1960

News that fighting had broken out in Saigon reached the Foreign Office on 10 November 1960. As ambassador Hohler was in Hong Kong,[28] his deputy, Cosmo Stewart, monitored the unfolding of events in the South Vietnamese capital. He reported that the fighting had started between 3.15 and 3.30 a.m. local time. Troops of a parachute regiment had surrounded but not taken the Presidential Palace.[29] The British learned from the State Department that the coup had taken the Americans by surprise. Washington was not very concerned about the move against Diem because the first reports from Saigon indicated that the

[25] Embtel 802: Durbrow (Saigon) to State Department. 15.10.60, and enclosures 1 and 2 to despatch 157: Durbrow (Saigon) to State Department. 15.10.60. Both in FRUS: 1958–1960, i, Vietnam, 595–604.
[26] Letter: Hohler (Saigon) to Warner (FO). 15.10.60. PRO: FO 371/152742, DV1015/66. Embtel 861: Durbrow (Saigon) to State Department. 20.10.60. USNA: RG 59, Central Files, 751k.00/10-2060. Embtel 868: Durbrow (Saigon) to State Department. 21.10.60. Ibid. 751k.00/10-2160.
[27] Minutes by Butler and Warner. 20.10.60. Minute by Lansdowne. 26.10.60. All in PRO: FO 371/152742, DV1015/66.
[28] Telegram 39: Hohler (Hong Kong) to FO. 11.11.60. Ibid. DV1015/70.
[29] Telegrams 377, 378, 387: Stewart (Saigon) to FO. 11.11.60. PRO: FO 371/152742, DV1015/70-76. For an account of the attempted coup, see Anderson, *Trapped by Success*, 192 ff.; Stanley Karnow, *Vietnam: A History* (New York: Viking, 1983), 235–7, and Kahin, *Intervention*, 123–5.

motives of the military figures behind the coup appeared to be firmly anti-communist.[30] The Foreign Office shared Washington's assessment. Frederick Warner briefed Lord Home on 11 November that neither the British nor the Americans needed to fear the rebels. The Americans were in 'friendly touch' with the coup leaders. Their aims seemed unexceptionable: they wanted to continue the fight against the communist insurgents and they had pledged to abolish the oppressive features of the Diem regime.[31]

However unexceptionable the rebels' aims were, they failed to take power. Still not completely certain about the outcome of the attempted coup, Stewart reported in the late afternoon (local time) of 12 November that it looked as if President Diem had once again 'pulled off a remarkable victory against what at one time seemed heavy odds'.[32] Two days later, Lord Home was informed that the rebellion had collapsed entirely and Diem had shown his 'usual tough character'. The turn of events had left the Americans embarrassed because they got 'rather deeply involved' and seemed to have been urging Diem to give in to some of the coup leaders' demands. To retrieve the situation, the United States made an official statement strongly congratulating Diem. In the Foreign Office's view it would suffice to state publicly that the British government was very glad that Diem had survived the attempted coup.[33]

The American 'embarrassment' stemmed from ambassador Durbrow's ostensibly neutral stance during the coup. Although Durbrow knew early on that pro-Diem forces from outside Saigon were on their way to relieve the siege of the Presidential Palace, he encouraged Diem to negotiate and arrive at a compromise with the rebels.[34] For Diem the negotiations were merely a means to gain time. When the tide was turning, Durbrow told Diem that he was 'extremely perturbed' that loyalist troops were closing in on the rebel forces although Diem had announced that he had reached an agreement with them.[35] The three coup leaders quickly realized their failure and escaped with sixteen of their supporters to Cambodia.[36] Three of them sought asylum in the United Kingdom eight months later, but the Foreign Office turned down their requests. London had no intention to allow anti-Diemists into the country and 'cause offence' to the South Vietnamese regime.[37]

[30] Telegram 2261: Caccia (Washington) to FO. 11.11.60. PRO: FO 371/152143, DV1015/79. Telegram 504: Forsyth (Saigon) to EA Canberra. 16.11.60. AUSNA: A1838/283, file 3014/2/1, part 14.

[31] Blue FO minute by Warner. 11.11.60. PRO: FO 371/152143, DV1015/95.

[32] Telegram 404: Stewart (Saigon) to FO. 12.11.60. Ibid. DV1015/86.

[33] Blue FO minute by Warner. 14.11.60. Ibid. DV1015/98.

[34] Embtels 1019 and 1025: Durbrow (Saigon) to State Department. 11.11.60. FRUS: 1958–1960, i, Vietnam, 634–8.

[35] Embtel 1040: Durbrow (Saigon) to State Department. 12.11.60. Ibid. 644–5. Telegram: McGarr (MAAG) to Felt (Manila). 12.11.60. Ibid. 648. Embtel 1049: Durbrow (Saigon) to State Department. 12.11.60. Ibid. 649–50. Kahin, *Intervention*, 124.

[36] Telegram 493: Forsyth (Saigon) to EA Canberra. 14.11.60. AUSNA: A1838/283, file 3014/2/1, part 14. Anderson, *Trapped by Success*, 192.

[37] Telegram 391: Garner (Phnom Penh) to FO. 12.7.61. PRO: FO 371/160161, DV1591/1. Letter: Southeast Asia Department (FO) to Chancery Phnom Penh. 29.8.61. Ibid. DV1591/3.

For Diem and his brother Nhu the coup confirmed their suspicions of the United States. Diem and Nhu openly criticized the Americans in a dinner conversation with Hohler and Lord Selkirk on 28 November. They charged that the United States 'may let us down as they did China'.[38] After meeting Diem and Nhu in mid-November 1960, ambassador Hohler realized how close the Ngo brothers were. He therefore told Durbrow that there was no point in trying to get rid of Nhu.[39]

As 1960 drew to a close the British found the political situation in Saigon not 'very cheering'. In the aftermath of the coup the Ngo family had shown that it was arrogant and incorrigible. Nhu would remain Diem's closest adviser and continue 'messing everything up'.[40] The regime talked of reform but did nothing. The American ambassador had lost all influence. Washington faced the dilemma that it could not threaten Diem with the withdrawal of its support.[41] The middle-class opposition was weaker than ever. It had behaved 'foolhardy in the extreme', as the British embassy put it. Seven Caravellists had decided to associate themselves with the rebels just when the revolt was about to collapse. They were subsequently arrested.[42] Whereas a clear split had developed between the pro-Diemists in the Pentagon and the anti-Diemists in the State Department, the British—in the absence of any military involvement—were united in their criticism of Diem. Ambassador Hohler and the Foreign Office were thoroughly disillusioned by Diem's government and the machinations of his brother. Yet by the end of 1960 it had become clear that neither the British nor the Americans could do anything about this: they were stuck with Ngo Dinh Diem.

The incoming Kennedy administration, influenced by Edward Lansdale's report of January 1961, was aware of Diem's view that the United States had been very close to those who had tried to kill him in November 1960. Thus ambassador Durbrow was soon replaced by Frederick Nolting, who was instructed to establish good relations with the South Vietnamese president. In addition, Vice-President Johnson was sent to Saigon in May 1961 to demonstrate Washington's commitment to the RVN and strengthen Diem's confidence in the United States.

---

[38] Embtel 1143: Durbrow (Saigon) to State Department. 1.12.60. USNA: RG 59, Central Files, 751k.00/12-160.

[39] Telegram 429: Hohler (Saigon) to FO. 19.11.60. PRO: FO 371/152743, DV1015/92. Airgram G-235: Durbrow (Saigon) to State Department. 29.11.60. USNA: RG 59, Central Files, 751k. 00/11-2960. Letter: Hohler (Saigon) to Warner (FO). 19.11.60. PRO: FO 371/152744, DV1015/108. Durbrow did not report this part of his conversation to Washington. He stated instead that Hohler had raised the 'question of entourage' with Diem, which the president resented. See airgram G-235: Durbrow (Saigon) to State Department. 29.11.60. USNA: RG 59, Central Files, 751k.00/11-2960. If Hohler indeed raised this subject, he did not seem to have reported it to London.

[40] Minute by Butler (FO). 7.12.60. PRO: FO 371/152744, DV1015/108.

[41] Despatch 64: Hohler (Saigon) to FO. 13.12.60. Minute by McGhie (FO). 22.12.60. Both in PRO: FO 371/152744, DV1015/114/G.

[42] Telegram 421: Hohler (Saigon) to FO. 15.11.60. PRO: FO 371/152743, DV1015/93. Despatch 59: Hohler (Saigon) to FO. 19.11.60. PRO: FO 371/152744, DV1015/104.

Behind these moves was the attempt at countering the effects of Durbrow's 'drastic action' and his equivocal attitude during the coup in November 1960.[43]

While ambassador Hohler was on leave in June 1961, Cosmo Stewart drew the Foreign Office's attention again to Diem's government. Stewart concluded that sooner or later another military coup would take place in Saigon. There were not only rumours in Saigon that a group of army generals was planning this, Stewart argued, but the ARVN would soon be in a stronger position to mount a coup. Diem and Nhu would not be able to avoid putting an experienced senior officer in overall charge of the counter-insurgency operations.[44] Moreover, the military was the Americans' only apparatus to provide assistance. 'It seems to me,' Stewart wrote, 'that in attempting to reinforce their support for President Diem the Americans are in serious danger of accelerating the process of militarization and thus paving the way for some military take-over.'[45]

The Foreign Office's Southeast Asia Department noted in response that a military coup was not necessarily a 'bad thing'. The removal of the Ngo family would produce a 'healthier atmosphere', and there was no reason to believe that 'the army would not provide better Government and more adequate prosecution of the emergency'.[46] Diem had certainly no friends in Whitehall. Still, however desirable his replacement, the dangers involved in a coup outweighed the advantages of an army regime in mid-1961. Frederick Warner was concerned about a possible civil war between right-wing groups if the rebels were not able to kill Diem and his family within the first forty-eight hours of a coup. The communists would benefit from this, as they had done in Laos.[47] A high-level Foreign Office meeting chaired by Lord Lansdowne, the Parliamentary Under-Secretary of State, endorsed Warner's views on 4 July 1961.[48] Stewart's subsequent idea of discussing a possible coup with the Americans was not followed up. Instead, Lord Home told his French and American colleagues in Paris in August 1961 that Britain, although unhappy about Diem's policy, saw no alternative to his regime.[49]

---

[43] Memorandum: Rostow to Bundy. 30.1.61. FRUS: 1961–1963, i, Vietnam I, 16–19. 'A Program of Action to Prevent Communist Domination of South Vietnam' by Cleveland (State Department). 1.5.61. Ibid. 97. NSAM 52. 11.5.61. Ibid. 132–3.

[44] Less than two months later Diem indeed appointed General Duong Van Minh as Commander with countrywide responsibility. Telegram 461: Hohler (Saigon) to FO. 2.8.61. PRO: FO 371/160115, DV1015/143/G.

[45] Letter: Stewart (Saigon) to Warner (FO). 10.6.61. PRO: FO 371/160112, DV1015/100/G.

[46] Minute by McGhie (FO). 19.6.61. Ibid. The views expressed by McGhie were not confined to the Foreign Office and the embassy in Saigon. Gordon Etherington-Smith, who was to become British ambassador in Saigon in 1963, also stated after a visit to the RVN in June 1961 that a military coup was not a 'bad thing'. Letter: Etherington-Smith (Singapore) to Peck (FO). 23.6.61. PRO: FO 371/160113, DV1015/116.

[47] Letter: Warner (FO) to Stewart (Saigon). 20.6.61. PRO: FO 371/160112, DV1015/100/G.

[48] Minute of Office Meeting on Southeast Asia. 4.7.61. PRO: FO 371/159701, D1015/15.

[49] Letter: Stewart (Saigon) to Warner (FO). 3.7.61. PRO: FO 371/160113, DV1015/116. Record of tripartite meeting held at the Quai d'Orsay at 10.30 a.m. 7.8.61. PRO: PREM 11/3736.

THE TOP PRIORITY: DEFEATING THE COMMUNIST INSURGENTS

Following the arrival of BRIAM in Saigon in September 1961, the military side of the conflict came to overshadow concerns about Diem's weaknesses. British policy was to 'hammer away' at the security problems and do what could be done to persuade Diem to improve his government.[50] In the wake of Kennedy's decision to step up American military aid, the British embassy in Saigon and the Foreign Office even concluded in early December 1961 that political reforms had become impractical. In Frederick Warner's opinion 'military measures must be given priority'.[51] Undoubtedly, Robert Thompson's thinking influenced the Foreign Office's stance. His first ideas on the pacification of the delta envisioned the further strengthening of Diem's position with the intention of giving him powers similar to those of the Director of Operations during the Malayan emergency.

This focus on the defeat of the insurgency did not mean that the Foreign Office completely neglected Diem's shortcomings. The Foreign Office came very close to discussing the removal of Diem with the Americans in the spring of 1962. Britain's concern was not the undemocratic nature of the regime. The crucial question was whether Diem could win the war. Ambassador Hohler was certain, and the Foreign Office agreed, that Diem's prestige and his confidence in subordinates had been further shaken in the wake of the attack on the Presidential Palace by two South Vietnamese air force planes on 27 February 1962.[52] In a conversation with his Australian colleague Brian Hill, the British ambassador wondered whether the Diem regime would now 'measure up to the task'.[53] Robert Thompson, too, regarded the attack as a 'tremendous blow' and was concerned about the effect it might have on the implementation of the delta plan.[54]

A still more important reason for London's toying with the idea of discussing Diem's removal with Washington was the South Vietnamese president's apparent unwillingness to implement Thompson's delta plan. Against this background, ambassador Hohler revealed in late March that he was inclined to believe that Diem was not capable of winning the war.[55] Hohler's views made Frederick Warner cry for Diem's head: 'I have been completely convinced . . . that we can make no progress [against the communist insurgents] until Diem is killed or removed.'[56] Before the Foreign Office approached the Americans with these

---

[50] Telegram 5336: London to EA Canberra. 6.11.61. AUSNA: A1209/134, file 1961/127, part 1.

[51] Telegram 772: Hohler (Saigon) to FO. 23.11.61. Letter: Warner (FO) to Hohler (Saigon). 1.12.61. Both in PRO: FO 371/160118, DV1015/227/G.

[52] Telegram 179: Hohler (Saigon) to FO. 27.2.62. Minute by McGhie (FO). 28.2.62. Both in PRO: FO 371/166700, DV1015/56.

[53] Despatch 2/62: Hill (Saigon) to Barwick. 5.3.62. AUSNA: A4231/2, file 1961–62, South East Asia.

[54] Letter: Thompson (BRIAM) to McGhie (FO). 28.2.62. PRO: FO 371/166701, DV1015/67/G.

[55] Telegram 231: Hohler (Saigon) to FO. 27.3.62. Minute by McGhie (FO). 28.2.62. PRO: FO 371/166702, DV1015/87.

[56] Minute by Warner (FO). 30.3.62. Ibid. DV1015/84. Warner also informed the Australians that, in his personal opinion, Diem could not win. Telegram 1356: Shann (London) to EA Canberra. 29.3.62. AUSNA: A1209/80, file 61/482, part 1.

conclusions, it decided to discuss the matter with Robert Thompson during his home leave in April 1962.[57] By then, Thompson had overcome the gloomy views on Diem he had voiced after the attack on the Presidential Palace in February. His essentially positive assessment of the South Vietnamese president did not only influence the British ambassador later on, but had an effect on the Foreign Office's thinking, too. Although Thompson had been sent to Vietnam as an 'idea's man' and was not expected to report on the overall situation in the RVN,[58] his ability to influence the Foreign Office's thinking on Diem demonstrated how seriously Thompson's views were taken in Whitehall. Simultaneously, his advice to stick with previous British policy was much easier to follow than initiating a change and work for Diem's dismissal. Therefore, Frederick Warner seemed much more positive about the situation in Vietnam in June. Reverting back to prioritizing the military aspect of the conflict, Warner stressed in a conversation with the Australians that Diem's main problem was not the lack of contact with his people, but the lack of capacity to protect them.[59] Still, had the Americans indicated that they were thinking of removing the Ngo family from power, the Foreign Office might well have followed the US lead. Yet Anglo-American talks on the subject ceased to be an option after W. Averell Harriman had told Warner in July that Washington saw no alternative to Diem and would back him 'up to the hilt'.[60] This did not prevent the Foreign Office from repeatedly instructing a reluctant ambassador Hohler that he should inform London about possible alternatives to Diem's regime.[61] Yet in September 1962, the Foreign Office concluded that Diem was 'as likely as any other' to prevent a communist victory in the RVN. It was too dangerous to encourage or even discuss with the Americans preparations for a successor as long as Diem remained in power.[62]

The British had no illusions about the shortcomings of Diem and his family, but the crucial question was whether Diem would be able to defeat the NLF forces. When ambassador Hohler temporarily regarded Diem's chances of winning the war as slim in the spring of 1962, the Foreign Office seemed prepared to abandon its support for Diem. Yet London shied away from discussing a change of government with the Americans. Robert Thompson's essentially positive view of Diem certainly influenced the Foreign Office. British deliberations on this issue revealed the deep-seated antipathy towards Diem in the Foreign Office, particularly in the Southeast Asia Department. Ambassador Hohler proved to be prone

[57] Minute by McGhie (FO). 3.4.62. Minute by Warner (FO). 4.4.62. Minute by Peck (FO). 5.4.63. All in PRO: FO 371/166702, DV1015/91/G.

[58] Letter: Scott (London) to EA Wellington. 15.12.61. NZNA: PM 478/4/1, part 14.

[59] Telegram 2759: Shann (London) to EA Canberra. 13.6.62. AUSNA: 1209/80, file 62/482, part 1.

[60] Note by Warner (FO) on his talk with Harriman in Geneva. 22.7.62. PRO: FO 371/166354, D1015/25.

[61] Blue FO minute by Warner. 26.7.62. PRO: FO 371/166706, DV1015/173/G. Letter: Hohler (Saigon) to Warner. 15.8.62. Letter: Warner (FO) to Hohler (Saigon). Both ibid. DV1015/170/G. Letter: Peck (FO) to Hohler (Saigon). 16.8.62. Letter: Burrows (Saigon) to Peck (FO). 23.8.62. Both ibid. DV1015/155/G. Despatch 43: Hohler (Saigon) to FO. 29.8.62. PRO: FO 371/166707, DV1015/181/G.

[62] Blue FO minute by Williams. 25.9.62. P, Ibid.

to changing his mind on the topic, and Robert Thompson became an increasingly staunch supporter of Diem. As in Washington, different opinions of Diem began to emerge in British deliberations. Those mainly concerned with the political aspects of the war were clearly more critical of Diem than Robert Thompson, whose main interest was the practical aspect of fighting the communist insurgents. At the same time it became obvious that the British would only approach the Americans about the question of removing Diem if they felt that the US government was also favouring his replacement. The Foreign Office was determined to let the Americans take the lead on this issue and keen to coordinate a possible change in Anglo-American policy on Diem.

THE BUDDHIST CRISIS

Robert Thompson had decided in early 1963 that South Vietnam was winning the war, and he had told President Kennedy so. Ambassador Hohler, whose tour in Saigon was due to end in July 1963, remained unconvinced. He became increasingly concerned about the political aspect of the war. Some officials in the State Department, Roger Hilsman and W. Averell Harriman in particular, shared similar concerns. They believed the war could not be won on the military front alone.[63] Against this background, the Buddhist crisis erupted on 8 May 1963 with a 'very ugly incident',[64] as the British embassy put it, opening the last chapter of the Diem era in South Vietnam.

The Buddhist community in Hué had been preparing considerable celebrations for Buddha's birthday, when the government decreed on 6 May that no Buddhist flags were to be flown on any except a few religious buildings. The flags were up already and the police made the rounds to ensure that they were taken down. Nevertheless, celebrations remained peaceful throughout the day. In the evening, however, the director of the government radio station refused to broadcast a Buddhist religious programme. The Buddhists had delivered it only ten minutes before the agreed time of transmission, which did not give the director enough time to learn of its content. Buddhist priests reacted angrily, talked of religious persecution and about three thousand Buddhist supporters marched to the radio station. The police failed to disperse the crowd, water hoses were tried without effect and eventually detachments of the army and the civil guard were called in. Tear gas was used, allegedly the civil guard shot into the crowd and a grenade was thrown, leaving eight people dead. Official reports claimed that the communists had thrown the grenade—a claim the British military attaché did not believe.[65] Throughout the Buddhist crisis the British held the view that the communists were not behind the protests. Reports that the Americans were conduct-

---

[63] Gelb and Betts, *The Irony of Vietnam*, 81–5.
[64] Letter: Murray (Saigon) to Williams (FO). 16.5.63. PRO: FO 371/170142, DV1781/3.
[65] Telegram MA/142: Lee (Saigon) to WO. 10.5.63. PRO: FO 371/170090, DV1015/28. Letter: Murray (Saigon) to Williams (FO). 16.5.63. PRO: FO 371/170142, DV1781/3.

ing an exercise to secure 'evidence' of communist support for the Buddhists were seen as an act of 'folly'.[66] Indeed, behind the scenes in Hanoi the authorities were very critical of the NLF because of its inability to influence the Buddhist movement and exploit the protests.[67]

In London, the events in Hué and the Saigon government's handling of the continuing protests evoked feelings of moral indignation. Frederick Warner was 'appalled', even more so when reports about the alleged use of blister gas reached the Foreign Office. Although Britain had been willing to stretch its support for South Vietnam a long way, 'this business of gassing Buddhists' was different. 'I feel', Warner went on, 'that [the South Vietnamese] should be made to see that there are some acts of foolishness in which they will get no backing at all from their allies.'[68] Robert Thompson phoned the Foreign Office from his home in Somerset, where he spent his leave, to express his concern about the reports that blister gas was used.[69] Colonel Lee, the military attaché in Saigon, spoke of a 'very serious' situation.[70] The British embassy in Saigon duly described the first immolation of a Buddhist monk on 11 June as a 'gruesome business'.[71]

This moral indignation was not translated into a change in Britain's policy towards the Saigon regime. Indeed, British policy between May and October was characterized by a reluctance to take any decisive political action. Given the Foreign Office's doubts about Diem and his brother between 1960 and 1962, this might seem surprising. Yet for London the Buddhist crisis came at an inopportune moment for two reasons. First and most importantly, between May and November 1963 the main trouble spot from the British point of view was the Malayan region. The same department in the Foreign Office dealt with Vietnam and all aspects of the formation of the new Federation of Malaysia, a move which Indonesia vehemently opposed. Malaysia was clearly a British interest and was at the forefront of political considerations. When the Buddhist crisis escalated in August, the Southeast Asia Department was preoccupied with ensuring the formation of Malaysia,[72] which was only achieved after a delay of more than two weeks on 16 September 1963. Frederick Warner repeatedly apologized to the Saigon embassy that he could not devote as much time to the situation in Vietnam as he would have liked.[73] Second, Henry Hohler was about to leave the RVN when the crisis escalated in June, and he seemed reluctant to counsel the

---

[66] Minute by Everard (FO). 19.7.63. PRO: FO 371/170091, DV1015/42. The American consul in Hué also shared the British view that the communists were not behind the incident. John J. Heble oral history interview. 5.4.96. Foreign Affairs Oral History Project. Lauinger Library, Georgetown University.

[67] Note for the record 114/63 by Matzke (Hanoi). 28.8.63. MfAA: A8570, ff. 227–31.

[68] Telegram 287: Hohler (Saigon) to FO. 4.6.63. Letter: Warner (FO) to Hohler (Saigon). 6.6.63. Both in PRO: FO 371/170142, DV1781/7.

[69] Minute by Peck. 5.6.63. Ibid. DV1781/9.

[70] Letter: Lee (Saigon) to Jones (WO). 6.6.63. PRO: FO 371/170134, DV1201/67.

[71] Letter: Murray (Saigon) to Williams (FO). 12.6.63. PRO: FO 371/170143, DV1781/23.

[72] Sir Edward Peck in interview with the author. 12.2.2002.

[73] Letter: Warner (FO) to Etherington-Smith (Saigon). 10.9.63. PRO: FO 371/170092, DV1015/73. Letter: Warner (FO) to Etherington-Smith (Saigon). 25.9.63. Ibid. DV1015/84.

abandonment of Britain's support for Diem during his last weeks in Saigon. Instead, he concluded after the first immolation that there was no sign of a coup. However, in his last dispatches he stressed that Diem was facing the most serious threat to his government since 1960. As the Buddhist demonstrations continued Hohler spoke of *the* crisis for South Vietnam.[74]

Moreover, Robert Thompson was on leave when the demonstrations began. When he returned to Vietnam on 14 June, he decided that it was best to continue BRIAM's work as before, especially as he thought the events in Saigon and Hué had not yet affected military campaigns.[75] Being the true adviser, he drafted recommendations for Diem on how to deal with the crisis, stressing that there was no reason to panic. The police should only use a minimum of force and Diem should make a radio address, in which he was to give a personal guarantee that there would be no discrimination against the Buddhists. Moreover, Diem should demonstrate his willingness to meet Buddhist leaders. Simultaneously, all processions should be banned for two months, but to make his regime more popular the ban on dancing—one of Madame Nhu's ideas—was to be relaxed and conscription done away with.[76] Thompson's recommendations were not implemented and it is doubtful if they made it all the way to Diem. The British embassy shared US ambassador Nolting's view that the South Vietnamese president appeared to become increasingly withdrawn within himself, and that his brother Nhu seemed to be taking over.[77]

Therefore, the relatively mild British reaction after the first immolation appears in a different light. Ngo Dinh Luyen, the RVN ambassador, was summoned to the Foreign Office on 17 June. Lord Home's brief for the meeting stressed that the Buddhist 'matter is of no concern of ours and we have tried to keep out of it'. Frederick Warner had suggested that Home should stress Britain's difficulty in defending Diem's treatment of the Buddhists if the Soviet Union brought the matter up as co-chairman of the Geneva conference. The Foreign Secretary, however, preferred to water this down. He told Luyen that the Soviet Union might raise the issue, and that the United Kingdom was 'very interested' that South Vietnam did not get a bad name. Therefore, he urged the South Vietnamese to make a conciliatory gesture.[78]

Unknown to Lord Home this gesture had already been made just hours before his meeting with Luyen. Diem and the Buddhists had arrived at a settlement with

[74] Letter: Hohler (Saigon) to Warner (FO). 13.6.63. PRO: FO 371/170090, DV1015/34. Despatch 35: Hohler (Saigon) to Home. 26.6.63. PRO: FO 371/170143, DV1781/35. Despatch 38: Hohler (Saigon) to Home. 6.7.63. PRO: FO 371/170144, DV1781/41.

[75] Letter: Lee (Saigon) to Jones (WO). 20.6.63. PRO: FO 371/170134, DV1201/72. Letter: Thompson (BRIAM) to Warner (FO). 24.6.63. PRO: FO 371/170101, DV1017/28. Letter: Williams (FO) to Thompson (BRIAM). 9.7.63. Ibid. DV1017/30. Letter: Farrell (Bangkok) to EA Wellington. 12.7.63. Letter: Ottawa to EA Wellington. 26.7.63. Both in NZNA: PM 478/4/1, part 17.

[76] Memorandum by Thompson (BRIAM). Undated. Attached to letter: Burrows (Saigon) to Warner. 25.7.63. PRO: FO 371/170144, DV1781/58.

[77] Telegram 371: Burrows (Saigon) to FO. 24.7.63. Ibid. DV1781/50.

[78] Brief for Home by Warner (FO). 13.6.63. PRO: FO 371/170143, DV1781/24. Telegram 485: FO to Saigon. 17.6.63. PRO: FO 371/170142, DV1781/14.

regard to the flying of flags on 16 June. Hohler quickly pointed out that the agreement was indeed merely a gesture as it only met minor grievances of the Buddhists. Moreover, nobody in the British and American embassies or in the British Advisory Mission believed that Diem would honour the agreement. Colonel Lee forecast that the Buddhist troubles would start again.[79]

As Diem's gestures indeed proved insufficient to placate the Buddhists, the Foreign Office finally concluded in late July that it might have to re-examine Britain's long-standing position on Vietnam. In a meeting on 25 July, Gordon Etherington-Smith, the ambassador designate to Saigon, was given the preliminary Foreign Office thinking on Vietnam. Past British policy had been that a coup against Diem would have split the anti-communist forces in Saigon, leading to NLF gains during the following period of disorganization. However, the outlook was now 'so black' for Diem that the RVN might not be worse off with a 'reasonably clear-cut and rapid change'.[80] The British increasingly took the Australians into their confidence and immediately informed them of their thinking. Clarifying London's views, Timothy Everard of the Southeast Asia Department agreed with the Australian observation that the 'hub of the matter' was whether a change could be clear-cut and rapid. In the same conversation, Everard was very interested in the Australian view that there might be a neutralist section in the South Vietnamese army, a danger the British had not taken into consideration.[81]

Whereas the exchange of views between Australia and Britain was frequent and frank, London again shied away from discussing the possible removal of Diem with the Americans. As a result of discussions with his embassy staff and Robert Thompson, Reginald Burrows, the British chargé d'affaires in Saigon, suggested urgent discussions with the Americans to find out whether they wanted to preserve the Diem regime. If Diem was to stay, Burrows thought the United States may need the support of their friends in pressing Diem to make the necessary overtures to the Buddhists. The Foreign Office, however, did not want to appear to be pressing the Americans, particularly as it was assumed that Washington would not do anything until the new ambassador, Henry Cabot Lodge, had arrived in Saigon.[82]

In his valedictory dispatch ambassador Hohler had expressed the hope that Lodge's appointment would improve the American diplomatic representation in Saigon. The British ambassador was very critical of the performance of his US colleagues. As for Elbridge Durbrow, Hohler pointed out that the US ambassador had been 'unwise enough to make an unsuccessful attempt to persuade

---

[79] Despatch 35: Hohler (Saigon) to Home. 26.6.63. PRO: FO 371/170143, DV1781/35. Despatch 38: Hohler (Saigon) to Home. 6.7.63. PRO: FO 371/170144, DV1781/41. Memorandum of conversation between Kennedy, Ball, Harriman, Bundy, Hilsman, Forrestal. 4.7.63. USNA: RG 59, Central Files, POL 27 S VIET.

[80] Letter: Warner (FO) to Trench (Washington). 29.7.63. PRO: FO 371/170144, DV1781/51.

[81] Telegram 3800: London to EA Canberra. 26.7.63. AUSNA: A1209/80, file 62/482, part 1.

[82] Telegram 372: Burrows (Saigon) to FO. 24.7.63. Letter: Warner (FO) to Trench. 29.7.63. Both in PRO: FO 371/170144, DV1781/51.

President Diem to exile Mr. and Mrs. Nhu'. Hohler conveniently forgot how close he himself had come in 1960 to urging Diem to get rid of his brother. With regard to Frederick Nolting, Hohler thought that he had made the 'opposite error to ingratiate himself' with Diem. Nolting's reward was nothing but South Vietnamese contempt, ingratitude, and hostility. What in Hohler's view was needed was a man with political rather than diplomatic experience, invested with pro-consul authority. In this respect Henry Cabot Lodge, an experienced Republican politician who had been Richard Nixon's running mate in the 1960 presidential election, seemed the ideal choice. The new British ambassador was due to arrive in Saigon on 20 August, and the potential 'pro-consul' two days later. Until then, the Foreign Office expected no major American initiative.[83]

In the weeks before the new American and British ambassadors arrived, the stream of negative reports from Vietnam did not cease. It became evident in August that a stalemate existed. The Buddhists had firmly 'dug themselves in', the British embassy reported, and faced the 'implacable' opposition of the Nhus. '[V]ulgar excesses' like Madame Nhu's talk of 'barbecued bonzes' in an interview on American television further underscored the Nhus' unreasonableness.[84] Moreover, Ngo Dinh Thuc, Diem's eldest brother and archbishop of Hué, gave a lecture on the Catholic attitude towards the Buddhist demands at the University of Hué on 9 August. This was another 'piece of political folly', which in the British embassy's opinion almost equalled Madame Nhu's performance. Only strong pressure from the apostolic delegate in Saigon dissuaded Thuc from making another lecture on Catholics and Buddhists.[85] The British military attaché predicted correctly in mid-August that the Buddhists would bait Diem and Nhu to such an extent that the brothers would resort to the use of force.[86]

Lord Selkirk's brief visit to Saigon in August confirmed the British impression that Diem and Nhu had no intention of meeting Buddhist demands. More importantly, Nhu revealed in his talk with Lord Selkirk on 10 August that he had regular contacts with Hanoi. This was the first time the British learned from Nhu's own lips that these contacts existed. He spoke of men of the 'Dien-Bien-Phu generation', who were nationalists first and communists second. 'I have had some of them sitting in this very room', Nhu told Selkirk. The British duly informed Washington of Nhu's revelation. The director of the State Department's Vietnam Task Force was interested to have this information, but thought that Nhu's intention was simply to frighten the United States. The British embassy in Washington felt it unlikely that this was Nhu's only intention, and the British in Saigon stressed that Nhu had mentioned his contacts to many people, including the Polish commissioner of the ICC. The Foreign Office did not seem worried about these possible contacts. Everard believed that if Nhu really thought he

    [83] Despatch 39: Hohler (Saigon) to Home. 6.7.63. PRO: FO 371/170091, DV1015/42.
    [84] Letter: Murray (Saigon) to Everard (FO). 8.8.63. PRO: FO 371/170145, DV1781/67.
    [85] Letter: Murray (Saigon) to Everard (FO). 15.8.63. Ibid. DV1781/69. Telegram 401: Burrows (Saigon) to FO. 15.8.63. Telegram 407: Burrows (Saigon) to FO. 16.8.63. Both ibid. DV1781/66.
    [86] Letter: Lee (Saigon) to Jones (WO). 15.8.63. PRO: FO 371/170135, DV1201/89.

could be the 'Man of Destiny' who would reunify Vietnam on his terms, he was clearly suffering from delusions.[87]

Gordon Etherington-Smith arrived in Saigon on 20 August 1963. At midnight on that day Donald Murray of the embassy drove him home from Reginald Burrows's house, where the new ambassador had been dining. They went past the Xa Loi pagoda. Everything was absolutely quiet around the pagoda and throughout Saigon. Ten minutes later Burrows phoned Etherington-Smith and informed him that South Vietnamese security forces had started a raid against the Xa Loi pagoda and other Buddhists centres.[88]

As after the first immolation, the initial Foreign Office reaction to the pagoda raids showed moral indignation. 'The gloves are now right off the Diem Government's campaign to suppress the Buddhist discontent by force', is how Frederick Warner summarized the events of 21 August. He regarded this move as 'suicidal folly' and argued that Britain could no longer appear to condone Diem's actions by remaining silent. Warner therefore suggested that London should answer any public inquiries by saying that Britain 'had been shocked by reports circulating in Saigon of inhumanity and police violence against those of Buddhist faith'. Lord Home, however, opposed any public statements. He saw no need to express 'a lot of moral indignation' in public.[89] Yet Home agreed to ask the Americans if the British should give Diem 'a useful jolt' by intimating that they, as co-chairman, would not defend the RVN's policy unless the Buddhist dispute was resolved peacefully. As a major reassessment of the situation in Vietnam was being made in Washington, the Americans were in no position to answer London's urgent inquiry. W. Averell Harriman therefore simply informed the British that the State Department was still analysing the situation.[90]

The pagoda raids of 21 August marked a watershed in Washington's relations with the South Vietnamese president. During his last days in Saigon, Nolting had pressed Diem to desist from any violent moves against the Buddhists. Diem had promised that nothing would be done and issued a public statement stressing that the policy of reconciliation with the Buddhists was irreversible.[91] The government clampdown on the Buddhists barely two weeks later reinforced the conviction of Diem's critics in Washington that the time had come to take action.

[87] Minute by Murray on Lord Selkirk's talk with Ngo Dinh Nhu on 10.8.63, attached to letter: Burrows (Saigon) to Warner (FO). 14.8.63. Letter: Trench (Washington) to Burrows (Saigon). 6.9.63. Letter: Burrows (Saigon) to Trench (Washington). 18.9.63. Minute by Everard (FO). 21.8.63. All in PRO: FO 371/170091, DV1015/53. See also Logevall, *Choosing War*, 6.

[88] Letter: Etherington-Smith (Saigon) to Warner (FO). 28.8.63. PRO: FO 371/170092, DV1015/73.

[89] Blue FO minute by Warner. 21.8.63. Draft of telegram to Washington by Warner. 21.8.63. Minute by Caccia (FO) after telephone conversation with Home. 21.8.63. All in PRO: FO 371/170091, DV1015/56.

[90] Telegram 8206: FO to Washington. 21.8.63. Telegram 2634: Greenhill (Washington) to FO. 22.8.63. Both ibid. DV1015/56.

[91] Embtel 189: Nolting (Saigon) to State Department. 7.8.63. Embtel 208: Nolting (Saigon) to State Department. 12.8.63. Embtel 253: Nolting (Saigon) to State Department. 14.8.63. All in FRUS: 1961–1963, iii, Vietnam 1963, 556–7 and 562–6. See also Herring, *America's Longest War*, 97, and Kahin, *Intervention*, 151.

However, the Kennedy administration remained deeply divided over what to do about Diem.

The somewhat infamous State Department cable of 24 August 1963 brought these divisions to the fore. It instructed Lodge to make a last attempt to persuade President Diem to rid himself of his brother Nhu and his wife. If Diem resisted, the United States was prepared to accept 'the obvious implication' that Diem could no longer be supported. Lodge was asked to convey the American position to the South Vietnamese generals and assure them of 'direct support in any interim period of breakdown of central government mechanism'.[92] Roger Hilsman drafted the cable. None of the principal politicians were in Washington at the time. Kennedy and Rusk approved it by telephone. McNamara's deputy signed it for the Pentagon, as did the deputy to John McCone, the CIA Director. Victor Krulak, the Joint Chiefs of Staff's Special Assistant for Counterinsurgency, gave the approval for the JCS. It later became clear that, in fact, McNamara, McCone, and General Taylor did not support the removal of Diem. They protested that they had not been fully and directly consulted in the drafting of the cable. Although this seemed to have troubled Kennedy, the instructions to Lodge were never rescinded. Diem's opponents in Washington had gained the upper hand. In effect, Hilsman's cable of 24 August turned out to be Diem's death sentence.[93]

The closest the British came to knowing of America's willingness to support a coup in Saigon at that point was on 27 and 28 August. Roger Hilsman talked to Dennis Greenhill of the British embassy in Washington on 27 August. Hilsman said that the State Department was thinking of trying to get a general into a leading position. As there was no suitable candidate in sight, the preferred solution was to encourage the formation of a junta of generals under the nominal leadership of Diem. On 28 August, ambassador Etherington-Smith met his American colleague in Saigon for the first time. Lodge revealed that he believed there was a possibility that the ARVN would take action against Diem. Although Lodge did not elaborate on this, Etherington-Smith got the impression that the Americans were working for a coup.[94]

Gordon Etherington-Smith certainly inherited a difficult task. The embassy staff appreciated his common sense and that he, in contrast to his predecessor, welcomed advice.[95] Good advice was badly needed in the first turbulent weeks of

---

[92] Deptel 283: Hilsman to Saigon. 24.8.63. FRUS: 1961–1963, iii, Vietnam 1963, 628–9.

[93] There are many accounts discussing Deptel 283. See for a detailed account, Kaiser, *American Tragedy*, 227–42. See also Blair, *Lodge in Vietnam*, 42. William Conrad Gibbons, *The United States and the Vietnam War: Executive and Legislative Roles and Relationships, 1961–1964*, ii (Princeton, NJ: Princeton University Press, 1986), 148–54. Bassett and Pelz, 'The Failed Search for Victory', 247. Francis X. Winters, *The Year of the Hare: America in Vietnam, January 25, 1963–February 15, 1964* (Athens: University of Georgia Press, 1997), 54–64. Many of the officials involved published memoirs. See William Colby and Peter Forbath, *Honorable Men: My Life in the CIA* (New York: Simon and Schuster, 1978), 210; Hilsman, *To Move a Nation*, 483–9; McNamara, *In Retrospect*, 52 ff.; and Maxwell D. Taylor, *Swords and Ploughshares: A Memoir* (New York: W. W. Norton, 1972), 292.

[94] Telegram 2680: Greenhill (Washington) to FO. 27.8.63. Telegram 481: Etherington-Smith (Saigon) to FO. 28.8.63. Both in PREM 11/4759.

[95] Reginald Burrows in interview with the author. 14.2.2002.

his term in Saigon. The new British ambassador was clearly unhappy about the situation, particularly about the 'curious' way American policy was handled in the wake of the pagoda raids. As a first reaction, Washington issued a statement that condemned the repressive action taken by Diem's government. However, US aid policy remained unchanged, at least until a broadcast of Voice of America indicated that American aid to South Vietnam might be cut. Similarly, the American radio station repeatedly stressed that Nhu had ordered the raids without the approval of the army. The British embassy was well aware of the anti-Nhu feelings in the State Department and in the American embassy in Saigon. Because of the public announcements Etherington-Smith thought that the Americans were instigating a coup. Three days later, on 31 August, however, the British ambassador concluded that the United States was 'just going hard on the view that Nhu must go' but had not yet made serious preparations to overthrow him. Etherington-Smith clearly had no knowledge of Lodge's earlier attempts to encourage the South Vietnamese generals to make a move against Diem. Not surprisingly, he found the uncertainty about American policy unsettling and asked the Foreign Office to make high-level approaches in Washington to find out what the Americans were up to.[96]

As a result, Roger Hilsman gave an outline of American policy to the British and Australians in Washington on 4 September. Hilsman seemed to have forgotten what he had told the British a week before about his preference for the establishment of a military junta. Instead, he stressed that all American public statements had been made for domestic consumption and that the risk of stimulating an army revolt by this publicity had to be run. Hilsman did not think that Diem would ever get rid of Nhu, and although the United States was not seeking the head of an individual, there would have to be changes. The British embassy in Washington concluded, therefore, that the United States would not make a dramatic move to bring about the fall of Diem for the time being. However, Nhu was clearly unacceptable to Washington, and Diem was also expendable. It could be expected that the Americans would support suitable opponents of the Nhus and would even cut economic aid unless Diem reconciled with the Buddhists.[97]

The development of immediate British thinking in the wake of the pagoda raid is all the more interesting because of the absence of a clear American policy. The strong public condemnation of the raids by the Americans on 21 August was taken as a green light to proceed with the idea of giving Diem 'a jolt' by threatening a changed British attitude to its co-chairmanship. When the South Vietnamese ambassador asked to see a Foreign Office minister on 22 August, Permanent Under-Secretary of State Peter Smithers took this opportunity to spell out that London would find great difficulty in defending the raids in exchanges with the Soviet co-chairman.[98]

---

[96] Letter: Etherington-Smith (Saigon) to Peck (FO). 31.8.63. PRO: FO 371/170092, DV1015/68/G.

[97] Telegram 2776: Greenhill (Washington) to FO. 5.9.63. PRO: PREM 11/4759.

[98] Blue FO minute by Williams. 22.8.63. PRO: FO 371/170092, DV1015/62. Telegram 680: FO to Saigon. 22.8.63. PRO: FO 371/170091, DV1015/56.

On the same day, Gordon Etherington-Smith presented his credentials to Diem. The new British ambassador expressed Home's concern about the situation and pointed out that the raids had created a highly damaging impression of the South Vietnamese regime abroad. As Diem indicated his willingness to receive Etherington-Smith for a longer interview, the Foreign Office instructed Etherington-Smith to speak to Diem on the same lines as Smithers had done to Luyen. Etherington-Smith met Nhu on 25 and Diem on 26 August. In both meetings the ambassador emphasized that it would be difficult for Britain as a co-chairman to defend Diem's actions if the Soviets raised the issue unless the dispute could be settled. Etherington-Smith urged the President to arrive at a full settlement, which satisfied Buddhist sentiment. In a long, defensive monologue Diem maintained that the Buddhist agitation had continued despite the fact that he as President had done all he could to come to an agreement. Then, the army had requested permission for the raid on the pagodas.[99]

The British did not believe this claim. They held Nhu responsible for the raids but admitted that the army had followed his instructions loyally. Possibly the British had similar information to those of the United States. Lucien Conein, the CIA operative who remained in close contact with the South Vietnamese generals and eventually helped to bring about the coup, talked to General Tran Van Don shortly after the raid. Don stressed that ten generals had asked Diem for martial law and the President went along with this request.[100] Nevertheless, Etherington-Smith found the two-hour long talk with Diem depressing: 'I could not help being reminded of those who had learned nothing and forgotten nothing.' The Foreign Office thought that Nhu in particular was becoming increasingly 'grotesque' and compared his behaviour with Hitler's during his last days in Berlin.[101]

However depressing Etherington-Smith found his talk with Diem, his first detailed assessment of the situation after the raids on 26 August was surprisingly different from the Foreign Office's initial stance. The British ambassador thought Diem and Nhu had been right in considering that the Buddhist protests could not be allowed to continue because they were undermining their authority. Although the pagoda raids were deplorable, Etherington-Smith regarded it as possible that the regime's 'strong action' would succeed and tensions would gradually relax. The ambassador concluded that great harm had been done to Diem's regime by the dispute but that something could still be saved if the situation were to be stabilized. Diem's policy of intending to reach an agreement with other Buddhists—after having disposed of the troublesome bonzes—could

---

[99] Telegram 439: Etherington-Smith (Saigon) to FO. 22.8.63. Telegram 684: FO to Saigon. 23.8.63. Telegram 463: Etherington-Smith (Saigon) to FO. 25.8.63. All in PRO: FO 371/170091, DV1015/60. Telegram 476: Etherington-Smith (Saigon) to FO. 26.8.63. PRO: FO 371/170092, DV1015/69.

[100] Kaiser, *American Tragedy*, 228.

[101] Telegram 476: Etherington-Smith (Saigon) to FO. 26.8.63. PRO: FO 371/170092, DV1015/69. Telegram 4384: London to EA Canberra. 24.8.63. AUSNA: A1838/334, file 3014/11/51, part 1.

achieve this stabilization. Etherington-Smith argued that the British should deplore the needless repression and encourage a solution based on an effective settlement with the Buddhist community, at least until the situation became clearer or the American attitude hardened.[102]

The Foreign Office found Etherington-Smith's thinking sound and decided to follow his line. Etherington-Smith regarded an army coup as unlikely because the military leaders seemed divided. The Foreign Office was still worried about the risk of splitting the anti-communist forces in Vietnam if the Americans were to encourage Diem's overthrow.[103] The attraction of this policy of inaction was, of course, that the British could avoid making any difficult decisions on changing a long-standing policy. This was all the more appealing as there was no clear lead from the United States on the issue, and neither the British ambassador in Saigon nor Robert Thompson were supportive of removing Diem. Moreover, Frederick Warner, who had advocated a stronger anti-Diem line when news of the pagoda raids had reached London, was not involved in the decision-making at this stage. He had, from the British point of view, more important problems to address in the last weeks of August and the first half of September. This was the crucial period in the run up to the formation of Malaysia. To help ensure the success of British policy, Warner was with the Commonwealth Secretary in Kuala Lumpur.[104] Lord Home also fully endorsed the cautious approach in early September 1963: 'I think we are right to lie fairly low. The Diem régime is not good but it is no use flushing it out if there is no alternative which there isn't.'[105]

In essence, the British decided to leave it to the Americans to make a move against Diem and his brother. They closely consulted with the Australians on the matter.[106] Everard informed Australia House of Etherington-Smith's assessment that the best course was to rally behind Diem for the time being. However, the Australians were left with the impression that Britain would give 'firm and sympathetic support to whichever decision [the] Americans make in these circumstances'.[107]

Harold Macmillan became personally interested in the situation in Vietnam when he read a Saigon telegram on French policy towards Diem. He asked for the Foreign Office's assessment of the situation and wanted to know whether London should 'take any part or send any views to Washington'.[108] The telegram that caught the Prime Minister's eye reported that Roger Lalouette, the French ambassador in Saigon, wanted to keep Nhu in power so that he could make use of his contacts to Hanoi and bring about a ceasefire. To Etherington-Smith this

---

[102] Telegram 466: Etherington-Smith (Saigon) to FO. 26.8.63. PRO: FO 371/170092, DV1015/67.

[103] Blue FO minute by Williams. 28.8.63. Telegram 725: FO to Saigon. 29.8.63. Telegram 487: Etherington-Smith (Saigon) to FO. 29.8.63. All ibid. DV1015/68/G.

[104] Letter: Warner (FO) to Gilchrist (Djakarta). 17.9.63. PRO: FO 371/169906, DH 1062/83.

[105] Minute by Home. 5.9.63. PRO: FO 371/170092, DV1015/68/G.

[106] Etherington-Smith's telegrams 439 and 443 on his conversations with Diem were passed on to EA Canberra instantly. AUSNA: 1209/80, 62/482, part 2.

[107] Telegram 4588: London to EA Canberra. 4.9.63. AUSNA: 1209/80, file 62/482, part 2.

[108] Letter: de Zulueta to Young (FO). 3.9.63. PRO: PREM 11/4759.

approach seemed consistent with General de Gaulle's policy. The French President had issued a statement on 29 August that called for allowing the Vietnamese people to settle their problems without outside interference. This statement marked the beginning of de Gaulle's advocacy of the neutralization of Vietnam.[109] Etherington-Smith did not believe that Nhu would be able to arrive at a settlement that would not hand South Vietnam to the communists. Moreover, he was certain that Nhu's alleged contacts with Hanoi had added to Washington's eagerness to get rid of Nhu. Yet the British ambassador hoped that the French, Americans, and British could agree to keep Diem in power and rebuild his position. If the Americans ousted Nhu, Etherington-Smith feared that France would come out in open opposition to Washington's efforts in Vietnam. While the British ambassador found some of Lalouette's thinking attractive, the Foreign Office quickly made its reservations clear, telegraphing that Etherington-Smith was not to put forward any British views on the matter.[110] Any moves in the direction of a negotiated settlement were still anathema to Whitehall, and even expressing views on the matter would be against the policy endorsed by Home that Britain should 'lie fairly low'.

In response to the Prime Minister's request, the Foreign Office painted a rosy picture of the situation in South Vietnam. Ambassador Etherington-Smith had stressed in his latest report that Diem had overwhelmed the opposition by a 'controlled show of violence' and was now making 'fulsome gestures' to the Buddhists.[111] The Foreign Office memorandum for the Prime Minister was yet more positive, pointing out that Diem and his family appeared united and as strong as ever. The pagoda raids were described as a 'bold move', which Diem and his family had survived unscathed. The army had cooperated, the country was now quiet and a settlement with the main body of the Buddhists was in sight. The United States was committed to the ouster of Nhu, Macmillan was informed, but Nhu's position had become stronger rather than weaker after the pagoda raids. The Americans faced the dilemma that their only real sanction, the withdrawal of assistance, could compromise the war effort. As for Britain, the Foreign Office stressed that it was reluctant to intervene in the Americans' search for a solution to their dilemma, and would only do so if Washington specifically asked for London's views. 'Not a very heroic line—but perhaps it is right', commented Philip de Zulueta, the Prime Minister's private secretary, when he received the Foreign Office note. Macmillan fully endorsed this passive, non-heroic attitude. He read the Foreign Office note one week before the new Federation of Malaysia was to be created. Indonesia was still opposed to the concept, and the UN

---

[109] Hammer, *A Death in November*, 225–32. Fredrik Logevall, 'De Gaulle, Neutralization and American Involvement in Vietnam, 1963–1964', *Pacific Historical Review*, 61/1 (1992), 78. De Gaulle's statement is also in telegram 582: Harpham (Paris) to FO. 30.8.63. PRO: PREM 11/4759.

[110] Telegram 489: Etherington-Smith (Saigon) to FO. 30.8.63. PRO: PREM 11/4759. Telegram 502: Etherington-Smith (Saigon) to FO. 4.9.63. Telegram 760: FO to Saigon. 5.9.63. All in PRO: FO 371/170092, DV1015/70/G.

[111] Despatch 46: Etherington-Smith to Home. 5.9.63. PRO: FO 371/170146, DV1781/87. This despatch was passed on to the Australians. AUSNA: A1209/80, file 62/482, part 3.

Secretary-General, who had undertaken to ascertain whether the peoples of northern Borneo wanted to join Malaya, had not yet issued his positive report. It was still uncertain if Malaysia could be created and how the Indonesians would react to this. 'With so many other troubles in the world', the Prime Minister therefore minuted, 'we had better keep out of the Saigon one.'[112] Completely ignoring the context and the contents of the submission on which Macmillan had scribbled this minute—and replacing 'Saigon' with 'Vietnam' in the quotation— Fredrik Logevall has concluded that the British Prime Minister decided that the United Kingdom should 'stay out' of the Vietnam conflict, diplomatically and militarily.[113] As we have seen, however, Macmillan was only referring to the question whether a coup against Diem should be supported and if Britain should voice an opinion on this.

On his return from Malaysia, Frederick Warner wrote to the British ambassador in Saigon and apologized for not always acknowledging and commenting on his 'excellent' reports as the department had been 'very busy . . . because of our troubles over Malaysia'.[114] 'The truth of the matter is that I have been concentrating so much on events in Malaysia and Indonesia that my ideas on Vietnam have become very rusty', Warner wrote in a subsequent letter. Etherington-Smith's reports had 'greatly cleared' his mind though. Warner agreed with Whitehall's Vietnam policy that had been decided in early September and this he boiled down to three main points. First, Britain should play a waiting game and express as few opinions as possible in public. Second, London should stay in line with American policy as nothing could be done contrary to Washington's efforts. Third, no dramatic gestures like the withdrawing of BRIAM should be made.[115]

ROBERT THOMPSON'S REPORT FOR JOHN F. KENNEDY

Despite the Buddhist crisis, Robert Thompson went about his business as usual and visited the provinces of the delta to check on the progress of the strategic hamlet programme. He saw no reason to reconsider his plan to leave Saigon for three weeks in late September to go via Kuala Lumpur to Australia and New Zealand. While he intended to talk to government officials in all capitals, his main motivation seemed to have been relaxation—he wanted to spend a few days with his fishing rod in the calm, untouched New Zealand countryside.[116] This

---

[112] FO note on Vietnam, attached to letter: Bridges (FO) to de Zulueta. 6.9.63. Minute by de Zulueta. 6.9.63. Minute by Macmillan. 10.9.63. All in PRO: PREM 11/4759.

[113] Logevall, *Choosing War*, 18–20.

[114] Letter: Warner (FO) to Etherington-Smith (Saigon). 10.9.63. PRO: FO 371/170092, DV1015/73.

[115] Letter: Warner (FO) to Etherington-Smith (Saigon). 25.9.63. PRO: FO 371/170093, DV1015/84.

[116] Letter: Thompson (BRIAM) to Peck (FO). 17.7.63. PRO: FO 371/170101, DV1017/32. Letter: Williams (Official Secretary of Governor) to McIntosh (EA Wellington). 27.5.63. NZNA: PM 478/4/1, part 16.

complacent attitude towards the crisis in Vietnam appears striking. The Department of Defence in Canberra, for instance, refused to grant any leave to its advisers in South Vietnam. The New Zealanders, who looked forward to Thompson's visit with much anticipation as their sources on the Vietnam situation were limited, were almost certain that Thompson would cancel the visit because of the Buddhist crisis. Yet Thompson did not.[117]

Robert Thompson endorsed the conclusions reached by the new British ambassador that Diem had to be supported for the time being. To what extent he influenced this decision remains unclear, as he refrained from sending his views of the situation immediately after the raids to London. It was not before mid-September that his latest assessment, albeit in a distorted form, became known to London, Washington, and the news media.

Henry Cabot Lodge invited Thompson to the American embassy for an hour-long talk on the morning of 12 September. Thompson argued that the Buddhist crisis had destroyed the atmosphere of confidence in Saigon. It would take six months, if not a year, to rebuild it. His latest visits to the countryside had shown the strong reaction of the NLF forces to the strategic hamlet programme. Overall the situation was serious, but not dangerous. Thompson did not share Lodge's concerns about the disaffection of the middle-classes and the professionals with the Diem regime. Diem had never been supported by them, Thompson pointed out. The support of the peasants and the lower-ranking officers was more important, and again Thompson disagreed with Lodge when the latter talked of the possibility that lower officers might also be affected by the Buddhist crisis. Thompson stressed that while westerners were shocked by Diem's use of violence against the Buddhists, the Vietnamese themselves were not. They were 'hard and callous people' and in Thompson's view 'the least attractive' of all the people in Asia. Therefore, the best line for Diem was to continue his conciliatory attitude towards the Buddhists who had not been arrested and to get on with the war. 'Nothing was as black and white as it might appear', Thompson told Lodge, and memories were fairly short. The west had to back Diem, at least until the war was won.[118]

Lodge and Thompson also discussed Ngo Dinh Nhu's contacts with Hanoi. The head of the British Advisory Mission thought it possible that Nhu might think of striking a deal with the DRV if the US brought excessive pressure onto him. As the RVN was in Thompson's view much stronger now than eighteen months ago, Saigon was in a position to exact a high price from Hanoi for getting the Americans out of Vietnam. Thompson admitted that he would not know what to do if the Americans were indeed asked to leave. At the end of their

[117] Army message (unnumbered): Canberra to Saigon. 7.8.63. AUSNA: A1209/80, file 62/482, part 2. Memorandum by Shanahan (EA Wellington). 10.7.63. COS(63)M.23. 18.7.63. Telegram 401: Bangkok to EA Wellington. 17.9.63. All in NZNA: PM 478/4/1, part 17. Letter: Thompson (BRIAM) to Williams (FO). 9.9.63. PRO: FO 371/170101, DV1017/32.

[118] Thompson (BRIAM) report on conversation with Lodge. 12.9.63. PRO: FO 371/170102, DV1017/41/G.

conversation Lodge again brought up the possible collapse of Diem's government. Thompson was certain that, if it came at all, this collapse would be gradual and that there would be sufficient warning. When Lodge finally asked Thompson to pass on to him any information he might obtain on a possible coup, the British adviser remained non-committal and stressed that his sources were inadequate. He had to rely on 'intuition and smell'.[119]

The British Advisory Mission's report of 17 September on the situation in the countryside put forward the same views that Thompson had expressed to Lodge. While essentially the war was being fought on the right lines, there were signs of overextension, and Thompson called for a period of consolidation. Similarly, Thompson repeated his view that the west should continue to back Diem in this serious situation in the covering letter to the report.[120] Those Americans who were involved in the strategic hamlet programme shared Thompson's assessment of the situation in the countryside. USOM's rural affairs officer in Phu Bon Province reported that 'the Viet Cong have lost their war in Phu Bon Province'. USOM's overall assessment in September 1963 was that the strategic hamlet programme continued to progress, albeit at a slower rate than before. Like Thompson the Americans called for a period of consolidation because of the 'program's overextension and lack of sound planning'.[121]

Thompson was certainly concerned about the situation, yet he did not seem too pessimistic. The American embassy's summary record of Thompson's meeting with Lodge, however, painted a different picture. It stated that Thompson thought the war could only be won if the Saigon government totally changed its conduct. Moreover, Thompson was reported as declaring that he had no hope that the situation would change for the better and that 'the only trump card Nhu had was the withdrawal of the US'. Hanoi would be willing to pay 'almost any price' for this.[122] Unfortunately, Fredrik Logevall in his recent study based his analysis of Thompson's views on this American embassy report and failed to compare it with Thompson's own record of the conversation and the reports he produced in the following weeks.[123]

At the time, the exaggerated US embassy report of Thompson's pessimism was leaked to the press. An article in the *Washington Post* stated that 'Thompson's pessimistic report made [a] profound impression on the President'.[124] In London,

[119] Ibid.

[120] Report by Thompson (BRIAM) on the situation in Vietnam. 17.9.63. Letter: Thompson (BRIAM) to Warner (FO). 18.9.63. Ibid.

[121] Memorandum by USOM Rural Affairs: 'Second informal appreciation of the status of the strategic hamlet program'. 1.9.63. Memorandum: Young (Rural Affairs, Phu Bon Province) to Phillips. 6.9.63. Both in HI: Lansdale Papers, folder: Vietnam correspondence, box 49.

[122] Embtel 496: Saigon to State Department. 12.9.63. FRUS: 1961–1963, iv, Vietnam, 204 footnote. Only excerpts of the telegram are printed. The original is still retained.

[123] Logevall, *Choosing War*, 7–12. This is particularly surprising as Logevall had access to British documents and used them to support his main arguments.

[124] The *Washington Post* article is quoted in telegram 554: Hindmarsh (BRIAM) to Thompson (BRIAM). 1.10.63. PRO: FO 371/170101, DV1017/40.

The Times ran a similar story. Correctly reporting the 'split right down the middle' of the Kennedy administration on the question whether Diem had to be replaced, the British newspaper also claimed that Thompson's 'rather pessimistic report' had made Kennedy dispatch General Taylor and Robert McNamara on a special mission to Vietnam.[125] There is no indication in the American record that this was indeed Kennedy's motivation. It seems rather that Taylor and McNamara were sent to Vietnam to ascertain Diem's capabilities of winning the war and helping Washington to arrive at an agreed policy. The divisions between pro-Diem forces in the Pentagon and the CIA and Diem's opponents in the State Department had hardened in September. An earlier fact-finding mission of Joseph Mendenhall of the State Department and the Pentagon's Victor Krulak had, predictably, reached completely opposite assessments of Diem's ability to win the war, prompting Kennedy to comment: 'The two of you did visit the same country, didn't you?'[126]

The leaking of Thompson's alleged pessimism, however, had two other effects. First, the Americans felt embarrassed, and ambassador Lodge once again revealed in a cable how highly Thompson was rated in American circles. It was feared that the leakage would undermine Thompson's position with Diem and hamper his excellent work.[127] Second, and more importantly, Kennedy's National Security Adviser, McGeorge Bundy, approached David Ormsby-Gore on 17 September 1963. Bundy stressed that Ormsby-Gore must be aware how much weight Kennedy attached to Thompson's views on Vietnam. Probably referring to the US embassy's report of Lodge's meeting with Thompson, Bundy said that the President had received a second-hand report on Thompson's views. Kennedy wanted something more 'authoritative', but it would be embarrassing to ask the American embassy in Saigon for a memorandum by Thompson.[128]

Although Robert Thompson received a Foreign Office telegram that requested another report on the situation for the Americans before his departure from Saigon on 23 September, he thought that it was sufficient to pass the general report he had just written to the Americans.[129] This was not, however, what the Foreign Office had in mind. Gordon Etherington-Smith was instructed to treat Kennedy's request in strict secrecy because of its 'delicate and important nature'. The other members of BRIAM were not to be informed. Thompson's memorandum should be on the lines of his 'usual excellent reports', but he should bear in mind that it was written for the American President.[130] Thompson had already

---

[125] 'U.S. Mission Faces Crucial Choice in Vietnam', *The Times*, 24.9.63, p. 10. The New Zealand High Commission commented on this report that Thompson was 'a good deal more sanguine than might have been expected'. Letter: Jermyn to EA Wellington. 30.9.63. NZNA: PM 478/4/1, part 18.

[126] Memorandum of Conversation at the White House (President Kennedy, Joseph Mendenhall, Major General Krulak among participants). 10.9.63. FRUS: 1961–1963, iv, Vietnam 1963, 162.

[127] Embtel 633: Lodge (Saigon) to State Department. 5.10.63. USNA: RG 59, Central Files, POL 27 S VIET.

[128] Telegram 2898: Ormsby-Gore (Washington) to FO. 18.9.63. PRO: FO 371/170101, DV1017/40.

[129] Blue FO minute by Warner. 23.10.63. PRO: FO 371/170102, DV1017/43/G.

[130] Letter: Peck (FO) to Etherington-Smith (Saigon). 23.9.63. Ibid. DV1017/42/G.

left Saigon for New Zealand when the Foreign Office's secret instructions reached Etherington-Smith. The Foreign Office admitted that, 'in the rush of the Indonesian crisis'—the British embassy in Jakarta had been burnt down on 18 September in reaction to the creation of Malaysia—it had been overlooked that the instructions by letter would take nine or ten days to reach Saigon. Ambassador Etherington-Smith indicated that he was not too keen on Thompson making his views known to President Kennedy. He suggested that the matter could wait until Thompson's return in late October.[131]

The further delay of more than three weeks was not acceptable to the Foreign Office. When Thompson arrived at Whenuapai airport in New Zealand on 3 October, a message from London was waiting for him. The Foreign Office requested a comprehensive review of the situation in South Vietnam, how the Buddhist crisis had affected it and what the chances of progress were under the current regime. It was stressed that the memorandum was for the highest level in Washington. Thompson drafted the report on his first day in New Zealand with the help of the British Information Service in Auckland. However, it took Thompson another week to reach Wellington, as he saw no reason to change his travel plans. He played golf and spent two days fishing on the Tongariro River. The diplomatic bag with his report for the American President finally left New Zealand on 10 October.[132]

In his memorandum for Kennedy, Thompson 'stuck out his neck', as he himself admitted, and came down strongly in favour of continuing the support for Diem. While the South Vietnamese president had not handled the Buddhist crisis well, there was no viable alternative to his regime. He stressed that he had seen no effect of the Buddhist crisis in the five or six delta provinces he had visited recently. If at all, there were more operations against NLF forces now than before. The west should stick to Diem's regime as its 'achievements of the last 18 months have been remarkable by any standard and progress is still being made'. Thompson predicted that decisive progress could probably be made in the next twelve months, and certainly within the next two years. He finally stressed that South Vietnam had to be held because it was vital 'to our global strategy against communism (and especially China)'.[133]

During his talks in Wellington and Canberra Thompson expanded his views on the situation and defended Diem's actions. He told officials of the Ministry of External Affairs and the New Zealand Joint Intelligence Committee that Diem had to take action against the Buddhists in late August. The Buddhist protests had developed into a political movement, with bonzes preaching sedition in the

[131] Letter: Peck (FO) to Etherington-Smith (Saigon). 9.10.63. Telegram 555: Etherington-Smith (Saigon) to FO. 1.10.63. Letter: Etherington-Smith (Saigon) to Peck (FO). 2.10.63. All ibid.

[132] Telegram 1377: CRO to Wellington (Peck to Thompson). 2.10.63. Ibid. Aerogram: Thompson (Wellington) to Peck (FO). 9.10.63. Ibid. DV1017/44. Letter: Thompson to Peck (FO). 5.11.63. Ibid. DV1017/48. EA Wellington note: 'Itinerary for Mr. R. G. K. Thompson'. 3.10.63. NZNA: PM 478/4/1, part 18. Thompson, *Make for the Hills*, 141.

[133] Memorandum by Thompson (BRIAM). 9.10.63. PRO: FO 371/170102, DV1017/43/G. Aerogram: Thompson (Wellington) to Peck (FO). 9.10.63. Ibid. DV1017/44.

pagodas. In Thompson's view things were now settling down in Saigon and it was likely that the Diem regime would be back in a position of strength after a while. Suggestions that Nhu held the real power in Saigon were unfounded. Overall, the war was being fought on the right lines and Thompson still believed that white areas could soon be proclaimed in the Vinh Long or Vinh Binh provinces. Contrary to his assessment in July,[134] and indeed his assertion in his report for Kennedy, he now claimed that the Buddhist disturbances had prevented the declaration of these provinces as 'white' earlier. The real danger, according to Thompson, was the deterioration of American–Vietnamese relations, which might push Diem and Nhu into seeking a deal with Hanoi.[135]

Talking to the Australian Chiefs of Staff Committee, Thompson made the same points as in Wellington. He added that if there were to be a coup in Saigon, the army was the only organization capable of arranging it. His view, however, was that a coup within the next few months would lead to the communists winning the war.[136] The Australians and New Zealanders were interested in Thompson's opinions, yet they noted that his 'fairly optimistic line' was in stark contrast to the latest assessments of the American embassy, which stressed that Diem and Nhu were in a 'dangerous and desperate' mood and that the regime could not contemplate any action other than the 'multiplication' of repressive police state measures.[137]

When Robert Thompson returned to Saigon on 23 October 1963, he found that his report for Kennedy had not yet been forwarded to Washington. A major policy reassessment had taken place in the British embassy and the Foreign Office during his absence. Strikingly similar to the split in the American administration, the British embassy and the Foreign Office now advocated Diem's ouster, whereas Thompson and his mission continued to support the Saigon regime. Those mainly involved in the political aspect of the war—the United States, British, and other western embassies and their ministries at home—had decided that a change was necessary. Those involved in the military and pacification side of the conflict—MACV, the CIA, and BRIAM—did not want to upset the situation.

Ambassador Etherington-Smith's position on Diem began to shift in the second half of September. In a letter that discussed the divisions between the MACV/CIA and the American embassy with regard to Diem and his ability to win the war, Etherington-Smith found that he and Thompson had their differences, too. Thompson's estimate of 17 September with regard to the prospects of the war was rosier than Etherington-Smith's. 'I am regretfully coming to the con-

<hr>

[134] Report on Vinh Long and Vinh Binh provinces by Thompson (BRIAM). 12.7.63. PRO: FO 371/170101, DV1017/31. In this report Thompson merely stated that progress in these provinces was slower than expected but still impressive. There was 'nothing to worry about provided that the advance continues steadily and methodically'.

[135] Memorandum by EA Wellington on the talks with Thompson. 17.10.63. NZNA: PM 478/4/1, part 18.

[136] Record of Meeting of COS Committee. 16.10.63. AUSNA: A1209/80, file 62/482, part 2.

[137] Letter: Shepherd (Canberra) to EA Wellington. 17.10.63. NZNA: PM 478/4/1, part 18.

clusion', Etherington-Smith wrote, 'that the war is unlikely to be won under the Diem régime.' The British ambassador might well have been influenced by his US colleague in arriving at this conclusion as he stressed that Henry Cabot Lodge held the same view.[138]

A week after this statement Etherington-Smith drafted a dispatch, which marked the turning point in his thinking on Diem. In the ambassador's opinion the regime had forfeited the support of large parts of the Vietnamese population, South Vietnamese–American relations were strained, Diem's ability to win the war seemed doubtful and there was even a chance that Nhu might 'double-cross' the west and make a deal with Hanoi. Moreover, disaffection was so widespread that an army coup could occur at any moment. For all these reasons, western policy should be 'directed towards the establishment of a more effective Government'. This could be encouraged if Britain disassociated itself from the policies of Diem's regime.[139] The British embassy had already been approached by some Vietnamese who were willing to overthrow the government,[140] yet the British ambassador thought it more prudent not to be implicated in anything. However, Britain should not denounce plots either. Etherington-Smith pointed out that Thompson would disagree with his assessment. Anticipating the position Thompson took in his report for Kennedy, the British ambassador stated that Thompson felt a coup would create a chaotic and dangerous situation. 'But Bob [Thompson] is not as fully in the local political picture as we are and my judgement (which is shared by a great many of my colleagues) is the other way.'[141]

Now that Thompson and Etherington-Smith had differing views on the situation in Vietnam, it was particularly awkward for the diplomatic mission to have another body in Saigon that was reporting to the Foreign Office as well. As in January when Henry Hohler expressed his more pessimistic opinion on the progress of the counter-insurgency effort, the embassy felt the need to point out that it was better informed than Thompson. Apart from contacts to the French, Reginald Burrows, Etherington-Smith's deputy, maintained good relations with foreign correspondents in Saigon, among them Dennis Warner and David Halberstam. Burrows also frequently travelled to the countryside. Ostensibly distributing British aid, like blankets, he used these tours to get an impression of the security situation in the hamlets. On one of his trips he found out first hand that the insurgents were far from being defeated. When he visited a village school to hand over technical equipment a grenade was thrown into the room through the window. Luckily, the explosive device did not go off. Information on the military side provided by Colonel Lee, the military attaché, also helped Etherington-Smith to make up his mind. The Colonel's relations with Thompson were

---

[138] Letter: Etherington-Smith (Saigon) to Warner (FO). 18.9.63. PRO: FO 371/170093, DV 1015/84.

[139] Despatch 53: Etherington-Smith (Saigon) to FO. 26.9.63. Ibid. DV1015/86/G.

[140] Telegram 2800: Washington to Canberra. 18.10.63. AUSNA: A1209/80, file 62/482, part 2.

[141] Letter: Etherington-Smith (Saigon) to Peck (FO). 9.10.63. PRO: FO 371/170093, DV1015/86/G.

strained, not least because of Lee's more critical appraisal of the progress of the strategic hamlet programme.[142]

Frederick Warner's first reaction to indications of Etherington-Smith's about-turn was incredulous. The Australians had learned from their ambassador in Saigon earlier than London that Etherington-Smith had changed his mind. Asked of his opinion, Warner said that he would be surprised if the British ambassador was arguing that Diem must go. It was more likely that he was merely arguing that there was no hope of winning the war if Diem remained in power.[143] Yet after receiving Etherington-Smith's full assessment, the Foreign Office quickly agreed with the ambassador. The long-standing reservations about Diem did not make it too difficult to endorse the ambassador's views. Frederick Warner pointed out to Lord Home that Etherington-Smith's latest dispatch marked a great change in Britain's attitude towards Diem. Previously the British had been afraid of an even more unstable South Vietnam and a split between the anti-communist forces in the aftermath of a coup—in other words a Laos-like situation. The ambassador in Saigon had now reached the firm conclusion that a change of regime was necessary. The British believed that Washington thought similarly, and the new US policy of cutting aid for selective projects, such as Nhu's elite forces, after McNamara's and General Taylor's visit to Saigon was taken as further proof of this.[144]

In fact, the conclusions of the McNamara–Taylor report were remarkably similar to Thompson's assessments. No initiative should be taken to encourage Diem's removal. The report stressed moreover that the military campaign had made 'great progress', indeed so much progress that one thousand US military advisers were superfluous and could return home in December 1963, and maybe all of them by 1965. By withholding some of the aid that was not essential for the war effort, the United States should make its disapproval of Diem's political programme clear.[145] Thompson therefore informed the Foreign Office of his broad agreement with the report, only the latter recommendation did not find Thompson's approval because he found that the withdrawal of aid was a 'straight invitation to a coup'.[146]

The changed British attitude towards Diem did not mean that London was giving up its passive policy. No British initiative was required, Warner stressed, and the embassy in Saigon should not get 'mixed up' in any plots. 'Our interest and influence in South Vietnam are slight and there is no sense of getting involved', Warner wrote. Interestingly, Sir Harold Caccia, Permanent Under-Secretary of State at the Foreign Office, did not quite agree that London's interest was only

---

[142] Reginald Burrows in interview with the author. 14.2.2002. Letter: Reginald Burrows to author. 21.2.2002.

[143] Telegram 5257: London to EA Canberra. 3.10.63. AUSNA: A1209/80, file 62/482, part 2.

[144] Blue FO minute by Warner. 8.10.63. PRO: FO 371/170093, DV1015/86/G.

[145] Memorandum from Taylor and McNamara to the President. 2.10.63. FRUS: 1961–1963, iv, Vietnam 1963, 336–46. The instructions for Lodge, including the freezing of aid to Nhu's security forces, are in deptel 534: Rusk to Saigon. 5.10.63. Ibid. 371–9.

[146] Letter: Thompson (BRIAM) to Peck (FO). 30.10.63. PRO: FO 371/170102, DV1017/47/G.

slight. He noted in the margin of the submission to Lord Home that Britain's interest in South Vietnam was 'indirect rather than direct'.[147] Caccia was certainly thinking of the problems over Malaysia and the possible repercussions that a communist victory in South Vietnam could have on London's position in the new federation. As a former ambassador in Washington, Caccia was also inclined to see Britain's interest and involvement in the RVN in the context of Anglo-American relations. If Britain supported the United States in Vietnam, the British could benefit from that in other areas.

The minute for Lord Home mentioned that Robert Thompson had been asked for his views, but that his report had not been received yet. Had Lord Home been apprised of Thompson's pro-Diem attitude, he might have reacted more forcefully. The Foreign Secretary was clearly not too happy about the sea change in the Saigon embassy but, preoccupied with his struggle for the leadership of the Conservatives and shortly before he left the Foreign Office to become Prime Minister,[148] he did nothing to reverse the new policy. 'I am very doubtful', Lord Home minuted on Warner's submission. 'Let the Americans play their hand if they like. I think any successor government might easily be worse.'[149]

The Vietnam desk officer in the Southeast Asia Department wanted to let Etherington-Smith know of Lord Home's reservations, but Warner found this unnecessary as Britain did not intend to get actively involved in any coup planning.[150] Even before Lord Home commented on the new policy, the Foreign Office had informed Etherington-Smith of its agreement with his conclusion: a change of regime in Saigon was desirable if it could be brought about rapidly and did not split the anti-communist forces. The ambassador was instructed not to become involved and make sure that 'all members of your staff keep their hands clean'. The Saigon embassy was reminded of the recent attacks on the British embassy in Jakarta, which showed the importance of utmost security and the necessity of destroying correspondence that could be misconstrued.[151]

Brian Hill, the Australian ambassador in Saigon, was one of those western colleagues who shared Etherington-Smith's views. London continued to keep the Australians well informed about the Foreign Office's thinking on Vietnam throughout October, and even told them about Kennedy's request for a report by Thompson, which had initially been treated with utmost secrecy.[152] The

---

[147] Blue FO minute by Warner. 8.10.63. Minute by Caccia. 10.10.63. Both in PRO: FO 371/170093, DV1015/86/G.

[148] Home became Prime Minister on 18 October 1963. On his preoccupation with Macmillan's succession after the latter's resignation on 9 October, see D. R. Thorpe, *Alec Douglas-Home* (London: Sinclair-Stevenson, 1996), 292 ff. and John Turner, *Macmillan* (London: Longman, 1994), 294–5.

[149] Minute by Home. 12.10.63. PRO: FO 371/170093, DV1015/86/G.

[150] Minutes by Everard (FO). 29.10.63 and 30.10.63. Ibid. DV1015/93/G.

[151] Letter: Peck (FO) to Etherington-Smith (Saigon). 9.10.63. Ibid. DV1015/86/G.

[152] Telegram 2800: Washington to EA Canberra. 18.10.63. AUSNA: 1209/80, file 62/482, part 2. Memorandum of Conversation between Beale (Australian ambassador) and Rusk. 16.9.63. USNA: RG 59, Central Files, POL S VIET.

Australians knew that Britain would welcome a coup if it came about by spontaneous Vietnamese action. Whereas Brian Hill wanted to inform the Americans of Australia's view that Diem's time was up, the British still preferred to keep their opinions to themselves. It was one thing to change the attitude towards Diem in private, and quite another to tell the Americans about it. Moreover, the British pointed out to the Australians on 19 October that they had not reached a *final* view yet. Four days later, Warner even told the Australians that the Foreign Office was unable to make up its mind on the prospects of a military victory in Vietnam because London had received conflicting advice from Etherington-Smith and Thompson.[153]

The Foreign Office received Thompson's report for Kennedy and ambassador Etherington-Smith's comments on it on 23 October. As expected, the two men's conclusions on a number of factors with regard to the situation in Vietnam were very different. As for the military prospects, Thompson saw no reason why the strategic hamlet programme could not be consolidated and some further progress be made. He did not expect a decisive turn for the better within the next three months but believed this could happen within twelve months and certainly within two years. Etherington-Smith found the value of the apparent progress with regard to strategic hamlets 'uncertain', and pointed out that there were increasing suggestions of subversion from within the hamlets. Etherington-Smith followed in his general assessment of the military prospects the line of the American ambassador. He saw no evidence that the war was being won, and he was certain that the disaffection of the middle classes with Diem's regime would sooner or later affect the war effort. 'I believe it is time for a change and that a change is essential', Etherington-Smith concluded. And he thought that by disassociating from the Diem regime the west could do something to help replace the regime. Thompson, however, thought that the west was 'stuck' with the legally constituted Saigon government and he stressed: 'This is not the moment for an upheaval.'[154]

It is true that, as the Australians were told, the British decided to postpone the production of a coordinated view on the situation in Vietnam until Thompson's next visit to London. However, the Foreign Office clearly sided with Etherington-Smith, as it refused to forward Thompson's report to Kennedy. Frederick Warner gave two reasons for this attitude. First, the report was outdated and Warner doubted that it would be of any value to the President. The Foreign Office knew that the McNamara–Taylor mission to Vietnam had already been followed up with a long directive to the US ambassador in Saigon, which set out the detailed policies of the United States, especially in terms of putting pressure on

---

[153] Savingram 154: Saigon to Canberra. 17.10.63. Telegram 5589: London to Canberra. 19.10.63. Telegram 5666: London to EA Canberra. 23.10.63. All in AUSNA: A1838/334, file 3014/11/51, part 1.

[154] Memorandum by Thompson (BRIAM). 9.10.63. Telegram 602: Etherington-Smith (Saigon) to FO. 23.10.63. 'Summary of Differences between Mr. R. G. K. Thompson and H.M. Ambassador, Saigon concerning the present situation in South Viet-Nam'. Enclosure to blue FO minute by Warner. 23.10.63. All in PRO: FO 371/170102, DV1017/43/G.

Diem by selectively cutting aid.[155] Second, and more importantly, Thompson's conclusions were different from Etherington-Smith's assessment. 'My feeling is', Warner wrote, 'that the Ambassador may well be right and Mr. Thompson wrong.' The head of the Southeast Asia Department concluded, and his superiors agreed, that Thompson's view should not be brought to Kennedy's attention.[156] Although Reginald Burrows described BRIAM in retrospect as a godsend to placate the Americans, he stressed—not without satisfaction—that his superiors in London finally sided with the embassy and not with Thompson, whom he regarded as more loyal to himself and Diem than to Her Majesty's Government. And however useful BRIAM was, the diplomatic establishment was not to be fooled: 'The Foreign Office does not fall for salesmen', Burrows pointed out.[157]

In Washington, David Ormsby-Gore completely disagreed with the Foreign Office's conclusions because he was keen to fulfil Kennedy's request. To the British ambassador in Washington it did not matter that Thompson's assessment differed from Etherington-Smith's opinion: '[W]hat [President Kennedy] has specifically asked for is Thompson's own views. It was very clearly understood when the Prime Minister agreed to this project that what Thompson had to say would not necessarily be in conformity with Her Majesty's Government's views.'[158] Because of Ormsby-Gore's intervention, the Foreign Office decided to ask Thompson to prepare an up-to-date report for the US President. This request was cabled to Saigon on 31 October.[159] Two days later Diem and Nhu were dead. There had been no time for Thompson to reiterate his support for Diem and make his views known to President Kennedy.

Naturally, it is difficult to say if the forwarding of Thompson's view would have made any impression on President Kennedy. Yet it does not seem completely unlikely. The divisions within the American administration on the removal of Diem had not been resolved, contrary to the Foreign Office's perception. Kennedy himself remained ambivalent about the coup. General Taylor and CIA director John McCone continued to oppose the ousting of Diem. They put their arguments to the President at a meeting on 29 October 1963. Robert Kennedy also doubted that working for the removal of Diem was the right policy. This appears to have almost swayed the President. In the end, however, Kennedy left the final decision to Lodge. If the US ambassador agreed with the latest CIA estimate that the pro- and anti-Diem military forces were evenly balanced, then, Kennedy decided, Lodge should be instructed to discourage a coup.[160] This was, of course, more a

---

[155] Deptel 534: Rusk to Saigon. 5.10.63. FRUS: 1961–1963, iv, Vietnam 1963, 371–9.

[156] Blue FO minute by Warner. 23.10.63. Minute by Peck. 24.10.63. Both in PRO: FO 371/170102, DV1017/43/G.

[157] Reginald Burrows in interview with the author. 14.2.2002.

[158] Telegram 3329: Ormsby-Gore (Washington) to FO. 28.10.63. PRO: FO 371/170102, DV 1017/46.

[159] Telegram 922: FO to Saigon. 31.10.63. Ibid.

[160] Memorandum by Bromley Smith of a conference with the President. 29.10.63. FRUS: 1961–1963, iv, Vietnam 1963, 468–71. On this meeting and Kennedy's contradictory signals to Lodge, see also McMaster, *Dereliction of Duty*, 39–41.

decision in favour of the removal of Diem than against it because of Lodge's conviction that Diem had to go.

The British quickly adapted to the new situation in Saigon after the overthrow of the Diem government. The embassy welcomed the change in the RVN and looked optimistically ahead. The British government recognized the new regime headed by General Duong Van Minh on 8 November.[161] Ambassador Etherington-Smith found that the Revolutionary Military Council had shown 'remarkable unity', and that its initial performance was 'impressive'.[162] The British military attaché, who enjoyed good relations with the ARVN, was the most optimistic. 'I feel for the first time since I have been here', he wrote, 'that at last this country has a chance to win the people to the Government and so win the war against the Viet Cong and Communism.'[163] Even Robert Thompson, although personally sorry about Diem's death, felt that the coup had been well executed. 'This augurs well for the future', he concluded, revealing his usual confidence.[164] There were, however, some more cautious voices. Brian Hill, the Australian ambassador, had been in favour of removing Diem. Yet only four days after Diem's death he felt that there was 'already some regret . . . over the irrevocable removal from the scene of Diem and Nhu'. As Lodge's attitude had had the 'most important bearing on [the] development of events', the onus was now on Lodge. The American task would not be easy, Hill stressed, as it was unlikely to find more talented leaders in South Vietnam than Diem and Nhu had been.[165]

AFTER DIEM: BRIAM IN DECLINE

In retrospect, the Buddhist crisis and the coup against Diem marked a turning point in Britain's Vietnam policy. The creation of Malaysia and its defence against hostile Indonesia were of first importance to the British government and refocused its attention from Indochina to the Malayan area. Because of the confrontation between Malaysia and Indonesia and the political chaos in the RVN, the British government had no intention to become more deeply involved in the Vietnam situation. London remained keen to give political support for American policy in Indochina and to appear to be a good ally. Yet in practical terms Britain was on the retreat in late 1963 and 1964, particularly as the political chaos in the RVN before and after the coup made it more difficult for BRIAM—still Britain's most visible commitment to the non-communist regime in Saigon—to continue to play a useful advisory role.

161 Telegram 678: Etherington-Smith (Saigon) to FO. 8.11.63. PRO: PREM 11/4759.
162 Letter: Etherington-Smith (Saigon) to Peck (FO). 13.11.63. PRO: FO 371/170095, DV1015/122.
163 Letter: Lee (Saigon) to Jones (WO). 14.11.63. PRO: FO 371/170137, DV1201/121.
164 Letter: Thompson (BRIAM) to Peck (FO). 5.11.63. PRO: FO 371/170102, DV1017/49/G. Thompson postscript of 4.11.63 on letter: Thompson (BRIAM) to Jockel (EA Canberra). 1.11.63. AUSNA: A1838/334, file 3014/11/51, part 1.
165 Savingram 167: Hill (Saigon) to EA Canberra. 6.11.63. AUSNA: A1838/280, file 3014/2/1, part 30B.

At first, however, Robert Thompson spoke of new opportunities for BRIAM after Diem's death. He hoped not only to give advice on emergency measures and the organization necessary to ensure the complete coordination between civil and military measures, but also on the future administrative structure of the Saigon government.[166] Yet these hopes were soon shattered. By December 1963 ambassador Etherington-Smith and Robert Thompson both agreed that the situation looked grim. Buddhist self-immolations continued, and the strategic hamlet programme was in deep trouble. In some areas like Vinh Long it was even disintegrating. Previous errors in the programme had been admitted, but due to the lack of firm direction from the new government nothing was being done to remedy the situation. Advances by NLF forces in the delta area were particularly worrying.[167] Thompson told the Australians in December that he had been 'taken aback by the steady rot' he had witnessed during his recent visit to the delta province of Kien Hoa. He thought the picture was 'pretty grim' and spoke of low morale and a 'highly-disturbing situation in the countryside'.[168] In an attempt to educate the new regime, Thompson drafted a memorandum on the principles of the strategic hamlet programme for the new government. The memorandum was also handed to the Australians and Americans.[169]

That Thompson was confronted with an increasingly depressing picture in the delta was only partly due to the incompetence of the new military junta in Saigon. Another consequence of Diem's ouster was Hanoi's renewed determination to bring down the regime in the south. In December 1963 it decided to escalate the military struggle, and the NLF forces were instructed to focus particularly on the delta area. In the first half of 1964 US intelligence also admitted that the strategic hamlet programme had stalled.[170] Faced with political turmoil in the wake of another coup in Saigon, Thompson's attempts at reviving the strategic hamlet programme throughout the first months of 1964 came to nothing. BRIAM's position had changed from that of an advisory mission to the Saigon government to that of a mission to the Americans in South Vietnam.[171] Thompson found this 'new' advisory role frustrating. He commented on an American invitation in February to their 'inner councils' in Saigon, that, regardless of this offer, the United States

[166] Letter: Thompson (BRIAM) to Peck. 5.11.63. PRO: FO 371/170102, DV1017/49/G.

[167] Telegram 725: Etherington-Smith (Saigon) to FO. 4.12.63. PRO: FO 371/170095, DV1015/132. Telegram 734: Etherington-Smith (Saigon) to FO. 9.12.63. Ibid. DV1015/136. Telegram 735: Thompson (BRIAM) to Peck (FO). 9.12.63. PRO: FO 371/170102, DV1017/52. Thompson (BRIAM) memorandum for General Le Van Kim. 9.12.63. Ibid. DV1017/55.

[168] Savingram 187: Hill (Saigon) to EA Canberra. 16.12.63. AUSNA: A1838/280, file 3014/2/1, part 30B. Telegram 3360: Washington to EA Canberra. 16.12.63. AUSNA: A1209/80, file 62/482, part 3. Savingram 192: Hill (Saigon) to EA Canberra. 17.12.63. AUSNA: A1838/280, file 3014/2/9, part 19.

[169] Thompson memorandum on strategic hamlets. 10.12.63. PRO: FO 371/170102, DV1017/55. A copy of the memorandum is also in HI: Lansdale Papers, folder: US Embassy Saigon, Senior Liaison Office, Subject file: British Advisory Mission, box 60; and in attachments to memorandum 1191: Hill (Saigon) to EA Canberra. 11.12.63. AUSNA: A1838/280, file 3014/2/9/1A, part 1.

[170] William J. Duiker, 'Hanoi's Response to American Policy, 1961–1965: Crossed Signals?' in Lloyd C. Gardner and Ted Gittinger (eds.), *Vietnam: The Early Decisions* (Austin: University of Texas Press, 1997).

[171] Letter: Thompson (BRIAM) to Peck (FO). 24.6.64. PRO: FO 371/175483, DV1017/23.

would make its decisions in its own particular way and his influence would be marginal.[172] Worse, only two weeks after his first attendance at a meeting of the American Pacification Committee in Vietnam, the committee had been abolished.[173] With the strategic hamlet programme in disarray, and no South Vietnamese government but only Americans to advise, a frustrated Thompson informed Edward Peck in May 1964 that there was no use for his services in Vietnam anymore. BRIAM had been able to do little more than merely observe the steady deterioration of the situation in Vietnam, Thompson complained. He therefore refused to renew his contract, which was due to expire in April 1965.[174]

By November 1964, Thompson was completely disillusioned with the situation in Vietnam. When he was in London at the beginning of the month, Edward Peck, the Assistant Under-Secretary of State at the Foreign Office, met Thompson and did his best 'to redress the balance of [Thompson's] gloomy prognosis by reminding him that the Americans still had in their hand the card of possible action against Hanoi and China as a last effort to persuade the North Viet-Namese to call off the war in South Viet-Nam'.[175] Yet the Foreign Office's more positive assessment—and Peck's view that playing this 'card' was indeed a viable option— did not persuade Thompson, and in late November he outlined in a long letter that, in his view, the war was lost. If the Americans continued to do more of what they had been doing, the NLF forces would succeed. If Washington escalated the conflict and started bombing the North, a policy he termed the 'bad-loser option', Hanoi would not give in, continue the struggle and eventually win. The only solution was to seek talks with the NLF and for the Americans to withdraw and leave South Vietnam to the communists. This would be, Thompson admitted, a disastrous defeat for the west as it would encourage the PRC's radical line and weaken the 'ex-Khrushchev' Soviet policy of peaceful co-existence in the context of the Sino-Soviet split. However, in the long run Thompson was certain that the Vietnamese, even if communist, would be hostile towards China because of their historical fear of being dominated by their more powerful neighbour.[176] In late 1964 in a reversal of roles it was Gordon Etherington-Smith who was more optimistic than Thompson. He maintained that the war had not been lost yet, stressing that 'something still can be done'. The British ambassador therefore insisted that the time had not come to decide for or against negotiations.[177] Ironically, Thompson seemed to have forgotten his prediction that Hanoi was bound to win when he returned to Vietnam in 1969 as President Richard Nixon's adviser on pacifica-

---

172 Letter: Thompson (BRIAM) to Peck (FO). 11.3.64. PRO: FO 371/175482, DV1017/10.

173 Letter: Thompson (BRIAM) to Peck (FO). 15.4.64. PRO: FO 371/175483, DV1017/15/G.

174 Minute by Peck (FO). 19.5.64. PRO: FO 371/175482, DV1017/19. Letter: Thompson (BRIAM) to Peck (FO). 5.8.64. PRO: FO 371/175483, DV1017/27.

175 Blue FO minute by Peck. 1.10.64. PRO: FO 371/175484, DV1017/44.

176 Letter: Thompson (BRIAM) to Peck (FO). 25.11.64. PRO: FO 371/175503, DV103145/217/G. See also Rolf Steininger, 'Großbritannien und der Vietnamkrieg 1964/65', *Vierteljahreshefte für Zeitgeschichte*, 45/4 (1997), 596–8.

177 Letter: Etherington-Smith (Saigon) to Peck (FO). 26.11.64. PRO: FO 371/175503, DV 103145/221/G.

tion.[178] Expressing his customary confidence after a brief visit to the RVN he told Nixon that the South Vietnamese government was in a 'winning position'.[179]

In August 1964, the Foreign Office noted with regret that Britain would lose its 'trump card' in Vietnam after Thompson's departure. Yet it agreed that BRIAM's 'usefulness had come to an end'.[180] The planned abandoning of BRIAM was concealed for as long as possible from the Americans, who increasingly urged their allies to step up their effort in support of the RVN. Four months after the Foreign Office had become resigned to the fact that BRIAM would have to be dissolved, the British still used the mission to stress that they were making a considerable effort in South Vietnam. During his first meeting with President Lyndon B. Johnson in December 1964, Harold Wilson, the new Labour Prime Minister, pointed out that 'Britain was already providing some reinforcements to the United States effort in Vietnam by maintaining the Thompson mission, by training Vietnamese troops in jungle warfare in Malaysian schools and by providing police in Saigon'. Wilson even added that Britain might be able to increase its 'effort in these directions to some extent'.[181] Not surprisingly, the American ambassador in Saigon was not happy when he was informed about BRIAM's termination just days after the Wilson–Johnson summit. In order to continue to have a presence in South Vietnam and to compensate for the termination of BRIAM, Britain had decided in October 1964 to send four British police advisers to work with USOM in 1965.[182] To placate the Americans, the Foreign Office thought it best that the four police advisers were to form a team, which, for presentational purposes, was named 'British Police Advisers Team, Viet-Nam'.[183]

CONCLUSION

From 1960 the Foreign Office and the Saigon embassy harboured serious doubts about Ngo Dinh Diem's ability to defeat the communist insurgency. The undemocratic nature of his government troubled the British only in so far as it could undermine the war effort, and winning against the communist insurgents was the prime objective. In 1961 for instance, many in the Foreign Office regarded a military government as the best solution for improving the RVN's chances to defeat the NLF forces. This showed once again that the British saw the Vietnam conflict very much through the prism of the Malayan emergency where the military Director of Operations had been invested with wide-ranging powers. Given the long-standing criticism of Diem and Nhu within British diplomatic circles, the

[178] For Thompson's role as Nixon's adviser, see Thompson, *Make for the Hills*, 158 ff.
[179] Jeffrey Kimball, *Nixon's Vietnam War* (Lawrence: University Press of Kansas, 1998), 179–80.
[180] Letter: Peck (FO) to Burrows (Saigon). 20.8.64. PRO: FO 371/175483, DV1017/27.
[181] Cabinet Office Record of a meeting held at the British Embassy in Washington, DC and later at the White House on 7 December 1964. 14.12.64. PRO: PREM 13/104.
[182] Letter: Etherington-Smith (Saigon) to Peck (FO). 4.8.64. PRO: FO 371/175483, DV1017/27. Blue FO minute by Murray. 16.10.64. PRO: FO 371/175484, DV1017/47.
[183] Blue FO minute by Murray. 16.12.64. Ibid. DV1017/53.

relatively mild reaction to the outbreak and escalation of the Buddhist crisis in May and June 1963 appears surprising. Yet the British reaction to the political crisis in Saigon from June 1963 reveals four important characteristics of Britain's policy towards the Vietnam war.

First and foremost, the Buddhist crisis and the subsequent coup marked a turning point in Britain's Vietnam policy. After actively seeking some involvement in the conflict between 1960 and early 1963, London took a step back from the Vietnam War. By May 1963, the problems the British were facing over the creation of Malaysia had begun to overshadow the crisis in Saigon, and Britain's main interests and responsibilities in Southeast Asia lay in Malaysia. Preoccupied with Indonesia's confrontation policy, the Foreign Office's decision to 'lie low' in South Vietnam appears understandable. In addition, the political chaos in the RVN after the coup undermined the British advisory role in Saigon. The strategic hamlet programme collapsed, BRIAM's advice and its members' Malayan experience were not needed anymore, Robert Thompson became disillusioned, and it was decided to terminate the mission.

Second, the British difficulty in formulating an agreed policy towards the Diem regime in the weeks before the coup and the subsequent breakdown of the strategic hamlet programme revealed the disadvantages of having established BRIAM. Interestingly, the division between BRIAM, on the one hand, and the British embassy in Saigon and the Foreign Office on the other, mirrored the splits in the Kennedy administration on Diem. As Harriman and Hilsman managed to gain the upper hand in Washington by sending the infamous cable of 24 August to Saigon that permitted ambassador Lodge to signal to the ARVN generals that the United States would support a coup, the Foreign Office silenced Robert Thompson. When Lord Home was made aware of the British policy reversal on Diem in October 1963, he was simply informed that Thompson's report that Kennedy had asked for had not been received. As Lord Home doubted the wisdom of removing Diem, Thompson's favourable assessment of the South Vietnamese President might have made a difference. Moreover, contrary to the Foreign Office's perception that the United States had made up its mind and was favouring a coup after the McNamara–Taylor mission, Thompson's report might have influenced Kennedy as the debate on the removal of Diem was still being waged in Washington at the end of October.

Third, Britain's policy towards the Diem regime showed that the Foreign Office was very reluctant to take any initiative that might not find Washington's approval. The British simply wanted to follow the Americans' lead, and there was no willingness to influence US policy on Diem one way or the other. This, again, highlights that Britain saw its involvement in Vietnam in the context of Anglo-American relations. Supporting American policy in Vietnam was to demonstrate that Britain was a reliable ally. A premature British suggestion to the Americans that Diem had to be replaced could have used up British 'credits' in Washington and endangered the 'special' relationship. In addition, and closely connected to the points made with regard to Britain's preoccupation with

Malaysia, by telling the Americans what their view was on Diem, the British would have taken on a responsibility for the situation in Vietnam they did not want. Therefore, it seemed more prudent to avoid any difficult decisions for as long as possible, wait until the United States had made up its mind, and then follow the American lead. This is what the British ambassador in Saigon was trying to do, and the Foreign Office was willing to follow his advice. Lord Home's remark that Britain should '[l]et the Americans play their hand if they like'[184] and make a move against Diem encapsulated Whitehall's feeling. The main difficulty for the British was, of course, to find out what American policy was in the first place—an almost impossible task given the splits within the Kennedy administration.

Fourth, in contrast to Britain's reluctance to discuss the Diem regime with the Americans, the exchanges on Vietnam between London and Canberra became more frequent and frank in 1963. The Australians were told that the main British worry until October 1963 was that a coup in Saigon might lead to more political instability and possibly a split between the non-communist forces in Vietnam. Similarly, Canberra was informed about Kennedy's request for a report by Thompson, a matter that had initially been treated with the utmost secrecy. What is more, when the British ambassador in Saigon changed his mind and supported the removal of Diem in October, his Australian colleague knew about this earlier than the Foreign Office. This Anglo-Australian closeness was certainly one of the benefits of Britain's Vietnam policy of the previous years. Canberra appreciated Whitehall's willingness to support the American counter-insurgency effort, and there was a sense of renewed trust in Britain's determination to make a contribution to the cold war struggle in Asia. Australia, in turn, became increasingly supportive of Britain's stance in Malaysia against Indonesian confrontation. And it was that confrontation that assumed centre stage in Britain's policy towards Southeast Asia in 1963.

---

[184] Minute by Home. 12.10.63. PRO: FO 371/170093, DV1015/86/G.

6

Defending the 'Back Door': *Konfrontasi* and the Vietnam War

WHILE THE BUDDHIST crisis was at its height and the Diem regime in serious trouble, Whitehall had to cope with rather different problems in Southeast Asia. On 18 September 1963, two days after Malaya and the British colonies of Singapore, North Borneo, and Sarawak had formed the Federation of Malaysia, mobs attacked and burnt down the British embassy in Jakarta. London strongly protested, but sought to avoid rupturing diplomatic relations with Jakarta.[1] Indonesia, however, refused to recognize the new federation and further escalated its conflict with newly formed Malaysia. President Sukarno announced the 'ganyang Malaysia' policy on 25 September 1963, which literally meant 'gobble Malaysia raw' but was usually translated as 'crush Malaysia'.[2] From 1963 to 1966, the confrontation between Malaysia and Indonesia provided a scenario which saw the last major involvement of British military forces in Southeast Asia. At the height of *konfrontasi*—the Indonesian expression for confrontation—Britain committed 68,000 personnel and a third of its entire surface fleet to the defence of Malaysia in honour of its treaty commitment.[3]

Faced with Indonesia's open opposition to the Malaysia plan, Macmillan and his cabinet opted for a policy of firmness. As a matter of fact, no other policy was seriously considered. There was no need to make concessions, it was thought, and even negotiating was deemed a sign of weakness. Who was Sukarno to disrupt orderly decolonization in Southeast Asia, that would leave Britain's influence—and its use of the Singapore military base—untouched? What would have been the message to the world if Britain could not even stand up to the challenge of a third-rate power like Indonesia?

Konfrontasi first began in January 1963 when Indonesia openly opposed the plan for a federation of the former British dependencies in Southeast Asia. Before the new Federation of Malaysia was established in September 1963, various attempts had been made to accommodate Jakarta's concerns. The analysis of Britain's response to Indonesia's confrontation policy in 1963 sheds further light on Whitehall's policy towards Southeast Asia. On the one hand, *konfrontasi*

---

[1] CC(63)55. 19.9.63. PRO: CAB 128/37.
[2] Merle C. Ricklefs, *A History of Indonesia: c.1300 to the present* (London: Macmillan, 1981), 261.
[3] Darwin, *Britain and Decolonisation*, 290; Peter Lowe, *Britain and the Far East* (London: Longman, 1981), 217; David Reynolds, *Britannia Overruled: British Policy and World Power in the 20th Century* (London: Longman, 1991), 228.

refocused the Foreign Office's attention—as pointed out in the previous chapter—from the Vietnam conflict to the Malayan area. On the other hand, Britain's uncompromising policy of firm resistance against Indonesia's opposition reflected the line the Macmillan government had taken over Vietnam in the previous years: the west had to make a stand against any further encroachments of its sphere of influence in Southeast Asia, and the pro-western regime in Malaya/Malaysia faced a challenge similar to that the RVN had to deal with. Indonesia, backed by communist bloc propaganda, was determined to wipe out first British and thereafter western influence in the region. As Kennedy left Lyndon B. Johnson with the legacy of an increased American commitment to a politically unstable RVN in the autumn of 1963, so Macmillan's successor, Sir Alec Douglas-Home, had to deal with Britain's defence commitment to the escalating conflict between Indonesia and Malaysia. In a postscript to this chapter it will be explored how the new political leaders coped with these legacies, and how and why they established a link between the two conflicts in Southeast Asia.

INDONESIAN *KONFRONTASI*

The plan to create Malaysia became firm British policy in late 1961. The formation of Malaysia provided a splendid opportunity for Britain to rid itself of its image as a colonial power in the region without sacrificing the rights to use the Singapore military base. Simultaneously, British forces would cease to be responsible for internal security in the former colonies and therefore substantial troop reductions could be made. Britain would be able to fulfil its commitments in the region at substantially reduced costs, and London would be in a position to maintain, or perhaps even increase, its prestige and political influence in Southeast Asia. That the peoples in North Borneo and Sarawak seemed fairly unenthusiastic about the scheme was brushed aside—the creation of Malaysia was in Britain's interest, and the consultations of the population in Borneo on the issue remained open to criticism.

Initially, the Malaysia scheme evoked little opposition from Indonesia.[4] In fact, the Indonesian Foreign Minister Subandrio stressed in a speech to the United Nations General Assembly in November 1961 that Indonesia 'had no objection to such a merger, based upon the will for freedom of the peoples concerned'.[5] The reason for Indonesia's initial stance was its preoccupation with the West Irian conflict, and its desire to prove that expansionism was not behind Jakarta's claim to the Dutch colony.[6] Nevertheless, in December 1961 the future Indonesian policy of confrontation was foreshadowed by a resolution of the Central Committee of the Indonesian Communist Party (PKI), which denounced Malaysia as a form of neo-colonialism.[7] The PKI was the biggest communist party outside the communist

---

[4] Mackie, *Konfrontasi*, 103. [5] Quoted from Boyce, *Malaysia and Singapore*, 67.
[6] Leifer, *Indonesia's Foreign Policy*, 76. [7] Mackie, *Konfrontasi*, 104.

bloc. President Sukarno's policy of 'guided democracy' was based on the balance of power between the army and the communists.[8]

The first hostile reaction to the Malaysia proposal on an international level did not, however, come from Indonesia but from the Philippines, whose President Diosdano Macapagal put forward a claim to North Borneo in June 1962. It was based on Manila's view that the Sultan of Sulu had merely leased, not ceded, this territory to the British in 1888, giving the Filipino government, as the Sultan's successor, rights over the disposition of North Borneo.[9] The Foreign Office, however, was far more concerned with Indonesia, warning that Jakarta posed 'by far the most serious potential challenge to Malaysia'. Yet in the summer of 1962 the Foreign Office considered it unlikely that Jakarta would interfere because of its weak 'internal position'.[10] As events were to prove, the British analysis of Indonesia's weak domestic position, as well as the limits it placed on Jakarta's willingness to intervene in Malaysia, failed to foresee that an external conflict would be seized upon by President Sukarno to cure those very domestic ills. Besides appealing to Indonesian nationalism and bolstering Sukarno's ideology of anti-imperialism, such a conflict would constitute a timely and welcome diversion from the country's economic problems.[11] Indeed, the Brunei revolt of late 1962 provided the Indonesian government with an opportunity too good to be missed.

On 8 December 1962 the military arm of Sheikh Ahmad Azahari's Partai Rakyat attacked police stations and seized British-owned oil refineries in Brunei, technically a British protectorate.[12] The Sultan requested the help of British forces. Gurkha units subdued the rebels, and Britain announced an end to the revolt on 16 December. Three thousand rebels were apprehended. The Sultan banned the Partai Rakyat, which opposed the Malaysia concept, and arrested hundreds of its supporters.[13] The British were convinced that Indonesia was involved in the rebellion. A week before the revolt, the British had received intelligence information that the Partai Rakyat was planning an insurrection. The British Governor in Sarawak reported that there was evidence of dumping of arms near the Indonesian border.[14] Moreover, the Indonesian General Nasution sympathized openly with Azahari.[15]

In Sukarno's view the rebellion proved that there was substantial opposition to the Malaysia concept, and that the whole idea was a neo-colonialist plot, thought out and imposed by the British.[16] Foreign Minister Subandrio announced on

[8] Letter: Whittington (Bangkok) to FO. 22.12.60. PRO: FO 371/152156, D1071/187. See also Smith, *International History of the Vietnam War*, ii. 138.

[9] Mackie, *Konfrontasi*, 145.   [10] FO Memorandum. 5.7.62. PRO: CAB 134/1951.

[11] Pamela Sodhy, 'Malaysian–American Relations during Indonesia's Confrontation against Malaysia, 1963–1966', *Journal of Southeast Asian Studies*, 19/1 (1988), 112.

[12] Leifer, *Indonesia's Foreign Policy*, 78.   [13] Mackie, *Konfrontasi*, 115.

[14] Telegram 900: Kuala Lumpur to CRO. 1.12.63. PRO: PREM 11/3869.

[15] Ricklefs, *History of Indonesia*, 260. Macmillan, *End of the Day*, 256. Chin, *Defence of Malaysia*, 66.

[16] Embtel 1317: Jones (Djakarta) to State Department. 27.2.63. USNA: RG 59, Central Files, POL 3 MALAYSIA.

20 January 1963 that Indonesia would 'henceforth pursue a policy of confrontation [against Malaya which] has lent itself to become tools of colonialism and imperialism'.[17] The statement was deliberately vague. The British expected that Indonesia would step up its propaganda directed at the local peoples of the Borneo territories.[18] Although an Indonesian invasion was ruled out, infiltration of guerrillas into North Borneo or Sarawak was considered likely.[19]

The British were very concerned about a possible conflict with Indonesia. During his talks with President Kennedy at Nassau in December 1962, which were dominated by negotiations on nuclear cooperation, Macmillan was reported to have stressed that Indonesia, and not Vietnam, was 'the most dangerous problem in the whole of Asia'.[20] Britain's response to Subandrio's announcement was that firm, frank, and friendly approaches were all that could be done on the diplomatic level for the time being. Consultations with the Americans and Australians were sought to discuss whether other forms of pressure might be put on Jakarta.[21]

THE BRITISH COMMITMENT TO DEFEND MALAYSIA

The Kennedy administration had welcomed the plan to form Malaysia in 1961, yet it had decided not to become involved in the details of setting up the new federation.[22] In the wake of the Brunei revolt the American ambassador in Kuala Lumpur, Charles Baldwin, saw a link between developments in Vietnam and Malaysia. He stressed that the communist 'element' in Indonesia was behind Jakarta's opposition to Malaysia and asked his government to give the Malaysia plan its full support. 'It now would be fruitless for [the United States Government] to make [a] vast effort [to] resist communist pressures in Vietnam and East Asia', he argued, 'and not strongly resist similar pressures elsewhere in [the] area even though they may be blended with local nationalism.'[23] However, Howard Jones, the US ambassador in Jakarta, did not share Baldwin's enthusiasm for Malaysia. Jones found that Britain had failed to make the necessary effort to 'sell' the Malaysia plan to Indonesia. He thought it possible that Indonesia would 'disengage' from the communist movement soon, thereby offering a stronger line of defence for the west than a Malaysia–Thailand line. It would be a mistake if

---

[17] Quoted from Boyce, *Malaysia and Singapore*, 70. 'Confrontation diplomacy' had been successfully pursued against the Dutch in the West Irian conflict. See Working Paper: 'Indonesian Objectives and Tactics in Southeast Asia'. Enclosure to airgram A-442: Whittington (Djakarta) to State Department. 20.11.63. USNA: RG 59, Central Files, POL 1 INDON.

[18] Letter: Wallace (CO) to Goode (North Borneo), 23.1.63. PRO: FO 371/169898, DH1061/23/G.

[19] Telegram 55: Fry (Djakarta) to FO. 21.1.63. PRO: PREM 11/4182.

[20] Cabinet Conclusion 1-63/2172. 2.1.63. CNA: RG 2, Series A-5-a, Vol. 6253.

[21] FO brief by Peck for Home. 18.1.63. PRO: FO 371/169690, D1061/2/G.

[22] Deptel 11: Rusk to Kuala Lumpur. 14.7.61. JFKL: NSF, Malaya & Singapore Country File, General, July 1961, box 140. See also Sodhy, 'Malaysian–American Relations', 111.

[23] Embtel 448: Baldwin (Kuala Lumpur) to State Department. 4.2.63. USNA: RG 59, Central Files, POL 3 MALAYSIA.

Washington threw its weight behind the Malaysia plan, which may become a 'losing proposition' at the cost of a hostile Indonesia.[24]

In Canberra, the Australian Ministry of External Affairs voiced similar doubts. Although in favour of the plan to create Malaysia, the Australians foresaw 'great difficulties in its successful implementation'. While Jakarta should not be permitted to develop its 'expansionist tendencies', External Affairs acknowledged that Indonesia had a 'legitimate interest' in the future stability and security of Borneo. Australia, therefore, could not content itself with forcing through Malaysia in the teeth of Indonesian hostility, thus leading to the prospect of having to support Malaysia indefinitely.[25]

Yet in London nobody talked of Indonesia's 'legitimate interest'. Instead, Britain's aim was to build a common front against Indonesia's confrontation policy. The United States, Australia, and New Zealand agreed to hold a secret quadripartite meeting on 11/12 February 1963. Frederick Warner, the head of the Foreign Office's Southeast Asia Department and his colleague from the Commonwealth Relations Office's Far Eastern Department, Anthony Golds, accordingly travelled to Washington. Warner was confident that Britain's allies would agree on Whitehall's perception of the Indonesian threat. He merely expected differences to arise over 'how beastly' the west should be to Indonesia.[26]

Shortly before the talks began, Averell Harriman, Assistant Secretary of State for Political Affairs, informed Warner of his doubts as to whether the British were really determined to prevent an Indonesian takeover of northern Borneo after Malaysia was established. Like ambassador Baldwin, he also linked the issue to the conflict in Indochina. Harriman, however, expressed his fear that in the end it would be up to the Americans to intervene on Malaysia's behalf, creating a second Vietnam for Washington.[27] Paul Nitze, Assistant Secretary of Defense for International Security Affairs, thought along the same lines. He doubted that the British were really prepared to undertake a commitment 'which may grow heavier and heavier as the months go by'.[28]

In response to Warner's report on Harriman's and Nitze's doubts, an emergency meeting of high officials from the Foreign Office, the Colonial Office, the Commonwealth Relations Office, and the Ministry of Defence was held on 11 February, which made the crucial decision to inform the Americans that Britain was indeed committed to bearing that burden. Sufficient British troops along with forces of the Commonwealth Strategic Reserve would remain in the region even after Malaysia Day. Moreover, extensive Indonesian subversive activities in

---

[24] Embtel 1196: Jones (Jakarta) to State Department. 5.2.63. USNA: RG 59, Central Files, POL 3 MALAYSIA.

[25] Telegram 217: EA Canberra to Washington. 4.2.63. AUSNA: A1838/287, file 2498/11, part 1.

[26] Embtel 2947: Jones (London) to State Department. 5.2.63. USNA: RG 59, Central Files, POL INDON.

[27] Telegram 448: Warner (Washington) to FO. 9.2.63. PRO: FO 371/169694, D1071/18/G. Memorandum of Conversation between Warner and Harriman. 8.2.63. USNA: RG 59, Central Files, POL 3 MALAYSIA.

[28] Letter: Warner (Washington) to Peck (FO). 11.2.63. PRO: FO 371/169695, D1071/25/G.

Malaysia would be grounds for bringing into effect Britain's obligations under the AMDA.[29]

At the quadripartite meeting Britain's allies approved of the Malaysia concept, but were reluctant to give London the full backing it sought. The United States agreed to intervene if there was open aggression against Malaysia. However, Washington would not assist in the fight against subversive infiltration. Australia and New Zealand did not exclude their participation in the defence of Malaysia, but at the same time would not give any guarantee of such assistance. Britain's allies stressed the need to preserve good relations with Indonesia. The Tunku should be asked to restrain his language, and he should consider making 'statesmanlike gestures' such as meetings with Sukarno and Macapagal.[30] 'The general impression left by the two days' discussion is that our allies are fearful of impending trouble', David Ormsby-Gore concluded. He pointed to the Australian and New Zealand policy of trying to obtain a firm American commitment to the region:

The Australians and New Zealanders see themselves as gradually being drawn in to any fighting necessary to keep the Indonesians out. They would be less anxious about this if they were sure that the Americans would be involved also. But the United States Government is determined to try and get the Commonwealth Countries to shoulder this burden alone while they themselves concentrate on Viet Nam.[31]

Washington at least departed from its policy of public 'cordial non-involvement',[32] and President Kennedy stated shortly after the quadripartite meeting that Malaysia was 'the best hope of security for that very part of the world'.[33] This public gesture, however, certainly did nothing to restrain Sukarno. The Americans had not committed themselves in any way and the American ambassador in Jakarta, who continued to be very critical of the British position, found ways to convey this to the Indonesians. Unknown to the British and without instructions from Washington, the American embassy in Jakarta reassured the Indonesians that Kennedy's statement simply reiterated American policy and that the United States had no intention of getting directly involved.[34] While the State Department basically agreed with this position, it was furious that the US embassy had conveyed it to the Indonesians and spelled out that, without specific instructions, the embassy should not 'water down U.S. positions to suit Indonesian feelings'.[35]

---

[29] Telegram 1665: FO to Washington. 11.2.63. PRO: FO 371/169694, D1071/18/G. Minute: Peck (FO) to Caccia (FO). 11.2.63. PRO: FO 371/169898, D1071/18.

[30] Telegram 471: Ormsby-Gore (Washington) to FO. 11.2.63. PRO: FO 371/169695, D1071/21. Telegram 481: Ormsby-Gore (Washington) to FO. 12.2.63. Ibid. D1071/23.

[31] Telegram 482: Ormsby-Gore (Washington) to FO. 12.2.63. PRO: PREM 11/4182.

[32] Peter Boyce, 'Canberra's Malaysia Policy', *Australian Outlook*, 17/2, (1963), 152.

[33] Kennedy interview of 14 February 1963. Quoted from Harold W. Chase and Allen H. Lerman (eds.), *Kennedy and the Press: The News Conferences* (New York: Crowell, 1965), 389.

[34] Embtel 1274: Galbraith (Djakarta) to State Department. 18.2.63. USNA: RG 59, Central Files, POL 3 MALAYSIA.

[35] Deptel 796: Rusk to Djakarta, 26.2.63. Ibid.

At the Washington quadripartite meeting Britain accepted the heavy burden of defending Malaysia for getting very little in return. The Kennedy administration continued its economic aid programme for Indonesia as well as its support of the Indonesian army in an attempt to maintain some influence in Jakarta. Not even the Australians were won over at this stage. The Ministry of External Affairs in Canberra thought that London was pushing ahead with the formation of Malaysia without regard for Indonesia's and the Philippines' concerns. Britain should seek to avoid the prospect of the new federation having to be supported indefinitely by the western powers against the PRC and its neighbours.[36]

Indeed, although the US administration and the Australian government were willing to support the Malaysia plan, their policy towards Indonesia was fundamentally different from Britain's policy. In late 1962 the Foreign Office had reached the conclusion that Indonesia posed a potential threat to the Borneo territories because the Soviet Union continued to supply it with weapons. Yet only a communist-controlled government in Indonesia was considered likely to lay claim to northern Borneo.[37] The British therefore seemed inclined to believe that Sukarno's confrontation policy was both expansionist and communist in character, and consequently his attempts at undermining the Malaysia concept had to be firmly resisted. Neither the Americans nor the Australians were prepared to support this view. In discussions with the United States, the British tried to put the confrontation into the larger context of the west's struggle against the spread of communism. The Americans were told that the overriding British motivation to push Malaysia through was the need to preserve the Singapore base, which was vital for the defence of the area and essential to assure 'free world control'. There was no advantage in making concessions to the Indonesians, and little reason to base British policy on the hope that an essentially unpredictable Indonesian government would become more friendly to the west.[38]

Similarly, the Malayan Minister of Defence, Tun Razak, played on the communist threat from Indonesia when he visited Washington in April 1963. He stressed the PKI's influence in Indonesia, made the communists responsible for Jakarta's confrontation policy, and drew the Americans' attention to the fact that the PRC had joined Indonesia in opposing the Malaysia concept. Neither the British nor the Malayan representations had any impact on Washington's position—the US administration still believed that Indonesia's claims could be accommodated, and that it was not yet lost to the communist bloc.[39]

---

[36] Telegram 481: Ormsby-Gore (Washington) to FO. 12.2.63. PRO: FO 371/169695, D1071/23.

[37] FO memorandum for Joint Intelligence Committee report on Indonesia. Not dated. PRO: DO 169/67. FO memorandum on talks with Japanese minister Ikeda. 11.11.62. PRO: FO 371/166354, D1015/34.

[38] Embtel 3025: Jones (London) to State Department. 7.2.63. USNA: RG 59, Central Files, POL 3 MALAYSIA.

[39] Memorandum of conversation between Tun Razak and Rusk. 23.4.63. Memorandum of conversation between Tun Razak and Hilsman. 23.4.63 Both ibid. Supplementary Talking Paper for Kennedy's meeting with Tun Razak. 23.4.63. USNA: RG 59, Central Files, POL 7 MALAYSIA.

Sir Garfield Barwick, the Australian Foreign Minister, also argued against the British assessment of Indonesia's policy when he was in London in April 1963. By charging that Malaysia was neo-colonialist, the British pointed out to him, Indonesia was using 'communist language' to put forward 'communist arguments'. Barwick disagreed and stressed that General Nasution, who was clearly anti-communist, was also a leading critic of the Malaysia concept. He thought that the Indonesians were genuinely afraid that Malaysia would take action against Sumatra or the Indonesian part of Borneo.[40] Although Sir Robert Menzies, the Australian Prime Minister, was inclined to back the firm British policy, Barwick's more cautious approach prevailed in Canberra in early 1963.[41] In March, Barwick encouraged the Indonesians and Filipinos to consider tripartite talks on Malaysia. The Filipinos, who had introduced the idea of tripartite talks, favoured his suggestion; the Indonesians, too, were willing to embark on talks. Barwick managed to elicit a non-binding concession from Subandrio that Indonesia might accept Malaysia. The Americans and New Zealanders immediately endorsed the Australian initiative.[42]

The British still preferred a firm policy towards Indonesia, believing that Sukarno could not be 'appeased'. However, they were keen on preserving their allies' support. The Foreign Office informed Macmillan that 'we are not trying to convert the Indonesians, but to justify ourselves in the eyes of our friends'.[43] The British ambassador in Jakarta, who was adamantly opposed to 'appeasing' Indonesia, was told that 'we do not mind annoying the Indonesians, but we do want to avoid appearing provocative to our friends'.[44] It is remarkable how quickly the Macmillan government had reached the position that only a policy of firmness could be pursued. Negotiations were anathema to London, and the concerns and differing assessments of Britain's allies were pushed aside. Indeed, there was a clear willingness to shoulder a potentially heavy military burden, a willingness that was consistent with London's policy towards the Vietnam conflict over the previous years. As Britain favoured a military solution to the Vietnam conflict, it was prepared to seek a similar solution to Indonesian confrontation if necessary. Britain was keen to prove to the Americans that it could look after its own interests in the region and that its military power was useful to the common western cause. Any further western retreats in Southeast Asia were unacceptable. Retreating in the face of Indonesian opposition would have done much damage to Britain's policy of orderly decolonization. It would have also done harm to the west's cold war interests for three reasons. First, the creation of Malaysia was, after all, designed to ensure Britain's use of the Singapore base to maintain its

---

[40] Record of conversation between Thomas and Barwick. 4.4.63. PRO: PREM 11/3868.
[41] Gregory Pemberton, *All the Way: Australia's Road to Vietnam* (Sydney: Allen & Unwin, 1987), 168.
[42] Letter: Barwick to Sandys. 18.3.63. Letter: Ormsby-Gore (Washington) to Caccia (FO). 19.3.63. Both in PRO: FO 371/169697, D1071/76.
[43] Minute: Bridges to de Zulueta. 26.4.63. PRO: PREM 11/4347.
[44] Letter: Warner (FO) to Gilchrist (Djakarta). 25.4.63. PRO: FO 371/169709, D1073/6.

contribution to the deterrent against China. Second, the new federation would solve the problem that an independent Singapore with its Chinese population would 'go communist'. Third, standing up to Indonesia's confrontation policy and backing the pro-western regime in Kuala Lumpur would prove the west's determination to support its allies, particularly against a challenge that was supported not only by local Indonesian communists but also by the PRC.

Equally remarkable was the broad support in Whitehall for the policy towards Indonesia that became obvious when Sir Burke Trend, the Cabinet Secretary, questioned the British approach. In a minute to Macmillan he asked: 'Should we not be devoting as much attention to the political problem of neutralising Indonesia . . . as to the military problem of defending Malaysia?' He went on to express his 'uneasy feeling' that Britain might find itself committed—perhaps against better judgement and certainly to its financial disadvantage—to carrying, single-handedly, a greater burden than the British government had contemplated before.[45] Macmillan agreed to send a minute voicing Trend's misgivings to all ministers concerned. The memorandum in answer to this minute by the Foreign Office, the Commonwealth Relations Office, and the Ministry of Defence dismissed Trend's concerns. The British government saw no alternative to its policy of firm support of Malaysia, was committed to the defence of the new federation, and was certain that, ultimately, Washington could not escape involvement.[46]

THE MANILA SUMMIT

Despite the different policies of its allies, London remained steadfast in its uncompromising opposition to Indonesia's confrontation policy. Yet negotiations between Indonesia, the Philippines, and Malaya went ahead, and after a series of preliminary meetings it was agreed to hold a summit in Manila in August. The Tunku, Indonesia's President Sukarno, and President Macapagal of the Philippines attended the summit. The British, pessimistic about the likelihood of an agreement, were prepared for the conference to break down.[47] Washington was aware of Britain's negative attitude and tried to prevent London from undermining the negotiations in Manila. Averell Harriman insisted that London should refrain from interfering with the Tunku during the meeting as that would look 'very much like a colonial effort'. The Americans and Australians were also in favour of a postponement of Malaysia Day, which would help save Sukarno's face. The State Department thought it would be 'the height of absurdity' for the British to stand in the way of an agreement at Manila by insisting on bringing Malaysia into being on 31 August.[48] Washington was putting pressure on London

    45   Minute: Trend to Macmillan. 2.4.63. PRO: PREM 11/4189.
    46   Joint FO, CRO, MOD memorandum for Macmillan. 16.4.63. Ibid.
    47   Draft CRO telegram to Tunku Abdul Rahman. 25.7.63. PRO: FO 371/169723, D1075/5.
    48   Deptels 773 and 790: Rusk to London. 1.8.63. Both in USNA: RG 59, Central Files, POL 3 MALAYSIA. Telegram 3957: London to EA Canberra. 4.8.63. AUSNA: A1838/287, 2498/11, part 1.

throughout the summit meeting to get agreement to the postponement of Malaysia Day. President Kennedy wrote to Macmillan suggesting that this would be necessary to give Sukarno a 'fig leaf'.[49] Yet Macmillan was not in the mood to give in to this pressure. He felt that the Americans had 'sold out' to the Indonesians. The Prime Minister, a keen reader of books on historic subjects, was in these days reading *The Appeasers*, a new study very critical of Chamberlain's appeasement policy prior to World War II.[50] In his diary Macmillan noted his high regard for a book that focused on one of the 'most shameful' periods of Britain's history.[51] Accordingly, Macmillan had no intention of repeating the mistakes of his predecessor and 'appease' a country that threatened vital British interests. He replied to Kennedy that he did not believe Sukarno could be bought off easily by postponing Malaysia Day. He added: 'There is an old French saying—what is postponed is lost.'[52]

When the British heard of the Tunku's inclination to postpone Malaysia Day, the Cabinet agreed to 'impress on the Tunku the importance of adhering to 31 August as the date for the formation of Malaysia and the dangers implicit in any further delay'.[53] The Tunku reassured the British and cabled: 'I realize too well that any postponement would be tantamount to a surrender.... You can rest assured that Malaysia will be announced on 31 August as scheduled.'[54]

The outcome of the summit, the Manila Agreement, showed that the Tunku had either misled the British or, in fact, surrendered. It was agreed that U Thant, the Secretary-General of the United Nations, should ascertain, prior to the establishment of the Federation of Malaysia, the wishes of the peoples of North Borneo and Sarawak.[55] U Thant made it clear to all parties that he would not be able to finish his mission before 31 August, and thus a short delay in proclaiming Malaysia of up to two weeks would be necessary.[56] While the Tunku's agreement to the postponement of Malaysia Day did not go down well in London, the Malayan Prime Minister could count on Washington's as well as Canberra's support for his decision.[57]

After the Manila Summit the British were not prepared to continue to sit back and leave the diplomatic arena to the Malayans. The top priority was to bring Malaysia into existence as soon as possible. On 5 August 1963 Prime Minister Macmillan stressed the urgency of the matter in a letter to Lord Selkirk, expressing his belief that Britain's position in Southeast Asia would become 'untenable'

[49] Personal message from Kennedy to Macmillan. 4.8.1963. FRUS: 1961–1963, xiii, Southeast Asia, 725.

[50] See Martin Gilbert and Richard Gott, *The Appeasers* (Boston: Houghton Mifflin, 1963).

[51] Macmillan diaries. 3.8.63, dep. d. 50, f. 25; and 5.8., dep. d. 50, f. 28.

[52] Personal message from Macmillan to Kennedy. 4.8.63. PRO: PREM 11/4593.

[53] CC(63)51. 1.8.63. PRO: CAB 128/37.

[54] Personal message from Tunku Abdul Rahman to Sandys. 3.8.63. PRO: FO 371/169724, D1075/25.

[55] Article 4 of Manila Agreement. Quoted from Rajinah Hussain, 'Malaysia and the United Nations', Ph.D. thesis (London, 1988), 101.

[56] Telegram 1206: Dean (New York) to FO. 8.8.63. PRO: PREM 11/4349.

[57] Telegram 3957: London to Canberra. 4.8.63. AUSNA: A1838/287, file 2498/11, part 1.

if Malaysia was not formed.[58] The Secretary of State for Commonwealth Relations and the Colonies, Duncan Sandys, insisted that the Tunku promised to go
ahead with Malaysia on whatever later date.[59] The Tunku readily agreed and informed London that he would like to form Malaysia on 16 September, 'irrespec-
tive of the nature of the Secretary-General['s] report'.[60] On 29 August Kuala
Lumpur indeed announced that Malaysia was to be created on 16 September.
The Philippines and Indonesia were informed of the new date shortly before it
was made public.[61] Although initially calm, both governments later sent a formal
note of protest. In announcing the firm date, Malaya gave the Indonesians and
Filipinos ammunition for challenging the UN enquiry and rejecting it.[62] Roger
Hilsman later called the announcement a 'blatant insult' to Manila and Jakarta.
In Hilsman's view, Duncan Sandys was the villain who had pressured the Tunku
into making the announcement.[63] That the Indonesians were 'really insulted' by
Britain's political manoeuvres was also the impression of the East German consulate in Jakarta. The East Germans thought that the premature announcement
of a firm new date for Malaysia Day had indeed provided Jakarta with excellent
'ammunition'. Moreover, they were also certain that Britain's uncompromising
stance would strengthen the communists in Indonesia and push Sukarno closer to
the communist bloc.[64]

U Thant's report concluded that the local elections of 1963, which had been
won by pro-Malaysia parties in North Borneo and Sarawak, had been free and
fair, and that Malaysia had been the dominant issue. His only criticism was of the
'premature' Malayan announcement of a new date for Malaysia, an unnecessary
action, which, he argued, had led to misunderstanding and even resentment in
Indonesia and the Philippines, who rejected his findings.[65] Implicitly criticizing
Britain, the Indonesians informed U Thant that 'if the Malayans had been left
alone an accommodation between them and the Indonesians and Filipinos would
have been easily reached'.[66]

Until the Manila Summit the British attempted to appear conciliatory in order
to please the Americans and Australians. Britain could neither prevent tripartite
meetings nor UN involvement, American economic aid to Jakarta was not
stopped, and the postponement of Malaysia Day seemed to endanger the whole
project. After the Manila Summit, the British, and Duncan Sandys in particular,
gave up any idea of restraint and assumed a more active role. The new strategy,
while helping to create Malaysia, only antagonized Indonesia further.[67] It also

[58] Letter: Macmillan to Selkirk (Singapore). 5.8.63. PRO: PREM 11/4188.
[59] Telegram 1926: Sandys to Kuala Lumpur. 8.8.63. PRO: PREM 11/4349.
[60] Telegram 1503: Kuala Lumpur to CRO. 9.8.63. The Tunku confirmed this position in writing
on the following day. Telegram 1514: Kuala Lumpur to CRO. 10.8.63. Both ibid.
[61] Telegram 1758: Kuala Lumpur to CRO. 29.8.63. Ibid.
[62] Hussain, 'Malaysia and the UN', 103.   [63] Hilsman, *To Move a Nation*, 403–4.
[64] Berichte von Kehr (Jakarta). 21.9.63; 18.10.63. MfAA: A16071.
[65] Boyce, *Malaysia and Singapore*, 74.
[66] Telegram 1431: Dean (New York) to FO. 12.9.63. PRO: PREM 11/4350.
[67] Australian telegram 2515: Washington to EA Canberra. 20.9.63. PRO: FO 371/169707,
D1071/272/G.

provided the communist bloc, and particularly the PRC, with new opportunities to forge closer relations with President Sukarno.[68]

Throughout 1963 the United States remained critical of Britain's uncompromising stance towards Indonesia's confrontation policy. London's hopes that Washington would avoid 'ambiguity' were in vain.[69] The American embassy in Jakarta especially doubted the wisdom of the Malaysia idea and showed understanding for Indonesia's claims. Although the State Department was reluctant to support this position, it intended to adopt an attitude that would give the Americans 'maximum flexibility' in dealing with the conflict.[70] The overriding US concern, shared by the Australian Ministry of External Affairs, was to keep Indonesia out of the communist bloc. This is why the Kennedy administration refused to threaten Sukarno with the cancellation of US aid to Indonesia. American deliveries of weapons and ammunition were only halted after mobs had burnt down the British embassy in Jakarta on 18 September 1963, two days after Malaysia Day. To Britain's annoyance, US economic aid continued to flow. The Americans hoped that this would keep channels to the Indonesian government open and give Washington some influence in Jakarta.[71]

Whereas Washington and Canberra thought that negotiating with Jakarta could resolve the dispute, the British were convinced that firm opposition to Sukarno's policy, which demonstrated his increasingly pro-communist tendency, was the only answer that would deter the Indonesian president from his expansionist policy. The Macmillan government adopted a 'Malaysia-first-attitude', and refused even to contemplate US and Australian arguments. Britain had committed its credibility and prestige to the establishment of Malaysia. The federation promised the ability to maintain Britain's military and political influence in the region, and had become as much a symbol of Britain's status as a world power as Vietnam had become a symbol of the American struggle to contain communism worldwide.

Yet Britain's military and economic resources were limited. One day after the creation of Malaysia, the Foreign Office sent a memorandum to the Ministry of Defence, inquiring about the forces required to meet expanded Indonesian subversive activity in northern Borneo.[72] In reply, the Chiefs of Staff pointed out that to achieve the necessary strength of eight army units, one unit had to be taken from either the Commonwealth brigade, the British units in Singapore, or from

---

[68]   Zhai, *China and the Vietnam Wars,* 117–19.

[69]   Embtel 3025: Jones (London) to State Department. 7.2.63. USNA: RG 59, Central Files, POL 3 MALAYSIA.

[70]   Embtel 1196: Jones (Djakarta) to State Department. 5.2.63. Deptel 357: Rusk to Kuala Lumpur. 21.2.63. Both ibid.

[71]   Record of a meeting held at the State Department: 'Indonesia'. 16.10.63. PRO: FO 371/169909, DH1071/31/G. Message: Rusk to Butler in telegram 3920: Washington to FO. 13.12.63. PRO: DO 169/70.

[72]   Minute: Bridges (FO) to Bligh (Admiralty House). 19.9.63, enclosing memorandum by Peck (FO): 'Implications of continued Hostilities in the Malaysian and Borneo Territories'. 17.9.63. PRO: PREM 11/4350.

the United Kingdom. Moreover, additional transport and fighter aircraft as well as helicopters were needed. The Chiefs of Staff therefore came to the conclusion that it appeared 'almost certain' that Britain would not be able 'to implement SEATO plans from either an army or an air force point of view'.[73] Peter Thorneycroft, the Minister of Defence, was concerned that Britain would be unable to maintain its forces for SEATO tasks. Yet he hoped that the SEATO allies would 'readily recognise' that Britain was making a significant contribution to SEATO defence 'since the defence of Malaysia against Indonesian aggression is essential to the defence of the SEATO area as a whole'.[74]

Prime Minister Macmillan had just resigned and Kennedy's last month in office was about to begin when Frederick Warner and Arthur Golds travelled to Washington for another round of quadripartite talks on Indonesia in mid-October 1963. The main British aim was to persuade the Americans to terminate their military and economic aid to Indonesia.[75] The steering briefs Warner and Golds took with them to Washington identified eight important western interests that Britain intended to defend and that formed the basis of Britain's firm opposition to Indonesia's challenge. First, the west had to secure as wide an area as possible in Southeast Asia in which it could deploy its military power in order to 'manoeuvre against the Communist threat'. Second, the west therefore needed to retain 'full use' of Britain's bases in Malaysia and American bases in the Philippines. Third, the western powers should aim to be able to concentrate on the communist threat 'from the North'—the DRV and the PRC—and avoid having to face a second front from Indonesia. Fourth, SEATO had to be maintained as an effective deterrent. Fifth, Australia and New Zealand had to be defended against Indonesian hostility. Sixth, the west should show that countries which were supported by western powers were 'inviolate'. Seventh, the west had to ensure that Malaysia would not fall into pieces, thereby preventing—as an eighth point—Singapore from becoming 'an outpost of Communist China'.[76] This reasoning reflected the growing British concern over the PRC. In 1960 the British had already been certain that the PRC's ultimate aim was to control Southeast Asia. Beijing's assertive and aggressive foreign policy in the early 1960s only reaffirmed this belief. As if the PRC's public support for Indonesia's claims against Malaysia and Chinese influence in the PKI were not enough[77]—the British spoke of a honeymoon in Indonesian/Chinese relations'[78]—the Foreign Office received reports in the latter half of 1963 that the number of Chinese military and technical advisers in Hanoi was increasing and that the Soviets seemed to be losing influ-

---

[73] COS 329/3. 27.9.63. PRO: DEFE 5/143.
[74] Minute: Thorneycroft to Macmillan. 2.10.63. PRO: PREM 11/4350. For a detailed analysis of British defence planning after Malaysia Day, see Easter, 'British Defence Policy', 141–4.
[75] Steering Brief No. 7 for Quadripartite Talks. Undated. PRO: FO 371/169909, DH1071/14/G. Telegram 5456: Hamilton (London) to EA Canberra. 11.10.63. AUSNA: A1838/287, file 2498/11, part 2. Deptel 716: Rusk to Djakarta. 31.12.63. LBJL: NSF, Country File Malaysia, Cables Vol. I, box 275.
[76] Steering Brief No. 7 for Quadripartite Talks. Undated. PRO: FO 371/169909, DH1071/14/G.
[77] Despatch 91: Gilchrist (Djakarta) to Home. 10.9.63. PRO: FO 371/169881, DH1015/47.
[78] Letter: Petersen (Djakarta) to Cable (FO). 5.6.63. PRO: FO 371/169884, DH103110/9/G.

ence in the DRV.[79] British suspicions seemed well-founded. At the time, the East Germans in Hanoi also noted that the DRV leadership became increasingly pro-Chinese.[80]

Cold war objectives dominated the British list of western interests in the region, yet Whitehall found it difficult to portray Sukarno as a communist. Although the PKI retained its independence and influence in Indonesia, the British admitted in October 1963 that the PKI needed the Indonesian President more than he needed the communists. However, whether communist or not, Indonesia in its 'present stage of development' was, the British concluded, 'necessarily hostile' to western powers and Jakarta's policies could not be moderated for the time being, 'except by disastrous concessions'. Therefore, American attempts to keep some influence in Indonesia were regarded as futile.[81]

While not disagreeing with the western interests the British identified, Washington did not share the assessment that Indonesia was 'necessarily hostile' to the west, and therefore refused to stop economic aid to Indonesia. Even the military assistance programme continued.[82] The Americans chose not to disclose the scope of their 'modest' military training programme in Indonesia to London, not least because they were certain that some aspects of the programme would 'make the British hair stand on end'.[83] London found the American attitude 'unsatisfactory'. High-level approaches by Lord Home to Dean Rusk and President Kennedy also failed to convince the Americans to discontinue all economic aid. The Kennedy administration stuck to its 'soft' policy on Indonesia. In early November, the British government therefore decided to delay a further high-level approach on the issue.[84] Two weeks later President Kennedy was assassinated in Dallas.

When Sir Alec Douglas-Home took office as Prime Minister, Britain had already committed itself to the defence of Malaysia against Indonesian subversion. Indeed, as Foreign Secretary Douglas-Home had not only agreed with the Macmillan government's line on Indonesia, he had actively promoted the policy of firmness. In 1963, British policies towards the Vietnam War and *konfrontasi* appeared consistent. No inch was to be given to the communists in South Vietnam, no concessions were to be made to Indonesia with regard to northern Borneo. London ruled out negotiated settlements of both conflicts for the time being and preferred military means to defend western interests. In comparison,

---

[79] FO brief for Commonwealth Prime Ministers Conference. 29.3.60. PRO: FO 371/152136, D1015/7. Letter: Everard (FO) to Atkinson (Hanoi). 25.7.63. PRO: FO 371/170134, DV1201/75. Letter: Atkinson (Hanoi) to Everard (FO). 2.9.63. PRO: FO 371/170135, DV1201/100.

[80] Memorandum by Bibow (Hanoi). 29.5.63. Stiftung Archiv Parteien und Massenorganisationen der DDR, Berlin (hereafter SAPMO): DY30, FB339/19824. Zhai confirmed the growing power of the pro-Chinese forces in the DRV in his recent study. Zhai, *China and the Vietnam Wars*, 123.

[81] Steering Brief No. 7 for Quadripartite Talks. Undated. PRO: FO 371/169909, DH1071/14/G.

[82] Record of a meeting held at the State Department: 'Indonesia'. 16.10.63. Ibid. DH1071/31/G. Message: Rusk to Butler in telegram 3920: Washington to FO. 13.12.63. PRO: DO 169/70.

[83] Memorandum: Forrestal (State Department) to M. Bundy (White House). 6.2.64. LBJL: NSF, Country File Indonesia, Memos, Vol. I, box 246.

[84] Minute: Garner (CRO) to Pritchard (CRO). 7.11.63. PRO: DO 169/70.

Washington's policy towards Southeast Asia seemed inconsistent—at least from Britain's point of view.[85] The Americans were determined to prevent a communist takeover in the RVN, but Washington would have liked to see a negotiated settlement of the conflict between Malaysia and Indonesia. In the autumn of 1963 Britain's policy towards Vietnam and Indonesia was a far cry from that of the peacemaker trying to restrain the belligerent Americans. In a curious reversal of the 'traditional' roles, it was the US administration that tried to restrain Britain with regard to Indonesia.

LINKING *KONFRONTASI* WITH THE VIETNAM WAR

The Douglas-Home government was not only confronted with American attempts to moderate the British position, it also had to deal with Canberra's and Wellington's lack-lustre support for London's policy towards Indonesia. Increased Australian and New Zealand military contributions played an important role in British military planning after Malaysia Day.[86] In August 1963, with the creation of Malaysia coming closer, Australia had committed itself to the defence of Malaysia by associating with the Anglo-Malaysian Defence Agreement (AMDA), and New Zealand had followed Canberra's example.[87] Ten days after Malaysia Day, Robert Menzies declared in Parliament that Australia would add its military assistance to Britain's efforts in the defence of Malaysia's territorial integrity and political independence.[88] Yet when Britain began to step up its military effort in Malaysia from September 1963 and asked for increased military contributions, the governments of Australian and New Zealand were not very forthcoming. The Australian Foreign Affairs and Defence Committee decided in December 1963 that there was no pressing need for increased Australian military assistance in Borneo.[89] Confronted with the reluctance of the Americans to curb their aid programme for Indonesia and the wavering of Australia and New Zealand, Douglas-Home became concerned about the somewhat one-dimensional, firm British policy towards Indonesia:

I am not sure that we have got our policy towards Indonesia in proper balance. I think the military, but negative aspect is right: that we defend Malaysia, hitting the Indonesians

---

[85]   Sir Edward Peck in interview with the author. 12.2.2002. See also letter: Foster (Washington) to Cable (FO). 7.7.64. PRO: FO 371/175063, D103145/31.

[86]   Minute: Thorneycroft to Macmillan. 2.10.63. PRO: PREM 11/4950. MOD memorandum: 'Present degree of military commitment'. 29.11.63. PRO: PREM 11/4905.

[87]   Telegram 322: EA Canberra to Washington. 14.8.63. AUSNA: A1838/287, file 2498/11, part 1.

[88]   *Australian Parliamentary Debates*, Vol. H. of R. 40, Session 1962–63, 25.9.63, 1339.

[89]   Minute: Wright (Private Secretary) to Douglas-Home. 17.12.63. PRO: PREM 11/4905. Decision No. 3(FAD): Foreign Affairs and Defence Committee. 19.12.63. The Australian Cabinet approved this decision: Cabinet Decision No. 15 'Indonesia and Malaysia'. 15.1.64. Both in AUSNA: A5828, Vol. 1. Telegram 545: Wellington to CRO containing message Holyoake to Douglas-Home. 19.12.63. Telegram 1317: Canberra to CRO containing message Menzies to Douglas-Home. 24.12.63. PRO: PREM 11/4905.

hard if they attack. But our policy seems to lack a positive, political aspect. We must defend Malaysia of course; but it will help neither Malaysia nor ourselves, nor the Western cause in general, if in the course of defending Malaysia we drive Indonesia into the arms of Communist Russia or China. It is probably considerations of this sort that make our friends and allies—Germany, Japan, the United States and even Australia and New Zealand—less than whole hearted in our support. Ought we not, in addition to our military readiness, be actively promoting a political solution? . . . Experience shows that is the only one that sticks.[90]

In response to the Prime Minister's questions Peter Thorneycroft warned that there was no long-term military solution to *konfrontasi*. Thorneycroft echoed the concerns the British Chiefs of Staff had voiced in September 1963, and pointed out that the strain on British military resources would be too big. Therefore, Britain would eventually have to look for a negotiated settlement. R. A. Butler, the new Foreign Secretary, on the other hand, still regarded a negotiated settlement with Indonesia as unlikely and counselled that Britain should maintain its present defensive policy. Both Thorneycroft and Butler, however, agreed that getting American backing for Britain's Indonesia policy was crucial, and both thought that establishing a link between the conflicts in Vietnam and the Malaysian area was the best way of doing this. Thorneycroft stressed that Washington would play a critical part in seeking a negotiated settlement. To draw Washington more closely into Britain's camp, he argued that the interdependence between a strong American presence in Southeast Asia and a stable Malaysia had to be made clear to the Americans.[91] Thorneycroft's reasoning was in line with his views on Britain's global defence role. He believed Britain could make a valuable contribution to western defence interests worldwide, yet without the support of the Americans and the coordination of Anglo-American defence efforts, London would not be able to afford its global role. If, in turn, the United States accepted this British role, Whitehall would be in a unique position to influence Washington's policy.[92]

Foreign Secretary Butler also undertook to bring the interdependence of the conflicts in Vietnam and the Malaysian area home to the Americans. He produced a 'reversed' version of the domino theory in a message to the US Secretary of State in January 1964. Butler argued that it would have serious repercussions in Thailand if the confrontation ended with a neutralized Malaysia. Bangkok might then reconsider its SEATO membership with the obvious consequence that this would weaken the west's position in Indochina.[93] Prime Minister Douglas-Home also established a link between *konfrontasi* and the Vietnam War at his first meeting with President Johnson in February 1964. One day before

[90] Minute: Douglas-Home to Butler. 19.12.63. Ibid.
[91] Telegram PT31: Thorneycroft (in Singapore) to Home. 7.1.64. Minute: Trend (Cabinet Secretary) to Douglas-Home. 8.1.64. Both ibid.
[92] Middeke, 'Britain's Interdependence Policy', 319–20.
[93] Telegram 962: FO to Washington containing message from Butler to Rusk. 21.1.64. PRO: PREM 4906.

the summit, Edward Peck, Assistant Under-Secretary of State at the Foreign Office, prepared the ground for Douglas-Home by reiterating the 'reversed' version of the domino theory at another round of quadripartite talks. He pointed out that 'the destruction of Malaysia by Indonesia would have repercussions on the situation in Vietnam'.[94] On the morning of 12 February 1964, Douglas-Home and Johnson discussed Vietnam and Malaysia. The British Prime Minister expressed the hope that Washington and London could see 'eye to eye on Indonesia in the future'.[95] Douglas-Home assured Johnson of his full support for US policy in Vietnam and stated categorically that he could see no alternative to the present American stance in Vietnam. He even said that Britain might be able to strengthen BRIAM if the United States so wished. This offer had the desired effect. Johnson seemed pleased and said he would be grateful if London could look into this.[96]

The Americans agreed to the British suggestion to highlight in the final communiqué of the summit both British support for US Vietnam policy and American support for the 'peaceful national independence of Malaysia'.[97] Two days later, in a meeting with officials from the White House, the State Department, and the Pentagon, the British stressed the linkage between the situations in Malaysia and Vietnam still more forcefully. Edward Peck pointed out that in Malaysia Britain was 'defending the back door' while the Americans 'defended the front' in Vietnam.[98] Peck was worried about Averell Harriman's reaction to this linkage and feared that the American veteran diplomat would react angrily, mainly because he seemed very tense at the beginning of the meeting. Harriman, however, remained nice and calm, and he seemed to understand the British position.[99]

In early 1965 the Foreign Office referred to the 'Malaysia/Viet-Nam bargain' that Douglas-Home and Johnson had struck at the summit meeting in February 1964.[100] Yet it is doubtful whether the link London tried to establish between the

---

[94] Record of Meeting. Quadripartite Talks, 10–11 February 1964. PRO: FO 371/175482, DV1017/6.

[95] Douglas-Home made this remark in the context of Robert Kennedy's attempt to mediate in the conflict. The British in Singapore were under the impression that their argument—that Sukarno was delivering Indonesia into the hands of the communists—made an impression on Robert Kennedy. Letter: Lord Moore of Wolvercote to author. 7.3.2002. For a more detailed discussion of Robert Kennedy's mission, see Easter, 'British Defence Policy', 167–9; Mackie, *Konfrontasi*, 225–7; Jeff Shesol, *Mutual Contempt: Lyndon Johnson, Robert Kennedy, and the Feud that Defined a Decade* (New York: W. W. Norton, 1997), 151–2; and Arthur M. Schlesinger, *Robert Kennedy and his Times* (London: Deutsch, 1978), 633–5.

[96] Record of Prime Minister's talks with President Johnson at the White House. 12.2.64. PRO: FO 371/175062, D103145/8. A copy of the record was also handed to the United States. LBJL: NSF, Country File United Kingdom, Home Visit, box 213.

[97] Record of a Meeting between Butler and Rusk at the White House. 12.2.64. PRO: PREM 11/4759. Telegram 653: Lord Harlech (Washington) to FO. 14.2.64. PRO: FO 371/175065, D1051/15. See also Memorandum of a Conversation at the White House between Douglas-Home, Butler, Johnson, Rusk. 12.2.64. FRUS: 1964–1968, i, Vietnam 1964, 68–70.

[98] Record of Meeting in Washington. 14.2.64. PRO: FO 371/175062, D103145/8.

[99] Sir Edward Peck in interview with the author. 12.2.2002.

[100] Letter: Peck (FO) to Trevelyan (Moscow). 17.2.65. PRO: FO 371/180215, D1072/3.

two conflicts in Southeast Asia did anything to influence Washington's Malaysia policy in the first half of 1964. Douglas-Home had clearly overplayed his hand in holding out the prospect of strengthening BRIAM. Moreover, London had been supportive of US Vietnam policy since 1960. There was no reason for the Americans to move closer to the British position on Indonesia just because the British had reiterated their support for US Vietnam policy. Throughout the first half of 1964, State Department and White House officials consequently continued to pursue the policy towards Indonesia that had been formulated under Kennedy. The link the Americans established between Vietnam and *konfrontasi* still stressed the need to prevent an escalation of the confrontation. Robert Komer, a member of the NSC staff, in particular warned time and again that the Indonesia–Malaysia conflict had to be kept from 'boiling over'.[101] He expressed his concern about the sending of Royal Navy ships through the Sunda Straits in reaction to the landing of several dozens of Indonesian paratroopers on the Malayan peninsula in September 1964. This British move was, in his view, a 'most provocative show of force', which could 'suck' the Americans into a 'nice mess' in Malaysia. He found that the British sounded 'as hysterical as Sukarno', particularly with regard to London's talk of Tonkin-Gulf-style retaliation.[102]

When the Johnson administration did move closer to the British position on the confrontation during the following months, this had not so much to do with Douglas-Home's representations at the February summit. It had more to do with Johnson's lack of patience with Sukarno, his different attitude towards neutralism in comparison with Kennedy and mounting Congressional pressure in favour of curbing the US aid programme in Indonesia.[103] On balance, the Foreign Office's talk of the 'deal' Johnson and Douglas-Home struck in February 1964 seems exaggerated. Rather, the summit led to 'a tacit understanding'—as Charles Baldwin, the US ambassador in Kuala Lumpur, described it later—between the British and Americans on the relationship between the two conflicts in Southeast Asia.[104] Even this 'understanding' was of great significance for the British government in its attempt to gain American recognition and appreciation for its role in the region and, ultimately, in the world.

In the second half of 1964 the Johnson administration became increasingly inclined to back Britain's firm stand against Indonesia.[105] The worsening situation in Vietnam in the wake of the Tonkin Gulf incidents certainly accounted for this,

[101] Memorandum: Komer to M. Bundy. 21.5.64. LBJL: NSF Country File Malaysia, Memos Vol. II, box 275. Background papers for visit of Tunku Abdul Rahman. 17.7.64. Ibid. Tunku Visit, Briefing Book and Memo, box 276.

[102] Memorandum: Komer to M. Bundy. 4.9.64. LBJL: NSF, Country File Malaysia, Memos Vol. III, box 275. Memorandum Komer to M. Bundy. 2.7.64. LBJL: NSF, Country File Indonesia, Cables and Memos, Vol. II, box 246.

[103] Johnson expressed his criticism of Sukarno and his concern about the pro-western government in Malaysia in telephone conversations with Senator Richard Russell on 10 January and 11 June 1964. The transcripts of the conversations are in Michael R. Beschloss (ed.), *Taking Charge: The Johnson White House Tapes, 1963–1964* (New York: Simon & Schuster, 1997), 157–8, 401–2.

[104] Charles Baldwin Oral History, 76. 13.3.69. LBJL: Oral Histories.

[105] Kaiser, *American Tragedy*, 313.

as well as the burgeoning relations between Indonesia and the PRC. Jakarta and Beijing, too, saw a link between the Vietnam War and the confrontation as both conflicts were part of the struggle against neo-colonialism.[106] Moreover, an international communist conference against imperialism in Hanoi adopted a resolution that supported the 'fight of the people of North Kalimantan [i.e. northern Borneo] for its independence' against the 'British imperialists'.[107]

When Britain had decided to make a firm commitment to the defence of Malaysia, this had not been done to provide the British government eventually with an excuse to refuse deeper involvement in the Vietnam War. From early 1964 it was clear that the confrontation had led to an overstretch in Britain's force deployments, and Britain admitted at an ANZAM committee meeting that it would have difficulties meeting its SEATO commitments on top of defending Malaysia.[108] Nevertheless, the Acting Chief of the Defence Staff considered sending British military forces to Vietnam shortly after the Tonkin Gulf incident in August 1964. He thought that Britain could send one infantry battalion group and/or one Royal Air Force fighter squadron. Whatever the British contribution would be, however, it had to be made sure that it would not prejudice Britain's ability to react to greater Indonesian pressure in northern Borneo.[109]

The defence of Malaysia was and remained Britain's clear priority in Southeast Asia. Increasingly the Foreign Office preferred to use its defence commitments in Malaysia to tell the Americans that London could not go beyond giving political support to the United States in Vietnam and was in no position to become involved militarily. One reason was the uncertainty of how much involvement a new British government would support after the British general elections in October 1964. In addition, the Foreign Office was keen to offset the potentially damaging consequences of BRIAM's phasing out. The desk officer in the Southeast Asia department stressed therefore that 'we could make more use of the argument that our major commitment in the area is in Malaysia, and tailor our aid projects accordingly'. However, there was no doubt in his mind that 'we shall not be able to withdraw entirely from supporting the Americans [in South Vietnam]'.[110]

In October 1964, the Foreign Office described the need for full American sympathy for Britain's policy of resisting *konfrontasi* as the 'real motive' for a British presence in South Vietnam. '[W]e cannot afford to let the Americans believe that our support for their determined policy in Viet-Nam is dwindling in enthusiasm', the Foreign Office concluded. 'It seems clear, therefore, that we can gain the best

---

[106] Mackie, *Konfrontasi*, 285–6.

[107] Resolution über die Unterstützung für den Kampf der Völker der Welt gegen Imperialismus und Kolonialismus (Resolution on the support for the struggle of the peoples of the world against imperialism and colonialism). 29.11.64. SAPMO: DY6/Vorl. 1047.

[108] COS(64), 17th meeting. 25.2.64. PRO: DEFE 4/165. See also Easter, 'British Defence Policy', 174.

[109] Annex to COS 2662/7/8/64. Minute by Acting Chief of Defence Staff to Chiefs of Staff. 7.8.64. PRO: DEFE 4/173.

[110] Minute by Simons (FO). 14.8.64. PRO: FO 371/175483, DV1017/27.

return for whatever effort we make by co-ordinating fully with the Americans and, if necessary, integrating our aid with theirs.'[111] After the Labour Party's victory in the elections, Harold Wilson, the new Prime Minister, was in the fortunate position that the Johnson administration was inclined to agree that Britain could not do much more in Vietnam because of its commitment in Malaysia. Britain's policy of firmness towards an increasingly radical Sukarno was described by McGeorge Bundy—and now also by Robert Komer—as the right strategy that had prevented the Indonesian president from embarking upon more dangerous adventures. Coming round to the British view, the United States believed that demonstrations of military strength would eventually make Sukarno back down and agree to a negotiated settlement of the conflict.[112] Although some members of the administration, for instance the Secretary of State, thought that Britain could do more in Vietnam and send token military forces, Lyndon B. Johnson himself appeared impressed by the argument that the confrontation precluded this option.[113]

According to an American intelligence report, the British had committed military forces to Malaysia to such an extent that they, 'even with the best will in the world', could not do more in Vietnam, and that it would be more beneficial to the United States if London and Washington continued to split the burden of defending Malaysia and South Vietnam. The report also observed that a small number of British forces in Vietnam would only help Washington politically, militarily they would not make a difference. However, if the British demanded as a *quid pro quo* a straightforward American military commitment to Malaysia, Washington would end up with a heavy and potentially costly responsibility that would outweigh the usefulness of a British military contribution in Vietnam.[114] Although McGeorge Bundy disagreed with this analysis and maintained that London should increase the number of 'Britishers' in Vietnam to one hundred, the intelligence assessment left an impression on him. He wrote to President Johnson shortly before his first meeting with Harold Wilson in December 1964:

The point of this memorandum is simply to make sure that you know how very hard it will be for Wilson to do as much for us in [South Vietnam] as we need him to. It is hard to treat a thing as our problem for 10 years and then try to get other people to take on a share of it, just because it is getting worse (though we choose not to say so).[115]

[111] FO memorandum: 'Future of British Advisory Mission in Viet-Nam'. 14.10.64. PRO: FO 371/175484, DV1017/44.

[112] Record of Discussion at the Foreign Office between Butler and Bundy. 17.9.64. PRO: FO 371/175063, D103145/35. Memorandum of Conversation between Butler and Bundy. 17.9.64. Memorandum: Komer to W. Bundy (State Department). 21.10.64. Both in LBJL: NSF, Country File Malaysia, Memos Vol. III, box 275. Deptel 715: Rusk to Djakarta. 22.10.64. Ibid. Cables Vol. III, box 275.

[113] Handwritten notes of meeting between Johnson, Rusk, Taylor, McNamara, and W. and M. Bundy. 1.12.64. LBJL: NSF, Meeting Notes File, Meeting with Foreign Policy Adviser on Vietnam, box 1.

[114] Memorandum: Assistant Deputy Director Intelligence to Bundy: 'The British in Vietnam'. 4.12.64. LBJL: NSF, Country File United Kingdom, PM Wilson Visit (I), box 214.

[115] Memorandum: Bundy to Johnson. 5.12.64. Ibid.

President Johnson raised the question of a British military contribution to the struggle in Vietnam on 7 December 1964. Johnson said that a 'few soldiers in British uniforms in South Vietnam . . . would have a great psychological effect and political significance'. The British Prime Minister pointed out that Britain could not do much more than it had been doing because the British 'faced exactly the same problem . . . in Malaysia'.[116] Secretary of State Rusk brought up Vietnam again on the following day. Rusk talked of the importance for American allies to 'show the flag' in Vietnam and he expressed his hope that the British would 'put people in the countryside'. Engineers, technicians, and military personnel were needed. His new British colleague, Patrick Gordon-Walker, reiterated that the American problem in Vietnam was essentially the same as the British problem in Malaysia. As the British had 'a battle of their own to fight', they could not put troops into Vietnam. All that Gordon-Walker did was to promise public support for US Vietnam policy and to stress that Britain would not agree to a conference on Vietnam without US consent.[117]

London's policy of linking the British commitment to Malaysia with the US effort in Vietnam had led to a result, which Wilson's Labour government with its precarious majority in the House of Commons could make good use of. The Johnson administration valued Britain's contribution towards looking after western interests in Southeast Asia, and urged the British government 'to give full weight to the role of Britain as a world Power beyond the NATO area'.[118] The British cabinet was therefore informed that the United States and Britain agreed that 'the British contribution to peace and stability outside Europe was more important than Britain's European role'.[119] The United States appreciated both the military role the British played in Malaysia, and its political support for US Vietnam policy. Although the Americans continued to ask for an increased British commitment in Vietnam, the pressure on London to get more heavily involved remained limited.

CONCLUSION

Faced with Indonesia's policy of confrontation, three successive British governments decided on a policy of firmness that ruled out any concessions to Jakarta's demands. Whitehall accepted the expensive consequences of its 'tough' stance. When the Americans spelled out that Malaysia could mean a heavy military commitment, and that Britain and its Commonwealth allies Australia and New

---

[116] Cabinet Office Record of a meeting held at the British Embassy in Washington, DC and later at the White House on 7th December 1964. 14.12.64. PRO: PREM 13/104.

[117] Memorandum of conversation at the White House: Wilson, Gordon-Walker, Johnson, and Rusk among the participants. 8.12.63. FRUS: 1964–1968, i, Vietnam 1964, 985–6.

[118] Cabinet Office Record of a meeting held at the British Embassy in Washington, DC and later at the White House on 7th December 1964. 14.12.64. PRO: PREM 13/104.

[119] CC(64), 14th meeting. 11.12.64. PRO: CAB 128/39.

Zealand had to shoulder that burden alone, the Macmillan government pledged its willingness to do so. Macmillan's successors, first Sir Alec Douglas-Home and then Harold Wilson, lived up to these promises.

Until the Manila Summit of August 1963, the British attempted to *appear* conciliatory to please the Americans and Australians. After the Manila Summit, the British, Duncan Sandys in particular, gave up this policy of restraint and assumed a more active role. The new strategy, while helping to create Malaysia, only antagonized Indonesia further. This attitude towards confrontation appeared to be remarkably similar to the American stand in South Vietnam. Firmness in the face of aggression, be it communist or a mixture between nationalism and communism, was of great importance. Although, or perhaps because, Britain was a declining world power, prestige was an essential ingredient in London's policy towards Indonesian confrontation. '[A]part from their military value', the British Defence Committee pointed out in early 1963, 'our forces in the Far East had political and prestige significance. Their withdrawal would be regarded as a major political defeat and, quite apart from its serious effect on Australia, New Zealand and the United States, would encourage the spread of communism.'[120]

Simultaneously, London's firm stand was a natural development of British policy in Southeast Asia, as reflected in Britain's attempts at maintaining the Singapore base and its policy towards the Vietnam War between 1961 and 1963. As Britain supported the uncompromising American stance, agreeing that communist expansion had to be stopped and that no negotiated solution on the Laos model would be acceptable in Vietnam, an attitude mirroring these convictions when Britain's direct interests were at stake appeared almost inevitable. London argued that its policies towards the conflicts in Southeast Asia were consistent, but pointed to the inconsistencies in US policy. How could the Americans urge restraint on the British with regard to their policy towards Indonesia when they themselves became increasingly inclined to escalate the conflict in Indochina? And how could they urge a negotiated solution, if they ruled out the reconvention of the Geneva conference to solve the Vietnam conflict?

Britain's uncompromising policy was all the more remarkable in the face of American reluctance to go along with it. Washington's foremost concern was to prevent another Vietnam-like commitment in Southeast Asia. Therefore, the link that Washington established in early 1963 between *konfrontasi* and the Vietnam War reinforced the argument of those forces within the American administration, particularly in the State Department, who wanted to accommodate Indonesia's claims to prevent Sukarno from turning even more to the communist bloc. The lack of US political support for Britain's policy towards Indonesia caused concern in Whitehall, yet it also provided an opportunity for Britain to show its ability to use its political and military power in Southeast Asia to safeguard its own interests, even without full American backing.

---

[120] D(63)3rd meeting. 9.2.63. PRO: CAB 131/28, f. 20.

Nevertheless, from early 1964 the British actively tried to link the two conflicts in Southeast Asia in order to win over the Americans to Britain's firm policy towards Indonesia and to prove the importance of Britain's military capabilities in the struggle against communism. In February 1964 the British government stressed its willingness to maintain or even increase its support for US Vietnam policy, in return for more unequivocal American political support for Malaysia. Although there was subsequently talk of a 'deal' or 'bargain' that had been struck between the British Prime Minister and the American President, no more than an informal understanding was reached in February 1964. The Johnson administration remained worried that the Malaysia–Indonesia conflict might 'boil-over'. Britain's increasingly aggressive and provocative stance found only limited support in Washington

By the latter half of 1964, however, the Johnson administration was slowly moving closer to Britain's views on the relationship between the two conflicts. In particular, American political support for Britain's firm policy against Sukarno became stronger after the escalation of the Vietnam conflict in the summer of 1964. The British now began to argue that their commitment in Malaysia made increased British involvement in Vietnam impossible. While the British argument did not convince the Johnson administration completely, it helped to keep Washington's pressure on Britain to commit token combat forces to Vietnam limited.

Conclusion

PRESIDENT JOHN F. KENNEDY decided that a communist victory in South Vietnam had to be prevented by military means. Between 1961 and 1963 the British government could have tried to restrain the Americans by pointing to alternative, perhaps non-military solutions to the conflict—as the Churchill government had done in 1954 or Macmillan himself worked for in regard to Laos in 1960–1. As co-chairman of the 1954 Geneva conference Britain could have attempted to revive the 'Geneva spirit' and could have called for negotiations. As a member of SEATO Britain could have resisted or at least slowed down contingency planning for SEATO intervention to counter the insurgency in Vietnam. In its relations with the South Vietnamese regime under Ngo Dinh Diem, the Macmillan government could have stressed the paramount need for democratic reform and could have publicly disapproved of Diem's brutality and ruthlessness. Faced with Diem's unpopular and repressive regime, it would have been easy for the British to throw up their hands in despair and walk away from the messy situation in Vietnam. In short, Britain could have opposed Kennedy's Vietnam policy, a policy that substantially deepened American involvement in the conflict and that left Kennedy's successor, Lyndon B. Johnson, with the choice of humiliating defeat or disastrous escalation in 1965.

British policy makers, however, chose to support Kennedy's Vietnam policy. When the Americans began to ignore the Geneva agreements, Whitehall used its special position as co-chairman of the Geneva conference to justify American action. There was no doubt in London that Washington's measures constituted a clear breach of the 1954 ceasefire agreement. There were doubts, however, about the reliability of the evidence produced by the South Vietnamese in the attempt to prove that Hanoi was behind the insurgency in the RVN. Yet these doubts were cast aside. The International Control Commission was singled out as a suitable instrument for putting the blame for the breakdown of the 1954 ceasefire agreement on the DRV, whether there was evidence or not. In its attempts to influence the ICC's decisions, the British showed particularly in 1961 that they were more impatient and more eager than the Canadians to get the ICC's condemnation of Hanoi's 'subversive activity' in the RVN. British as well as American and Canadian pressure on India, the chairman of the ICC, bore fruit in June 1962. The ICC's Special Report condemned first the DRV for supporting communist subversion in the RVN and then the United States for stepping up its military aid in late 1962. This facilitated western governments' efforts to portray the American involvement as a purely defensive reaction to 'outside' aggression. The ICC also provided a shield against calls for a negotiated settlement in Vietnam. The British government was adamantly opposed to a negotiated solution to the Vietnam War between 1961 and 1963, and rejected ideas of reconvening the Geneva conference to deal with Vietnam. Whereas the Macmillan government had worked for a negotiated solution to the Laos crisis, Britain had no intention of playing the role of the peacemaker in Vietnam. Instead, British policy was designed to support the United States in its attempt to seek a military solution to the Vietnam conflict.

There is no evidence to suggest that Britain would have favoured SEATO involvement in the military struggle against NLF forces. However, there are indications that the British would have taken part in SEATO intervention in Indochina if the United States had insisted. Despite doubts about the alliance, Britain's policy of preventing a communist victory in the RVN found its expression even within SEATO. Once the Laos crisis had been defused and the conflicting parties brought to the conference table in Geneva in May 1961, Britain went along with SEATO's counter-insurgency planning for Vietnam. Concerns were voiced in London about provocative aspects of SEATO Plans 6 and 7. Plan 6 provided for amphibious landings in the DRV if Hanoi attacked the RVN. Plan 7, the counter-insurgency plan, called for a large deployment of SEATO forces close to the 17th parallel. But Whitehall was never prepared to express these concerns within SEATO. Instead, Britain took part in SEATO's contingency planning and declared forces to both plans.

It did not really matter to the British that Ngo Dinh Diem's regime was repressive, undemocratic, and corrupt. What did matter was that the South Vietnamese President was a staunch anti-communist and, as there was nobody else who was suitable, that he embodied the best hope of defeating the insurgency. It goes without saying that the British would have preferred a well-organized, well-liked, and truly democratic pro-western regime in Saigon. What caused real concern in London was Diem's narrow power base, the lack of popular support, and, above all, his regime's apparent ineffectiveness in dealing with the insurgency. Defeating the NLF forces was the priority, and if Diem proved incapable of leading a successful counter-insurgency campaign he was dispensable. In 1961 and 1962 the British were at times convinced that Diem would not be able to 'deliver'. Some Foreign Office officials began to pin their hopes on the South Vietnamese army taking over from Diem. The British, however, were never prepared to share these views with the Americans and discuss Diem's removal. Ultimately, Britain was afraid that Diem's replacement might lead to a split of the anti-communist forces in Vietnam that would further strengthen the position of the NLF.

The most striking manifestation of Britain's willingness to assist the RVN in its military struggle against the insurgency was the decision to establish the British Advisory Mission in Saigon in 1961. Not only were the Americans not putting pressure on the British to increase their involvement in Vietnam at this stage, but Britain actually had to overcome the US military's resistance to forming BRIAM. The sending of the mission to Saigon demonstrated, on the one hand, Britain's growing concern about the situation in Vietnam and the hope that the communist challenge could be thwarted. On the other hand, it showed the inter-ministerial consensus behind Britain's Vietnam policy. The Foreign Office's eagerness to establish BRIAM was supported by the Commonwealth Relations Office, the Prime Minister, and the Treasury. Equally uncontroversial was the decision to extend the life of the Mission for another two years in 1963. Overall, the Prime Minister and his Cabinet were content to leave the formulation of British Vietnam policy to the relevant departments in the Foreign Office and the embassies in Washington and Saigon. Macmillan and Lord Home never initiated a reassessment of Britain's policy or questioned the line that emerged from the Foreign Office's departments.

What was behind the British government's willingness to support Kennedy's Vietnam policy? From the outset the British compared the Vietnam War with the Malayan emergency, and they pointed to the similarities between these two conflicts. The British had defeated the communist-led guerrilla campaign in Malaya and they were convinced that the same could be done in Vietnam. British officials in the area stressed that the American military was not experienced enough to deal with a guerrilla campaign. In their view, the fact that US military advisers had trained the ARVN to fight a conventional war proved this point. The British, on the other hand, thought they knew all that had to be known about defeating an insurgency, and that their experience gained in Malaya could be put to good use in Vietnam. One important consideration behind sending BRIAM and offering ARVN officers training courses in Malaya's jungle warfare schools was the hope that the benefit of British advice on counter-insurgency measures could tip the balance in favour of the anti-communist forces in Vietnam.

The Vietnam conflict was never seen in isolation, and wider political considerations were crucial in determining British Vietnam policy. The maintenance of Britain's political influence in Southeast Asia was an important aim of the Macmillan government. If Britain wanted to be taken seriously, it had to keep sufficient military forces in the area to fulfil its commitments with regard to SEATO, AMDA, and ANZAM. The unhampered use of the Singapore base for as long as possible was considered vital. The creation of Malaysia promised the continued use of the base. Consequently, the British government embraced the Malaysia plan in late 1961 when the Tunku agreed to leave Britain's rights to the Singapore base untouched. Prime Minister Macmillan in turn was prepared to push the Borneo territories, on which the Tunku had set his eyes, into the new federation with little regard for the concerns of the local peoples.

From mid-1961 Kennedy was all the more prepared to stand firm in Vietnam because of his decision to seek a negotiated settlement to the Laos crisis. A further western 'retreat' in the face of communist expansion could not be tolerated. Britain drew similar conclusions from the Laos crisis for two reasons. First, accepting the logic of the domino theory, the British feared that the fall of Saigon would have dire consequences for the western position in Southeast Asia. Communist pressure on Thailand would grow. Bangkok might lose faith in the west and seek an accommodation with the communist bloc. SEATO would break up and Malaya would become the last line of defence against the spread of communism. Second and more importantly, Britain could not afford to be perceived as being 'soft' on communist expansion again. The Macmillan government's stance on Laos had antagonized many Americans and it had also led to concerns in Australia. To counter this, Britain was willing to prove that it was prepared to play its part in the cold war struggle in Asia, and there was no better place than Vietnam to demonstrate its resolve. Supporting the western cause in Vietnam was to strengthen Canberra's, Wellington's, and Kuala Lumpur's belief in Commonwealth defence. The British knew that in the long run only the United States was in a position to satisfy Australia's and New Zealand's security needs. Yet in the short run the Macmillan government wanted to preserve the special military relations with the two 'old' Commonwealth countries. Britain was therefore determined to maintain its commitment to SEATO. A retreat from the alliance or even any lack of resolve in supporting contingency planning within SEATO would have shaken Australia's and New Zealand's belief in Britain's willingness to live up to its defence commitments in Southeast Asia, including its Commonwealth defence obligations.

Indeed, the Commonwealth was of great importance in achieving the Macmillan government's aim to preserve Britain's role as a world power. Consequently, a close political and military relationship with Australia and New Zealand was essential, particularly at a time when Canberra grew increasingly suspicious of Britain's commitment to the Commonwealth. The Australians not only doubted Britain's resolve to stand up to the communist challenge in Southeast Asia in the wake of the Laos crisis; Macmillan's application to join the EEC and the possible concessions the British would make at the expense of the old Dominions put a strain on Anglo-Australian relations. Macmillan was also convinced that open Australian or New Zealand opposition would endanger, if not completely destroy, the British EEC application.[1] Proving to the Australians and New Zealanders that Britain had no intention to go back on its defence obligations in Southeast Asia, despite its overtures towards Europe, was therefore very important to counter the perception that Britain was on the retreat from its global role. In Vietnam the British could prove that the opposite was true, and sending BRIAM to Vietnam was clearly designed to reassure Britain's Commonwealth allies. 'At the present time our friends in Australia, New Zealand and Pakistan feel that we are not sufficiently interested in the problems of Southeast Asia', Commonwealth Secretary Duncan Sandys wrote in July 1961, shortly after the start of the conference on Laos. 'The counter-insurgency mission [BRIAM] would be a timely reminder', Sandys went on, 'that we are ready to play a helpful part in that part of the world.'[2]

No doubt, there were also concerns about Chinese communist expansion in the area. The British were convinced that it was the PRC's ultimate aim to dominate Southeast Asia. The formation of Malaysia was to thwart a potential communist takeover of Singapore with its mainly Chinese population. The growing

---

[1] Macmillan, *At the End of the Day*, 129.
[2] Minute: Sandys to Lloyd. 25.7.61. PRO: DO 169/109.

influence of the Chinese in the DRV at the expense of the potentially less aggressive Soviets deeply worried the Foreign Office, and Lord Home stressed in July 1961 that Britain 'could not afford, for strategic and economic reasons, to stand by while virtually the whole of Indo-China fell into Communist hands'.[3] These 'strategic' reasons were not confined to Home's conviction that deterring communist expansion and defending the Commonwealth countries in the area were linked. For Britain's strategic position in Southeast Asia it was also essential to play a part in the effort to resist a communist victory in the RVN in order to strengthen Anglo-American relations. Indeed, it can hardly be overemphasized how fundamental maintaining or even improving Anglo-American relations was to British deliberations on Vietnam.

Sending BRIAM would therefore not only reassure the Australians, but also remind Washington that Britain was 'with the United States' in the RVN, that Britain was able to play a role outside Europe, and that it had a lot to offer: ample experience in counter-insurgency and jungle warfare schools close by in Malaya. The maintenance of British forces in Singapore, including the nuclear deterrent against the PRC, was also regarded as essential to be in a position to influence US policy if necessary. Politically, the British would only be able to use this influence if the United States was willing to listen to British advice. Harold Macmillan was very concerned about the state of Anglo-American relations, particularly shortly before John F. Kennedy became President, and he was keen to promise Kennedy in December 1960, well before Kennedy's lofty inaugural speech, that Britain would not 'shrink from sacrifice'[4] in the cold war. From 1961 the British were well on their way to proving this in Southeast Asia.

In 1961, Britain was willing to get more deeply involved in Vietnam before Washington even asked for it, and certainly before any other American ally—including Australia—showed an inclination to step up assistance to the RVN. Therefore, the Macmillan government's Vietnam policy had the desired salutary effect on Anglo-American relations, mainly because of BRIAM. Robert Thompson quickly overcame the initial difficulties with the American military and the US embassy in Saigon, and he established himself as one of the most important, if not the most important, foreign adviser to Diem's government. The South Vietnamese President appeared to be prepared to listen to Thompson's advice. The Kennedy administration also readily accepted Thompson's special advisory role. Particularly in 1962 and 1963 American officials in Washington and Kennedy himself were keen to get Thompson's assessment of the situation in Vietnam. The Foreign Office therefore regarded BRIAM as a success, and the British ambassador in Saigon concluded that a 'special' Anglo-American relationship was developing in Vietnam.

While Thompson's assessments and his views on counter-insurgency left an impression on the Americans, BRIAM's impact on the anti-guerrilla campaign

---

[3] Minute: Home to Lloyd. 21.7.61. PRO: PREM 11/3736.
[4] Letter: Macmillan to Kennedy. 19.12.60. PRO: FO 371/152108, ZP8/63/G.

was limited. Thompson's advocacy of Malayan-type measures in Vietnam helped to pave the way for Washington's acceptance of the strategic hamlet programme, yet it is conceivable that the South Vietnamese and the Americans would have pursued a similar policy in any case. The strategic hamlet programme contained elements of Thompson's delta plan, but President Diem and his brother Ngo Dinh Nhu had shown an inclination to implement a scheme based on defending villages and hamlets and regrouping parts of the population well before Thompson's arrival in Saigon. Thompson himself was not informed of the announcement of the programme in February 1962, and the British did not greet it with enthusiasm. They were even concerned that Thompson might be associated with a strategy he had not devised. Yet as the strategic hamlet programme became the order of the day—and appeared to have a positive impact— the British refrained from discouraging the impression that Thompson was behind the programme. Indeed, Thompson quickly adapted to the new situation after February 1962 and strove to influence the strategic hamlet programme as best he could. Ultimately, he seemed content with the partial implementation of his concepts. Thompson went along with the South Vietnamese decision to disregard important elements of his advice, particularly with regard to constructing strategic hamlets in secure areas first, and then slowly expand into areas under NLF control. Similarly, he could not be satisfied with the coordination of the civil and military campaign. In fact, his approach reflected the Kennedy administration's way of dealing with the Saigon regime. Thompson as well as the Americans found it impossible to persuade President Diem to implement all elements of their advice. Kennedy's attempt in December 1961 to link increased US military assistance with Diem's acceptance of more US administrative and political influence in Saigon failed. Diem agreed to American military aid but successfully resisted pressure for administrative reform. Likewise, Thompson initially worked for Diem's adoption of his delta plan. Eventually, however, he went along with the South Vietnamese approach. The delta plan got lost in the strategic hamlet programme and the delta became no more than a priority area within the programme, which was to be pushed ahead throughout the country.

Even if optimism and confidence was part of Thompson's strategy, by 1963 he began to play down the difficulties the Americans and South Vietnamese were still facing. He had begun to identify himself closely with the counter-insurgency struggle. 'We are winning', was the message Thompson personally delivered to Kennedy in 1963. Thompson's problem was not only that he did not keep a healthy distance from the counter-insurgency effort, but that, more importantly, the three premises upon which he based his approach to the Vietnam conflict were flawed. First, he believed that the Vietnamese peasants would reject communism. Second, all the South Vietnamese people wanted was good government—a smoothly working administrative machinery was therefore more important than political support for the government. Third, Thompson was certain that the insurgency in Vietnam could be defeated by the same measures the British had applied in Malaya. This boils down to the fact that Thompson did not find it necessary to devise original anti-guerrilla schemes designed to fit the Vietnamese situation.

As a consequence of establishing BRIAM, the British faced a dilemma similar to the one Kennedy had to deal with. From October 1961 the British had two missions in Saigon, one closely involved in the practical aspects of the military struggle against the NLF forces, and, of course, the diplomatic mission. Whitehall was eventually confronted with divergent assessments from these missions with regard to Diem's government, just as Kennedy had to deal with conflicting advice from the various US missions in Saigon and their counterparts in Washington. The British ambassador's view, expressed in October 1963, that Diem had to be replaced may have been an indication of the influence his US colleague had on him. Similarly, Robert Thompson's pro-Diem stance may have been the result of his cooperation with the American military advisers who also supported Diem. On the other hand, it seems more likely that the differing assessments reflected the decisions that would inevitably have been reached from the missions' different perspectives on the Vietnam war. In any case, in Washington and in London the support for the diplomatic/political perspective was dominant.

The months before the coup against Diem also illustrated that however 'special' the British ambassador thought Anglo-American relations were in Vietnam, they were not sufficiently 'special' to discuss the future of the Diem regime. Whitehall showed no desire to become involved in the ugly business of unseating the Saigon government for various reasons. First and foremost, the British were increasingly prepared to simply follow the American lead on Vietnam, particularly as they became preoccupied with Indonesia's confrontation policy. Second, the Foreign Office found it difficult to make up its mind whether Diem had to be ousted or not. For these two reasons Britain had no real desire to influence American thinking on Diem and possibly upset Anglo-American relations with advice that parts of the US administration would resent. Consequently, the report by Thompson that Kennedy had asked for was not forwarded to Washington, and Kennedy, who had not made up his mind completely with regard to Diem, was deprived of the possibility to listen to another voice that opposed the removal of Diem.

Although the Americans undoubtedly appreciated Britain's supportive stance in Vietnam, the salutary effect British Vietnam policy had on Anglo-American relations in Southeast Asia was limited. When the British government found itself confronted with Indonesia's opposition to the Malaysia plan, the lack of strong American political support disappointed the Macmillan government. The Kennedy administration never agreed with Britain's tough and at times aggressive policy towards Indonesia. Washington wanted to accommodate Jakarta's concerns in an attempt to maintain American influence in Indonesia and prevent President Sukarno from moving still closer to the communist bloc. The British government believed that a policy of firmness was the only answer to the confrontation. Sukarno would not understand anything else, and his anti-Malaysia policy proved that he had already embarked on an essentially expansionist and anti-western—if not even pro-communist—foreign policy.

As the immediate future of Britain's role in Southeast Asia hinged upon the maintenance of the Singapore base within the Federation of Malaysia, a lot was at stake for the British. What is more, Britain could not allow a third-rate power like Indonesia to put pressure on Britain. These reasons were sufficient to justify the decision of February 1963 to inform the Americans that Britain was committed to defending Malaysia against Indonesian subversion. British Vietnam policy from 1961 showed that London was determined to use military means if necessary to maintain the western position in the area. It was only logical to show the same determination in the Malayan area. Indeed, the Foreign Office pointed out to the Americans in 1964 that British policy towards Southeast Asia was more consistent than America's. Whitehall had always supported the firm American stance in Vietnam, and Britain now pursued a firm policy to thwart Indonesia's expansionist designs. The British government was against negotiations with regard to both conflicts. Laos had been the last compromise solution the west would accept, and firm opposition to any further challenges became an essential ingredient of Britain's policy of maintaining the western position in Asia. The anti-communist governments in the RVN and Malaysia had to be kept in power to forestall the west's gradual loss of influence in the area.

The British government did not try to establish a link between the conflicts in Vietnam and Malaysia in 1963 because it had nothing to gain from such a move. Offering British support in Vietnam in exchange for American backing of Britain's uncompromising stance towards Indonesia would not have made sense as Britain had been supportive of Kennedy's Vietnam policy throughout his presidency. In fact, the Americans were reluctant to underwrite British policy towards confrontation *because* of their problems in Vietnam. The United States wanted to avoid the outbreak of another Vietnam-like war in Southeast Asia. Not being sucked into a second anti-guerrilla conflict was more important to the Americans than safeguarding Britain's support in Vietnam, which Washington already had in any case. This American attitude only changed slowly and was mainly brought about by Sukarno's increasing radicalism, which in part was a reaction to Britain's uncompromising policy towards *konfrontasi*, and the escalating Vietnam conflict.

Although the British tried to link the confrontation and the Vietnam War in 1964, presenting a 'reversed' domino theory to the United States, holding out the prospect of a larger British role in Vietnam and talking of defending Vietnam's 'back door' in Malaysia, there never was a clear-cut Anglo-American deal with regard to linking US support for Malaysia with Britain's support for US Vietnam policy. Yet Britain's involvement in the confrontation brought three benefits. First, the Americans increasingly accepted the British argument that the British effort in Malaysia and the American effort in Vietnam were related. Second, the number of British troops in the Malayan area provided a credible excuse, particularly for Harold Wilson's government, not to send British combat forces to Vietnam. Third, the Americans began to appreciate Britain's global role, and increasingly regarded the British military presence east of Suez as equally, if not more, important than Britain's role in Europe.

These gains, however, were only short term. In the long run Britain's Malaysia policy revealed the weakness of Britain and the limits of its power. In effect, the attempt to maintain a credible British military presence through its base in Singapore undermined the British strategy of maintaining SEATO and Commonwealth defence commitments at reduced costs by adopting a strategy that relied on the mobility and not on the size of the forces. The conflict with Indonesia never gave this strategy a chance. By 1964 the British also concluded that, despite the build-up, they had insufficient forces in the area to take part in SEATO operations without weakening the defence of Malaysia. Confrontation proved not only costly, but also demonstrated that British forces were overstretched.

The conflicts in Southeast Asia eventually brought the reality of the limits of Britain's power home to Whitehall. Not that these limits were new to British policy makers—intellectually it had long been realized that Britain would not be able to remain a world power. Yet colonial mindsets and political instincts made decision makers search for ways to stay in the power game. Former US Secretary of State Dean Acheson remarked in 1962 that 'Great Britain has lost an Empire and has not yet found a role'.[5] This oft-repeated quote, however, seems misleading. Finding a role on the world stage would not have been a problem for the Macmillan government and its successors: the empire would have become the Commonwealth, colonies would have become clients, EEC membership would have ensured prosperity, and the special relationship with the US security, plus a say in matters involving war and peace worldwide. The problem was to be accepted in that role by friends and foes alike. Consequently, British policy in the early 1960s was designed to prove that the United Kingdom qualified for that role. Faced with the French veto against Britain's EEC membership, the other aspects of the envisaged role gained importance. The former empire as a 'cultural and ethnic frame of reference'[6] made it easier to pull away from Europe and look to other parts of the world. Southeast Asia seemed the ideal choice: the Malayans remained good friends who listened to British advice, and Singapore was still a formidable military base, a base 'that was always a pleasure to visit', as Minister of Defence Harold Watkinson remembered.[7] Contrary to Mark Curtis's view that the desire to use the world's economic resources lay at the root of Britain's aim of upholding its great power status,[8] economic interests, although important, did not play a crucial role in Southeast Asia. The region was simply one of the few left in the world where Britain could play the role of a great power, militarily and diplomatically. Decades of colonial experience, many government officials with Southeast Asian expertise, and considerable military forces, it was here where the British could cling to the role they had played for a century and wanted to continue to play.

---

[5] Reynolds, *Britannia Overruled*, 225.   [6] Ibid. 303.

[7] Harold Watkinson, *Turning Points: A Record of our Times* (London: Michael Russel, 1986), 127.

[8] Mark Curtis, *The Ambiguities of Power: British Foreign Policy since 1945* (London: Zed Books, 1995), 12.

Against this background, Britain's stance in Vietnam could not have come as a complete surprise. British policy towards the Vietnam War between 1961 and 1963 illustrates that London agreed with and was supportive of Kennedy's Vietnam policy. While there were significant concerns about communist expansion in Asia and while Britain was prepared to contribute to the deterrent of the PRC, a more important reason for the Macmillan government to support Kennedy's Vietnam policy was to demonstrate to its allies that it was not 'soft' on communism. Proving Britain's resolve in the cold war was essential to maintain and improve Anglo-American relations as well as relations with the Commonwealth, particularly with Australia and New Zealand. Britain would only be able to maintain its role as a world power if Washington, Canberra, and Wellington were convinced that Britain was capable and determined to defend western political and military interests.

Yet, there was nothing cynical in Britain's support for Kennedy's Vietnam policy between 1961 and 1963. Britain was adamantly opposed to a negotiated solution to the conflict and willing to fight the war for the Americans on the diplomatic front because the British indeed thought that there was nothing to negotiate about and that the Vietnam situation was quite different from Laos. Like the Americans, the British preferred a military solution to the conflict and believed that the communist insurgents in Vietnam could be defeated. And like the Americans, the British were willing to help the South Vietnamese government in its struggle and give advice in the counter-insurgency field. London had no alternative to offer to Kennedy's policy of looking for a military victory in Vietnam. Rather, Britain's policy towards Vietnam and Southeast Asia encouraged the Kennedy administration to seek victory in Vietnam, just as the British had sought and achieved victory in Malaya, and were trying to achieve in the confrontation. Between 1961 and 1963, Britain did not play the role of the peacemaker in Indochina. Instead, the British chose to adopt the role of the loyal cold war and Commonwealth ally that believed not only in the need to prevent the fall of the pro-western regime in Saigon, but also in the possibility of defeating the communist insurgency. Britain did nothing to steer Washington away from the path that led to the Vietnam quagmire.

Bibliography

I. UNPUBLISHED DOCUMENTS

(a) Australia

National Archives of Australia, Canberra (AUSNA)

Department of Defence (CA 46)
  A1945   Correspondence Files, 1949–1978
  A5799   Defence Committee, agenda, 1932–
  A5954   The Shedden Collection: Department of Defence (III), Central Office
Department of External Affairs (CA 18)
  A4231   Bound volumes of despatches from overseas posts, 1940–
  A1838   Correspondence Files, 1948–1989
  A4531   Australian Embassy, Saigon, Correspondence Files, 1952– (CA2773)
  A2908   Australian High Commission, United Kingdom, Correspondence Files (CA241)
Cabinet Office (CA 3)
  A4940   Cabinet files 'C' single number series, 1958–1967
  A5827   Cabinet submissions and associated decisions, 1963–66
Prime Minister's Department (CA 12)
  A463   Correspondence files, general
  A1209   Correspondence files, annual single number series, 1957–
  A4231   Bound volumes of despatches from overseas posts

(b) Canada

National Archives of Canada, Ottawa (CNA)

  RG 2   Records of the Privy Council
  RG 25   Records of the Department of External Affairs

(c) Germany

Bundesarchiv Berlin: Stiftung Archiv Parteien und Massenorganisation der Deutschen Demokratischen Republik (SAPMO)

  DY 6   Nationalrat der Nationalen Front der DDR
  DY 30   Sozialistische Einheitspartei Deutschlands
  DY 34   Freier Deutscher Gewerkschaftsbund

Bundesarchiv: Militärarchiv, Freiburg (BArchMA)

  VA   Akten des Ministeriums für Nationale Verteidigung der DDR

Politisches Archiv des Auswärtigen Amtes der Bundesrepublik Deutschland

Archiv Berlin (MfAA): Akten des Ministeriums für Auswärtige Angelegenheiten der Deutschen Demokratischen Republik
  Aktenserie A und C

Archiv Bonn (PA): Akten des Auswärtigen Amtes der Bundesrepublik Deutschland
  Ref. 709 (IB5) Abteilung Süd- und Ostasien: Malaya
  Ref. 710 (IB5) Abteilung Süd- und Ostasien: Vietnam
  Ref. 304 (IA5) Abteilung Großbritannien, Gemeinsame Fragen des Commonwealth, Australien, Neuseeland

(d) New Zealand

National Archives of New Zealand, Wellington (NZNA)

Department of External Affairs, SEATO Files (EA 1, W2668, subseries 120, PM series) Ministry of External Relations and Trade/Ministry of Foreign Affairs and Trade (ABHS Series 950, W4627, PM series)

(e) United Kingdom

Public Record Office, Kew (PRO)

CAB 128	Cabinet: Minutes (CM and CC Series)
CAB 129	Cabinet: Memoranda (CP and C Series)
CAB 130	Cabinet: Miscellaneous Committees. Minutes and Papers (GEN, MISC, and REF Series)
CAB 131	Cabinet: Defence Committee: Minutes and Papers (DO, D, and DC Series)
CAB 133	Cabinet Office: Commonwealth and International Conferences and Ministerial Visits to and from the UK. Minutes and Papers (ABC and other Series)
CAB 134	Cabinet Office: Defence Committee. Minutes and Papers (General Series)
CAB 148	Cabinet Office: Defence and Oversea Policy Committees and Sub-committees. Minutes and Papers (DO, DOP, and OPD Series)
CO 936	Colonial Office: International Relations. Original Correspondents
CO 947	Commission of Enquiry in North Borneo and Sarawak Regarding Malaysian Federation (Cobbold Commission, 1962)
CO 1030	Colonial Office: Far East Department. Original Correspondence
DEFE 4	Ministry of Defence: Chiefs of Staff Committee. Minutes
DEFE 5	Ministry of Defence: Chiefs of Staff Committee. Memoranda
DEFE 6	Ministry of Defence: Chiefs of Staff Committee. Joint Planning Staff Reports
DEFE 7	Ministry of Defence: Registered Files
DEFE 11	Ministry of Defence: Chiefs of Staff Committee. Registered Files
DEFE 13	Ministry of Defence: Private Office. Registered Files (MO, D/M, and D/Min Series)
DO 35	Dominions Office and Commonwealth Relations Office. Original Correspondence
DO 164	Commonwealth Relations Office: Defence. Registered Files
DO 169	Commonwealth Relations Office: Far East and Pacific Department. Registered Files (FE Series)

FO 371   Foreign Office: Political Departments. General Correspondence
FO 800   Lord Selkirk Papers
FO 1109   Foreign Office: Lord Butler of Saffron Walden. Papers
PREM 11   Prime Minister's Office: Correspondence and Papers, 1951–1964
PREM 13   Prime Minister's Office: Correspondence and Papers, 1964–1970

Private Collections

Sir William Goode Papers. Rhodes House Library, Oxford
Harold Macmillan Papers: Political Diaries. Bodleian Library, Oxford
Earl Mountbatten Papers. University of Southampton
Duncan Sandys Papers. Churchill Archives Centre, Cambridge
Field Marshal Gerald Templer Papers. National Army Museum, London
Sir Alexander Waddell Papers. Rhodes House Library, Oxford

(d) *United States*

National Archives of the United States, College Park, Maryland (USNA)

RG 59   Records of the Department of State
RG 84   Records of the Foreign Service Posts of the Department of State
RG 111   Records of the office of the chief signal officer
RG 306   Records of the United States Information Agency (USIA)

Hoover Institution on War, Revolution and Peace, Palo Alto, California (HI)

Edward G. Lansdale Papers

John F. Kennedy Presidential Library, Boston, Massachusetts (JFKL)

National Security Files (NSF)
   Meetings and Memoranda Series
   Malaya & Singapore Country Series
   Trip and Conference Series
   Vietnam Country Series
Presidential Office Files (POF)
   Roger Hilsman Papers
   White House Photographs
Oral Histories: David E. Bruce, Dean Rusk, Sir Alec Douglas-Home, Frederick Nolting,
Maxwell Taylor, Peter Thorneycroft

Lauinger Library, Georgetown University, Washington, DC

Foreign Affairs Oral History Collection
Oral Histories: John Heble, Joseph A. Mendenhall, William Trueheart

Lyndon B. Johnson Presidential Library, Austin, Texas (LBJL)

National Security File (NSF)
   Country File Australia
   Country File China
   Country File Indonesia
   Country File Malaysia
   Country File United Kingdom

Declassified and sanitized documents from unprocessed files (DSDUF)
    Files of McGeorge Bundy
    Files of Alfred Jenkins
    International Travel and Meeting File
    Meeting Notes File
    Memos to the President
    NSC Histories: Presidential Decisions—Gulf of Tonkin attacks
    Papers of Francis Bator
    Papers of Walt W. Rostow
    Security File: National Security Council
    Security File: Travel File
    Vice Presidential File
George Ball Papers
McGeorge Bundy Papers
Oral History Collection: David Bruce, William Colby, Chester L. Cooper, Elbridge Durbrow, Paul Harkins, W. Averell Harriman, Roger Hilsman, U. Alexis Johnson, Lyan Lemnitzer, William Trueheart
White House Central File: Confidential File
    The White House Tapes

II. INTERVIEWS AND CORRESPONDENCE

Reginald Burrows (interview on 14 February 2002 and correspondence)
Lord Douglas-Hamilton (correspondence)
Lord Moore of Wolvercote (correspondence)
Isabel Oliphant (interview on 13 February 2002)
Sir Edward Peck (interview on 12 February 2002 and correspondence)
Sir Reginald Secondé (correspondence)

III. PUBLISHED DOCUMENTS

(a) United Kingdom

Command Papers
    Cmnd. 9239, Miscellaneous No. 20: Further Documents Relating to the Discussion of Korea and Indochina at the Geneva Conference (London: HMSO, 1954)
    Cmnd. 1755, Vietnam No. 1: Special Report to the Co-Chairmen of the Geneva Conference on Indo-China, 2 June 1962 (London: HMSO, 1962)
    Cmnd. 2834, Documents Relating to British Involvement in the Indo-China Conflict 1945–1965 (London: HMSO, 1965)
House of Commons Debates, 5th Series

(b) United States

BESCHLOSS, MICHAEL R. (ed.), *Taking Charge: The Johnson White House Tapes, 1963–1964* (New York: Simon & Schuster, 1997).

GRAVEL, MIKE, *The Pentagon Papers: The Defense Department History of the United States Decisionmaking on Vietnam*, 5 vols. (Boston: Beacon Press, 1972).

HERRING, GEORGE C. (ed.), *The Secret Diplomacy of the Vietnam War: The Negotiating Volumes of the Pentagon Papers* (Austin: University of Texas Press, 1983).

US Department of Defense, *United States–Vietnam Relations, 1945–1967 [The Pentagon Papers]*, 12 vols. (Washington, DC: US Government Printing Office, 1971).

US Department of State, *Foreign Relations of the United States, 1952–1954*, xvi. *The Geneva Conference: Korea and Indochina* (Washington, DC: US Government Printing Office, 1981).

——*Foreign Relations of the United States, 1961–1963*, i. *Vietnam 1961* (Washington, DC: US Government Printing Office, 1988).

——*Foreign Relations of the United States, 1961–1963*, ii. *Vietnam 1962* (Washington, DC: US Government Printing Office, 1990).

——*Foreign Relations of the United States, 1961–1963*, iii. *Vietnam January–August 1963* (Washington, DC: US Government Printing Office, 1991).

——*Foreign Relations of the United States, 1961–1963*, iv. *Vietnam September–December 1963* (Washington, DC: US Government Printing Office, 1991).

——*Foreign Relations of the United States, 1964–1968*, i. *Vietnam 1964* (Washington, DC: US Government Printing Office, 1992).

——*Foreign Relations of the United States, 1961–1963*, xxiii. *Southeast Asia* (Washington, DC: US Government Printing Office, 1995).

(c) Other

Australian Parliamentary Debates: House of Representatives
Canadian House of Commons Debates

BOYCE, PETER, *Malaysia and Singapore in International Diplomacy. Documents and Commentaries* (Sydney: Sydney University Press, 1968).

CHASE, HAROLD W., and LERMAN, ALLEN H. (eds.), *Kennedy and the Press: The News Conferences* (New York: Crowell, 1965).

GRANVILLE, JOHN A. S., and WASSERSTEIN, BERNARD, *The Major International Treaties since 1945: A History and Guide with Texts* (London: Methuen, 1987).

WESTAD, ODD ARNE, CHEN JIANG, et al. (eds.), *77 Conversations between Chinese and Foreign Leaders on the Wars in Indochina, 1964–1977* (Washington, DC: Cold War International History Project Working Paper No. 22, 1998).

IV. NEWSPAPERS

The Guardian
The Times

V. MEMOIRS

BALL, GEORGE, *The Past Has Another Pattern: Memoirs* (New York: W. W. Norton, 1982).

BOWLES, CHESTER, *Promises to Keep: My Years in Public Life 1941–1969* (New York: Harper & Row, 1971).

BUTLER, RICHARD A. B., *The Art of the Possible: The Memoirs of Lord Butler* (London: Hamilton, 1971).

COLBY, WILLIAM, and FORBATH, PETER, *Honorable Men: My Life in the CIA* (New York: Simon & Schuster, 1978).

COOPER, CHESTER, *The Lost Crusade: America in Vietnam* (New York: Dodd, Mead, 1970).

COUVE DE MURVILLE, MAURICE, *Une politique étrangère, 1958–1969* (Paris: Plon, 1971).

DE GAULLE, CHARLES, *Memoirs of Hope: Renewal and Endeavour* (London: Weidenfeld & Nicolson, 1971).

EDEN, ANTHONY, *Full Circle: The Memoirs* (London: Cassell, 1960).

GALBRAITH, JOHN K., *Ambassador's Journal: A Personal Account of the Kennedy Years* (Boston: Houghton Mifflin, 1969).

GORDON-WALKER, PATRICK (ed. by R. Pearce), *Patrick Gordon-Walker Political Diaries, 1932–1971* (London: Historians' Press, 1991).

GORE-BOOTH, Baron PAUL, *With Great Truth and Respect* (London: Constable, 1974).

HILSMAN, ROGER, *To Move a Nation: The Politics of Foreign Policy in the Administration of John F. Kennedy* (Garden City, NY: Doubleday, 1967).

HOME, Baron ALEC DOUGLAS-HOME, *The Way the Wind Blows: An Autobiography* (London: Collins, 1976).

JOHNSON, LYNDON B., *The Vantage Point: Perspectives of the Presidency, 1963–1969* (New York: Holt, Rinehart & Winston, 1971).

JOHNSON, U. ALEXIS, and OLIVARIUS, JEF, *The Right Hand of Power* (Englewood Cliffs, NJ: Prentice-Hall, 1984).

JONES, HOWARD PALFREY, *Indonesia: The Possible Dream* (Singapore: Mas Aju, 1973).

LANSDALE, EDWARD G., *In the Midst of Wars: An American's Mission to South-east Asia* (New York: Harper & Row, 1972).

LEE KUAN YEW, *The Singapore Story: Memoirs of Lee Kuan Yew* (Singapore: Times Education, 1998).

MACMILLAN, HAROLD, *At the End of the Day, 1961–1963* (London: Macmillan, 1973).

MCNAMARA, ROBERT S., *In Retrospect: The Tragedy and Lessons of Vietnam* (New York: Vintage Books, 1995).

MANELI, MIECZYSLAW, *War of the Vanquished* (New York: Harper & Row, 1971).

NIXON, RICHARD M., *RN: The Memoirs of Richard Nixon* (London: Sidgwick & Jackson, 1978).

NOLTING, FREDERICK, *From Trust to Tragedy: The Political Memoirs of Frederick Nolting, Kennedy's Ambassador to Diem's Vietnam* (New York: Praeger, 1988).

RAHMAN PUTRA AL-JAL, Tunku Abdul, *Malaysia, the Road to Independence* (Petaling Jaya, Selangor: Pelanduk Publications, 1984).

ROSTOW, WALT W., *The Diffusion of Power: An Essay in Recent History* (New York: Macmillan, 1972).

RUSK, DEAN, and RUSK, RICHARD, *As I Saw It* (New York: W. W. Norton, 1990).

STEWART, MICHAEL, *Life and Labour: An Autobiography* (London: Sidgwick & Jackson, 1980).

TAYLOR, MAXWELL, *Swords and Plowshares: A Memoir* (New York: W. W. Norton, 1972).

THOMPSON, ROBERT G. K., *Make for the Hills: Memoirs of Far Eastern Wars* (London: Leo Cooper, 1989).

WATKINSON, HAROLD, *Turning Points: A Record of our Times* (London: Michael Russel, 1986).

WESTMORELAND, WILLIAM C., *A Soldier Reports* (Garden City, NY: Da Capro Press, 1976).

WILSON, HAROLD, *The Labour Government, 1964–1970: A Personal Record* (London: Weidenfeld & Nicolson, 1971).

VI. BOOKS

ALDOUS, RICHARD, and LEE, SABINE (eds.), *Harold Macmillan and Britain's World Role* (Basingstoke: Macmillan Press, 1996).

ALI, S. MAHMUD, *Cold War in the High Himalayas: The USA, China and South Asia in the 1950s* (New York: St. Martin's Press, 1999).

ANDERSON, DAVID L., *Trapped by Success: The Eisenhower Administration and Vietnam, 1953–1961* (New York: Columbia University Press, 1991).

——(ed.), *Shadow on the White House: Presidents and Vietnam, 1953–1961* (Lawrence: University of Kansas Press, 1993).

APPADORAI, A., and RAJAN, M. S., *India's Foreign Policy and Relations* (New Delhi: South Asian Publishers, 1985).

ARNETT, PETER, *Live from the Battlefield: From Vietnam to Baghdad. 35 Years in the World's War Zones* (New York: Simon & Schuster, 1994).

AVANT, DEBORAH D., *Political Institutions and Military Change: Lessons from Peripheral Wars* (Ithaca, NY: Cornell University Press, 1994).

BARCLAY, GLEN ST. J., *A Very Small Insurance Policy: The Politics of Australian Involvement in Vietnam, 1954–1967* (St. Lucia: University of Queensland Press, 1988).

BARRETT, DAVID M., *Uncertain Warriors: Lyndon Johnson and his Vietnam Advisers* (Lawrence: University of Kansas Press, 1993).

BARTLETT, CHRISTOPHER J., *The Long Retreat: A Short History of British Defence Policy, 1945–1970* (London: Macmillan, 1972).

——*British Foreign Policy in the Twentieth Century* (Basingstoke: Macmillan Education, 1989).

——*'The Special Relationship': A Political History of Anglo-American Relations since 1945* (London: Longman, 1992).

BAYLIS, JOHN, *Anglo-American Defence Relations, 1939–1984: The Special Relationship* (London: Macmillan, 1984).

——*Ambiguity and Deterrence: British Nuclear Strategy, 1945–1964* (New York: Clarendon Press, 1995).

BELL, CORAL, *Dependent Ally: A Study in Australian Foreign Policy*, 3rd edn. (Canberra: Allen & Unwin, 1994).

BERMAN, LARRY, *Planning a Tragedy: The Americanization of the War in Vietnam* (New York: W. W. Norton, 1982).

——*Lyndon Johnson's War: The Road to Stalemate in Vietnam* (New York: W. W. Norton, 1989).

BESCHLOSS, MICHAEL R., *Kennedy v. Khrushchev: The Crisis Years, 1960–1963* (London: Faber & Faber, 1991).

BILL, JAMES A., *George Ball: Behind the Scenes in U.S. Foreign Policy* (New Haven: Yale University Press, 1997).

BILLINGS-YUN, MELANIE, *Decision against War: Eisenhower and Dien Bien Phu, 1954* (New York: Columbia University Press, 1988).

BLACKBURN, ROBERT M., *Mercenaries and Lyndon Johnson's 'More Flags': The Hiring of Korean, Filipino, and Thai Soldiers in the Vietnam War* (Jefferson, NC: McFarland, 1994).

BLAIR, ANNE E., *Lodge in Vietnam: A Patriot Abroad* (New Haven: Yale University Press, 1995).

BLAUFARB, DOUGLAS S., *Counterinsurgency Era: U.S. Doctrine and Performance, 1950 to the Present* (New York: Free Press, 1977).

BOWER, TOM, *The Perfect English Spy: Sir Dick White and the Secret War, 1935–1990* (London: Heinemann, 1995).

BRANDS, H. W., *India and the United States: The Cold Peace* (Boston: Twayne Publishers, 1990).

——*The Wages of Globalism: Lyndon Johnson and the Limits of American Power* (New York: Oxford University Press, 1995).

BRECHER, MICHAEL, *India and World Politics: Krishna Menon's View of the World* (London: Oxford University Press, 1968).

BRIDGE, CARL (ed.), *Munich to Vietnam: Australia's Relations with Britain and the United States since the 1930s* (Carlton: Melbourne University Press, 1991).

BRODIE, SCOTT, *Tilting at Dominoes: Australia and the Vietnam War* (Brookvale: Child & Associates, 1987).

BUSZYNSKI, LESZEK, *SEATO: The Failure of an Alliance Strategy* (Singapore: Singapore University Press, 1983).

BUZZANCO, ROBERT, *Masters of War: Military Dissent and Politics in the Vietnam Era* (New York: Cambridge University Press, 1996).

——*Vietnam and the Transformation of American Life* (Malden, Mass.: Blackwell, 1999).

CABLE, JAMES, *The Geneva Conference of 1954 on Indochina* (Basingstoke: Macmillan, 1986).

CABLE, LARRY E., *Conflict of Myths: The Development of American Counterinsurgency Doctrine and the Vietnam War* (New York: New York University Press, 1986).

——*Unholy Grail: The United States and the War in Vietnam* (London: Routledge, 1991).

CAIN, P. J., and HOPKINS, A. G., *British Imperialism: Crisis and Deconstruction, 1914–1990* (London: Longman, 1993).

CAIRNCROSS, ALEC, and EICHENGREEN, BARRY, *Sterling in Decline: The Devaluations of 1931, 1949, and 1967* (Oxford: Blackwell, 1983).

CAMPBELL, DUNCAN, *The Unsinkable Aircraft Carrier: American Military Power in Britain* (London: Paladin, 1986).

CARVER, MICHAEL, *Tightrope Walking: British Defence Policy since 1945* (London: Hutchinson, 1992).

CASTLE, TIMOTHY N., *At War in the Shadow of Vietnam: US Military Aid to the Royal Lao Government, 1955–1975* (New York: Columbia University Press, 1993).

CHALLINOR, DEBORAH, *Grey Ghosts: New Zealand Vietnam Vets Talk about their War* (Auckland: Hodder Moa Beckett, 1998).

CHANDLER, DAVID P., *The Tragedy of Cambodian History: Politics, War and Revolution since 1945* (New Haven: Yale University Press, 1993).

CHEN MIN, *The Strategic Triangle and Regional Conflicts: Lessons from the Indochina Wars* (Boulder, Colo.: Lynne Rienner Publishers, 1992).

CHEW, ERNEST C. T., and LEE, EDWIN, *A History of Singapore* (Oxford: Oxford University Press, 1991).

CHIN KIN WAH, *The Defence of Malaysia and Singapore: The Transformation of a Security System 1957–1971* (Cambridge: Cambridge University Press, 1983).

CHOMSKY, NOAM, *Rethinking Camelot: JFK, the Vietnam War, and US Political Culture* (London: Verso, 1993).

CLOAKE, JOHN, *Templer, Tiger of Malaya: The Life of Field Marshal Sir Gerald Templer* (London: Harrap, 1985).

COATES, JOHN, *Suppressing Insurgency: An Analysis of the Malayan Emergency, 1948–1954* (Boulder, Colo.: Westview Press, 1992).

COHEN, WARREN I. (ed.), *Pacific Passage: The Study of American–East Asian Relations on the Eve of the Twenty-First Century* (New York: Columbia University Press, 1996).

——and BERNKOPF TUCKER, NANCY, *Lyndon Johnson Confronts the World: American Foreign Policy, 1963–1968* (Cambridge: Cambridge University Press, 1994).

COLBY, WILLIAM, *Lost Victory: A Firsthand Account of America's Sixteen-Year Involvement in Vietnam* (Chicago: Contemporary Books, 1989).

COLVIN, JOHN, *Volcano under Snow: Vo Nguyen Giap* (London: Quartet, 1996).

COOPEY, R., and FIELDING, S. (eds.), *The Wilson Governments 1964–1970* (London: Pinter, 1993).

CURREY, CECIL B., *Edward Lansdale: The Unquiet American* (New York: Houghton Mifflin, 1985).

CURTIS, MARK, *The Ambiguities of Power: British Foreign Policy since 1945* (London: Zed Books, 1995).

DALLEK, ROBERT, *Flawed Giant: Lyndon Johnson and his Times, 1961–1973* (New York: Oxford University Press, 1998).

DARBY, PHILLIP, *British Defence Policy East of Suez, 1947–1968* (London: Oxford University Press, 1973).

DARWIN, JOHN, *Britain and Decolonisation* (Basingstoke: Macmillan, 1988).

——*The End of the British Empire: The Historical Debate* (Oxford: Blackwell, 1991).

DALLOZ, JACQUES, *La Guerre d'Indochine 1945–1954* (Paris: Le Seuil, 1987).

DEVILLERS, PHILIPPE, and LACOUTURE, JEAN, *End of a War: Indochina 1954* (New York: Praeger, 1969).

DICKIE, JOHN, *Inside the Foreign Office* (London: Chapmans, 1992).

——*'Special' No More: Anglo-American Relations: Rhetoric and Reality* (London: Weidenfeld & Nicolson, 1994).

DIMBLEBY, DAVID, and REYNOLDS, DAVID, *An Ocean Apart: The Relationship between Britain and America in the Twentieth Century* (London: BBC Books, 1988).

DOBSON, ALAN P., *The Politics of the Anglo-American Economic Special Relationship* (Brighton: Wheatsheaf, 1988).

——*Anglo-American Relations in the Twentieth Century: Of Friendship, Conflict and the Rise and Decline of Superpowers* (London: Routledge, 1995).

DOMMEN, ARTHUR J., *Conflict in Laos: The Politics of Neutralization* (London: Pall Mall Press, 1964).

DUIKER, WILLIAM J., *The Communist Road to Power in Vietnam* (Boulder, Colo.: Westview Press, 1981).

——*U.S. Containment Policy and the Conflict in Vietnam* (Stanford, Calif.: Stanford University Press, 1994).

——*Sacred War: Nationalism and Revolution in a Divided Vietnam* (New York: McGraw-Hill, 1995).

——*Ho Chi Minh* (New York: Hyperion, 2000).

DUNCANSON, DENNIS J., *Government and Revolution in Vietnam* (London: Oxford University Press, 1968).

DUNN, PETER M., *The First Vietnam War* (London: C. Hurst, 1985).

EAYRS, JAMES, *In Defence of Canada. Indochina: Roots of Complicity* (Toronto: Toronto University Press, 1983).

EDWARDS, PETER, with PEMBERTON, GREGORY, *Crises and Commitments: The Politics and Diplomacy of Australia's Involvement in Southeast Asian Conflicts 1948–1965* (North Sydney: Allen & Unwin, 1992).

FALL, BERNARD B., *The Two Vietnams* (New York: Praeger, 1963).

FARMER, ALAN, *Britain: Foreign and Imperial Affairs, 1939–1964* (Sevenoaks: Hodder & Stoughton, 1994).

FERGUSON, NIALL, *Virtual History: Alternatives and Counterfactuals* (London: Picador, 1997).

FINEMAN, DANIEL, *A Special Relationship: The United States and Military Government in Thailand, 1947–1958* (Honolulu: University of Hawai'i Press, 1997).

FRANKEL, JOSEPH, *British Foreign Policy 1945–1973* (London: Oxford University Press, 1975).

FREEDMAN, LAWRENCE, *Kennedy's Wars: Berlin, Cuba, Laos, and Vietnam* (New York: Oxford University Press, 2000).

GADDIS, JOHN LEWIS, *The Long Peace: Inquiries into the History of the Cold War* (New York: Oxford University Press, 1987).

——*Strategies of Containment: A Critical Appraisal of U.S. National Security Policy* (New York: Oxford University Press, 1987).

——*We Now Know: Rethinking Cold War History* (Oxford: Clarendon, 1997).

GAIDUK, ILYA V., *The Soviet Union and the Vietnam War* (New York: Ivan R. Dee, 1996).

GARDNER, LLOYD C., *Approaching Vietnam: From World War II through Dienbienphu* (New York: Norton, 1988).

——*Pay Any Price: Lyndon Johnson and the Wars for Vietnam* (Chicago: Ivan R. Dee, 1995).

——and GITTINGER, TED (eds.), *Vietnam: The Early Decisions* (Austin: University of Texas Press, 1997).

GEARSON, JOHN P. S., *Harold Macmillan and the Berlin Wall Crisis, 1958–1962* (London: Macmillan, 1998).

GELB, LESLIE, and BETTS, RICHARD K., *The Irony of Vietnam: The System Worked* (Washington, DC: Brookings Institute, 1979).

GIBBONS, WILLIAM CONRAD, *The United States and the Vietnam War: Executive and Legislative Roles and Relationships, 1961–1964,* ii (Princeton: Princeton University Press, 1986).

GIGLIO, JAMES N., *The Presidency of John F. Kennedy* (Lawrence: University of Kansas Press, 1991).

GILBERT, MARTIN, and GOTT, RICHARD, *The Appeasers* (Boston: Houghton Mifflin, 1963).

GILL, RANJIIT, *Of Political Bondage: An Authorised Biography of Tunku Abdul Rahman* (Singapore: Sterling Corporate Services, 1990).

GLASSER, JEFFREY D., *The Secret Vietnam War: The United States Air Force in Thailand* (London: McFarland, 1995).

GLOVER, RUPERT G., *New Zealand in Vietnam: A Study of the Use of Force in International Law* (Palmerston North: Dunmore Press, 1986).

GOODMAN, ALAN E., *The Lost Peace: America's Search for a Negotiated Settlement* (Stanford, Calif.: Hoover Institution Press, 1978).

GRAYLING, CHRISTOPHER, *Just Another Star? Anglo-American Relations since 1945* (London: Harrap, 1988).

GREENE, T. N. (ed.), *The Guerrilla and How to Fight Him* (New York: Praeger, 1962).

HALBERSTAM, DAVID, *The Making of a Quagmire* (New York: Random House, 1964).

——*The Best and the Brightest*, 4th edn. (New York: Ballantine Books, 1993).

HALLIN, DANIEL C., *The 'Uncensored War': The Media and Vietnam* (New York: Oxford University Press, 1986).

HAMILTON, DONALD W., *The Art of Insurgency: American Military Policy and the Failure of Strategy in Southeast Asia* (Westport, Conn.: Praeger, 1998).

HAMMER, ELLEN J., *A Death in November: America in Vietnam, 1963* (New York: E. P. Dutton, 1987).

HANNAH, NORMAN B., *The Key to Failure: Laos and the Vietnam War* (Lanham, Md.: Madison Books, 1987).

HAYES, SAMUEL P., *The Beginning of American Aid to Southeast Asia: The Griffin Mission of 1950* (Lexington, Va.: DC Heath, 1971).

HENNESSY, PETER, *Whitehall* (London: Fontana Press, 1990).

HERRING, GEORGE C., *America's Longest War: The United States and Vietnam, 1950–1975*, 2nd edn. (New York: Knopf, 1986).

——*LBJ and Vietnam: A Different Kind of War* (Austin: University of Texas Press, 1995).

HESS, GARY R., *The United States' Emergence as a Southeast Asian Power* (New York: Columbia University Press, 1987).

——*Vietnam and the United States: Origins and Legacy of War* (Boston: Twayne, 1990).

HETCHER, PATRICK, *Suicide of an Elite: American Internationalists and Vietnam* (Stanford, Calif.: Stanford University Press, 1990).

HOGAN, MICHAEL J., *America in the World: The Historiography of American Foreign Relations since 1941* (Cambridge: Cambridge University Press, 1995).

HOLLAND, ROBERT F., *Emergencies and Disorder in European Empires after 1945* (London: Frank Cass, 1995).

HORNE, ALISTAIR, *Macmillan, 1957–1986* (London: Macmillan, 1989).

HUNT, MICHAEL H., *The Genesis of Chinese Communist Foreign Policy* (New York: Columbia University Press, 1996).

——*Lyndon Johnson's War: America's Cold War Crusade in Vietnam, 1945–1965* (New York: Hill & Wang, 1996).

HUNT, RICHARD A., *Pacification: The American Struggle for Vietnam's Hearts and Minds* (Boulder, Colo.: Westview, 1995).

IMMERMAN, RICHARD H. (ed.), *John Foster Dulles and the Diplomacy of the Cold War* (Princeton: Princeton University Press, 1990).

JAMES, HAROLD, and SMALL, DENIS S., *The Undeclared War: The Story of Indonesian Confrontation, 1962–1966* (London: Leo Cooper, 1971).

JOES, ANTHONY J., *The War for South Vietnam, 1945–1975* (New York: Praeger, 1989).

JONES, MATTHEW, *Conflict and Confrontation in South East Asia, 1961–1965: Britain, the United States and the Creation of Malaysia* (Cambridge: Cambridge University Press, 2002).

KAHIN, GEORGE McT., *Intervention: How America Became Involved in Vietnam* (New York: Knopf, 1986).

KAISER, DAVID, *American Tragedy: Kennedy, Johnson, and the Origins of the Vietnam War* (Cambridge, Mass.: Harvard University Press, 2000).

KAPLAN, LAWRENCE, ARTAUD, DENISE, and RUBIN, MARK (eds.), *Dien Bien Phu and the Crisis of Franco-American Relations, 1954–1955* (Wilmington, Del.: Scholarly Resources, 1990).

KARNOW, STANLEY, *Vietnam: A History* (New York: Viking, 1983).

KEARNS, DORIS, *Lyndon Johnson and the American Dream* (New York: Harper & Row, 1976).

KEITH, RONALD C., *The Diplomacy of Zhou Enlai* (Basingstoke: Macmillan, 1989).

KHONG YUEN FOONG, *Analogies at War: Korea, Munich, Dien Bien Phu, and the Vietnam Decisions of 1965* (Princeton: Princeton University Press, 1992).

KIMBALL, JEFFREY, *Nixon's Vietnam War* (Lawrence: University of Kansas Press, 1998).

KINNARD, DOUGLAS, *The Certain Trumpet: Maxwell Taylor and the American Experience in Vietnam* (Washington, DC: Brassey's, 1991).

KISSINGER, HENRY, *Diplomacy* (New York: Simon & Schuster, 1994).

KOLKO, GABRIEL, *Anatomy of a War* (New York: Random House, 1985).

KOMER, ROBERT W., *Bureaucracy at War: U.S. Performance in the Vietnam Conflict* (Boulder, Colo.: Westview, 1986).

——*The Malayan Emergency in Retrospect: Organizing of a Successful Counterinsurgency Effort* (Santa Monica, Calif.: RAND, 1972).

LAMB, RICHARD, *The Macmillan Years, 1957–1963: The Emerging Truth* (London: John Murray, 1995).

LAU, ALBERT, *The Malayan Union Controversy* (Singapore: Oxford University Press, 1991).

——*A Moment of Anguish: Singapore in Malaysia and the Politics of Disengagement* (Singapore: Time Academic Press, 1998).

LEE, STEPHEN HUGH, *Outposts of Empire: Korea, Vietnam, and the Origins of the Cold War in Asia, 1949–1954* (Liverpool: Liverpool University Press, 1995).

LEIFER, MICHAEL, *Indonesia's Foreign Policy* (London: Allen & Unwin, 1983).

LEVANT, VICTOR, *Quiet Complicity: Canadian Involvement in the Vietnamese War* (Toronto: Between the Lines, 1986).

LEVINE, ALAN J., *The United States and the Struggle for Southeast Asia, 1945–1975* (Westport, Conn.: Praeger, 1995).

LEVY, DAVID, *The Debate Over Vietnam* (Baltimore: Johns Hopkins University Press, 1991).

LOGEVALL, FREDRIK, *Choosing War: The Lost Chance for Peace and the Escalation of War in Vietnam* (Berkeley: University of California Press, 1999).

LOMPERIS, TIMOTHY J., *From People's War to People's Rule: Insurgency, Intervention, and the Lessons of Vietnam* (Chapel Hill: University of North Carolina Press, 1996).

LOWE, PETER, *Britain and the Far East* (London: Longman, 1981).

LUDLOW, N. PIERS, *Dealing with Britain: The Six and the First UK Application to the EEC* (Cambridge: Cambridge University Press, 1997).

MCINTYRE, W. DAVID, *Background to the ANZUS Pact* (London: Macmillan Press, 1995).

MACKIE, JAMES A. C., *Konfrontasi: The Indonesia–Malaysia Dispute, 1963–66* (Kuala Lumpur: Oxford University Press, 1974).

MCMAHON, ROBERT J. (ed.), *Major Problems in the History of the Vietnam War* (Lexington, Va.: D. C. Heath, 1990).

——*The Cold War on the Periphery: The United States, India and Pakistan* (New York: Columbia University Press, 1994).

MCMASTER, HERBERT R., *Dereliction of Duty: Lyndon Johnson, Robert McNamara, the Joint Chiefs of Staff, and the Lies That Led to Vietnam* (New York: HarperPerennial, 1998).

McNeill, Ian, *Australian Army Advisers in Vietnam, 1962–1972* (Canberra: Australian War Memorial, 1984).

——*To Long Tan: The Australian Army and the Vietnam War, 1950–1966* (St. Leonards: Allen & Unwin, 1993).

Maga, Timothy P., *John F. Kennedy and the New Pacific Community, 1961–1963* (New York: St. Martin's, 1990).

Marr, David G., *Vietnam 1945: The Quest for Power* (Berkeley: University of California Press, 1995).

Milner, A. C., *The Invention of Politics in Colonial Malaya* (Cambridge: Cambridge University Press, 1995).

Mockaitis, Thomas R., *British Counter-Insurgency 1919–1960* (Manchester: Manchester University Press, 1960).

Modelski, George (ed.), *SEATO: Six Studies* (Melbourne: F. W. Cheshire for the Australian National University, 1962).

Moïse, Edwin E., *Tonkin Gulf and the Escalation of the Vietnam War* (Chapel Hill: University of North Carolina Press, 1996).

Moss, George D., *Vietnam: An American Ordeal*, 2nd edn. (Englewood Cliffs, NJ: Prentice-Hall, 1994).

Murphy, John, *Harvest of Fear: A History of Australia's Vietnam War* (Sydney: Allen & Unwin, 1993).

Newman, John M., *JFK and Vietnam: Deception, Intrigue, and the Struggle for Power* (New York: Warner Books, 1992).

Ninkovic, Frank, *Modernity and Power: A History of the Domino Theory in the Twentieth Century* (Chicago: University of Chicago Press, 1994).

Nixon, Richard M., *No more Vietnams* (London: W. H. Allen, 1986).

Northedge, Frederick, *Descent from Power: British Foreign Policy 1945–1973* (London: Allen & Unwin, 1974).

Nunnerley, David, *President Kennedy and Britain* (London: Bodley Head, 1972).

Olson, James S., and Roberts, Randy, *Where the Domino Fell: America and Vietnam, 1945–1990* (New York: St. Martin's Press, 1991).

Ongkili, James P., *Nation-building in Malaysia* (Singapore: Oxford University Press, 1985).

Osborne, Milton, *Sihanouk: Prince of Light, Prince of Darkness* (Sydney: Allen & Unwin, 1994).

Paterson, Thomas G. (ed.), *Kennedy's Quest for Victory: American Foreign Policy, 1961–1963* (New York: Oxford University Press, 1989).

Pearson, Mark, *Paper Tiger: New Zealand's Part in SEATO, 1954–1977* (Wellington: New Zealand Institute of International Affairs, 1989).

Pemberton, Gregory, *All the Way: Australia's Road to Vietnam* (Sydney: Allen & Unwin, 1987).

Pickering, Jeffrey, *Britain's Withdrawal from East of Suez: The Politics of Retrenchment* (Basingstoke: Macmillan, 1998).

Pike, Douglas, *PAVN: People's Army of Vietnam* (Novato, Calif.: Presidio Press, 1986).

——*Vietnam and the Soviet Union: Anatomy of an Alliance* (Boulder, Colo.: Westview Press, 1987).

Pimlott, Ben, *Harold Wilson* (London: HarperCollins, 1992).

Post, Ken, *Revolution, Socialism and Nationalism in Viet Nam*, iv. *The Failure of Counter-Insurgency in the South* (Aldershot: Dartmouth, 1990).

PRADOS, JOHN, *The Blood Road: The Ho Chi Minh Trail and the Vietnam War* (New York: John Wiley, 1999).

PROCHNAU, WILLIAM, *Once upon a Distant War: David Halberstam, Neil Sheehan, Peter Arnett: Young War Correspondents and their Early Vietnam Battles* (New York: Vintage Books, 1996).

RACE, JEFFREY, *War Comes to Long An: Revolutionary Conflict in a Vietnamese Province* (Berkeley: University of California Press, 1973).

RAMSDEN, JOHN, *Winds of Change: Macmillan to Heath, 1957–1975* (London: Longman, 1996).

RANDLE, ROBERT F., *Geneva 1954: The Settlement of the Indochinese War* (Princeton: Princeton University Press, 1969).

RECORD, JEFFREY, *The Wrong War: Why We Lost in Vietnam* (Annapolis, Md.: Naval Institute Press, 1998).

REEVES, RICHARD, *President Kennedy: Profile of Power* (London: Papermac, 1994).

REMME, TILMAN, *Britain and Regional Co-operation in Southeast Asia 1945–49* (London: Routledge, 1995).

REYNOLDS, DAVID, *Britannia Overruled: British Policy and World Power in the 20th Century* (London: Longman, 1991).

RICKLEFS, MERLE C., *A History of Modern Indonesia: c. 1300 to the Present* (London: Macmillan, 1981).

ROSS, DOUGLAS A., *In the Interests of Peace: Canada and Vietnam* (Toronto: Toronto University Press, 1984).

ROTTER, ANDREW J., *The Path to Vietnam: Origins of the American Commitment to Southeast Asia* (Ithaca, NY: Cornell University Press, 1987).

——*Light at the End of the Tunnel: A Vietnam Anthology* (New York: St. Martin's Press, 1991).

RUANE, KEVIN, *War and Revolution in Vietnam, 1930–75* (London: University College London Press, 1998).

RUISCO, ALAIN, *La Guerre française d'Indochine* (Bruxelles: Editions Complexe, 1992).

RUST, WILLIAM, and Editors of US News Books, *Kennedy and Vietnam* (New York: Scribners, 1985).

SANDERS, DAVID, *Losing an Empire, Finding a Role: British Foreign Policy since 1945* (Basingstoke: Macmillan Education, 1990).

SANGER, CLYDE, *Malcolm MacDonald: Bringing an End to Empire* (Montreal: McGill-Queen's University Press, 1995).

SARDESAI, DAMODAR R., *Indian Foreign Policy in Cambodia, Laos and Vietnam 1947–1964* (Berkeley: University of California Press, 1968).

——*Vietnam: The Struggle for National Identity*, 2nd edn. (Boulder, Colo.: Westview Press, 1992).

SCHLESINGER, ARTHUR M., *A Thousand Days: John F. Kennedy in the White House* (Boston: Houghton Miffin, 1965).

——*Robert Kennedy and his Times* (London: Deutsch, 1978).

SCHOENBAUM, THOMAS J., *Waging Peace and War: Dean Rusk in the Truman, Kennedy and Johnson Years* (New York: Simon & Schuster, 1988).

SCHWAB, ORRIN, *John F. Kennedy, Lyndon Johnson, and the Vietnam War, 1961–65* (Westport, Conn.: Praeger, 1998).

SCOTT, L. V., *Macmillan, Kennedy and the Cuban Missile Crisis: Political, Military and Intelligence Aspects* (Basingstoke: Macmillan, 1999).

SHAFER, D. MICHAEL, *Deadly Paradigms: The Failure of U.S. Counterinsurgency Policy* (Princeton: Princeton University Press, 1988).

SHAPLEY, DEBORAH, *Promise and Power: The Life and Times of Robert McNamara* (Boston: Little, Brown, 1993).

SHARMA, ARCHANA, *British Policy Towards Malaysia, 1957–1967* (London: Sangam, 1993).

SHESOL, JEFF, *Mutual Contempt: Lyndon Johnson, Robert Kennedy, and the Feud that Defined a Decade* (New York: W. W. Norton, 1997).

SHORT, ANTHONY, *Communist Insurrection in Malaya* (London: Muller, 1975).

—— *The Origins of the Vietnam War* (New York: Longman, 1989).

SMITH, RALPH B., *An International History of the Vietnam War*, 3 vols. (New York: St. Martin's Press, 1981–91).

SOPIEE, MOHAMED N., *From Malayan Union to Singapore Separation* (Kuala Lumpur: Penerbit Universiti Malaya, 1974).

STUBBS, RICHARD, *Hearts and Minds in Guerrilla Warfare: The Malayan Emergency, 1948–1960* (Singapore: Oxford University Press, 1989).

SUMMERS, HARRY G., *On Strategy: A Critical Analysis of the Vietnam War* (Novato, Calif.: Presidio Press, 1984).

TARLING, NICHOLAS, *The Fall of Imperial Britain in Southeast Asia* (Singapore: Oxford University Press, 1993).

TAYLOR, JAY, *China and Southeast Asia: Peking's Relations with Revolutionary Movements* (New York: Praeger, 1974).

THAKUR, RAMESH CHANDRA, *Peacekeeping in Vietnam: Canada, India, Poland, and the International Commission* (Edmonton: University of Alberta Press, 1984).

THAYER, CARLYLE, *War by Other Means: National Liberation and Revolution in Viet-Nam, 1954–1960* (Cambridge: Unwin Hyman, 1989).

THOMPSON, ROBERT G. K., *Defeating Communist Insurgency: Experiences from Malaya and Vietnam* (London: Chatto & Windus, 1966).

—— *No Exit from Vietnam* (London: Chatto & Windus, 1969).

—— *Revolutionary War in World Strategy, 1945–1969* (London: Secker & Warburg, 1970).

—— *Peace Is Not at Hand* (London: Chatto & Windus, 1974).

THORNE, CHRISTOPHER, *The Far Eastern War; States and Societies, 1941–45* (London: Unwin, 1986).

THORPE, D. R., *Alec Douglas-Home* (London: Sinclair-Stevenson, 1996).

TØNNESSON, STEIN, *The Vietnamese Revolution of 1945: Roosevelt, Ho Chi Minh and de Gaulle in a World at War* (London: Sage Publications, 1991).

TURNER, JOHN, *Macmillan* (London: Longman, 1994).

TURNER, KATHLEEN, *Lyndon Johnson's Dual War: Vietnam and the Press* (Chicago: University of Chicago Press, 1985).

VANDEMARK, BRIAN, *Into the Quagmire: Lyndon Johnson and the Escalation of the Vietnam War* (New York: Oxford University Press, 1991):

VAN DER KROEF, JUSTUS M., *The Lives of SEATO* (Singapore: Institute of Southeast Asian Studies, 1976).

VANDIVER, FRANK E., *Shadows of Vietnam: Lyndon Johnson's Wars* (College Station: Texas A&M University Press, 1997).

VERTZBERGER, YAACOV I., *Misperceptions in Foreign Policymaking: The Sino-Indian Conflict, 1959–1962* (Boulder, Colo.: Westview Press, 1984).

WARBEY, WILLIAM, *Ho Chi Minh and the Struggle for an Independent Vietnam* (London: Merlin Press, 1972).

——*Vietnam: The Truth* (London: Merlin Press, 1965).

WATT, DONALD C., *Succeeding John Bull: America in Britain's Place, 1900–1975* (Cambridge: Cambridge University Press, 1984).

WEDEMAN, ANDREW H., *The East Wind Subsides: Chinese Foreign Policy and the Origins of the Cultural Revolution* (Washington, DC: Washington Institute Press, 1987).

WINTERS, FRANCIS X., *The Year of the Hare: America in Vietnam, January 25, 1963– February 15, 1964* (Athens: University of Georgia Press, 1997).

YOUNG, JOHN W. (ed.), *The Foreign Policy of Churchill's Peacetime Administration* (Leicester: Leicester University Press, 1988).

—— *Britain and European Unity, 1945–1992* (Basingstoke: Macmillan, 1993).

——*Winston Churchill's Last Campaign: Britain and the Cold War, 1951–1955* (Oxford: Clarendon Press, 1996).

YOUNG, MARILYN B., *The Vietnam Wars, 1945–1990* (New York: HarperCollins, 1991).

ZHAI QIANG, *China and the Vietnam Wars, 1950–1975* (Chapel Hill: University of North Carolina Press, 2000).

ZIEGLER, PHILIP, *Harold Wilson: The Authorised Biography of the Life of Lord Wilson of Rievaulx* (London: Weidenfeld & Nicolson, 1993).

ZUBOK, VLADISLAV M., and PLESHAKOV, CONSTANTINE, *Inside the Kremlin's Cold War: From Stalin to Khrushchev* (Cambridge, Mass.: Harvard University Press, 1996).

VII. SELECTED ARTICLES AND THESES

BARCLAY, GLEN ST. J., ' "The Light that Failed": Australia and the Vietnam War', *History Today*, 38 (February 1988), 18–22.

BECKETT, IAN, 'Robert Thompson and the British Advisory Mission to South Vietnam 1961–65', *Small Wars and Insurgencies*, 8/2 (1997), 41–63.

BERMAN, LARRY, 'Coming to Grips with Lyndon Johnson's War', *Diplomatic History*, 17/4 (1993), 519–37.

BOYCE, PETER, 'Canberra's Malaysia Policy', *Australian Outlook*, 17/2 (1963), 149–61.

BUSZYNSKI, LESZEK, 'SEATO: Why It Survived until 1977 and Why It was Abolished', *Journal of Southeast Asian Studies*, 12/2 (1981), 287–96.

CHANG, GORDON, 'JFK, China and the Bomb', *Journal of American History*, 74/4 (1988), 1287–310.

CHEN JIAN, 'China and the First Indo-China War, 1950–54', *China Quarterly*, 133 (1993), 85–110.

——'China's Involvement in the Vietnam War, 1964–1969', *China Quarterly*, 142 (1995), 356–87.

COMBS, ARTHUR, 'The Path Not Taken: The British Alternative to U.S. Policy in Vietnam, 1954–1956', *Diplomatic History*, 19/1 (1995), 33–57.

DALLEK, ROBERT, 'Lyndon Johnson and Vietnam: The Making of a Tragedy', *Diplomatic History*, 20/2 (1996): 147–62.

DINGMAN, ROGER, 'John Foster Dulles and the Creation of the South-East Asia Treaty Organisation in 1954', *International History Review*, 11/3 (1989), 457–77.

DOBSON, ALAN P., 'The Years of Transition: Anglo-American Relations 1961–67', *Review of International Studies*, 16/3 (1990), 239–58.

DUMBRELL, JOHN, 'The Johnson Administration and the British Labour Government, Vietnam, the Pound and East of Suez', *Journal of American Studies*, 30/2 (1996), 211–31.

DUNCANSON, DENNIS J. 'Ho-chi-Minh in Hong Kong, 1931–32', *China Quarterly*, 5 (1974), 84–100.

EASTER, DAVID, 'British Defence Policy in South East Asia and the Confrontation, 1960–66', Ph.D. thesis (London School of Economics, 1998).

FIELDING, JEREMY, 'Coping with Decline: US Policy toward the British Defense', *Diplomatic History*, 23/4 (1999), 633–56.

GARVER, JOHN W., 'Chinese-Indian Rivalry in Indochina', *Asian Survey*, 27/11 (1987), 1205–19.

HERRING, GEORGE C., and IMMERMAN, RICHARD H., 'Eisenhower, Dulles and Dien Bien Phu', *Journal of American History*, 71/2 (1984), 343–63.

HOPKINS, MICHAEL F., 'Focus of a Changing Relationship: The Washington Embassy and Britain's World Role since 1945', *Contemporary British History*, 12/3 (1998), 103–14.

HORNER, DAVID, 'The Australian Army and Indonesia's Confrontation with Malaysia', *Australian Outlook*, 43/1 (1989), 61–76.

HUSSAIN, RAJINAH, 'Malaysia and the United Nations: A Study of Foreign Policy Priorities, 1957–1987', Ph.D. thesis (London, 1988).

IMMERMAN, RICHARD H., 'The United States and the Geneva Conference', *Diplomatic History*, 14/1 (1990), 43–66.

KEAR, SIMON, 'The British Consulate-General in Hanoi, 1954–1973', *Diplomacy and Statecraft*, 10/1 (1999), 215–39.

KUNZ, DIANE B., ' "Somewhat Mixed Up Together": Anglo-American Defence and Financial Policy during the 1960s', *Journal of Imperial and Commonwealth History*, 27/2 (1999), 213–32.

LOGEVALL, FREDRIK, 'De Gaulle, Neutralization and American Involvement in Vietnam, 1963–1964', *Pacific Historical Review*, 61/1 (1992), 69–102.

MCCRAW, DAVID, 'Reluctant Ally: New Zealand's Entry into the Vietnam War', *Australian Journal of Politics and History*, 34/3 (1988), 308–19.

MCLEAN, DAVID, 'American and Australian Cold Wars in Asia', *Australasian Journal of American Studies*, 9/2 (1990), 33–46.

MAGA, TIMOTHY P., 'The New Frontier vs Guided Democracy: JFK, Sukarno and Indonesia, 1961–1963', *Presidential Studies Quarterly*, 20/1 (1990), 91–102.

MAHAGANI, USHA, 'The Malaysia Dispute: A Study in Mediation and Intervention', *Australian Outlook*, 20/2 (1966), 177–92.

MEANS, GORDON, 'Malaysia—A New Federation in Southeast Asia', *Pacific Affairs*, 36/2 (1963), 138–59.

MIDDEKE, MICHAEL, 'Britain's Interdependence Policy and Anglo-American Cooperation on Nuclear and Conventional Force Provisions, 1957–1964', Ph.D. thesis (London School of Economics, 1999).

MILNE, R. S., 'Malaysia', *Asian Survey*, 4/2 (1964), 695–701.

RABEL, ROBERTO, 'The Vietnam Decision Twenty-Five Years On', *New Zealand International Review*, 15 (May/June 1990), 8–11.

——'Vietnam and the Collapse of the Foreign Policy Consensus', in Malcolm McKinnon (ed.), *New Zealand in World Affairs 1957–1972* (Wellington: New Zealand Institute of International Affairs, 1991), 40–63.

REYNOLDS, DAVID, 'A "Special Relationship"? America, Britain, and the International Order since the Second World War', *International Affairs*, 62/1 (1986), 1–20.

ROSS, DOUGLAS A., 'Middlepowers as Extra-Regional Balancer Powers: Canada, India, Indochina 1954–1962', *Pacific Affairs*, 55/2 (1982), 185–209.

RUANE, KEVIN, 'Anthony Eden, British Diplomacy and the Origins of the Geneva Conference of 1954', *Historical Journal*, 37/1 (1994), 152–72.

——'Refusing to Pay the Price: British Foreign Policy and the Pursuit of Victory in Vietnam, 1952–1954', *English History Review*, 110/435 (1994), 70–92.

——'Containing America: Aspects of British Foreign Policy and the Cold War in South-East Asia, 1951–54', *Diplomacy and Statecraft*, 7/1 (1996), 141–74.

SELBY, IAN, 'British Policy towards Indochina: South Vietnam and Cambodia, 1954–1959', Ph.D. thesis (Cambridge, 1998).

SHAO KUO-KANG, 'Zhou Enlai's Diplomacy and the Neutralization of Indochina 1954–55', *China Quarterly*, 107 (1986), 483–504.

SODHY, PAMELA, 'Malaysian–American Relations during Indonesia's Confrontation against Malaysia, 1963–1966', *Journal of Southeast Asian Studies*, 19/1 (1988), 111–36.

SOPIEE, MOHAMED N., 'The Advocacy of Malaysia before 1961', *Modern Asian Studies*, 7/4 (1973), 717–32.

STEININGER, ROLF, '"The Americans Are in a Hopeless Position": Great Britain and the War in Vietnam, 1964–1965', *Diplomacy and Statecraft*, 8/3 (1997), 237–85.

——'Großbritannien und der Vietnamkrieg 1964–65', *Vierteljahreshefte für Zeitgeschichte*, 45/4 (1997), 589–624.

STOCKWELL, ANTHONY J., 'Malaysia: The Making of a Neo-Colony?', *Journal of Imperial and Commonwealth History*, 26/2 (1998), 138–56.

TILMAN, ROBERT O., 'Elections in Sarawak', *Asian Survey*, 3/10 (1963), 507–18.

WARNER, GEOFFREY, 'President Kennedy and Indo-China: The 1961 Decision', *International Affairs*, 70/4 (1994), 685–700.

——'The United States and the Fall of Diem', Part I: 'The Coup That Never Was', *Australian Outlook*, 28/3 (1974), 245–58.

WILLIAMS, JOHN, 'ANZUS: A Blow to Britain's Self-Esteem', *Review of International Studies*, 13/4 (1987), 243–63.

WILSON, CRAIG, 'Rhetoric, Reality and Dissent: The Vietnam Policy of the British Labour Government, 1964–1970', *Social Science Journal*, 23/1 (1986), 17–31.

YOUNG, JOHN W., 'The Wilson Government and the Davies Peace Mission to North Vietnam, July 1965', *Review of International Studies*, 24/4 (1998), 545–62.

ZHAI QIANG, 'China and the Geneva Conference of 1954', *China Quarterly*, 129 (1992), 103–22.

——'Transplanting the Chinese Model: Chinese Military Advisers and the First Vietnam War, 1950–1954', *Journal of Military History*, 57/4 (1993), 689–715.

List of Office Holders

Abdul Rahman Putra, Tunku
Prime Minister of Malaya, 1957–63; Prime Minister of Malaysia, 1963–70

Azahari, Sheikh Ahmad
President Brunei Partai Rakyat, 1955–62

Bao Dai
Emperor of Annam, 1932–45; Emperor of Vietnam, 1949–55

Barwick, Sir Garfield
Australian Minister for External Affairs, 1961–64

Beale, Sir Howard
Australian Ambassador to the United States, 1958–64

Bonesteel, General Charles H.
US Army, Assistant to the Chairman of the Joint Chiefs of Staff 1960–61; Commanding General, 7th Corps, 1961–62

Brook, Norman
British Secretary to the Cabinet, 1947–62

Brubeck, William H.
US Deputy Executive Secretary, Executive Secretariat, Department of State, 1961–62; Special Assistant to the Secretary of State and Executive Secretary 1962–63

Bruce, David K. E.
US Ambassador to the United Kingdom, 1961–73

Bundy, McGeorge
US Special Assistant to the President for National Security Affairs, 1961–66

Bundy, William
US Deputy Assistant Secretary of Defense for International Security Affairs, 1961–63; Deputy Assistant Secretary for East and Pacific Affairs, State Department, 1963–64; Assistant Secretary for East and Pacific Affairs, State Department 1964–69

Bunting, John
Australian Secretary of Prime Minister's Department, 1959–68

Burrows, Reginald A.
British Counsellor and Consul-General in the RVN, 1961–64

Butler, Richard (Rab)
British Secretary of State for Foreign Affairs, 1963–64

Cable, James
Assistant, Southeast Asia Department, FO, 1961–63; Head of Southeast Asia Department, 1963–66

Caccia, Sir Harold
British Ambassador to the United States, 1958–61
Permanent Under-Secretary of State, FO, 1962–65

Cleveland, Robert G.
US Deputy Director, Office of Southeast Asian Affairs, State Department, 1962

Cox, Gordon
Canadian commissioner, ICC Vietnam, 1962–64

Critchley, Thomas
Australian High Commissioner to Malaya and Malaysia, 1957–65

Dean, Sir Patrick
Permanent United Kingdom Representative to the United Nations at New York, 1960–64

De Gaulle, Charles
President of France, 1958–69

Denson, John B.
British First Secretary in Washington embassy, 1959–63

Diefenbaker, John
Canadian Prime Minister, 1957–63

Durbrow, Elbridge
US Ambassador to the RVN, 1957–61

Eisenhower, Dwight D.
President of the United States, 1953–61

Etherington-Smith, Gordon
British Ambassador to the RVN, 1963–66

Everard, Timothy J.
Assistant, Southeast Asia Department, FO, 1962–63

Felt, Admiral Harry D.
US Commander in Chief, Pacific, 1958–64

Festing, Francis
British Chief of the Imperial General Staff, 1958–61

Ford, Joseph F.
British Consul-General in the DRV, 1960–62

Forrestal, Michael V.
Member of the US National Security Council Staff, 1962–64

Forsyth, William
Australian Ambassador to the RVN, 1959–61

Fry, Sir Leslie
British Ambassador to Indonesia, 1959–63

Galbraith, John Kenneth
US Ambassador to India 1961–63

Gilchrist, Sir Andrew
British Ambassador to Indonesia, 1963–66

Gilpatric, Roswell L.
US Deputy Secretary of Defense, 1961–64

Golds, Anthony
Head of Far East and Pacific Department, CRO, 1962–64

Goode, Sir William
British Governor of North Borneo, 1960–63

Gordon-Walker, Patrick
British Secretary of State for Foreign Affairs, 1964–65

Harkins, General Paul
Commander MACV, 1962–64

Harriman, W. Averell
US Ambassador-at-large 1961; Assistant Secretary of State for Far Eastern Affairs, 1961–63; Under-Secretary of State for Political Affairs, 1963–65

Head, Lord Anthony
British High Commissioner to Malaysia, 1963–66

Herter, Christian A.
US Secretary of State, 1959–61

Hill, Brian
Australian Ambassador to the RVN, 1961–64

Hilsman, Roger
US Director of the Bureau of Intelligence and Research, Department of State, 1961–63; Assistant Secretary of State for Far Eastern Affairs, 1963–64

Hohler, Henry A.
British Ambassador to the RVN, 1960–63

Holyoake, Keith
Prime Minister of New Zealand and Minister for Foreign Affairs, 1960–72

Home, Lord (Alexander Frederick Douglas)
British Secretary of State for Commonwealth Relations, 1955–60; Secretary of State for Foreign Affairs, 1960–63, Prime Minster, 1963–64

Hood, Viscount Samuel
Minister of the British Embassy in the United States, 1957–62

Hooton, Jeffrey
Canadian commissioner, ICC Vietnam, 1961–62

Hull, General Sir Richard
British Commander-in-Chief Far East Land Forces, 1958–61

Johnson, Lyndon B.
Vice President of the United States, 1961–1963; President of the United States, 1963–69

Johnson, U. Alexis
US Ambassador to Thailand, 1958–61; Deputy Under-Secretary of State for Political Affairs, 1961–64

Kennedy, John F.
President of the United States, 1961–63

Kennedy, Robert
US Attorney General, 1961–64

Khrushchev, Nikita Sergeyevich
Chairman of the Council of Ministers of the Soviet Union and First Secretary of the
Central Committee of the Communist Party, 1953–64

Kohler, Foy D.
US Assistant Secretary of State for European Affairs, 1961–62

Komer, Robert W.
Member of the US National Security Council staff, 1961–66

Laking, George
New Zealand Ambassador to the United States, 1961–67

Lansdale, Brigadier General Edward
US Deputy Assistant for Special Operations to the Secretary of Defense, 1960–61; from
1961 Assistant for Special Operations to the Secretary of Defense

Lee Kuan Yew
Prime Minister of Singapore, 1959–90

Lloyd, Selwyn
British Secretary of State for Foreign Affairs, 1955–60, Chancellor of the Exchequer,
1960–62

Lodge, Henry Cabot
US Ambassador to the RVN, 1963–64

Luce, Sir David
British Commander-in-Chief, Far Eastern Station, 1960–62; Commander-in-Chief, Far
Eastern Command, 1962–64

Macapagal, Diosdano
President of the Philippines, 1961–65

McConaughy, Walter P.
US Assistant Secretary of State for Far Eastern Affairs, 1961

McCone, John A.
US Director of Central Intelligence, 1961–65

MacDonald, Malcom
Head of the British delegation at the Geneva conference on Laos, 1961–62

Macleod, Iain
British Secretary of State for the Colonies, 1959–61

Macmillan, Harold
British Prime Minister, 1957–63

McNamara, Robert S.
US Secretary of Defense, 1961–68

Maudling, Reginald
British Chancellor of the Exchequer, 1962–64

Mendenhall, Joseph
Counsellor, US embassy Vietnam, 1961–63

Menon, Gopala
Indian chairman, ICC Vietnam, 1960–61

Menzies, Sir Robert
Australian Prime Minister, 1949–66; Minister of External Affairs, 1960–61

Mountbatten of Burma, Lord Louis
British Chief of the Defence Staff, 1959–65

Nasution, General Abdul
Indonesian Minister of Defence and People's Security, 1959–66

Nehru, Jawaharlal
Prime Minister of India, 1947–64

Ngo Dinh Diem
Prime Minister of the State of Vietnam, 1954–55, President of the RVN, 1955–63

Ngo Dinh Nhu
Ngo Dinh Diem's Adviser, 1954–63

Nitze, Paul H.
US Assistant Secretary of Defense for International Security Affairs, 1961–63

Nolting, Frederick
US ambassador in Vietnam, 1961–63

Ormsby-Gore, Sir David (Lord Harlech)
British Ambassador to the United States, 1961–65

Parkes, Roderick
British Ambassador to the RVN, 1957–60

Parthasarathi, G.
Indian chairman, ICC Vietnam, 1961–62

Peck, Edward
British Assistant Under-Secretary of State, FO, 1961–66

Perth, Lord
British Minister of State for Colonial Affairs, 1957–62

Pike, Sir Thomas
British Chief of the Air Staff, 1960–63

Pilcher, John
British Ambassador to the Philippines, 1959–63

Pritchard, Neil
British Deputy Under-Secretary of State, CRO, 1963–67

Razak Bin Hussain, Tun Abdul
Malayan/Malaysian Deputy Prime Minister and Minister of Defence, 1959–69

Rostow, Walt Whitman
Deputy Special Assistant to the US President for National Security Affairs 1961; Counsellor of the Department of State and Chairman of the Policy Planning Council, 1961–66

Rusk, Dean
US Secretary of State, 1961–69

Sandys, Duncan
British Minister of Defence, 1957–59; Minister of Aviation, 1959–60; Secretary of State for Commonwealth Relations, 1960–64, and for the Colonies, 1962–64

Scott, Sir Robert
British Permanent Secretary, MOD, 1961–64

Selkirk, Lord George
British Commissioner for Singapore and Commissioner-General for Southeast Asia, 1959–63

Shann, Keith
Australian External Affairs Office, London, 1959–62; Ambassador to Indonesia, 1962–66

Subandrio, Raden
Indonesian Foreign Minister, 1957–66

Sukarno, Achmed
President of Indonesia, 1945–67

Taylor, General Maxwell D.
US President's Military Representative, 1961–62; Chairman of the Joint Chiefs of Staff, 1962–64; Ambassador to the RVN, 1964–65

Thant, U
UN Secretary-General, 1962–71

Thompson, Robert G. K.
Head of British Advisory Mission to Vietnam, 1961–65

Thorneycroft, Peter
British Minister of Defence, 1962–64

Tory, Sir Geofroy
British High Commissioner to Malaya, 1957–63

Townley, Athol Gordon
Australian Minister of Defence, 1958–63

Trend, Sir Burke
British Secretary to the Cabinet, 1963–73

Vu Van Mau
RVN Foreign Minister, 1955–1963

Waddell, Sir Alexander
British Governor of Sarawak, 1960–63

Waller, J. Keith
Australian First Assistant Secretary, External Affairs, 1961–64

Warner, Frederick
British Head of the Southeast Asia Department, FO, 1960–63

Wilson, Harold
British Prime Minister, 1964–70

Woodsworth, Charles
Canadian commissioner, ICC Vietnam, 1960–61

De Zulueta, Philip
Private Secretary to British Prime Minister, 1955–64

Index